KU-650-692

THE OXFORD BOOK OF
CAROLS

THE OXFORD BOOK OF CAROLS

Percy Dearmer
R. Vaughan Williams
Martin Shaw

No. 68 version 2.
No. 176
No. 175
No. 181

OXFORD
OXFORD UNIVERSITY PRESS
NEW YORK TORONTO

Oxford University Press, Walton Street, Oxford OX2 6DP
London New York Toronto
Delhi Bombay Calcutta Madras Karachi
Kuala Lumpur Singapore Hong Kong Tokyo
Nairobi Dar es Salaam Cape Town
Melbourne Auckland
and associated companies in
Beirut Berlin Ibadan Mexico City Nicosia

Oxford is a trade mark of Oxford University Press

First published 1928
Twenty-Fifth Impression Re-engraved and Reset 1964
Thirty-Third Impression 1984

ISBN 0 19 353314 6

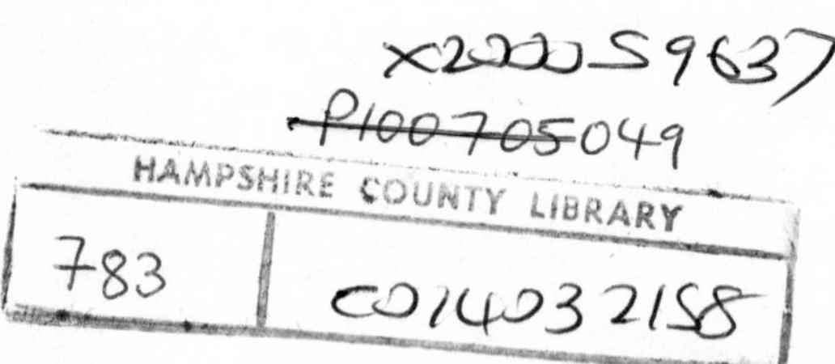

Printed in Great Britain by
R. J. Acford Ltd. Chichester, Sussex

PREFACE

CAROLS are songs with a religious impulse that are simple, hilarious, popular, and modern. They are generally spontaneous and direct in expression, and their simplicity of form causes them sometimes to ramble on like a ballad. Carol literature and music are rich in true folk-poetry and remain fresh and buoyant even when the subject is a grave one. But they vary a good deal: some are narrative, some dramatic, some personal, a few are secular; and there are some which do not possess all the typical characteristics. Simplicity, for instance, was often lost in the conceits of Jacobean poets, who yet wrote some charming carols.

Hilarity also has been sometimes forgotten, or obscured in the texts. The word 'carol' has a dancing origin, and once meant to dance in a ring: it may go back, through the old French *caroler* and the Latin *choraula*, to the Greek *choraules*, a flute-player for chorus dancing, and ultimately to the *choros* which was originally a circling dance and the origin of the Attic drama. The carol, in fact, by forsaking the timeless contemplative melodies of the Church, began the era of modern music, which has throughout been based upon the dance. But, none the less, joyfulness in the words has been sometimes discarded by those who were professionally afraid of gaiety. Some French carols were rewritten by well-meaning clergymen into frigid expositions of edifying theology; some of the English tunes were used by excellent Methodists of the eighteenth century to preach their favourite doctrines. Before their time the British tendency to lugubriousness had occasionally shown itself in the folk-carol: but even in such cases the dancing tunes remained, happily to belie the words; and in France behind the ecclesiastical propriety of modern noëls there lurk many carols like 'Guillô, pran ton tamborin' (No. 82) to bear witness to the spirit of a more spontaneous and undoubting faith.

The typical carol gives voice to the common emotions of healthy people in language that can be understood and music that can be shared by all. Because it is popular it is therefore genial as well as simple; it dances because it is so Christian, echoing St. Paul's conception of the fruits of the Spirit in its challenge to be merry — 'Love and joy come to you'. Indeed, to take life with real seriousness is to take it joyfully, for seriousness is only sad when it is superficial: the carol is thus all the nearer to the ultimate truth because it is jolly. So, on the one hand, the genius of the carol is an antidote to the levity of much present-day literature, music, and drama, made by men who are afraid to touch the deeper issues of life because seriousness is associated in their minds with gloom; for its jubilant melodies can encircle the most solemn of themes: on the other hand, it is an antidote to pharisaism, the formalism which is always morose, as Paul Sabatier says in his life of Francis of Assisi — that most Christian of saints, who as scenic artist at the Greccio crib, and as the sweet-voiced troubadour of the Holy Spirit, the 'joculator Dei', was the precursor if not the parent of the carol: 'Le formalisme religieux, dans quelque culte que ce soit, prend toujours des allures guindées et moroses. Les pharisiens de tous les temps se défigurent le visage, pour que nul ne puisse ignorer leurs dévotions: François non seulement ne pouvait souffrir ces simagrées de la fausse piété, mais il mettait la gaieté et la joie au nombre des devoirs religieux . . . le maître alla jusqu'à en faire un des préceptes de la Règle. Il était trop bon général pour ne pas savoir qu'une armée joyeuse est toujours une armée victorieuse. Il y a dans l'histoire des premières missions franciscaines des éclats de rire qui sonnent haut et clair.'

Carols, moreover, were always modern, expressing the manner in which the ordinary man at his best understood the ideas of his age, and bringing traditional conservative religion up to date: the carol did this for the fifteenth century after the collapse of the old feudal order, and should do the same for the twentieth. The charm of an old carol lies precisely in its having been true to the period in which it was written, and those which are alive to-day retain their vitality because of this sincerity; for imitations are always sickly and short-lived. A genuine carol may have faults of grammar, logic, and prosody; but one fault it never has—that of sham antiquity.

1. History of the Carol

Because the carol was based upon dance music, it did not appear until the close of the long puritan era which lasted through the Dark Ages and far into the Medieval period. The word meant something Terpsichorean and evil in the seventh century, as we can see in St. Ouen's *Life* of the contemporary St. Eligius (ii. 15): 'Nullus in festivitate S. Joannis, vel quibuslibet sanctorum solemnitatibus, solstitia aut ballationes vel saltationes aut *caraulas* aut cantica diabolica exerceat': the people evidently wanted to dance on saints' days, especially on Midsummer Day, and the *caraula* was condemned with the *ballatio*: from this latter example of Late Latin our 'ballad' is derived, and 'ball' (and ultimately 'ballet'). St. Augustine uses the verb *ballare* of David dancing before the ark; but David's example was ignored, and the dance reprobated under all three names—*ballatio*, *saltatio*, and *caraula*. By the fourteenth century, however, the word 'carol' had changed its meaning, and, though it retained its dancing associations, had become respectable. Dante, in the 24th canto of the *Paradiso*, could use it of the dancing band of saints in glory: 'Così quelle carole differentemente danzando': here 'carola' means a choir, but it is a choir that dances.

Therefore the carol made its appearance late in Christian history—not, indeed, until the modern spirit of humanism had dawned upon the Middle Ages. It was a creation of the fifteenth century. Popular singers and reciters had of course always existed; and the curious early thirteenth-century Anglo-Norman wassail song, 'Seignors ore entendez a nus', shows, as we should expect, that minstrels did not avoid the baronial hall at Christmas time; but it was not till the fourteenth century that English poetry developed from the homiletic verse, the metrical chronicle, and the melancholy elegiac poetry of the preceding two hundred years into the metrical romance, and Chaucer arrived with his Italian humanism and his new demonstration of the possibilities of verse. There was a marked growth of the democratic spirit in the fourteenth century; and religious literature in the vernacular, including hymns, spread as a result of this and of the activity of the preaching friars. Only in the lifetime of Chaucer are there signs of the carol beginning to emerge as something different from a poem, or from a sequence like 'Angelus ad virginem' (52) which can be treated as a carol only because of its enchanting melody. It is difficult, if not impossible, to find any example of an authentic carol which can with certainty be dated earlier than 1400 (Chaucer's roundel of *c.* 1382, No. 128, has to be arranged in order to be sung as a carol). Professor Saintsbury, indeed, says definitely that the oldest of our carols date from the fifteenth century.

The carol was in fact a sign, like the mystery play, of the emancipation of the people from the old puritanism which had for so many centuries suppressed the dance and the drama, denounced communal singing, and warred against the tendency of the people to disport themselves in church on the festivals. Instances abound of the struggle, as for instance when John of Salisbury in the twelfth century denounced the *mimi, balatroni, praestigiatores*, and others of an age which he declares 'non modo aures et cor prostituit vanitate sed oculorum et aurium voluptate suam mulcet desidiam', and no doubt in the Middle Ages, as under the Roundheads, such objections often found justification in the excesses of popular merriment. But even in the twelfth century and even in church the instinct for dramatic expression was in revolt, and we find Abbot Aelred of Rievaulx complaining of chanters who gesticulated and grimaced while singing the sacred offices, and imitated the sound of thunder, of women's voices, and of the neighing of horses. In other and more seemly ways anthems, sequences, and tropes were sung with increasing dramatic emphasis, till from them the mystery play developed. The struggle went on, and the Muses gradually won: about the time when the English barons rose against King John, Pope Innocent III forbad 'ludi theatrales' in church, and his order was repeated by Gregory IX. St. Francis, their contemporary, by his jovial singing as well as by his invention of the Christmas crib, gave, as we have said, a great impetus to the new conception of music and drama in the thirteenth century. We get a glimpse of the transition in such descriptions as that printed by Petit de Julleville in his *Histoire de Théâtre en France* of the crib ceremonies at Rouen in the fourteenth century: the crib was behind the altar, the shepherds came in by the great gates of the choir, a child on a platform represented the angel, and 'two priests of the first rank wearing dalmatics will represent the midwives and stand by the crib'. But by this time the mystery play had become in many places a real form of drama, performed outside the church. France, which was ahead of England with the play (as Germany seems to have been more than a generation ahead with the carol), had a secular drama in the thirteenth century, four examples of which, by Adam the Hunchback (*d.* 1288) and others, survive. English drama in the literary sense dates from about the year 1300; the Guilds took up the mystery play and brought it to full flower, gradually increasing the secular element at the same time: the York and Towneley Plays date from 1340 to 1350, the Chester Plays are *c.* 1400, and the Coventry Plays ran from 1400 to 1450; the old drama thus reached the top of its vigour in the fifteenth century. Such developments led naturally to the writing of religious songs in the vernacular, as in the 'Coventry Carol' (22), and also to the gradual substitution of folk-song and dance tunes for the winding cadences of liturgical music. The time was ripe for the carol.

People were now accustomed to think vividly of many of the Bible stories: the influence of the constant dramatic visualization of such scenes as the annunciation, the visit of the shepherds ('And farewell, Joseph, with thy round cap') and of the legendary three kings, or the misdeeds of Herod, 'that moody king'—who was often out-Heroded long before *Hamlet* was written—is evident in many old carols, as well as in sculpture and painting; and some carols, like the two of which the tunes are preserved, the 'Coventry Carol' (22) and the German 'Joseph lieber' (77), were definitely written for the mystery play or crib. Plainsong antiphons were not very suitable for the drama, and they gradually disappeared; for the fifteenth century was a great era also of musical development both in prick-song and counterpoint, and in the latter England for a while led the way for the Netherlands under the influence of composers like John Dunstable, who had a European reputation twenty years before he died in 1453: 'What tidings bringest thou, messenger' (40) is from his school, if not by him. The fifteenth century was also the special time of ballad production in England—there was little, if any, before—and the ballad is another example of popular tradition: a narrative poem of communal origin, the ballad began in the dramatic singing of a throng of people under a leader, and in its earlier form was sung with a refrain: 'ballad', as we have seen, means a dancing song, just as 'carol' does.

There was thus a drawing together, with a new music, in what was still almost a new language, of minstrel, literary, and folk poetry in the fifteenth century. Chaucer was dead; and it was not a great age of English verse, except for the ballads and songs, and for the carols—those 'masterpieces of tantalizing simplicity', as Professor Manly calls them. The ballad was one of the forms in which many of our traditional carols have been cast, as for instance, 'The Carnal and the Crane' (53-5) and 'The Cherry Tree Carol' (66). The lyric also sometimes takes on a new religious grace, a 'harp of Ariel' quality in such a poem as 'I sing of a maiden' (183), and thus becomes so much a carol that Professor Saintsbury quotes it in his *Short History of English Literature* as the typical carol of the age, though this is perhaps to go a little too far, since we do not know how or even whether it was sung. There also emerges a new form of verse with a lilting rhythm, evidently devised for singing (like 'Adam lay ybounden', 180). This form, with a refrain for the chorus to sing, is the carol *par excellence*, and the following are instances of it, all from between the years 1430 and 1460: 'When Christ was born of Mary free' (178), 'This Endris Night' (39), 'Welcome Yule' (174). One version of the last named occurs in the collection of John Audlay (*c.* 1430), the blind chaplain of Haughmond Abbey in Shropshire, who 'at the end of a tedious versifying of the whole duty of man', as Sir Edmund Chambers says, suddenly changes his key: 'the gladdened scribe marks it with red letters':

I pray you, Sirs, both more and less
Sing these carols in Christèmas.

Here a priest is helping on the new movement. Another form of carol is the macaronic, in which lines of Latin, generally from the well-known office hymns, are interspersed with vigorous phrases in the vernacular, as in 'Make we joy' (23) and the famous 'In dulci jubilo' (86), both of which have retained their melodies. This last class has suggested to some writers the activity of innovating parsons; but the Latin often consists of tags like *A solis ortus cardine* (the first line of the hymn for Evensong on Christmas Day as well as for Lauds), which were familiar to anyone who paid the least attention in church; and Latin was used by most people who were acquainted with letters in any form. Parsons doubtless wrote some of these carols and some of other kinds; but there were other classes in which poets and composers were found, not least the *scholares vagantes*, light-hearted products of all the universities of Europe, 'equally at home in ale-house, in hall, in market-place, or in cloister', who were busy making songs both secular and religious, and singing them (often improperly, as in the case of No. 36) to tunes both religious and secular. The truth is that carols are a national creation; if they represent the layman's contribution to religion, the clergy also have contributed much, though less from the musical side: like Gothic architecture they are unclerical in the sense that they are the work of all the people combined—including many parsons, who in this as in all succeeding ages of carol-making had their share with musicians, poets, and peasant folk.

The carol arose with the ballad in the fifteenth century, because people wanted something less severe than the old Latin office hymns, something more vivacious than the plainsong melodies. This century rang up the modern era: it was the age of the all-pervading Chaucerian influence and of the spread of humanism in England, where it culminates in the New Learning under Grocyn, Warham, Linacre, and Colet: in Italy the fifteenth century began with the full flood of the Renaissance, and Leonardo was in his prime when it ended: before its close, printed books were familiar objects, and the New World had been discovered. Our earliest carols are taken from manuscripts of this century and from the collection which Richard Hill, the grocer's apprentice (36, *note*), made at the beginning of the sixteenth. The earliest printed collection which has survived (and that only in one of its leaves containing one of the Boar's Head Carols, No. 19, and 'a caroll of huntynge') was issued in 1521 by Wynkyn de Worde, Caxton's apprentice and successor. A later extant collection was printed by Richard Kele, *c*. 1550. The metre of these earlier carols is most commonly a one-rime iambic tercet, eight syllables to each line, with a refrain (as in 'Tyrley, Tyrlow', 169), which is near to the familiar long measure of the vast majority of the ancient Latin hymns, and when the refrain is also in eight syllables (as in 'In Bethlehem, that fair City', 120, and 'Out of your Sleep', 177) is, but for the rime of the refrain, exactly in long measure. This metre continued in use—it is that, for instance, of the seventeenth-century 'The First Nowell' (27), with the addition of a refrain and some tripping extra syllables here and there. But the later traditional carols tend to employ the ordinary ballad metre or common measure, in which the second and fourth lines have six syllables only (as in 'The Holy Well', 56, and 'The moon shines bright', 46), and sometimes the D.C.M. (as 'The first good joy', 70) and other metres. The prevalent iambic metre of the old carols, and the rarity of feminine endings to lines, are the reason why English words which have lost their tunes can only occasionally be fitted to foreign substitutes; and for this reason new words have generally to be found for foreign tunes.

The carol continued to flourish through the sixteenth century, and until the recrudescence of puritanism in a new form suppressed it in the seventeenth. In the year 1644 the unfortunate people of England had to keep Christmas Day as a fast, because it happened to fall on the last Wednesday in the month—the day which the Long Parliament had ordered to be kept as a monthly fast. In 1647 the Puritan Parliament abolished Christmas and other festivals altogether. The new Puritan point of view is neatly expressed by Hezekiah Woodward, who in a tract of 1656 calls Christmas Day 'The old Heathen's Feasting Day, in honour to Saturn their Idol-God, the Papist's Massing Day, the Profane Man's Ranting Day, the Superstitious Man's Idol Day, the Multitude's Idle Day, Satan's—that Adversary's—Working Day, the True Christian Man's Fasting Day. . . . We are persuaded, no one thing more hindereth the Gospel work all the year long, than doth the observation of that Idol Day once in a year, having so many days of cursed observation with it.'

Thus, most of our old carols were made during the two centuries and a half between the death of Chaucer in 1400 and the ejection of the Reverend Robert Herrick from his parish by Oliver Cromwell's men in 1647.

The old masques and carols did not recover after the Restoration. New carols so-called continued indeed to be printed, throughout the eighteenth century, in such publications as *Poor Robin's Almanack* (1663-1776); but they were mere eating-songs about pork and pudding. Indeed, almost the only contribution of this static era was to print Nahum Tate's 'While Shepherds Watched' in the *Supplement* of *c*. 1698 to the *New Version*, as is mentioned in our foot-note to carol 33, and 'Hark! the herald angels' (altered from Charles Wesley's finer original of 1739) in the *Supplement* of 1782.

Meanwhile the old carols travelled underground and were preserved in folk-song, the people's memory of the texts being kept alive by humble broadsheets of indifferent exactitude which appeared annually in various parts of the country. The carol was ignored by the formal and prosaic world of the eighteenth century, and was slowly losing ground among the poor, though there is evidence of its continuance in many parts of England. Goldsmith in 1766 says that the parishioners of *The Vicar of Wakefield* 'kept up the Christmas carol'. A writer in the *Gentleman's Magazine* for May 1811 states that in the North Riding of Yorkshire he was awakened about six o'clock on Christmas Day 'by a sweet singing under my window', and looking out he saw six young women and four men singing. The American visitor, Washington Irving, in 1820 was surprised one Christmas night, also in Yorkshire, to hear beautiful music from rustics: 'I had scarcely got into bed', he writes in his *Sketch Book*, 'when a strain of music seemed to break forth in the air just below the window. I listened, and found it proceeded from a band, which I concluded to be the waits from some neighbouring village. They went round the house playing under the windows'; he listened with 'hushed delight', and notes half apologetically that 'even the sound of the waits, rude as may be their minstrelsy, breaks upon the mid-watches of a winter night with the effect of perfect harmony'.

The forgotten wealth of beauty was not restored by the pioneers of the Romantic Revival, nor even by that great rediscoverer of Christmas (and author of *A Christmas Carol*, which was magnificent but not a carol), Charles Dickens. Indeed, when Dickens was a boy the carol seemed to be on the verge of extinction, and William Hone, the author of *The Every Day Book*, anticipated that carol-singing would entirely disappear in a few years. At the same time, in 1822, Davies Gilbert published the first modern collection of traditional carols: he was a many-sided man—M.P. for Bodmin, he had given early help to Sir Humphry Davy, he chose Brunel's design for Clifton Suspension Bridge, and became

President of the Royal Society. A second edition of his *Collection of Christmas Carols* was called for in 1823. But he also spoke of the carol as a thing of the past: these Cornish examples of his were sung, he said, 'in churches on Christmas Day, and in private houses on Christmas Eve, throughout the West of England up to the latter part of the late century'. The next collector, William Sandys, the solicitor antiquary, in his *Christmas Carols Ancient and Modern*, 1833, did not take a much more hopeful view; carol singing, he wrote, still existed 'in the Northern counties and some of the Midland'; but he added that the practice appeared 'to get more neglected every year'.

Indeed, the very meaning of the word 'carol' came to be forgotten. In 1831 a book called *Christmas Carols* was published by J. W. Parker for the S.P.C.K., and reprinted until 1857: it consisted entirely of new Christmas hymns, very poor in quality (and now forgotten), while the music included only one carol tune. We have before us another book, dated 1848, which, although it is called *Christmas Carols A Sacred Gift*, is really an anthology of poems on the Nativity without any musical suggestions whatever. 'Carol' had come to mean printed matter suitable for Christmas.

The broadsheets, however, continued to preserve the tradition among the common people, though they were deteriorating. W. H. Husk, in his *Songs of the Nativity*, 1868, reported that carols were still sung, but that the broadsheets showed that their printers, especially in London, 'find the taste of their customers rather incline towards hymns, mostly those in use amongst dissenting congregations, than to the genuine Christmas carol'. This was true also of the collection *The Christmas Box*, published as early as 1825 by the Religious Tract Society (mentioned in our note to No. 119), which contains several 'new carols' of a hymn-like description, including 'another new carol' for Spring, and a recast of 'God rest you merry', with 'merry' left out, but still appointed to be sung 'To the old tune,– *God rest you merry, Gentlemen*'; but beyond this and a second recast of the same, there is little that is not of a solemn and didactic character, addressed to 'Ye young and ye gay, ye lovers of sin, Who sportive with play, each new year begin': there are no real traditional carols, and the little book was evidently intended to supplant them.

In spite of such efforts of superior people, the neglected folk-carol continued to exist. Two examples may serve to give an idea of the position between about 1830 and 1870. We have before us a small paper book, *A New Carol Book*, published at Birmingham by J. Guest: it is undated, but does not look much later than 1830. It consists of forty-eight pages and contains, among several long compositions of no merit, 'Hark! the herald angels', 'On Christmas night all Christians sing' (our No. 24), 'Dives and Lazarus' (57), 'The moon shines bright' (46), 'God rest you merry' (11), and 'The holly and the ivy' (38). Our second example is from an article in the *Leisure Hour* for December 1869, which dwells on the enormous circulation of broadsheets at that time, but consoles its readers with unconscious irony, 'Village schools and village choirs have enlarged the rustic knowledge and improved the rustic ear'. The article reprints in full a typical broadsheet of the year, called *The Evergreen: Carols for Christmas Holidays*: its contents are 'God rest you merry', 'In friendly love and unity', 'The moon shines bright', 'Now cruel Herod', 'The first good joy' (our

No. 70), and 'As I sat upon a sunny bank' (3). It is important to note that the people with their 'rustic' ears could always be depended on for the tunes.

But from another side a succession of scholars had been preparing the way for revival since the middle of George III's reign, as is shown by the names of Bishop Percy (whose *Reliques of Ancient English Poetry* had been published as far back as 1765), Joseph Ritson (his *Ancient Songs* were dated 1790), the Rev. John Brand (*d.*1806), Sir Walter Scott (*d.*1832), and William Hone (*d.*1842). The work went on: in 1836 Thomas Wright began printing fifteenth-century *Songs and Carols* (from the Sloane MS. 2593), published more in 1847, and was still publishing ancient carols in 1856. Other scholars followed; and the valuable work of societies like the Percy Society and the Early English Text Society has assisted them down to our own day. Musicians began at last to be interested: in 1855-9 William Chappell published his two volumes of old music, but he ignored the living folk-song, alas, when it was still abundant. E. F. Rimbault, who did some useful but not always trustworthy work for music, had begun with a *Little Book of Carols* in 1846, though his more important small collections did not appear till 1863 and 1865.

Such was the position in the middle of the last century. In 1847 a genuine collector of folk-carols had published anonymously the valuable little book, *A Good Christmas Box*, at Dudley, unfortunately without tunes; and in 1852 Sandys added some new material in *Christmas Tide* to his first admirable collection. Thus, seventy years ago, when the folk-carol was slowly dying (in spite of the continuance of the broadsheets), at the other end of the scale the carol was being recovered: scholarly foundations had already been laid, and enough music had been published by Gilbert and Sandys to make carol-singing possible among the few educated people who were interested in it. The only men who were in touch with both sides and might therefore be able to effect a national revival were the clergy; and, as it happened, the new movement in the Church was causing some of the young high-church parsons to think wistfully about carols. But the first great impulse in the Church arose from an unexpected quarter.

A very rare Swedish book had come into the possession of the editors of the *Hymnal Noted* of 1852, the Rev. J. M. Neale and the Rev. T. Helmore: it was called *Piae Cantiones*, and was full of exquisite sixteenth-century tunes (see 141 *n.*). Neale translated some of the carols or hymns therein, and in 1853 he and Helmore published *Carols for Christmas-tide*, twelve carols, with music from the old book. This they followed up next year with twelve *Carols for Easter-tide*—the first recognition since old times of the carol apart from Christmas. Thus some of our finest carols both in words and music were given to the Church: the misfortune was that the traditional carols of this country were ignored, and their recovery was retarded. The Rev. J. E. Vaux indeed wrote in *Church Folk Lore*, 1894 (apparently without disapproval), that Neale and Helmore 'have done much to lead to the disuse of certain old favourites, which probably in a few years will be forgotten'; and he mentions that 'A Virgin unspotted' had been dropped at Grasmere about 1860, though recently it had been revived again 'to the great joy of the people'. But glamour at that time was sought among things ancient and foreign, and it is probable that Neale and Helmore hit upon the only way to recover prestige for the carol. Also they published their collection in cheaper form for use in church, and thus began to rebuild the broken bridge between poets and people. Fired by their example, Edmund Sedding published in 1860 nine *Antient Christmas Carols*, to which he added seven more in 1863, including a few English with some good Dutch and other foreign examples (e.g. 153). But Neale died in 1866 when he was only forty-eight, and Sedding followed him two years later. It was doubtless these men and their supporters whom Husk had in mind when in 1868 he said that 'a certain section of the clergy' had made attempts to revive a taste for the use of Christmas carols amongst their parishioners. 'But their efforts have been too intermittent and spasmodic to produce any successful result.' Anyhow the first chapter in the revival was ended.

The second chapter of the revival in the nineteenth century opens in 1871 with the publication of forty-two *Christmas Carols New and Old* by the Rev. H. R. Bramley, Fellow of Magdalen College, Oxford, and Dr. John Stainer, then organist of the college. The influence of this book was enormous: it placed in the hands of the clergy (who were perhaps not so 'intermittent' in their efforts as Husk had thought) a really practicable tool, which came into general use, and is still in use after nearly sixty years. The great service done by this famous collection was that it brought thirteen traditional carols, with their proper music, into general use at once. There was another side, it is true. Twenty-four of the numbers were composed by contemporary Church musicians, and it was the heyday of *Hymns Ancient and Modern*; of these, little perhaps, except the tune by Sir John Goss (30)*, deserves to survive; the traditional melodies also lost some of their freshness and strength in the inappropriate harmonies which were made for them. Moreover, it must be confessed that the mantle of Neale had not fallen upon Bramley; the new words were but sorry pietistic verse for the most part. It is nevertheless mainly to Bramley and Stainer that we owe the restoration of the carol; and if they obscured as well as restored, the age must be blamed rather than the editors. With their fifteen or sixteen old carol tunes, and two more from Neale and Helmore (thus popularizing our No. 136) they repaired the breach: afterwards they made up their total to seventy, which increased the modern compositions to forty-three, and the traditional to twenty-seven.

Many other new carols and some collections were produced in the last quarter of the nineteenth century, for carol singing had now become popular; but none of these attained to the standard of Bramley and Stainer. There is a carol-book, for instance, of 1875 which contains over sixty modern pieces—with poor tunes, and words pitifully jejune—to less than forty that can be called carols—and these often obscured almost out of recognition. Indeed, Bramley and Stainer's book supplied nearly all that there was, until in 1901 and 1902 Dr. G. R. Woodward in two editions of the *Cowley Carol Book* (First Series) reprinted twenty-one of Neale's carols, and thus reopened the precious little vein of foreign music which had been discovered fifty years before by Neale and Helmore.

The carol, in fact, was still in jeopardy fifty years ago, and even later. Our churches were flooded with music inspired by the sham Gothic of their renovated interiors: 'carol services' are indeed not infrequently held even today

*O.B.C. No. 190 (1964 edition)

at which not a single genuine carol is sung. On this bad music let us quote Sir Henry Hadow and have done with it. He writes, in his little book, *Church Music* (1926): 'There has probably been no form of any art in the history of the world which has been so overrun by the unqualified amateur as English church music from about 1850 to about 1900. Many of our professional musicians at this time stood also at a low level of culture and intelligence and were quite content to flow with the stream. . . . Thirty years ago we were perhaps at our lowest ebb. This music was deplorably easy to write, it required little or no skill in performance, it passed by mere use and wont into the hearts of the congregation, it became a habit like any other, and it is only during comparatively recent years that any serious attempts have been made to eradicate it.'

Fortunately, however, some two dozen real carols had also become generally known, and these have won their way by their intrinsic merit. The position in 1875, when the flood of bad carols had but recently begun, was correctly described by a writer in the *Guardian* that year, who noted that some 'hearty' persons were bringing carols into 'the sacred precincts' and actually using them as an act of worship; he added that, 'During the last few years carol-singing has been extensively revived. It had never indeed quite died out in our rural districts, in which roughly printed broadsides, with grotesque woodcuts were, and are to this day, annually purchasable at the village shop. These broadsides are issued from the neighbourhood of Seven Dials, in a type, or rather in a conglomeration of odd specimens of type, which would fairly shock the nerves of a good compositor; yet their circulation is enormous, and, if their printers cannot excite our admiration, they at least deserve our gratitude, for they have sustained the very existence of some of the most beautiful carols during the long period of neglect at the hands of musicians and men of letters.'

It was not, however, till the last decade of the nineteenth century that folk music began to be systematically collected. Indeed, the Folk-Song Society was not founded till 1898; and Cecil Sharp, in his *English Folk-Songs: Some Conclusions* (1907), says that 'Twenty years ago it was only by a very few people that folk-songs were known to exist in this country', and the very word 'folk-song' does not seem to have been coined (from *Volkslied*) till after 1880. England, almost alone among the countries of Europe, had not produced a book of national songs; for we were supposed to be an unmusical people, 'Das Land ohne Musik'. At last it was realized that England, as well as Scotland and Germany, and the rest of the civilized world, had its songs; and that folk-music (from which art-music is derived as literature is derived from popular speech) had existed in England all along—tunes originally of individual invention having been gradually shaped to the communal feeling of the race, here not less than in other countries. Then began the search among the memories of old people in the country-side, only just in time; and to this we owe the recovery of one lost carol tune after another. So many have been discovered that there is now a fairly wide scope for the selection of those which are best and most distinctive.

It is a thrilling history, full of significance. Something transparently pure and truthful, clean and merry as the sunshine, has been recovered from under the crust of artificiality which had hidden it. The English-speaking peoples are now getting back what once belonged to them, both in poetry and in music, through the researches of a few scholars and through the conservatism of old village folk and the work of a few musicians who could recognize beauty when they saw it. The carol is established again, and not the carol only; for the work that men like Cecil Sharp did for traditional song and dance is being spread to many ends by the primary and secondary schools throughout the country; the deadly effects of imitation and affectation are passing away, and, by the recovery of our national music which the musicians had lost, an inspiration has come which has already restored English music to the position it held in Europe before the eighteenth century.

2. Selection and Arrangement

The selection of carols is not so easy a task as perhaps might be imagined. There are some genuine old tunes which no one would ever sing; others, like those of William Byrd in collections published in 1588, 1589 and 1611, which are really motets; there are also far more genuine old texts than could possibly be made use of; and, as we have said, there is a large body of recovered folk-carol tunes; there is, moreover, a debatable land between the hymn and the carol; and besides all this there are hundreds of foreign carols. Furthermore, new carols are produced every year, and there is a large accumulation of inferior material, especially imitative work of the self-conscious and artificial type and sentimental verses written for foreign tunes not of the first rank. Much of the labour in any comprehensive collection must therefore be directed to elimination; and this is ungrateful work which has to be done for conscience' sake, since it produces no visible result and may even give the impression that matter has been overlooked which in reality has been carefully considered. One carol, for instance, has recently obtained a certain vogue because it was ascribed to a famous historical personage (a man, by the way, who would have been surprised to find his work associated with so slight a tune): it was evident that the words as they stood were at best but an unskilled translation remote from the supposed original, but a long search had to be made before we could be sure that the historical personage was entirely innocent of the thing in any form whatever.

From the great body of foreign carols it has been our task to discover, so far as we could, the finest tunes, selecting only those which for beauty and distinction seemed to belong to all mankind, and translating or paraphrasing so far as possible the words. Although in a carol the tune generally has precedence, and not the text as in a hymn, this is no reason why perfunctory libretto or meaningless doggerel should be given to a fine melody; we have therefore sought the co-operation of poets in order that both the words and music of the foreign carols might be as good as we could manage. In some cases where no good text seemed to have survived, we have asked our collaborators to write entirely new words: there are therefore some twentieth-century poems in this book; and we hope they are as true to their age, as fresh and direct, as the fifteenth-century poems were. Some modern tunes are also included, most of them in order to carry a specially good fifteenth- or sixteenth-century carol whose tune has been lost. There is, indeed, no reason why the art of carol-making should die.

To avoid, however, a confusion between old and new weddings of tunes to words we have arranged the *Oxford Book of Carols* in a special way. In the First Part we have placed traditional carols which still have their proper tunes (excluding cases that are perhaps on the border-line, such as Nos. 114, 130, and 137, and those texts in Part III which are only based on foreign originals); in the Second Part, traditional carol tunes set to their traditional or old texts; in the Third, the words are not traditional; in the Fourth, the tunes are by modern composers; and in the Fifth are a few entirely modern carols. We have not attempted a further chronological arrangement, since any such attempt would be misleading; but the carols are grouped according to their seasons, and in this Music Edition there is a complete table of carols arranged for use throughout the year.

3. The Texts

We have kept as close as possible to the original texts, and have endeavoured to avoid changing their character or modernizing them into dullness; but sometimes texts have to be slightly altered to make them singable. The problem is more confused than that of hymns; for every fifteenth-century carol that appears in more than one manuscript is in more than one form, and every traditional carol that has been recovered from the people is more or less changed or truncated, while the broadsides are by no means trustworthy. Again, the fifteenth-century carols lose their rhymes if all archaic words are changed, and their character if the sounded 'e' is always replaced by an epithet; but we have altered such things sometimes when the character of the line did not seem to suffer by the change, since this is not a collection of texts but a practical book for choir and people. Especially when a carol is well known, as 'A babe is born all of a may' (116), it would seem perverse to restore 'A merye song then sungyn he', when 'A merry song that night sang he' (or they) has been familiar for the last fifty years, and gives to a reader of today more of the character of the original than would the original words themselves, which in fact were not at all archaic to the author. On the other hand, carols like 'Lullay my liking' (182) and 'Adam lay ybounden' (180) would lose their character if the sounded 'e' were eliminated; they are perfectly intelligible as they stand, and they are not popularly associated with any other version.

The best texts of traditional carols can only be arrived at by copying from the more trustworthy collections, which are few in number, and sometimes by collating various versions. Davies Gilbert in 1822 evidently wrote down the words almost as he heard them, and like William Sandys he sometimes preserved the tunes. Sandys's collection of 1833 is larger; he was a scholarly editor and preserves the character of the originals, though he must have smoothed them a little. The anonymous editor of *A Good Christmas Box*, Dudley, 1847, did in a modest way for the Midlands what Gilbert had done for Cornwall, and seems to have taken down exactly what he heard. W. H. Husk (*Songs of the Nativity*, 1868) deserves much credit for having made use of the broadsides. Most other compilers of the nineteenth century copied from these and from one another; and though some of them recovered a few more old carols, they tried so much to improve on their originals that their texts have seldom much value. Indeed, few subjects have suffered more than the traditional carol from the want of careful research and accurate presentation. The Hanoverian and Victorian scholars and musicians, with a few exceptions, ignored it; and some collections were made by people not well fitted for the task: there was, indeed, only just enough good work—in this country as distinct from Germany—to carry what was left of the old tunes and texts precariously over the gulf. Not even today does there yet exist a standard book on the carol, nor anything like a complete and trustworthy collection. On this subject the *Encyclopaedia Britannica* fails,* and even the *Cambridge History of English Literature* stumbles a little. One result of these misfortunes is that when people give lectures or addresses about carols, few of their statements are correct; another is that the task of workers in the field is heavy, and beset with pitfalls.

Nonetheless, during the nineteenth century the learned societies were active in printing the old manuscripts, and towards the end of the century some work was done for the later carols which was more worthy of the beginning made by Gilbert and Sandys. A. H. Bullen produced his volume of *Carols and Poems* in 1885; and on another side the Folk Song Society has brought accurate and thorough methods into a department which had suffered long from the lack of them. Among editors of varying degrees of accuracy at the present day Edmund K. Chambers and Frank Sidgwick stand out for their scholarly methods (*Early English Lyrics*, 1921), and lead us to hope that such flawless work may be extended, and that one day there may appear a complete collection of English carols of all ages in trustworthy form. This is not such a collection, but a practical book of carols intended to be sung. We have, indeed, supplied footnotes, but only so far as seemed necessary to make each number as intelligible and interesting as the space allowed.

4. Carol Music

The tunes in this book are real carol tunes, and we have endeavoured to secure that their harmonies shall be appropriate to their character, preserving the freshness and buoyancy of the true carol. We have made it a principle not to attempt to provide words for other traditional music. It would be possible to take thousands of folk-tunes like 'The Raggle-taggle Gipsies' or 'Mowing the Barley' and write interminable new instalments of *pastiche* verses for them; but the result would be counterfeits and not carols. When an old tune like 'Greensleeves' (28) or 'Nous voici dans la ville' (91) has been for ages associated both with a carol and a folk-song, it can rightly be claimed as a carol tune; but to go beyond this class is to incur the danger of that artificiality which is still the great enemy of the carol.

There is a point where carols overlap with hymns, especially on their musical side. We have included 'While shepherds watched' (33) because of the traditional carol tune which belongs to it; and, passing over hymns like 'Christians, awake', we have also included for the sake of their carol music 'O little town' (138), 'In the bleak mid-winter' (187), and 'How far is it' (142) from the *English Hymnal* and *Songs of Praise*. A few outstanding carol tunes (Nos. 39, 76, 77, 78, 79), which are set to other words in these two books, we have also included because we think that no carol-book would be complete without them.

Variety in the method of singing is even more important with carols than with hymns, and the verses should never be sung straight through all in the same way. The first and last verses, for instance, can be sung in unison, and other verses

*No exception can be taken to the article in the current *Encyclopaedia Britannica*. J.A.P. (1964).

also in the case of long carols; a fine antiphonal effect can often be got by the alternate singing of choir and people. Sometimes a carol can be treated as a solo, the harmonies being sung *bouche fermée* by the choir; and sometimes the organ or orchestra can be brought in with fine effect after it has been silent during two or three verses. Suggestions for variations of this sort, as well as varied harmonies and fa-burdens, will be found in this Music Edition of the *Oxford Book of Carols*. Whatever is to be done should be thought out beforehand and announced before the carol is sung, so that the people can do their part with confidence. Choir and people alike will be greatly helped if the choirmaster stands in a place from which he can conduct them both. Since a few carols are very short and others even after abridgement are long, and since the music enjoys a certain precedence, a very short carol like 'A little child' (74) may well be sung twice over, and the first verse at least repeated in a carol like 'Patapan' (82) or 'Rocking' (87), while a long carol like 'A New Dial' (64) may be more summarily abbreviated than is advisable in the case of a hymn.

5. The Use of Carols

By no means all the old carols are about Christmas. If, for instance, we analyse Richard Hill's typical manuscript collection (described under No. 36), we find that his 62 sacred songs in the Early English Text Society edition—all true carols with refrains—can be classified thus: A. *Carols of a general character* suitable at any time of the year, 18 (there are no narrative ballad carols and no May carols in the collection). B. *Carols bearing on the Nativity*, specifically Christmas, 17; Christmastide saints, 4; Epiphany, 2; Nativity, 4, one of these being mainly on the Passion; to the Virgin, 2; on the Annunciation, 5 (making a total in Section B of 34). C. *Carols on other subjects*, Baptism of Christ, 1; the Passion, 6; the Eucharist, 3. In other parts of the book are the Corpus Christi Carol (61 *n.*), 'Nay, nay ivy', and several devotional poems unconnected with Christmas. The absence of Easter is remarkable; for carols represent those aspects of religion in which the fifteenth-century Englishman was most interested: there are many foreign Easter carols, but abroad as well as in England the great subjects commemorated in the festivals after Easter evoked little or no lyrical response. The iconography of painting, as a visit to any picture gallery will show, has much the same characteristics, and evinces the same absence of interest in the works and teaching of Christ. This last subject appears in English seventeenth-century carols, in which also Easter finds mention as the sequel to the Passion.

There seems to have been a constant tendency of the people to sing carols all the year, and of those in authority (at least as early as the sixteenth century) to restrict festivities to the Twelve Days. After the Epiphany, labourers and apprentices were required to settle down to work again for the rest of the year—reluctantly, poor things: the young men used to hinder the maids by setting fire to their flax on the 7th of January, 'St. Distaff's Day', as Herrick tells us:

Partly work and partly play,
You must on Saint Distaff's day
From the plough soon free your team,
Then come home and fodder them:
If the maids a-spinning go
Burn the flax and fire the tow.

After this stolen day they 'bid Christmas sport goodnight'; and, concludes Herrick, 'next morrow, every one To his own vocation'. It is easy to see how the carol came to be restricted at least in its more festive aspects to Christmas, and occasional holidays like May Day, so that before the nineteenth century the conveniently alliterative title 'Christmas Carol' held the field. Bramley and Stainer completed the temporary disappearance of other carols by the popularity of their *Christmas Carols*, and thenceforward authors seldom attempted carols on any theme outside the Twelve Days.

The old people in the villages, however, held on to the other carols, and thus many have been recovered in recent years. In earlier days the waits, as they tottered towards extinction, had apparently found that some excuse was needed for singing such carols, since we can hardly account otherwise for the tags about Christmas or New Year which occur sometimes at the end of Passion and General Carols. Poor rustics! ever since the Methodist Revival people had been teaching them to drop carols altogether. The fact that so much has survived in the little private repertories of peasants and gipsies down to our own day is a tribute to the quality of the folk-carol. It should be easily possible to restore such spontaneous and imperishable things to general use, in the home as well as in church, and to have the waits at work again, not only out of doors but in halls and public rooms, all the year round.

Carols have been used in more than one way—out of doors, in church, at masques and concerts, in the home. As early as Chaucer, the Clerk of Oxenford could sing his carol-like sequence (52) 'So swetely that al the chambre rong'; and we hope that the lovely old tunes in this book will be more and more sung by people in their own homes. We hope also that they will be increasingly sung in halls, from the modest village institute to the fully equipped concert hall. The revival of village life and the desire to relieve the hideous secularity of our great towns may well lead to a demand for the use of carols in out-door processions and festivities in spring and summer as well as at Christmas. Clubs, guilds, women's institutes should find carols a constant source of happiness and inspiration.

We think also that carols might be continuously sung in ordinary parish churches and in chapels, where the choir often try to emulate the too difficult anthem of cathedral and collegiate churches. On p. 871 of the Music Edition of *Songs of Praise* we gave a list of hymns that are suitable to be sung instead of the anthem so often disastrous to the normal parish choir. What might not be done with carols? On every Sunday, in the place of the anthem, or after service, glorious carols can be sung by the choir, the people joining in the refrains, or singing the third and subsequent alternate verses. Perhaps nothing is just now of such importance as to increase the element of joy in religion; people crowd in our churches at the Christmas, Easter, and Harvest Festivals, largely because the hymns for those occasions are full of a sound hilarity; if carol-books were in continual use, that most Christian and most forgotten element would be vastly increased, in some of its loveliest forms, all through the year.

P.D.
1928

ACKNOWLEDGEMENTS

(1928)

BESIDES those whose contributions we gratefully acknowledge below, the translators, poets, and musicians who have taken so much trouble in helping us, we owe special thanks to Mr. Walter Gandy for his prolonged musical and literary researches; to the late Professor Röntgen for the Dutch and Flemish carols (73, 74); to Mr. J. B. Trend for Spanish carols (81,113); to Canon R. E. Roberts for Welsh carols (9, 34, 50, 59); to the Rev. G. H. Doble and Mr. H. Jenner for Cornish carols (35, 41); to Miss Lucy Broadwood (45, 55); and especially to Miss Karpeles, the literary executrix to Cecil Sharp, for the English traditional carols acknowledged below. Also to Mr. J. H. Arnold, Miss E. Maconchy, and Dr. Geoffrey Shaw, for harmonizing melodies; to many who have helped and encouraged us, especially to Mr. Frank Sidgwick for his very kind help, and Mrs. Alexander Ferguson and Miss Violet Latford for their careful clerical assistance.

We acknowledge here the copyright texts under the initials A.F.D., A. G., B. M. G., E. B. G., G. D., L. M., N. S. T., O. B. C., S.P.; as well as those texts, melodies, and harmonies under the names of the Editors. Our thanks are due to Messrs. Stainer and Bell for allowing the reprinting of the following folk carols collected by Mrs. Leather and R. Vaughan Williams, 7, 43, 53, 57, 115, 131 (copyright, U.S.A. 1920, by Stainer & Bell, Ltd.); and by R. Vaughan Williams, 17, 24, 47, 51, 61, 68 (copyright, U.S.A. 1919, by Stainer & Bell, Ltd.); Messrs. Novello & Co. Ltd., for the following collected by Cecil Sharp, 8, 54, 60 (melody and words), and by Mr. W. P. Merrick and R. Vaughan Williams, 60 (3). Also to Messrs. Boosey for Miss Broadwood's Folk Carol, 45; Messrs. J. Curwen & Sons, Ltd., for tunes 78 (Curwen Edition, No. 71655, copyright, U.S.A. 1924, by Gustav Holst), 137 (Curwen Edition, No. 71656, copyright, U.S.A. 1924, by Gustav Holst), 172 (Curwen Edition, No. 2418, copyright, U.S.A. 1926, by Martin Shaw), 176 (Curwen Edition, No. 80663, copyright, U.S.A. 1928, by Armstrong Gibbs), also 182 and 189; also to Messrs. J. M. Dent & Sons, Ltd., for the late G. K. Chesterton's carol, 143; Miss Maud Karpeles for melody of 142; Messrs. Macmillan & Co., Ltd., for Christina Rossetti's carol, 187; Messrs. A. R. Mowbray & Co., Ltd., for tunes 22 (2), 29, 58, 178 (2), 184, 194, 195; Messrs. Novello & Co. Ltd., for tune 192, and the Caniedydd Committee, Welsh Congregational Union, for tunes 34 and 59.

Our heavy debt to the late Cecil Sharp is shown by our notes in many parts of the book, especially under Nos. 4, 8, 24, 32, 38, 44, 54, 60, 65, 70; our debt to the late Professor Julius Röntgen for help over Dutch tunes extends beyond the two numbers we have mentioned; and to Miss Jacubičková we owe the two Czech carols (87, 103) which she collected. Dr. Grattan Flood kindly gave us permission for Nos. 6 and 14 before he died; and to Trinity College, Dublin, we owe the permission to photograph the manuscript of No. 30. The Rev. J. R. Van Pelt kindly communicated the tune of No. 143; and Archdeacon Kewley gave permission for the melody of the Manx tune No. 167 collected by the late Dr.

John Clague. Mr. H. J. L. J. Massé has helped us all by his publication of foreign carols, especially in *A Book of Old Carols*, which he edited in 1907 and 1910 with Mr. Charles Kennedy Scott.

We offer our best thanks to those who have made or translated carols for this book, or who have allowed their work to be included here: the Rev. H. N. Bate (191, 193); the Rev. Maurice F. Bell (75, 83); Mr. Laurence Binyon (161); Mr. Patrick R. Chalmers (101, 108, 110); the late G. K. Chesterton (143); Mrs. G. K. Chesterton (142); the Rev. J. M. C. Crum (149); Mr. Geoffrey Dearmer (111, 154, 155, 157); Mr. Walter de la Mare (163); Miss Eleanor Farjeon (88, 91, 97, 133, 158, 188); Miss Rose Fyleman (156); Mr. Robert Graves (80, 84); Mr. Selwyn Image (192, 194); Mr. Frank Kendon (140, 146); Professor George H. Leonard (145); Mr. A. A. Milne (106); Mrs. Roberts (9, 34, 50, 59); Mr. A. H. Fox-Strangways (95); Mr. R. C. Trevelyan (73, 74); Mr. H. T. Wade-Gery (179); and Mr. Steuart Wilson (98, 162, 164, 166, 167). Also to the following composers for permission to use their tunes: Mr. Rutland Boughton (168); Mr. E. Rubbra (175); Mr. Harry Farjeon (188); Mr. Armstrong Gibbs (176); the late G. Holst (187); Mr. John Ireland (170); Mr. R. O. Morris (190); Mr. S. H. Nicholson (174); and the late Peter Warlock (169, 180, 181); and to the following for their harmonizations: Miss E. Maconchy (56, 69); and Dr. Geoffrey Shaw (2, 30, 48, 83, 92, 95, 98, 102, 105, 120, 135, 141, 148, 150, 151, 152, 158).

The arrangements of most of the tunes by (M. S.) and (R. V. W.), also No. 186, are the copyright of the Musical Editors. Also tunes Nos. 103, 123, 130, 177, and 183 are copyright, U.S.A. 1928, by Martin Shaw; and tunes Nos. 173, 185, and 196 are copyright, U.S.A. 1928, by R. Vaughan Williams. Tunes Nos. 169, 175, 180, 181, and 188 are copyright, U.S.A. 1925, and Nos. 21 and 67 are copyright, U.S.A. 1928, by the Oxford University Press. The following tunes are also the copyright of the Oxford University Press: Nos. 60 (2), 178 (1), 57 (2).

We wish to take this opportunity of acknowledging our gratitude to the memory of J. M. Neale and the other pioneers in the revival of the carol: and also to all those old people in the villages of England who preserved and communicated so many traditional carols for our use today.

EXPLANATORY NOTES

AN ASTERISK suggests verses that may conveniently be omitted, but it is not intended to negative still further omissions. *Tr.* means 'translated by', and *Pr.* 'paraphrased by'. The nature of the music is briefly stated at the head of each carol on the right side in all editions, and that of the words on the left side. *Ibid.* means that the words and tune are in the same book or other source or sources. In the Music Edition the composers of the harmonies, &c., are indicated by names or initials within brackets at the head of the music.

NOTE TO 1964 IMPRESSION

THE original words of most of the translated carols have been added. Translations have been provided for those few carols which the original editors left in the vernacular and, in one or two cases, alternative English words of proven value have also been included.

John Goss's well-known tune for No. 190, copyright when the *Oxford Book of Carols* was first published, has now been included. Three medieval carols (Nos. 21, 52, and 67) have been transcribed afresh from the original sources. Since the 1928 edition there has been much research into early carols, and all early publications in this field have been outdated by Dr. R. L. Greene's *The Early English Carols* (1935) and Dr. J. E. Stevens' *Medieval Carols* (Musica Britannica, Vol. IV) (1952). References to these two books have been added to the footnotes throughout the book.

Thanks are due to Mr. John A. Parkinson for his valuable help in the preparation of the 1964 impression. We are also grateful to Mr. Paul Arma and Les Editions Ouvrières for permission to include the French words of Nos. 88, 108, 140, 154, and 166.

CONTENTS

PART I
TRADITIONAL CAROLS
WITH TUNES PROPER TO THEM

1. ENGLISH, WELSH, AND IRISH

1 CHRISTMAS EVE

Traditional
FIRST TUNE
Ibid.
(M.S.)
SOPRANO
ALTO
TENOR
BASS
1. The_ Lord at first did_ A-dam make Out of the dust and clay,___ And_ in his nos-trils_ brea-thed life, E'en as the scrip-tures say. And then in E - den's_ pa - ra - dise He pla-ced him to dwell, That he with-in it___ should re-main, To dress and keep it
2. Now_ mark the good-ness_ of the Lord Which he to man-kind bore;___ His_ mer-cy soon he_ did ex - tend, Lost man for to_ re-store: And then, for to re - deem our souls From death and hell-ish thrall, He said his_ own dear_ Son should be The Sa - viour of___ us

CHORUS
well:
all:
Now let good Christ- ians _ all be - gin An ho - ly life to

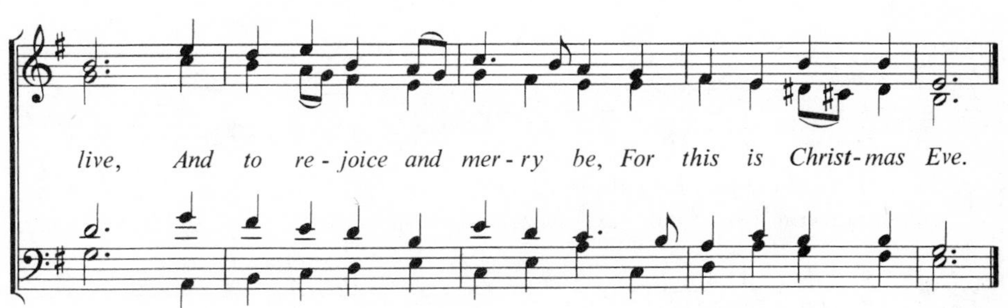
live, And to re - joice and mer - ry be, For this is Christ-mas Eve.

3 Now for the blessings we enjoy,
  Which are from heaven above,
Let us renounce all wickedness,
  And live in perfect love:
Then shall we do Christ's own command,
  E'en his own written word;
And when we die, in heaven shall
  Enjoy our living Lord:

Now let good Christians etc.

4 And now the tide is nigh at hand,
  In which our Saviour came;
Let us rejoice and merry be
  In keeping of the same:
Let's feed the poor and hungry souls,
  And such as do it crave;
Then when we die, in heaven we
  Our sure reward shall have:

Now let good Christians etc.

In Davies Gilbert's West-country collection, *Some Ancient Christmas Carols*, 1822, seven verses, with the first tune. The second tune is from Sandys, *Christmas Carols*, 1833.

1 CHRISTMAS EVE

SECOND TUNE

Traditional
Ibid.
(M.S.)
SOPRANO
ALTO
TENOR
BASS
1. The Lord at_first did_ A-dam make Out of the dust and_clay, And
2. Now mark the good-ness_ of the Lord Which he to man-kind_bore; His
in his_ nos-trils_ brea-thed life, E'en as the scrip-tures_ say. And_
mer-cy_ soon he_ did ex-tend, Lost man for to re-store: And_
then in_ E-den's pa-ra-dise He pla-ced_ him to dwell, That_
then, for_ to re-deem our souls From death and_hell-ish thrall, He_
he with-in it should_ re-main, To dress_and keep_it_ well:
said his own dear Son_ should be The Sa-viour of_us_ all:

CHORUS
Now let good Christ-ians all be - gin An ho - ly— life— to live, And—

to re - joice and mer - ry— be, For this is— Christ-mas Eve.

3 Now for the blessings we enjoy,
Which are from heaven above,
Let us renounce all wickedness,
And live in perfect love:
Then shall we do Christ's own command,
E'en his own written word;
And when we die, in heaven shall
Enjoy our living Lord:

Now let good Christians etc.

4 And now the tide is nigh at hand,
In which our Saviour came;
Let us rejoice and merry be
In keeping of the same:
Let's feed the poor and hungry souls,
And such as do it crave;
Then when we die, in heaven we
Our sure reward shall have:

Now let good Christians etc.

In Davies Gilbert's West-country collection, *Some Ancient Christmas Carols*, 1822, seven verses, with the first tune. The second tune is from Sandys, *Christmas Carols*, 1833.

2 A CHILD THIS DAY
(CHRISTMAS)

Traditional | Ibid. (G.S.)

The harmonies to verse 1 may be used throughout, if desired

With vigour
SOPRANO ALTO
TENOR BASS
1. A child this·day is born, A child of high re-nown, Most wor-thy of a scep-tre, A scep-tre and a crown:
2. These tid-ings shep-herds heard, In field watching their fold, Were by an an-gel un-to them That night re-veal'd and told:
CHORUS
Now-ell, Now-ell, Now-ell, Now-ell, sing all we may, Be-cause the King of all kings Was born this bless-ed day.
Be-cause the King Was born this day.
Be-cause the King of all kings Was born this bless-ed day.
Fine
3. To whom the an-gel spoke, Say-ing, 'Be not a-fraid; Be
4. 'For lo! I bring you tid-ings Of glad-ness and of mirth, Which
(Altos and Tenors, lightly)
Now-ell, Now-ell, Sing all we

Repeat CHORUS
glad, poor sil - ly shep - herds–Why are you so dis - mayed?'
com - eth to all peo - ple by This ho - ly in - fant's birth':
may This bless - ed, This bless - ed, bless - ed day.
dim.
5. Then was there with the an - gel An host in - con - ti - nent Of
7. And as the an - gel told them, So to them did ap - pear; They
Repeat CHORUS
hea - ven - ly bright sol - diers, Which from the High-est was sent:
found the young child, Je - sus Christ, With Ma - ry, his mo - ther dear:
6. Laud - ing the Lord our God, And his ce - les - tial King; All
(Two bass parts)
Now - ell, Now - ell, Sing all we
Repeat CHORUS
Now-
Now - ell, Now-ell, Now - ell,
glo - ry be in pa - ra-dise, This heav'n-ly host did sing:
Now - - -
may This bless - ed, This heav'n-ly host did sing. Now -

3. Silly—originally 'blessed' (*selig*), had still in the seventeenth century the meaning of 'simple'.
Words and tune from William Sandys, *Christmas Carols*, 1833 (West of England). The usual seven out of twenty-one verses are here given.

3 SUNNY BANK
(CHRISTMAS)

Traditional

Ibid.
(M.S.)

SOPRANO
ALTO
TENOR
BASS
1. As I sat on a sun - ny bank, a sun - ny bank, a sun - ny bank, As I sat on a sun - ny bank,
2. I spied three ships come sail - ing by, come sail - ing by, come sail - ing by, I spied three ships come sail - ing by,
On Christ - mas Day in the morn - ing.

3 And who should be with those three
But Joseph and his fair lady! [ships

4 O he did whistle, and she did sing,
On Christmas Day in the morning.

5 And all the bells on earth did ring,
On Christmas Day in the morning.

6 For joy that our Saviour he was born
(that he was born, that he was born,)
On Christmas Day in the morning.

Cf. No. 18. Melody, with some of the verses, taken by Mr. J. H. Blunt, in 1916, from Mr. Samuel Newman, at Downton, Wilts. 'A Sunny Bank' (either thus or as 'I saw three ships') is in most old broadsides and modern collections. It has been found in the North, and West, and Midlands; Cecil Sharp noted two versions, one in Worcestershire, and Bullen found it in Kent. There is an early version in Forbes's *Cantus* (Aberdeen), 1666. We print the usual broadside version of this form as given by Husk.

4 A VIRGIN MOST PURE

(CHRISTMAS)

FIRST TUNE

Traditional

Ibid. (M.S.)

SOPRANO
ALTO
TENOR
BASS
1. A — vir - gin — most — pure, as the pro - phets do
tell, Hath — brought — forth — a — ba - by, as it — hath — be -
-fel, To be our Re - deem - er from death, hell, — and
sin, Which — A - dam's — trans - gres - sion hath wrap-ped us in:

4—A Virgin most Pure

CHORUS
Aye and there - fore be mer - ry, re - joice and be you
and be you
mer - ry, Set sor - rows a - side; Christ
Je - sus our Sa - viour was born on this tide.
Fine
VERSES 2-7
SOPRANO
ALTO
TENOR
BASS
2. At Beth - lem in Jew - ry a ci - ty there
3. But when they had en - ter'd the ci - ty so
was, Where Jo - seph and Ma - ry to - ge - ther did
fair, A num - ber of peo - ple so migh - ty was

pass, And there to be___ tax - ed with ma - ny___ one
there, That Jo - seph and___ Ma - ry, whose sub - stance was
Repeat CHORUS
mo', For___ Cae - sar___ com - man - ded the same should be so:
small, Could find in___ the___ inn there no lodg - ing at all:

4 Then were they constrained in a stable to lie,
Where horses and asses they used for to tie;
Their lodging so simple they took it no scorn:
But against the next morning our Saviour was born:

Aye and therefore etc.

5 The King of all kings to this world being brought,
Small store of fine linen to wrap him was sought;
And when she had swaddled her young son so sweet,
Within an ox-manger she laid him to sleep:

Aye and therefore etc.

6 Then God sent an angel from heaven so high,
To certain poor shepherds in fields where they lie,
And bade them no longer in sorrow to stay,
Because that our Saviour was born on this day:

Aye and therefore etc.

7 Then presently after the shepherds did spy
A number of angels that stood in the sky;
They joyfully talkèd, and sweetly did sing,
To God be all glory, our heavenly King:

Aye and therefore etc.

2. mo'—more.

Davies Gilbert, *Some Ancient Christmas Carols*, 1822. There is a printed version of 1734. Sandys (1833) prints a slightly different version with an eighth verse. Three versions are printed by W. H. Husk, *Songs of the Nativity*, 1868 (pp. 30, 56, 65). There are many tunes. The first we give from Gilbert; the second from Cecil Sharp's *English Folk Carols*, noted by him from Mr. Henry Thomas at Chipping Sodbury. The third was noted by Cecil Sharp in Shropshire, 1911, and printed in the *Journal of the Folk-Song Society*, vol. v., p. 24.

For other 'Virgin Unspotted' tunes see Nos. 114 and 139.

4 A VIRGIN MOST PURE
(CHRISTMAS)
SECOND TUNE

Traditional | Ibid. (M.S.)

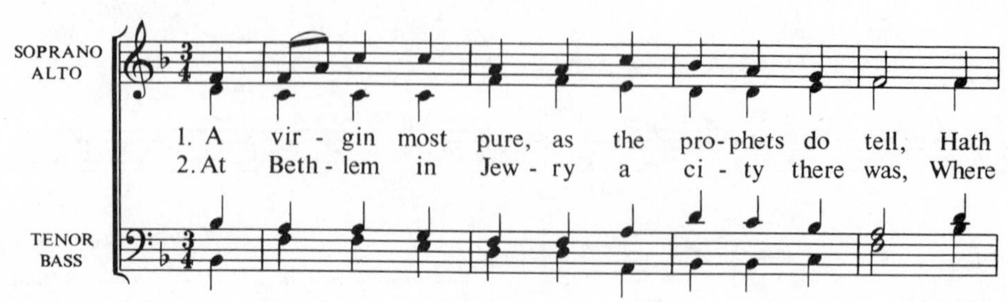
SOPRANO
ALTO
1. A vir - gin most pure, as the pro-phets do tell, Hath
2. At Beth - lem in Jew - ry a ci - ty there was, Where
TENOR
BASS

brought forth a ba - by, as it hath be - fel, To
Jo - seph and Ma - ry to - ge - ther did pass, And

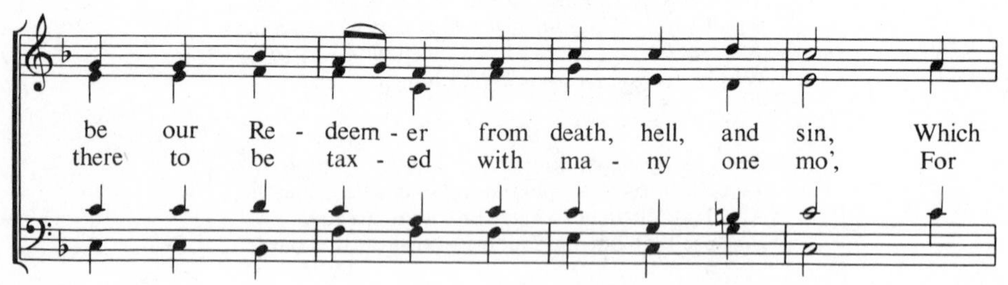
be our Re - deem - er from death, hell, and sin, Which
there to be tax - ed with ma - ny one mo', For

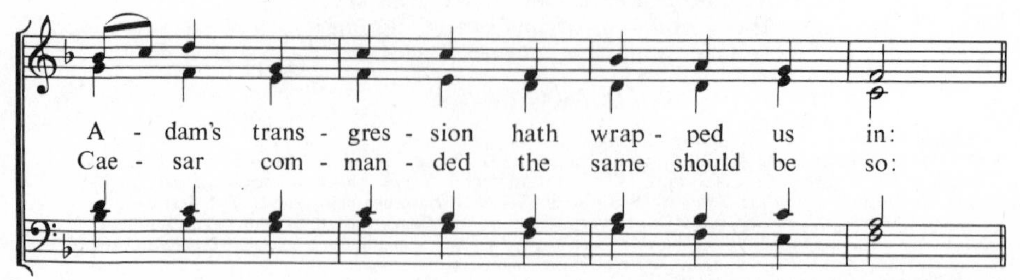
A - dam's trans - gres - sion hath wrap - ped us in:
Cae - sar com - man - ded the same should be so:

CHORUS
And there-fore be mer - ry, set sor - rows a - side; Christ

Je - sus our Sa - viour was born on this tide.

3 But when they had entered the city so fair,
A number of people so mighty was there,
That Joseph and Mary, whose substance was small,
Could find in the inn there no lodging at all:

And therefore be merry, etc.

4 Then were they constrained in a stable to lie,
Where horses and asses they used for to tie;
Their lodging so simple they took it no scorn:
But against the next morning our Saviour was born:

And therefore be merry, etc.

5 The King of all kings to this world being brought,
Small store of fine linen to wrap him was sought;
And when she had swaddled her young son so sweet,
Within an ox-manger she laid him to sleep:

And therefore be merry, etc.

6 Then God sent an angel from heaven so high,
To certain poor shepherds in fields where they lie,
And bade them no longer in sorrow to stay,
Because that our Saviour was born on this day:

And therefore be merry, etc.

7 Then presently after the shepherds did spy
A number of angels that stood in the sky;
They joyfully talkèd, and sweetly did sing,
To God be all glory, our heavenly King:

And therefore be merry, etc.

2. mo'—more.
For note on this carol see p. 11.

4 A VIRGIN MOST PURE

(CHRISTMAS)

THIRD TUNE

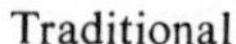

Traditional

Ibid.
(R.V.W.)

Voices in unison (or solo)
ACCT.
1. A— vir - gin most— pure, as the— pro - phets— do
2. At— Beth - lem in— Jew - ry a— ci - ty—there

tell, Hath—brought forth a ba - by, as— it hath be - fel,
was, Where—Jo - seph and Ma - ry to - ge - ther did pass,

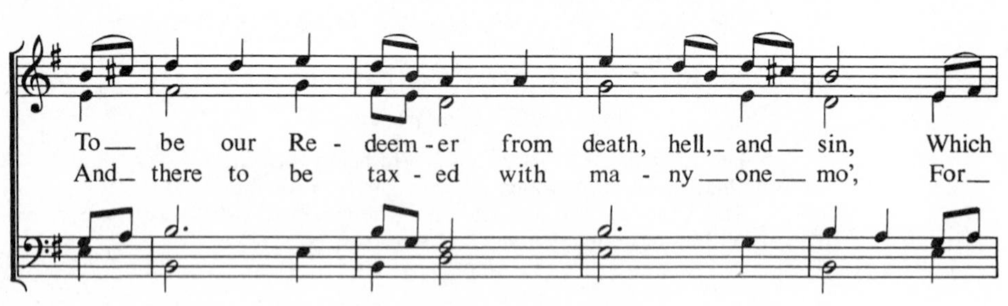
To— be our Re - deem - er from death, hell,—and—sin, Which
And—there to be tax - ed with ma - ny—one—mo', For—

A - dam's trans - gres - sion hath— wrap - ped— us in:
Cae - sar com - man - ded the— same should be so:

CHORUS
And— there-fore be mer - ry, set sor - rows— a - side; Christ

Je - sus our— Sa - viour was— born on— this tide.

3 But when they had entered the city so fair,
A number of people so mighty was there,
That Joseph and Mary, whose substance was small,
Could find in the inn there no lodging at all:

And therefore be merry, etc.

4 Then were they constrained in a stable to lie,
Where horses and asses they used for to tie;
Their lodging so simple they took it no scorn:
But against the next morning our Saviour was born:

And therefore be merry, etc.

5 The King of all kings to this world being brought,
Small store of fine linen to wrap him was sought;
And when she had swaddled her young son so sweet,
Within an ox-manger she laid him to sleep:

And therefore be merry, etc.

6 Then God sent an angel from heaven so high,
To certain poor shepherds in fields where they lie,
And bade them no longer in sorrow to stay,
Because that our Saviour was born on this day:

And therefore be merry, etc.

7 Then presently after the shepherds did spy
A number of angels that stood in the sky;
They joyfully talkèd, and sweetly did sing,
To God be all glory, our heavenly King:

And therefore be merry, etc.

2. mo'—more.
For note on this carol see p. 11.

5 THE PRAISE OF CHRISTMAS

(ADVENT: CHRISTMAS)

T. Durfey and others

Traditional (M.S.)

SOPRANO
ALTO
TENOR
BASS
1. All hail to the days that me - rit more praise Than
2.'Tis ill for a mind to an - ger in - clined To
all the rest of the year, And wel - come the nights that
think of small in - jur - ies now; If wrath be to seek, do not
dou - ble de - lights As well for the poor as the peer! Good
lend her thy cheek, Nor let her in - ha - bit thy brow. Cross
for - tune at - tend each mer - ry man's friend That
out of thy books ma - le - vo - lent looks, Both

doth but the best that he may, For - get - ting old wrongs with
beau - ty and youth's de - cay, And_ whol - ly con - sort with

ca - rols and songs, To drive the cold win - ter a - way.
mirth and with sport, To drive the cold win - ter a - way.

3 This time of the year is spent in good cheer,
And neighbours together do meet,
To sit by the fire, with friendly desire,
Each other in love to greet.
Old grudges forgot are put in the pot,
All sorrows aside they lay;
The old and the young doth carol this song,
To drive the cold winter away.

4 When Christmas's tide comes in like a bride,
With holly and ivy clad,
Twelve days in the year much mirth and good cheer
In every household is had.
The country guise is then to devise
Some gambols of Christmas play,
Whereat the young men do best that they can
To drive the cold winter away.

There is a black-letter copy of this wholesome song (of which twelve verses exist) in the Pepysian Collection. Rimbault preserved the tune. The first two verses are by Tom Durfey (1653-1723), the dramatist and friend of Charles II, in his *Pills to Purge Melancholy*, 1719.

6 IRISH CAROL
(CHRISTMAS)
Irish traditional
Ibid.
(M.S.)
SOPRANO
ALTO
TENOR
BASS
1. Christ-mas Day is come; let's all pre-pare for mirth, Which
2. But why should we re-joice? Should we not ra-ther mourn To
(Bass) Ding dong, ding dong, etc.
fills the heav'ns and earth at this a-maz-ing birth. Through
see the hope of na-tions thus in a sta-ble born? Where
both the joy-ous an-gels in strife and hur-ry— fly, With
are his crown and scep-tre, where is his throne sub-lime, Where
Sop. {In
{Is
glo-ry and ho-san-nas, 'All Ho-ly'— do they cry,
A.+T. Ding
is his train ma-jes-tic that should the— stars out-shine?
heav'n the Church tri-um-phant a-dores with all her choirs, The
there no sump-tuous pa-lace nor a-ny inn at all To
dong, ding dong, ding dong, ding dong, ding dong,— ding— dong, ding

mi - li-tant on earth— with hum - ble faith ad - mires. In
lodge his heav'n-ly mo - ther— but in a fil - thy stall? Is
1st time
dong, ding dong, ding dong, with hum - ble— faith— ad - mires. Ding
but in a — fil - thy— stall?
(Bass) Ding dong, ding dong, ding dong, ding
hum - ble faith ad - mires.
in a fil - thy stall?
2nd time
hum - ble— faith— ad - mires, with— hum - ble— faith— ad - mires.
in a— fil - thy— stall, but— in— a— fil - thy— stall?
dong, ding dong, ding dong, ding dong, ding dong, ding dong.

3 Oh! cease, ye blessèd angels, such clamorous joys
to make!
Though midnight silence favours, the shepherds are
awake;
And you, O glorious star! that with new splendour
brings
From the remotest parts three learnèd eastern kings,
Turn somewhere else your lustre, your rays elsewhere
display;
For Herod he may slay the babe, and Christ must
straight away.

4 If we would then rejoice, let's cancel the old score,
And, purposing amendment, resolve to sin no more—
For mirth can ne'er content us, without a conscience
clear;
And thus we'll find true pleasure in all the usual cheer,
In dancing, sporting, revelling, with masquerade and
drum,
So let our Christmas merry be, as Christians doth
become.

The words and tune kindly communicated by Dr. Grattan Flood. The words in their original form were probably written for the tune in the seventeenth century, when Bishop Luke Wadding (1588-1657) wrote many hymns and carols for folk-tunes which had become associated with 'coarse' words. Since then carols of this kind have been traditional in Kilmore, South Wexford. Cf. No. 14.

The English Carol (Routley) p. 218 gives alternative words by Anne Scott, 'Come ye thankful people'.

7 HEREFORD CAROL

(CHRISTMAS)

Traditional

Ibid. (R.V.W.)

SOPRANO
ALTO
TENOR
BASS
1. Come all you — faith-ful Christ-ians That dwell here on — earth,
2. Be - hold the — an - gel Ga - bri - el, In scrip-ture it is said,
Come — ce - le - brate the mor - ning Of our dear Sa - viour's birth.
Did — with his — ho - ly mes - sage Come — to the — vir - gin maid:
This — is — the hap - py mor - ning, This — is the bles - sed morn: —
'Hail, — blest — a - mong all wo - men!' He — thus did greet her then, —
To — save our souls from ru - in, The — Son of — God was born.
'Lo, — thou shalt — be the mo - ther Of the Sa - viour — of all men.'

3 Her time being accomplished,
She came to Bethlehem,
And then was safe delivered
Of the Saviour of all men.
No princely pomp attended him,
His honours were but small;
A manger was his cradle,
His bed an ox's stall.

4 Now to him that is ascended
Let all our praises be;
May we his steps then follow,
And he our pattern be;
So when our lives are ended,
We all may hear him call—
'Come, souls, receive the kingdom,
Preparèd for you all.'

Collated (with the omission of several verses) from three sources: (1) Mr. Hirons, Haven, Dilwyn; (2) Mr. Gallet, Leigh Linton, Worcestershire; (3) A ballad sheet published by R. Elliot, Hereford. Melody from Mr. Hirons. From *Twelve Traditional Carols from Herefordshire* (Leather and Vaughan Williams), Stainer & Bell.

8 SOMERSET CAROL
(CHRISTMAS)

Traditional
Ibid.
(M.S.)
SOPRANO
ALTO
TENOR
BASS
1. Come all you wor - thy gen - tle-men That may be stan-ding by,
2. ___ Christ our bless - ed Sa - vi - our Now in the man-ger lay—
3. God bless the ru - ler of this house, And long on may he reign,
___ Christ our bless - ed Sa - vi - our Was born on Christ-mas Day.
He's ly - ing in the man - ger, While the ox - en feed on hay.
___ Ma - ny hap - py Christ-mas - es He live to see a - gain!
1,2) The bless - ed Vir - gin Ma - ry Un - to the Lord did say,
3) God bless our ge - ne - ra - tion, Who live both far and near,
1,2) O we wish_ you the com - fort and ti - dings of joy!
3) And we wish_ them a hap - py, a hap - py New Year!

Cf. No. 11. Taken from Mr. Rapsey of Bridgwater, by Cecil Sharp, *Folk Songs from Somerset* (No. 126), and *English Folk Carols*, No. XI (by permission of Novello & Co. Ltd.). Mr. Rapsey was taught the carol by his mother, and as a child used to sing it with other children in the streets of Bridgwater at Christmas time.

9 DARK THE NIGHT
(EPIPHANY: GENERAL)

Tr. K.E. Roberts

Melody by CANON OWEN JONES
Harmonized by Dr. CARADOG ROBERTS

SOPRANO
ALTO

TENOR
BASS

1. Dark the night lay, wild and drea-ry Moaned the wind-by Mel-chior's tower,
2. Now, Lord Je-sus, hear our call-ing, Deep the dark-ness where we stray;

Sad the sage, while pon-d'ring wea-ry O'er the doom of— Ju-dah's power:
How shall we, mid boul-ders fall-ing, Know for thine the-rough-hewn way?

When be-hold, the clouds are part-ed—West-ward, lo, a—light gleams far!
Lo, a light shines down to guide us Where thy saints and-an-gels are!

Now his heart's-true quest has start-ed, For his eyes-have-seen the star.
Now we know—thy love be-side—us; For our eyes-have-seen the star.

A free translation of a Welsh carol by the Rev. W. Lloyd. The tune and original Welsh words first appeared in *Carolan Nadolig* by Canon Owen Jones.

10 COME, LOVE WE GOD!

(CHRISTMAS: EPIPHANY)

Shann MS.
Ibid.
SOPRANO
ALTO
TENOR
BASS
1. Come, love we God! of might is most The Fa-ther, the
2. The herd-men came with their off'-ring For to — pre-
Son, the Ho-ly Ghost, *Reg-nan-te jam in ae-the-ra;* The
-sent that pret-ty thing *Cum sum-ma re-ve-ren-ti-a.* They
which made man, both more and less, And cre-ate him to his like-
gave their gifts that child un-til; They were re-cei-ved with good-
v.4: *De-o — Pa-tri,*
-ness, *O quan-ta, O quan-ta sunt haec op-e-ra.*
-will; *Quam gra-ta, quam gra-ta sunt haec mu-ne-ra!*

3 Three kingès came from the east country,
Which knew they by astronomy,
Et Balam vaticinia;
They offered him gold, myrrh, incense;
He took them with great diligence:
Quam digna est infantia!

4 They turned again full merrily,
Each came unto his own country:
O Dei mirabilia,
They had heaven's bliss at their ending,
The which God grant us old and young.
Deo Patri sit gloria.

1. *Regnante*, &c.—Now reigning in the sky. *O quanta*, &c.—O how great are these works.
2. *Cum*, &c.—With utmost reverence. *Quam*, &c.—How welcome are these gifts.
3. *Et Balam*, &c.—And by the prophecy of Balaam. *Quam*, &c.—How worthy is the infancy.
4. *O Dei*, &c.—O wonderful (works) of God. *Deo Patri*, &c.—Glory be to God the Father.

The tune and a selection from the partly illegible ten verses of the original are from 'Certaine pretie songes hereafter followinge drawn together by Richard Shanne, 1611', in the MS. of the Shann family of Methley, Yorks, now B.M., Add. 38599. Among various songs, some with music, is this: it is headed 'A Christmas Carroll maid by Sir Richard Shanne, priest', who may have been much earlier, since this has the characteristics of a fifteenth-century carol, and the tune is in a style contemporary with the words. We have altered the error 'These kinges' in v. 3 to *Three* (the number of course is legendary); 'and sence' to *incense*. V. 4 has 'younge', but the original which Shann transcribed probably had 'ying'.

11 GOD REST YOU MERRY
(CHRISTMAS)

Traditional (usual version)
FIRST VERSION
Traditional (M.S.)
SOPRANO ALTO
TENOR BASS
1. God rest you mer-ry, gen-tle-men, Let no-thing you dis-may,
2. In Beth-le-hem in Jew-ry This bless-ed babe was born,
For Je-sus Christ our Sa-viour Was born up-on this day,
And laid with-in a man-ger, Up-on this bless-ed morn;
To save us all from Sa-tan's power When we were gone a-stray:
The which his mo-ther Ma-ry No-thing did take in scorn:
CHORUS
O tid-ings, O tid-ings of com-fort and joy,
For

For Je-sus Christ our Sa - viour Was born on Christ-mas Day.
Je - sus Christ our Sa - viour Was born on Christ - mas_ Day.

3 From God our heavenly Father
  A blessèd angel came,
And unto certain shepherds
  Brought tidings of the same,
How that in Bethlehem was born
  The Son of God by name:

O tidings, O tidings etc.

4 'Fear not,' then said the angel,
  'Let nothing you affright,
This day is born a Saviour,
  Of virtue, power, and might;
So frequently to vanquish all
  The friends of Satan quite':

O tidings, O tidings etc.

5 The shepherds at those tidings
  Rejoicèd much in mind,
And left their flocks a-feeding,
  In tempest, storm and wind,
And went to Bethlehem straightway
  This blessèd babe to find:

O tidings, O tidings etc.

6 But when to Bethlehem they came,
  Whereat this infant lay,
They found him in a manger,
  Where oxen feed on hay;
His mother Mary kneeling,
  Unto the Lord did pray:

O tidings, O tidings etc.

7 Now to the Lord sing praises,
  All you within this place,
And with true love and brotherhood
  Each other now embrace;
This holy tide of Christmas
  All others doth deface:

O tidings, O tidings etc.

12 GOD REST YOU MERRY
(CHRISTMAS: NEW YEAR)

SECOND VERSION

Traditional, London

Ibid.

SOPRANO
ALTO
TENOR
BASS
1. God rest you mer-ry gen-tle-men, Let no-thing you dis-may, Re-mem-ber Christ our Sa - viour Was born on Christ-mas Day, To save poor souls from Sa-tan's power Which had long time gone a - stray,
2. From God that is our Fa - ther, The bless-ed an-gels came, Un-to some cer-tain shep-herds, With ti-dings of the same; That there was born in Beth-le-hem, The Son of God by name.
And it's tid - ings of com - fort and joy, com-fort and joy: And it's tid - ings of com - fort and joy, com-fort and joy.
joy.
joy.

3 Go, fear not, said God's angels,
  Let nothing you affright,
For there is born in Bethlehem,
  Of a pure virgin bright,
One able to advance you,
  And throw down Satan quite.
And it's tidings of comfort and joy.

4 The shepherds at those tidings,
  Rejoiced much in mind,
And left their flocks a feeding
  In tempest storms of wind,
And strait they came to Bethlehem,
  The Son of God to find.
And it's tidings of comfort and joy.

5 Now when they came to Bethlehem,
  Where our sweet Saviour lay,
They found him in a manger,
  Where oxen feed on hay,
The blessed Virgin kneeling down,
  Unto the Lord did pray.
And it's tidings of comfort and joy.

6 With sudden joy and gladness,
  The shepherds were beguil'd,
To see the Babe of Israel,
  Before his mother mild,
On them with joy and chearfulness,
  Rejoice each mother's child.
And it's tidings of comfort and joy.

7 Now to the Lord sing praises,
  All you within this place,
Like we true loving brethren,
  Each other to embrace,
For the merry time of Christmas,
  Is drawing on a pace.
And it's tidings of comfort and joy.

8 God bless the ruler of this house,
  And send him long to reign,
And many a merry Christmas
  May live to see again.
Among your friends and kindred,
  That live both far and near,
And God send you a happy New Year.

'God rest you merry', which is, as Bullen says, 'the most popular of Christmas carols', has two magnificent tunes, and deserves to be given in two versions.

The first version, No. 11, gives the best-known text, as in Sandys, 1833, accepting Bullen's correction of 'Whereas' in v. 6. Sandys gives 'friends' in v. 4, though we fancy that the alternative 'fiends' was the word more generally sung. 'God rest you merry' means 'God keep you merry', but the comma after 'merry' is generally misplaced. There is a version in the *Roxburgh Ballads*, vol. iii, *c*. 1770.

The second version, No. 12 (with the tune 'as sung', said Rimbault, a century ago, 'in the London streets'), we have reprinted from a broadside printed by J. & C. Evans, Long-lane, London, some fifty years before Rimbault. In this case we have reproduced the spelling and punctuation, only correcting the misprint 'comforts' in the first occurrence of the refrain; otherwise the carol is exactly as in the broadside, except that we have numbered the verses, and omitted some capital letters.

Rimbault stated that the tune printed by Sandys of the first version is from Cornwall.

The words of No. 11 can be sung to the London tune (No. 12), by singing 'O tidings of comfort and joy' twice for the refrain.

13 GOD'S DEAR SON
(CHRISTMAS: EPIPHANY)

Traditional
Ibid.
(M.S.)
SOPRANO
ALTO
TENOR
BASS
1. God's dear Son with-out be-gin-ning, Whom the wick-ed
2. In Beth-le-hem, King Da-vid's ci-ty, Ma-ry's babe had
priests did scorn, — The on-ly wise, with-out all sin-ning,
sweet cre-a-tion; God and man en-dued with pi-ty,
On this bless-ed day was born; — To save us all from
And a Sa-viour of each na-tion. Yet Jew-ry land with
sin and thrall, When we in Sa-tan's chains — were — bound, And
cru-el hand Both first and last his power de-nied; Where

shed his blood to do us good, With ma - ny a pur - ple bleed - ing wound.
he was born they did him scorn, And showed him_ ma - lice when he died.

3 No kingly robes nor golden treasure
Decked the birthday of God's Son;
No pompous train at all took pleasure
To this King of kings to run.
No mantle brave could Jesus have
Upon his cradle for to lie;
No music charms in nurse's arms,
To sing the babe a lullaby.

4 Yet as Mary sat in solace,
By our Saviour's first beginning,
Hosts of angels from God's palace
Sounded sweet from heaven singing;
Yea, heaven and earth, at Jesus' birth,
With sweet melodious tunes abound,
And everything for Jewry's King
Upon the earth gave cheerful sound.

5 *Then with angel-love inspirèd,
Three wise princes from the East,
To Bethlehem as they desirèd,
Came where as our Lord did rest:
And there they laid before the maid,
Unto her son, her God, her King,
Their offerings sweet, as was most meet,
Unto so great a power to bring.

6 Now to him that hath redeemed us
By his precious death and passion,
And us sinners so esteemed us,
To buy dearly this salvation,
Yield lasting fame, that still the name
Of Jesus may be honoured here;
And let us say that Christmas Day
Is still the best day in the year.

In Gilbert (eight verses), with tune, 1822. A rougher version in nine verses is in *A Good Christmas Box*, Dudley, 1846. Here, as elsewhere, we have removed an accusation against the Jews.

14 WEXFORD CAROL
(CHRISTMAS)

English and Irish traditional
Irish traditional (M.S.)
SOPRANO ALTO
TENOR BASS
3
1. Good peo- ple all, — this Christ-mas-time, Con - si - der well — and bear in mind What our good — God — for us has done, In send - ing his — be - lo - ved Son. With Ma - ry ho - - ly we should pray To — God with love — this Christ-mas Day; In
2. The night be - fore — that hap - py tide, The no-ble Vir - gin and her guide Were long time — seek - ing up and down To find a lodg - ing in the town. But mark how all — things came to pass: From e - v'ry door — re - pell'd, a - las! As

Beth - le - hem— up - on that morn There was a bless-ed Mes - si - ah born.
long fore - told,— their re - fuge all Was but an hum - ble ox- 's stall.

3 Near Bethlehem did shepherds keep
Their flocks of lambs and feeding sheep;
To whom God's angels did appear,
Which put the shepherds in great fear.
'Prepare and go', the angels said,
'To Bethlehem, be not afraid;
For there you'll find, this happy morn,
A princely babe, sweet Jesus born.'

4 With thankful heart and joyful mind,
The shepherds went the babe to find,
And as God's angel had foretold,
They did our Saviour Christ behold.
Within a manger he was laid,
And by his side the virgin maid,
Attending on the Lord of life,
Who came on earth to end all strife.

5 There were three wise men from afar
Directed by a glorious star,
And on they wandered night and day
Until they came where Jesus lay.
And when they came unto that place
Where our beloved Messiah was,
They humbly cast them at his feet,
With gifts of gold and incense sweet.

Kindly communicated, with No. 6, by Dr. Grattan Flood. The words (subsequently revised) and tune were taken down from a traditional singer in County Wexford. The words seem to have come from England: the first four and a half verses are in Shawcross's *Old Castleton Christmas Carols*, and the first verse was taken by R. Vaughan Williams from Mr. Hall, Castleton, Derbyshire (*Eight Traditional English Carols*, No. 7), with another tune. For another version see Sharp's *English Folk Carols*, viii.

15 WASSAIL SONG

(CHRISTMAS: NEW YEAR)

FIRST TUNE

North of England traditional
Ibid. (M.S.)
SOLO
1. Here we come a - was - sail - ing A - mong the leaves so green, Here we come a - wan - der - ing, So fair to be seen:
2. *Our was - sail cup is made Of the rose - - ma - ry tree, And so is your beer Of the best bar - ley:
3. We are not dai - ly beg - gars That beg from door to door, But we are neigh-bours' chil - dren Whom you have seen be - fore:
4. *Call up the but - ler of this house, Put on his gol - den ring; Let him bring us up a glass of beer, And bet - ter we shall sing:
Acct. (or voices humming)
CHORUS
S. A.
Love and joy come to you, And to you your was - sail
T. B.
Love and joy come to you, And to

too, And God bless you, and send— you A hap - py New
you your was - sail too, And God send— you

Year, And God send— you A hap - py New Year.

SOLO
5. We have got a lit - tle purse Of stretch - ing lea - ther
6. *Bring us out a ta - - ble, And spread it with a
7. God bless the mas - ter of this house, Like - wise the mis - tress
8. Good mas - ter and good mis - tress, While you're sit - ting by the

skin; — We want a lit-tle of your mon-ey To line — it well with - in:
cloth; — Bring us out — a moul-dy cheese, And some of your Christ-mas loaf:
too; — And all the lit - tle chil - dren That round the ta - ble go:
fire, — Pray think of us — poor chil-dren Who are wand-'ring in the mire:

For Editors' notes see second tune, p. 35.

16 GOOD-BYE

17th century

GOD bless the master of this house,
The mistress also,
And all the little children
That round the table go:

Love and joy, etc.

2 And all your kin and kinsfolk,
That dwell both far and near;
I wish you a merry Christmas,
And a happy New Year.

Love and joy, etc.

15 WASSAIL SONG
(CHRISTMAS: NEW YEAR)

SECOND TUNE (LEEDS)

North of England traditional
Ibid.
(M.S.)
SOPRANO SOLO
1. Here we come a - was - sail - ing A - mong the leaves so green, Here we come a - wan - der - ing, So fair to be seen:
2.*Our was - sail cup is made Of the rose - ma - ry tree, And so is your beer Of the best bar - ley:
3. We are not dai - ly beg - gars That beg from door to door, But we are neigh-bours' chil - dren Whom you have seen be - fore:
4.*Call up the but - ler of this house, Put on his gol - den ring; Let him bring us up a glass of beer, And bet - ter we shall sing:
(Acct.)
A.
T.
B
Here we come, we come,
Here we come, we come.
A hap-py New Year, we come, we come.
In each verse the three under parts sing the same words during the solo
CHORUS
S.
A.
Love and joy come to you, And to you your was - sail
T.
B.
Love and joy come to

too, And God bless you, and send you A hap - py— New Year.—
you,

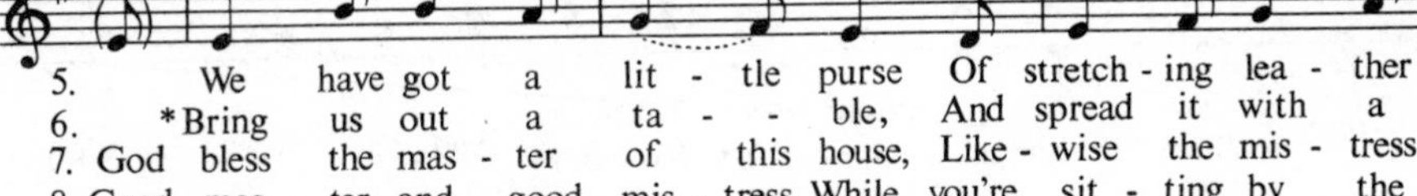
SOLO
5. We have got a lit - tle purse Of stretch - ing lea - ther
6. *Bring us out a ta - - ble, And spread it with a
7. God bless the mas - ter of this house, Like - wise the mis - tress
8. Good mas - ter and good mis - tress, While you're sit - ting by the

skin;— We want a lit-tle of your mo-ney To line— it well with - in:
cloth;——Bring us out— a moul-dy cheese, And some of your Christ-mas loaf:
too;—And all the lit - tle chil - dren That round— the ta - ble go:
fire,—Pray think of us poor chil-dren Who are wand -'ring in the mire:

No. 16 might be sung to the second tune when the first tune is used for No. 15.

The starred verses are not suitable when the carol is sung in church, but they give a vivid picture of the Waits of old times. Text from Husk's *Songs of the Nativity*, 1868, where he refers to a Yorkshire copy of the carol in a broadsheet printed at Bradford as late as c. 1850, and to a Lancashire copy in a Manchester chap-book. The first tune from Yorkshire has been familiarized by Stainer. The second tune was learnt by Martin Shaw when a boy from his father, James Shaw, who had often heard it in the streets of Leeds in the eighteen-fifties; the Rev. J. T. Horton of Bradford reported some fifty years ago that it was still often sung by the Waits in the West Riding.

The charming seventh verse is also printed by Ritson in his *Ancient Songs and Ballads*, 1829, where he seems to have copied it from some source of the reign of James I or Charles I; he gives two verses only. Shakespeare may well have heard them sung outside his house on a Christmas night. We print them separately below, exactly as Ritson gave them, since they make a good conclusion to a carol-concert, and we have two tunes at our disposal:

16 GOOD-BYE

17th century

God bless the master of this house,
The mistress also,
And all the little children
That round the table go:

Love and joy, etc.

2 And all your kin and kinsfolk,
That dwell both far and near;
I wish you a merry Christmas,
And a happy New Year.

Love and joy, etc.

17 ALL IN THE MORNING

Part 1 (Christmas)

Traditional

Ibid. (R.V.W.)

SOPRANO
ALTO
TENOR
BASS
1. It was on Christ-mas Day,
2.*It was on New Year's Day,
And all in the morn-
-ing, Our Sa - viour was born,
They circum - cised our Sa-viour
And our hea - - v'nly
King: And was not this a joy - ful
thing? And sweet Je - - sus they called him by name.

3 It was on the Twelfth Day,
And all in the morning,
The wise men were led
To our heavenly King:

And was not this etc.

4 *It was on Twentieth Day,
And all in the morning,
The wise men returned
From our heavenly King:

And was not this etc.

5 *It was on Candlemas Day,
And all in the morning,
They visited the Temple
With our heavenly King:

And was not this etc.

17 ALL IN THE MORNING

PART 2 (LENT TO EASTER)

Traditional

Ibid.
(R.V.W.)

SOPRANO
ALTO
TENOR
BASS
6. It was on Holy Wednesday, And all in the morning, That Judas betrayed Our dear heav'nly King:
7.* It was on Sheer Thursday, They plaited a crown of thorns For our heav'nly
V.7
And was not this a woeful thing? And sweet Jesus we'll call him by name.

8 It was on Good Friday,
And all in the morning,
They crucified our Saviour,
And our heavenly King:

And was not this etc.

9 It was on Easter Day,
And all in the morning,
Our Saviour arose,
Our own heavenly King;
The sun and the moon
They did both rise with him,
And sweet Jesus we'll call him by name.

The text has been completed from *Old Castleton Christmas Carols*, edited by the late Rev. W. H. Shawcross. Melody and first verse of text from Mr. Hall, Castleton, Derbyshire. From *Eight Traditional English Carols* (Vaughan Williams), Stainer & Bell.

18 I SAW THREE SHIPS
(CHRISTMAS)

Traditional

Ibid. (M.S.)

SOPRANO
ALTO
1. I saw three ships come sail - ing in,
2. And what was in those ships all three? On
3. Our Sa - viour Christ and his la - dy.
TENOR
BASS
Christ - mas Day, on Christ - mas Day,
I saw three ships come
And what was in those
Our Sa - viour Christ and
sail - ing in,
ships all three? On Christ - mas Day in the morn - ing.
his la - dy.

4 Pray, whither sailed those ships all three?

5 O, they sailed into Bethlehem.

6 And all the bells on earth shall ring,

7 And all the angels in heaven shall sing,

8 And all the souls on earth shall sing.

9 Then let us all rejoice amain!

Cf. No. 3, 'As I sat on a sunny bank'. In one or other version this is in all the broadsides, sharing its popularity with 'God rest you merry' and 'The Seven Joys'. The version above (in Sandys, 1833) differs only in v. 3 from the Derbyshire version with our first tune in Bramley & Stainer, *Christmas Carols New and Old*, 1871. A unique version introducing the Passion ('As I sat by my old cottage door') was taken down by Cecil Sharp in Worcestershire. Our second tune is from Sharp's *English Folk Carols*. There is another tune in the *English Carol Book*, Second Series (P. Dearmer and M. Shaw), Mowbray.

19 BOAR'S HEAD CAROL

(CHRISTMAS, Secular)

Traditional
(M.S.)
Queen's College, Oxford, version
SOLO VOICE
1. The boar's head in hand bear I, Be-decked with bays and rose-ma-ry; And I
pray you, my mas-ters, be mer-ry, *Quot es-tis in con-vi-vi-o:*
CHORUS
S.
A.
Ca-put a-pri de-fe-ro, Red-dens lau-des Do-mi-no.
End here.
T.
B.
SOLO VOICE
2. The boar's head, as I un-der-stand, Is the rar-est dish in all this land, Which
Repeat CHORUS
thus bedecked with a gay gar-land, Let us *ser-vi-re can-ti-co:*
3. Our stew-ard hath pro-vi-ded this, In hon-our of the King of bliss, Which
Repeat CHORUS
on this day to be ser-ved is, *In Re-gi-nen-si a-tri-o:*

1. *Quot*, &c.—So many as are in the feast. *Caput*, &c.—The boar's head I bring, giving praises to God. 2. *Servire*, &c.—Let us serve with a song. 3. *In*, &c.—In the Queen's hall.

This version, as sung every Christmas at Queen's College, Oxford, is in Dibden's *Typog. Antiq.*, 1812, ii. 252, whence A. H. Bullen reprinted it in *Carols and Poems*, 1885 (p. 171), together with a version (p. 267) from Joseph Ritson's *Ancient Songs*, 1790 (from MS. Add. 5665 in the British Museum), the Wynkyn de Worde version correctly given with modern spelling (p. 170), and a quite different Boar's Head Carol (p. 172) sung at St. John's College, Oxford, in 1607. The carol in Hill's MS. (see No. 36) is a variant of the contemporary version of Wynken.

Jan van Wynken, of Worth, was Caxton's apprentice and successor: of his *Christmasse Carolles*, 1521, only the last leaf survives; it fortunately includes the colophon and is preserved in the Bodleian Library, Oxford: the text is reprinted with the original spelling in E. Flügel's *Neuenglisches Lesebuch*, 1895. Miss Rickert in *Ancient English Christmas Carols*, 1914, prints also three boar's head carols of the fifteenth century, but without references.

20 YEOMAN'S CAROL

(CHRISTMAS)

Church-gallery Book

Ibid. (M.S.)

SOPRANO
ALTO
1. Let Christ - ians all with joy - ful mirth, Both young and
2. No pa - lace, but an ox - 's stall, The place of
TENOR
BASS
old, both great and small,— Now think up - on our Sa - viour's birth,
his na - ti - vi - ty;—— This tru - ly should in - struct us all
Who brought sal - va - tion to us all:
To learn of him hu - mi - li - ty:
This day did Christ man's soul from
death— re - move, With glo - rious saints to dwell‿in heav'n a - bove.—

3 Then Joseph and the Virgin came
Unto the town of Bethlehem,
But sought in vain within the same
For lodging to be granted them:
This day etc.

4 A stable harboured them, where they
Continued till this blessèd morn.
Let us rejoice and keep the day,
Wherein the Lord of life was born:
This day etc.

5 He that descended from above,
Who for your sins has meekly died,
Make him the pattern of your love;
So will your joys be sanctified:
This day etc.

The words and tune are from an old church-gallery tune-book, Dorset, and were discovered by the Rev. L. J. T. Darwall.

21 SIR CHRISTÈMAS
(CHRISTMAS, Secular)

c. 1500

Ibid.
(John A. Parkinson)

The two-part sections should be sung by soli, and the three-part sections by the full choir.

SOPRANO (or ALTO)
No - well, No - - - well, No - - well, No - - - well, No - - - - - - - - - - - - - well.

TENOR
No - well, No - - well, No - - well, No - - well, No - - - - - - - - - - - - well.

SOPRANO (ALTO)
Who is there that sing - eth so, No - well, No - - well, No - - - - - - - - - - - - well?

TENOR I
Who is there that sing-eth so, No - - well, No - - well, No - - - - - - well?

TENOR II
Who is there that sing-eth so, No - - well, No - - well, No - - - - - well?

S. or A.
I am here, Sir Chris-te - - mas.

T.
I am here, Sir Chris-te - - mas.

21—Sir Christèmas

S. or A.
Wel-come, my lord Sir Chris-te - mas! Wel - come to us
T. I
Wel-come, my lord Sir Chris-te - mas! Wel - come to us
T. II
Wel-come, my lord Sir Chris-te - mas! Wel - come to us
all, both more and less! Come near, No - - well.
all, both more and less! Come near, No - well.
all, both more and less! Come near, No - - well.
S. or A.
1. Dieu vous garde, beaux sieurs, ti - dings I you
2. Christ is now born of a pure
3. Bu - vez bien par toute la com - - - pa - -
T.
1. Dieu vous garde, beaux sieurs, ti - dings I you
2. Christ is now born of a pure
3. Bu - vez bien par tou - te la com - - - pa - -
bring: A maid hath borne a child full young,
maid; In an ox - stall he is laid,
-gnie. Make good cheer and be right mer - - ry,
bring: A maid hath borne a child full young,
maid; In an ox - stall he is laid,
-gnie. Make good cheer and be right mer - - - - ry,

The which caus - - - - - eth you for
Where - fore sing we all
And sing with us now
The which caus - - eth you
Where - fore sing we
And sing with us
to sing:
at a brayde:
joy - ful - ly:
No - - - - - - - - well.
for to sing:
all at a brayde:
now joy - ful - - ly:
No - - - - - - - - well.
D.S.
S. or A.
T. I
T. II
No - - - - - - well. - No - well, No - -
No - - - - - - well. No - well, No - -
No - - - - - - well. No - well, No - -
- well, No - - - - - - well, No - - - - - - - - well.
- well, No - - - - - - well, No - - - - - - - - - - well.
- well, No - - - - - - - well, No - - - - - - - - well.

2. more and less—great and small. 3. *Dieu*, &c.—God keep you, fair gentlemen. 4. brayde—to start, here 'all at once'. 5. *Buvez*, &c.—Drink well, through all the company.

Words and music from the MS. Add. 5665, which consists of English and Latin songs with music, dating probably from Edward IV to the early years of Henry VIII; this carol is attributed to Richard Smart, rector of Plymtree, Devon, from 1435-1477. The original pitch is a tone higher. See *Medieval Carols*, No. 80.

22 COVENTRY CAROL

(CHRISTMAS: INNOCENTS)

FIRST VERSION

Pageant of the Shearmen and Tailors, 15th century

Original version of 1591

SOPRANO

TENOR BASS

Lul - ly, lul - la, thou lit - tle tiny child, By by, lul - ly lul - lay, thou lit - tle tiny child, By by, lul - ly lul - lay.

1. O sis - ters too, How may we do For to pre- serve this day This poor young-ling, For whom we do sing, By by, lul - ly lul - lay?
2. He - rod, the king, In his rag - ing, Char- ged he hath this day His men of might, In his ___ own sight, All young chil - dren to slay.
3. That woe is me, Poor child for thee! And e - ver morn and day, For thy part- ing Neither say ___ nor sing By by, lul - ly lul - lay!

The only surviving source of this carol is the rough facsimile of the 1591 manuscript published by Thomas Sharp in his *Dissertation on the Pageants at Coventry* (1825), where it is found, together with the Shepherds' Carol 'As I outrode' as part of the Pageant of the Shearmen and Tailors. This carol gives added poignancy to the scene in which Herod's soldiers come in to slay the innocent children.

In the original version the tenor part in bar 24 is written a third higher, but the whole copy is too inaccurate for the resultant discord to be acceptable. For a discussion of these carols see *Monthly Musical Record*, November 1959.

22 COVENTRY CAROL
(CHRISTMAS: INNOCENTS)

SECOND VERSION

Pageant of the Shearmen and Tailors, 15th century

Modern version of tune (M.S.)

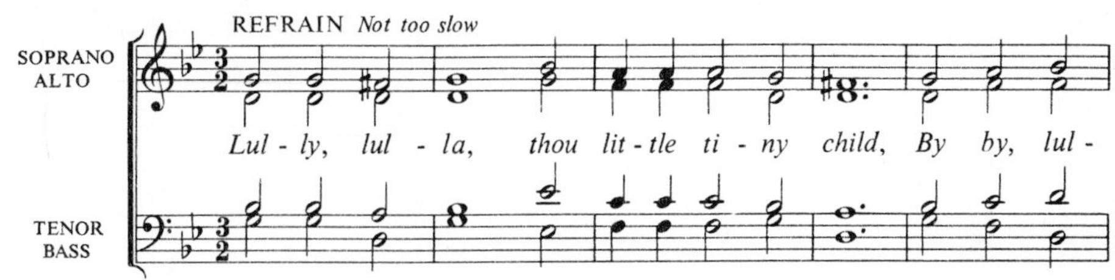
REFRAIN *Not too slow*
SOPRANO
ALTO
TENOR
BASS
Lul - ly, lul - la, thou lit - tle ti - ny child, By by, lul -

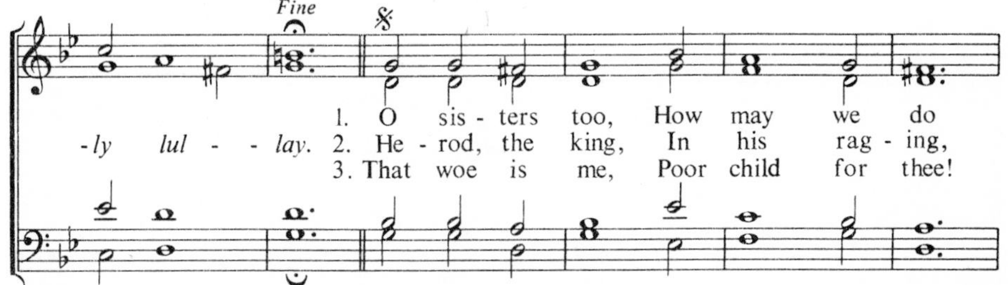
Fine
-ly lul - - lay.
1. O sis - ters too, How may we do
2. He - rod, the king, In his rag - ing,
3. That woe is me, Poor child for thee!

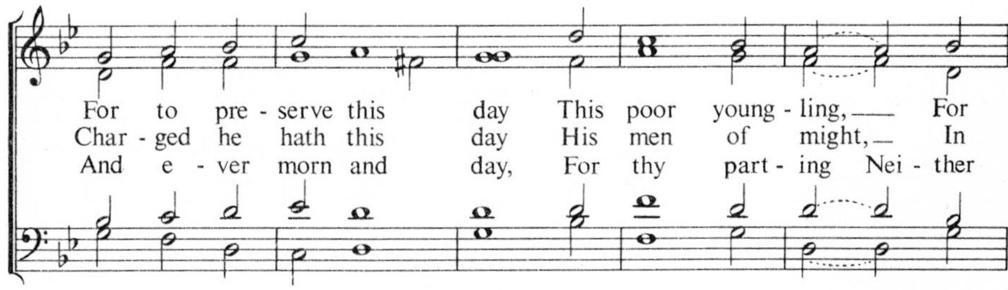
For to pre - serve this day This poor young - ling, For
Char - ged he hath this day His men of might, In
And e - ver morn and day, For thy part - ing Nei - ther

After 3rd verse, sing Refrain again
whom we do sing, By by, lul - ly lul - - lay?
his own sight, All young chil - dren to slay.
say nor sing By by, lul - ly lul - - lay!
D.S.

The text is that of Robert Croo, 1534, reprinted by E. Rhys, *Everyman and other Plays*. The Coventry plays were witnessed by Margaret, Queen of Henry VI, in 1456, by Richard III in 1484, by Henry VII in 1492, and we hear of the Smiths' play being performed in 1584, which brings us near to the date where the tune appears.

See the note on p. 44.

23 MAKE WE JOY
(CHRISTMAS: EPIPHANY)

15th century

Ibid.
(M.S.)

SOPRANO
ALTO
TENOR
BASS
Make we joy now in this feast In quo Chris - tus
na - tus est: E - - - - - - - - - - - - ya!
1. A
2. Ag -
Pa - tre u - ni - ge - - ni - tus Through a
-nos - cat om - ne se - - cu - lum: A bright star
maid - en is come to us: Sing we of him and
made three king - ès come, For to seek with

D.S.
say 'Wel - come, Ve - ni Re - demp-tor gen - ti - - um.'
their pre - sents Ver - bum su - per - num pro - di - - ens:

3 *A solis ortus cardine,*
So mighty a lord was none as he:
He on our kind his peace hath set,
Adam parens quod polluit:

4 *Maria ventre concipit,*
The Holy Ghost was ay her with:
In Bethlehem yborn he is,
Consors paterni luminis:

5 *O lux beata, Trinitas!*
He lay between an ox and ass,
And by his mother, maiden free.
Gloria tibi, Domine!

1. *In quo Christus*, &c.—On which Christ was born. *A Patre*, &c.—From the Father only-begotten. *Veni Redemptor*, &c.—Come, Redeemer of the nations (*English Hymnal*, 14). 2. *Agnoscat*, &c.—Let every age acknowledge (thee). *Verbum*, &c.—The celestial word proceeding (*E.H.*2). 3. *A solis*, &c.—Risen from the quarter of the sun (*E.H.*18). *Adam parens*, &c.—Which the parent Adam defiled. 4. *Maria ventre*, &c.—Mary conceived in her womb. *Consors*, &c.—Consort of the Father's light. 5. *O lux*, &c.—O blessed light, O Trinity (*E.H.*164). *Gloria*, &c.—Glory to thee, O Lord.

Words (slightly altered in third lines of verses 1, 3 and 5) and melody from the Selden MS., B.26 (Southern English, *c.* 1450), which came to the Bodleian *c.* 1659. Facsimile and transcription in Stainer's *Early Bodleian Music*, and a more modern transcription in *Medieval Carols*, No. 26.

24 SUSSEX CAROL

(CHRISTMAS)

FIRST TUNE

Traditional

Ibid.
(R.V.W.)

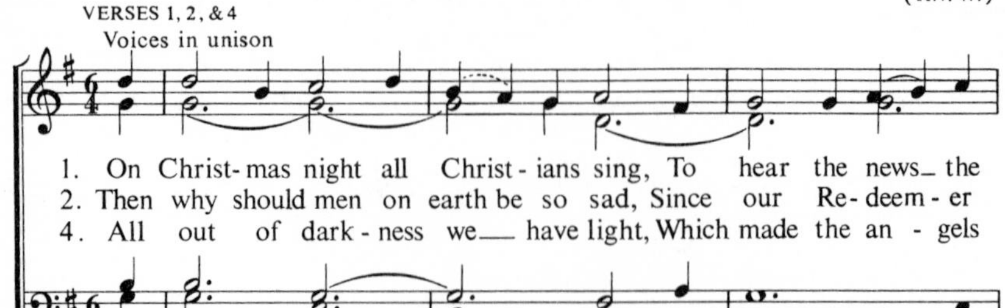
VERSES 1, 2, & 4
Voices in unison
1. On Christ-mas night all Christ-ians sing, To hear the news_ the
2. Then why should men on earth be so sad, Since our Re-deem-er
4. All out of dark-ness we_ have light, Which made the an-gels

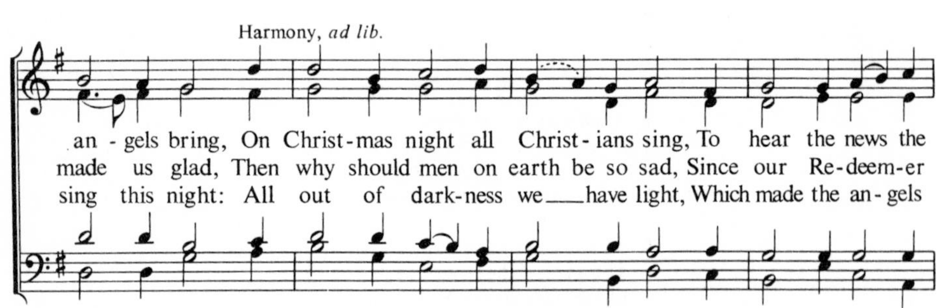
Harmony, *ad lib.*
an-gels bring, On Christ-mas night all Christ-ians sing, To hear the news the
made us glad, Then why should men on earth be so sad, Since our Re-deem-er
sing this night: All out of dark-ness we_have light, Which made the an-gels

Unison
an-gels bring— News of great joy,_ news of_ great mirth,
made_ us glad, When from our sin_ he set_ us free,
sing_this night: 'Glo-ry to God_ and peace_ to men,

Harmony, *ad lib.*
News of our mer-ci-ful_ King's birth.
All for to gain our li-ber-ty?
Now and for e-ver-more._ A-men.'

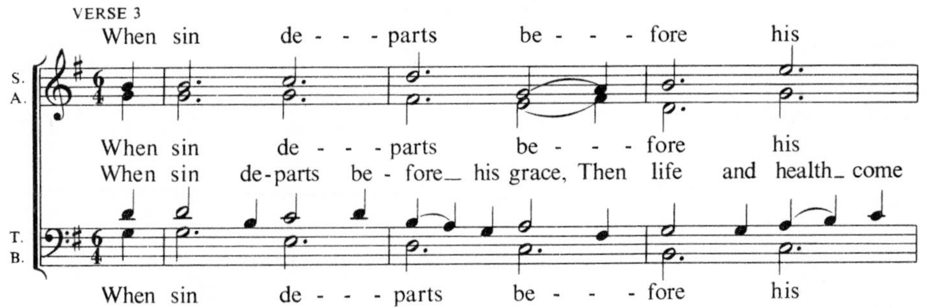
VERSE 3
When sin de - - - parts be - - - fore his
S.
A.
When sin de - - - parts be - - - fore his
When sin de-parts be - fore his grace, Then life and health come
T.
B.
When sin de - - - parts be - - - fore his

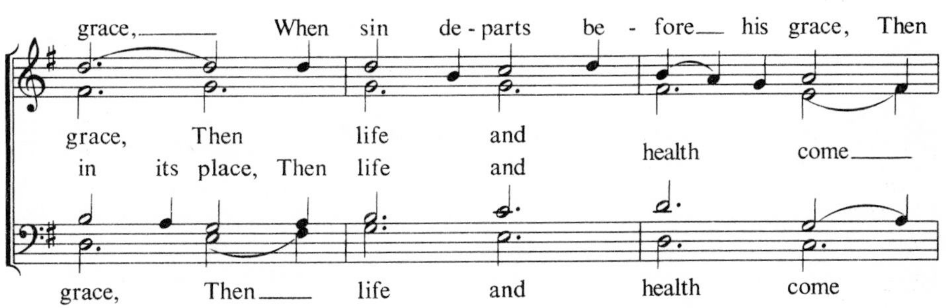
grace, When sin de - parts be - fore his grace, Then
grace, Then life and
in its place, Then life and
health come
grace, Then life and health come

life and health come in its place; An - gels and men with joy may
in its place; An - gels may
in its place;

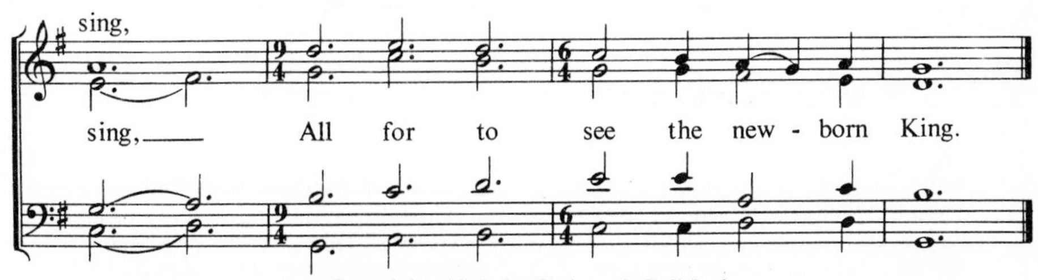
sing,
sing, All for to see the new - born King.

Melody and text from Mrs. Verrall, Monks Gate, Sussex. Other versions in *Journal of the Folk Song Society*, vol. ii, p. 127, and Cecil Sharp, *English Folk-Carols*, No. X. Arrangement for unaccompanied singing in *Eight Traditional English Carols* (Vaughan Williams), Stainer & Bell.

24 SUSSEX CAROL
(CHRISTMAS)

Traditional

SECOND TUNE

Ibid.
(R.V.W.)

Slow
VOICES IN UNISON (or SOLO)
ORGAN
1. On Christ-mas night all Christ-ians sing, To hear the news the an-gels bring News of great joy, news of great mirth, News of our mer-ci-ful King's birth.
2. Then why should men on earth be so sad, Since our Re-deem-er made us glad, When from our sin he set us free, All for to gain our li-ber-ty?

3 When sin departs before his grace,
Then life and health come in its place;
Angels and men with joy may sing,
All for to see the new-born King.

4 All out of darkness we have light,
Which made the angels sing this night:
'Glory to God and peace to men,
Now and for evermore. Amen.'

Tune noted by the late Dr. Culwick in 1904, from his mother, who had heard it many years previously in the streets of Dublin. The tune is printed in the *Journal of the Folk Song Society*, vol. ii, p. 126.

25 A GALLERY CAROL
(CHRISTMAS: EPIPHANY)

Church-gallery Book

Ibid. (M.S.)

SOPRANO ALTO

TENOR BASS

1. Re - joice and be mer - ry in songs and in mirth! O praise our Re - deem - er, all mor - tals on earth! For this is the birth - day of Je - sus our King, Who brought us sal - va - tion— his prai - ses we'll sing!

2. A hea - ven - ly vi - sion ap - peared in the sky; Vast num - bers of an - gels the shep - herds did spy, Pro - claim - ing the birth - day of Je - sus our King,

3 Likewise a bright star in the sky did appear,
Which led the wise men from the East to draw near;
They found the Messiah, sweet Jesus our King,
Who brought us salvation—his praises we'll sing!

4 And when they were come, they their treasures unfold,
And unto him offered myrrh, incense, and gold.
So blessèd for ever be Jesus our King,
Who brought us salvation—his praises we'll sing!

The words and tune, from an old church-gallery book, discovered in Dorset, like No. 20, by the Rev. L. J. T. Darwall.

26 SAINT STEPHEN
(DEC. 26 AND OTHER OCCASIONS)

Traditional
Ibid. (M.S.)
SOPRANO ALTO
TENOR BASS
1. Saint Ste-phen was a ho-ly man, En-dued with heav'n-ly might, And ma-ny won-ders he did work Be-fore the peo-ple's sight;
2. Be-fore the el-ders was he brought His answer for to make; But they could not the spi-rit with-stand, Where-by this man did speak.
And by the bless-ed Spi-rit of God, Which did his heart in-flame,
Whilst this was told, the mul-ti-tude, Be-hold-ing him a-right,
(1.) He spa-red not, in e-v'ry place,
(2.) His come-ly face be-gan to shine
1.) He spa-red not, in e-v'ry place, To
2.) His come-ly face be-gan to shine Most
(1.) He spa-red not, in e-v'ry place,
(2.) His come-ly face be-gan to shine
1.) He spa-red not, in e-v'ry place,
2.) His come-ly face be-gan to shine

CHORUS
preach God's holy name:
like an angel bright:
O man, do never faint nor fear, When God the truth shall try,
But mark how
But
But mark how
Stephen, for Christ's sake, Was willing for to die.
But
mark how Ste-phen, for Christ's sake,
Stephen, for Christ's sake,
Was willing for to die.
mark how Ste-phen, for Christ's sake, Was willing for to die.

3 Then Stephen did put forth his voice,
And he did first unfold
The wondrous works which God hath wrought,
Even for their fathers old;
That they thereby might plainly know
Christ Jesus should be he,
That from the burden of the law
Should quit us frank and free:

O man, etc.

4 'But, O,' quoth he, 'you wicked men!
Which of the prophets all
Did not your fathers persecute
And keep in woeful thrall?'
But when they heard him so to say
Upon him they all ran,
And then without the city gates
They stoned this holy man:

O man, etc.

5 There he most meekly on his knees
To God did pray at large,
Desiring that he would not lay
This sin unto their charge;
Then yielding up his soul to God,
Who had it dearly bought,
He lost his life, whose body then
To grave was seemly brought:

O man, etc.

Both the tune and words of this carol were preserved by Sandys, from whom we have taken the last two verses; the rest are exactly as in the older and slightly different version of Gilbert, but we have shortened the original, which is in eight verses.

27 THE FIRST NOWELL
(EPIPHANY : CHRISTMAS)

Traditional
Ibid.
(M.S.)
VERSES 1, 2, 4, 5, 7, 8, & 9
†
SOPRANO
ALTO
TENOR
BASS
1. The first — No - well the — an - gel did say Was to cer - tain poor shep - herds in fields as they lay; In — fields — where — they lay, — keep - ing their sheep, In a cold win - ter's night — that was — so deep:
2. They look - ed up and — saw — a star, Shin - ing in — the east, — be - yond — them far; And to — the — earth it — gave — great light, And — so it con - tin - ued both day — and night:
REFRAIN
No - well, — No - well, No - well, No - well, Born is the King — of Is - - - ra - el!

†It is suggested that the organ remain silent until the refrain in one or more verses.

3 And by the light of that same star,
Three wise men came from country far;
To seek for a king was their intent,
And to follow the star wheresoever it went:

Nowell, etc.

4 This star drew nigh to the north-west;
O'er Bethlehem it took its rest,
And there it did both stop and stay
Right over the place where Jesus lay:

Nowell, etc.

5 *Then did they know assuredly
Within that house the King did lie:
One entered in then for to see,
And found the babe in poverty:

Nowell, etc.

6 Then entered in those wise men three,
Fell reverently upon their knee,
And offered there in his presénce
Both gold and myrrh and frankincense:

Nowell, etc.

7 *Between an ox-stall and an ass
This child truly there born he was;
For want of clothing they did him lay
All in the manger, among the hay:

Nowell, etc.

8 Then let us all with one accord
Sing praises to our heavenly Lord,
That hath made heaven and earth of naught,
And with his blood mankind hath bought:

Nowell, etc.

9 *If we in our time shall do well,
We shall be free from death and hell;
For God hath preparèd for us all
A resting place in general:

Nowell, etc.

ALTERNATIVE HARMONIZATION

FOR VERSES 3 AND 6 (MELODY IN TENOR)

VERSES 3 & 6
S.
A.
T.
B.
3. And_ by the light of that_ same
6. Then_ en - - tered in those wise_ men
3. And_ by___ the_ light of___ that___ same star, Three
6. Then en - - tered in those wise___ men three, Fell_
3. And by___ the_ light of_ that___ same star, Three wise_ men
6. Then en - tered in those wise___ men three, Fell_ rev - 'rent -
No - well, No - well, No - well, No -

27—The First Nowell

star, Three wise men came from far; To seek for a king was
three, Fell rev - 'rent - ly on knee, And of - - fered there in
wise men came from coun - try far;
rev - 'rent - ly up - on their knee,
No - well, No -
came from coun - try far; To seek for a king was their in -
-ly up - on their knee, And of - fered there in his pres -
-well, No - well, No - well, No - well,
their in - tent, And to fol - low the star where-so - ev - er it went:
his pres - ence Both gold and myrrh and frank - in - cense:
No -
-well, No - well, No - well, No - well, No - well, No - well,
-tent, And to fol-low the star where-so - ev - er it went:
-ence Both gold and myrrh and frank - in-cense:
No - well, No -
No - well,
-well, No - well, No - well, No - well, No - well, No - well.
No - well, No - well, No - well, No - well, No - well.
-well, No - well, No - well, Born is the King of Is - - ra - el!
No - well, No - well, No - well, No - well.

As in Sandys, 1833 (except 'certain' for 'three' in v. 1), with tune. Gilbert (1822) is rougher. The carol cannot be later than the seventeenth century. We have restored the verses omitted by Bramley in 1871, marking them with an asterisk: they are good, and will be sometimes very useful, for this carol makes a fine processional in the Epiphany season. Verse 2 is not quite historical: the carol is more for Epiphany than Christmas.

28 GREENSLEEVES
(NEW YEAR)

1642 | Traditional (M.S.)

Sopranos sing words

1. The old year now— a-way is fled,—The new year it— is
2. The name-day now— of Christ we keep, Who for our sins did
3. And now with New—Year's gifts each friend Un-to each o-ther

SOPRANO
ALTO
A.T.B. hum
TENOR
BASS

en-ter-ed, Then let us now— our sins down-tread,—And joy-ful-ly all— ap-pear:
of-ten weep; His hands and feet—were wound-ed deep, And his bless-ed side with a spear;
they do send: God grant we may all our lives a-mend,—And that—the truth may ap-pear.

All sing words

Let's mer-ry be this day,—And let us now—both sport and play:
His head they crowned with thorn,—And at him they—did laugh and scorn,
Now, like—the snake, your skin—Cast off, of e-vil thoughts and sin,

Hang grief,—cast care a-way!—God send you a hap-py New Year!—
Who for—our good was born: God send us a hap-py New Year!—
And so—the year be-gin:—God send us a hap-py New Year!—

A Waits' carol. There are three more verses, appealing to 'Jack, Tom, Dick, Bessy, Mary and Joan', and also to the dame of the house, rather pathetically pleading for good cheer. From *New Christmas Carols*, 1642 ('to the tune of Greensleeves'), in the unique black-letter collection of Antony à Wood, now in the Bodleian. We have had to alter some words for the sake of choral singing.

29 THIS NEW CHRISTMAS CAROL
(CHRISTMAS: EPIPHANY)

Traditional

Ibid. (M.S.)

SOPRANO
ALTO
TENOR
BASS
1. This new Christ-mas ca - rol Let us cheer - ful - ly
2. Now the proud may come hi - ther And ___ per - fect - ly
sing, To the hon - our and glo - ry Of our hea - ven - ly
see The most ex - cel - lent pat-tern Of ___ hu - - mi - li - -
King, Who was born of a vir - gin, Bless - ed Ma - - ry by
-ty; For in - stead of a cra - dle, Decked with or - - na - ments
name; For poor sin - ners' re - demp-tion To the world_ here he came.
gay, Here the great King of glo - ry In a man - ger he lay.
v 5

3 As the shepherds were feeding
Of their flocks in the field,
The sweet birth of our Saviour
Unto them was revealed
By blest angels of glory,
Who those tidings did bring,
And directed the shepherds
To their heavenly King.

4 *When the wise men discovered
The bright heavenly star,
Then with gold and rich spices
Straight they came from afar,
In obedience to worship
With a heavenly mind,
Knowing that he was born
For the good of mankind.

5 *Let us learn of those sages,
Who were wise, to obey.
Nay, we find through all ages
They have honoured this day,
Ever since our Redeemer's
Blest nativity,
Who was born of a virgin
To set sinners free.

In Gilbert, 1822; in Sandys with tune, 1833. A new version, with the melody of the third phrase a tone lower, will be found in *The English Carol Book* (Mowbray's), No. 10.

30 LUTE-BOOK LULLABY
(NATIVITY)

W. Ballet (17th century)
Ibid.
(G.S.)
SOPRANO
ALTO
TENOR
BASS
1. Sweet was the song the Vir - gin sang,
When
When she to Beth - lem Ju - - da came
And
she to Beth - lem Ju - - - - da
came
was de - liv - ered of a son,
That bless - ed
Je - sus hath to name:
'Lul - la, lul - la,
lul - la, lul - la - by,
Lul - la, lul - la, lul - la, lul - la - by.' 2. 'Sweet
lul - la - by,

babe,' sang she, 'my son, And eke a
Saviour born, Who hast vouchsafed from on
high To visit us that were for-
To visit us, us that were for-
-lorn: La-lu-la, la-lu-la, la-lu-la-by. Sweet babe,' sang
-lorn: La-lu-la, la-lu-la, la-lu-la-by, Sweet babe,' sang
she, And rocked him sweetly on her knee.

From the MS. *Lute Book* by William Ballet, early seventeenth century, Trinity College, Dublin. B.M. Add. 17786-91 also contains a version for five voices or viols. We do not know that this Lullaby was ever in traditional use, but it belongs more to our First Part than to any other.

31 GLOUCESTERSHIRE WASSAIL
(CHRISTMAS AND NEW YEAR, Secular)

Traditional

Ibid. (R.V.W.)

In quick time
SOPRANO
ALTO
TENOR
BASS
1. Was - sail, was - sail, all o - ver the town! Our toast it is white, and our ale it is brown, Our bowl it is made of the white ma - ple tree; With the was - - - - sail - ing bowl we'll drink to thee.
2. So here is to Cher - ry and to his right cheek, Pray God send our mas - ter a good piece of beef, And a good piece of beef that may we all see; With the was - - - - sail - ing bowl we'll drink to thee.

3 And here is to Dobbin and to his right eye,
Pray God send our master a good Christmas pie,
And a good Christmas pie that may we all see;
With our wassailing bowl we'll drink to thee.

4 So here is to Broad May and to her broad horn,
May God send our master a good crop of corn,
And a good crop of corn that may we all see;
With the wassailing bowl we'll drink to thee.

5 And here is to Fillpail and to her left ear,
Pray God send our master a happy New Year,
And a happy New Year as e'er he did see;
With our wassailing bowl we'll drink to thee.

6 *And here is to Colly and to her long tail,
Pray God send our master he never may fail
A bowl of strong beer; I pray you draw near,
And our jolly wassail it's then you shall hear.

7 *Come, butler, come fill us a bowl of the best,
Then we hope that your soul in heaven may rest;
But if you do draw us a bowl of the small,
Then down shall go butler, bowl and all.

8 *Then here's to the maid in the lily white smock,
Who tripped to the door and slipped back the lock!
Who tripped to the door and pulled back the pin,
For to let these jolly wassailers in.

Wassail, Wes hal, Old English, 'Be thou whole' (hale); a form of salutation, and hence a festive occasion. Cf. 'wassail bowl', cup, or horn.

Cherry and Dobbin are horses. Broad May, Fillpail and Colly are cows.

Sung by an old person in the county to R. Vaughan Williams. A variant was taken from Mr. William Bayliss at Buckland, Glos., and (5, 6, 7) from Mr. Isaac Bennett at Little Sodbury, Glos., by Cecil Sharp, *English Folk-Carols*, Novello. Collated with Sandys, &c. Other versions in Cecil Sharp's *Folk Songs from Somerset*, Nos. 128-30. Also found in Hone and in Chappell's *Collection of Anc. Eng. Melodies*. Brand recorded a hundred-and-sixty years ago that it was sung in Gloucestershire by wassailers carrying a great bowl dressed up with garlands and ribbon; Husk, that it was sung in 1864 in Over, near Gloucester, by a troop of wassailers from the neighbouring village of Minsterworth.

32 SOMERSET WASSAIL
(CHRISTMAS AND NEW YEAR, Secular)

Traditional
Ibid.
(M.S.)
In quick time
Voices in unison (Semi-chorus)
PIANO
or
ORGAN
1. Was - sail,— and was - sail,— all o - - ver the town! The cup— it is white and the ale— it is brown; The cup— it is made of the good— ash - en tree, And— so— is the malt of the best— bar - -
2. O mas - ter and mis - sus, are you— all with- -in? Pray o - - pen the door— and let— us come in; O mas - ter and mis - sus a - sit - ting by the fire, Pray— think up - on poor trav - 'llers, a - trav-'lling in the

CHORUS
-ley: For it's your was - sail, and it's our was - -
mire:
-sail! And it's joy— be to you, and a jol - ly was-sail!

3 O where is the maid, with the silver-headed pin,
To open the door, and let us come in?
O master and missus, it is our desire
A good loaf and cheese, and a toast by the fire:

For it's your wassail, etc.

4 There was an old man, and he had an old cow,
And how for to keep her he didn't know how,
He built up a barn for to keep his cow warm,
And a drop or two of cider will do us no harm:

No harm, boys, harm; no harm, boys, harm;
And a drop or two of cider will do us no harm.

5 The girt dog of Langport he burnt his long tail,
And this is the night we go singing wassail:
O master and missus, now we must be gone;
God bless all in this house till we do come again:

For it's your wassail, etc.

This Wassail was noted about twenty years ago by Cecil Sharp from the Drayton wassailers in Somerset, and we print it separately because of its fine tune and distinctive words. Sharp thought that the great dog of Langport was a reference to the Danes whose invasion of Langport is not yet forgotten in that town.

33 WHILE SHEPHERDS WATCHED
(CHRISTMAS)

Nahum Tate
Traditional
(M.S.)
SOPRANO
ALTO
TENOR
BASS
1. While shep-herds watched their flocks by night, All seat - ed on the
ground, The an - gel of the Lord came down, And
glo - ry shone a - round. 'Fear not,' said he— (for
migh - ty dread Had seized their troub - led mind); 'Glad
ti - dings of great joy I bring To you and all man - kind.

2 'To you in David's town this day
Is born of David's line
A Saviour, who is Christ the Lord;
And this shall be the sign:
The heavenly babe you there shall find
To human view displayed,
All meanly wrapped in swathing bands,
And in a manger laid.'

3 Thus spake the seraph: and forthwith
Appeared a shining throng
Of angels praising God, who thus
Addressed their joyful song:
'All glory be to God on high,
And to the earth be peace;
Good-will henceforth from
heaven to men
Begin and never cease.'

This carol, which is better known as a hymn because of its inclusion in all the hymnals, is here printed for the sake of the traditional tune proper to the words. It is, of course, now usually sung to 'Winchester Old' from *Este's Psalter* of 1592. The words first appeared in the *Supplement* to the *New Version*, the metrical version of the Psalms called 'Tate and Brady' by our forefathers, which appeared in 1696 and was 'allowed' by the King in Council, in place of the *Old Version* of 1556 ('Sternhold and Hopkins'); the earliest *Supplement* was in 1700 and contained 'While shepherds watched'; the *Supplement* of 1782 added 'Hark the herald' and four others. Soon after 1807, 'Jesus Christ is risen today' and 'Glory to thee, my God, this night' were added.

34 POVERTY
(NATIVITY)

Tr. K.E. Roberts

Welsh
(Dr. Caradog Roberts)

SOPRANO
ALTO
TENOR
BASS
1. All poor men and_ hum-ble, All lame men who stum-ble, Come
For Je - sus, our_ trea-sure, With love past all mea-sure, In
haste ye, nor_ feel ye a - fraid; 2. Though wise men who found him Laid_
low - ly poor_ man-ger was laid. 3. Then haste we to show him The_
rich gifts a - round him, Yet ox - en they gave_ him their hay:
prai - ses we owe_ him; Our ser - vice he ne'er_ can des - pise:
And Je - sus in___ beau - ty Ac - cep - ted their
Whose love still is___ a - ble To show us that
du - ty; Con - ten - ted in___ man - ger he lay.
sta - ble Where soft - ly in___ man - ger he lies.

By permission of the Caniedydd Committee, Welsh Congregational Union.

A free translation of the Welsh Carol 'O Deued Pob Cristion'.

35 SANS DAY CAROL

(NATIVITY: PASSIONTIDE TO EASTERTIDE)

Cornish

Ibid (M.S.)

SOPRANO ALTO

1. Now the hol - ly bears a ber - ry as white as the milk, And Ma - ry bore Je - sus, who was wrapped up in silk:
2. Now the hol - ly bears a ber - ry as green as the grass, And Ma - ry bore Je - sus, who died on the cross:
3. Now the hol - ly bears a ber - ry as black as the coal, And Ma - ry bore Je - sus, who died for us all:
4. Now the hol - ly bears a ber - ry, as blood is it red, Then trust we our Saviour, who rose from the dead:

And Ma - ry bore Je - sus Christ our Sa - viour for to be, And the first tree in the green-wood, it was the hol - ly, hol - ly, hol - ly! And the first tree in the green - wood, it was the hol - ly!

TENOR BASS

The Sans Day or St. Day Carol has been so named because the melody and the first three verses were taken down at St. Day in the parish of Gwennap, Cornwall. St. Day or St. They was a Breton saint whose cult was widely spread in Armorican Cornwall. We owe the carol to the kindness of the Rev. G. H. Doble, to whom Mr. W. D. Watson sang it after hearing an old man, Mr. Thomas Beard, sing it at St. Day. A version in Cornish was subsequently published ('Ma gron war'n gelinen') with a fourth stanza, here translated and added to Mr. Beard's English version.

36 THE SALUTATION CAROL
(NATIVITY: ANNUNCIATION)

15th century
Ibid.
(R.V.W.)
SOPRANO
ALTO
TENOR
BASS
BURDEN
No - well, No-well, No - well, No-well! This is the sal - u - ta - ti - on of th'an-gel Ga - bri - el.
Fine
VERSE
1. Tid - ings true there be come new, Sent from the Trin - i - ty By Ga - bri - el to Naz - a - reth, Ci - ty of Gal - i - lee. 'A clean mai-den, a pure vir-gin, By her hu-mil - i - ty Shall
2. When he first pre - sen - ted was Be - fore her fair vi - sage, In most de-mure and good - ly wise He did to her ho - mage; And said, 'La - dy, from heav'n so high, That Lord - es he - ri - tage, The

Repeat Burden
now con - ceive the Per - son Se - cond in de - i - ty.'
which of thee born would be I am sent on mes - sage.

3 'Hail, virgin celestiál,
  The meek'st that ever was!
Hail, temple of the Deity!
  Hail, mirror of all grace!
Hail, virgin pure! I thee ensure,
  Within a little space
Thou shalt conceive, and him receive
  That shall bring great soláce.'

4 Then bespake the maid again
  And answered womanly,
'Whate'er my Lord commandeth me
  I will obey truly.'
With '*Ecce sum humillima*
  Ancilla Domini;
Secundum verbum tuum,'
  She said, '*fiat mihi.*'

Salutation—an old name for the Annunciation. 2. demure—in its earlier sense of 'grave, sober'. 4. '*Ecce sum*', &c.—'Lo, I am the most humble handmaid of the Lord. According to thy word,' she said, 'be it done to me.'

Source: Bodleian Library, MS. Eng. poet e.i. (late 15th century) contains words and music for one voice, transcribed in *Early Bodleian Music*, vol. II, p. 183. The words are also found in the Sloane MS. 2593 and in Richard Hill's *Commonplace Book* (Balliol MS. 354), although these contain no music.

Richard Hill's MS. has been printed (so far as the verse is concerned) by R. Dyboski for the Early English Text Society, *Extra Series*, c. I, 1908. It was discovered c. 1850, having been concealed behind a bookcase for a great number of years. Our carols, Nos. 39, 118, 120, 169, 172, occur in it, and other versions of Nos. 19, 38, 61 (and 184), 70, 116.

Richard Hill was 'servant' or apprentice of John Wyngar, grocer, who became an alderman of the City of London in 1493 and mayor in 1504. Hill married in 1518 Margaret, daughter of Harry Wyngar, haberdasher. The earliest part of the book was written before 1504, the latest date in it is 1536; the carols seem all to have been transcribed together about 1504. This precious MS. contains also English, French, and Latin poems, romances, extracts from Gower, &c., mixed with commercial entries, tables of weights, prices, dates of fairs, medical and cooking recipes (including a 'medicen for a doge that is poysent', and 'a good medycyne for a cutt' which begins 'Take a pynte of good ale'), a form for making letters of attorney, a list of diaper table-cloths, &c. for the mayor's annual feast at the Guildhall, rules for purchase of land, the bread assize, a treatise on wine, dates of his children, pious ejaculations and reflections, notes on the breaking in of horses, the 'crafte to brewe bere', forms for business letters in English and French, riddles, puzzles, with many humorous and satirical verses.

37 THE ANGEL GABRIEL
(NATIVITY: ANNUNCIATION)

Traditional
Ibid.
(M.S.)
SOPRANO
ALTO
TENOR
BASS
1. The an-gel Ga-bri-el from God Was sent to Ga-li-lee, Unto a vir-gin fair and free, Whose name was called Ma-ry. And when the an-gel thi-ther came, He fell down on his knee, And look-ing up in the vir-gin's face, He said, 'All hail, Ma-ry':
2. Ma-ry a-non looked him up-on, And said, 'Sir, what are ye? I mar-vel much at these ti-dings Which thou hast brought to me. Mar-ried I am un-to an old man, As the lot fell un-to me; There-fore, I pray, de-part a-way, For I stand in doubt of thee':
CHORUS
Then sing we all, both

great and small, 'No - well, No - well, No - well'; We may re - joice to
hear the voice Of the an - gel — Ga - bri - el.

3 'Mary,' he said, 'be not afraid,
But do believe in me:
The power of the Holy Ghost
Shall overshadow thee;
Thou shalt conceive without any grief,
As the Lord told unto me:
God's own dear Son from heaven shall come,
And shall be born of thee':

Then sing we all, etc.

4 *This came to pass as God's will was,
Even as the angel told,
About midnight an angel bright
Came to the shepherds' fold,
And told them then both where and when
Born was the child our Lord,
And all along this was their song,
'All glory be given to God':

Then sing we all, etc.

5 Good people all, both great and small,
The which do hear my voice,
With one accord let's praise the Lord,
And in our hearts rejoice;
Like sister and brother, let's love one another
Whilst we our lives do spend,
Whilst we have space let's pray for grace,
And so let my carol end:

Then sing we all, etc.

As in Sandys, 1833; Stainer gives the tune from Devonshire. The 'lot' in v. 2 is an allusion to the apocryphal Gospel of the Birth of Mary where Joseph is chosen out from the other suitors by the budding of his rod; the legend is introduced into the tenth play (Mary's Betrothal) of the so-called *Ludus Coventriæ*, and is familiar in pictures, e.g. in Raphael's *Sposalizio* in the Brera.

38 THE HOLLY AND THE IVY

(NATIVITY: LENT: AUTUMN)

Traditional

Ibid. (M.S.)

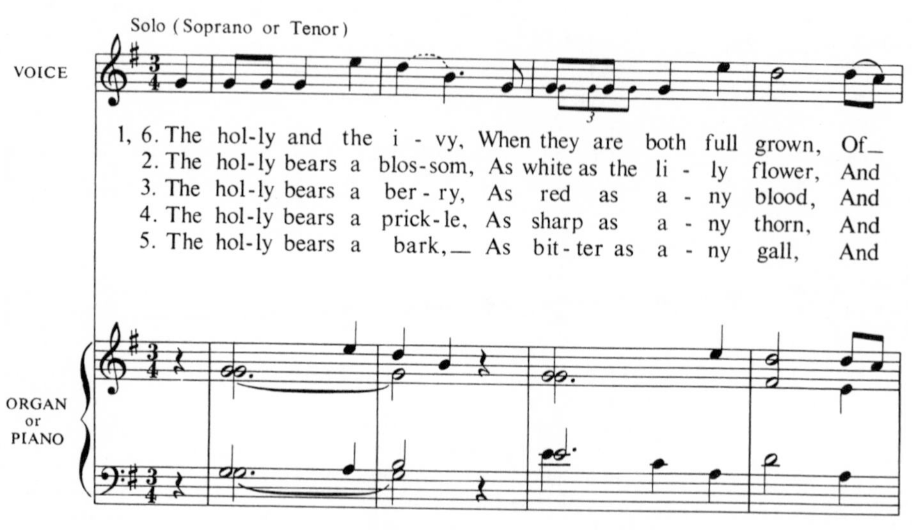

Solo (Soprano or Tenor)
VOICE
1, 6. The hol-ly and the i - vy, When they are both full grown, Of
2. The hol-ly bears a blos-som, As white as the li - ly flower, And
3. The hol-ly bears a ber - ry, As red as a - ny blood, And
4. The hol-ly bears a prick-le, As sharp as a - ny thorn, And
5. The hol-ly bears a bark, As bit-ter as a - ny gall, And
ORGAN or PIANO

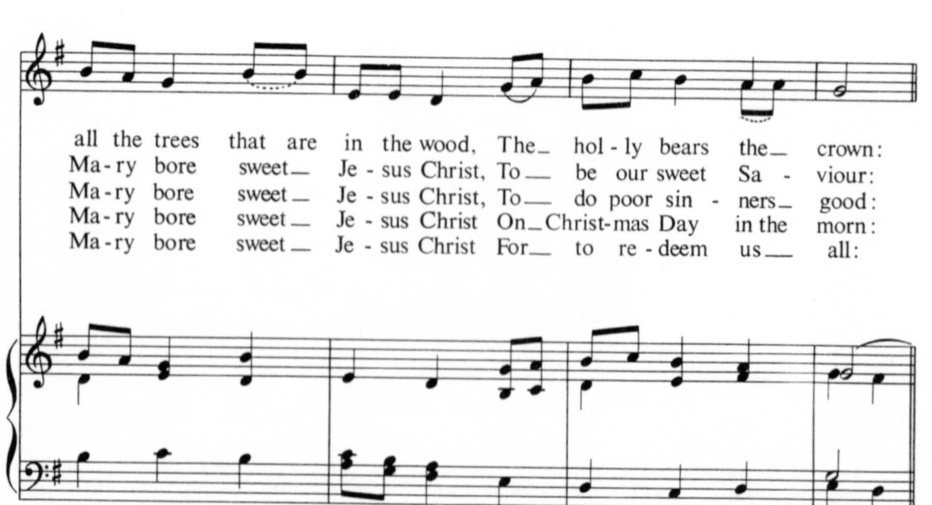

all the trees that are in the wood, The hol - ly bears the crown:
Ma-ry bore sweet Je - sus Christ, To be our sweet Sa - viour:
Ma-ry bore sweet Je - sus Christ, To do poor sin - ners good:
Ma-ry bore sweet Je - sus Christ On Christ-mas Day in the morn:
Ma-ry bore sweet Je - sus Christ For to re - deem us all:

CHORUS
S.
A.
The ris-ing of the sun— And the run-ning of the deer, The—
T.
B.
(Small notes, Organ or Piano)

play-ing of— the— mer-ry or - gan, Sweet sing-ing in the choir.

This carol may be sung with or without accompaniment

Cf. Nos. 35 and 63. Words and melody taken from Mrs. Clayton at Chipping Campden, Glos. (supplemented by words from Mrs. Wyatt, East Harptree, Somerset), by Cecil Sharp, *English Folk-Carols* (Novello). Another version is in Bramley and Stainer, and in the *English Carol Book* (Mowbray's) set to a French carol tune. 'Joshua Sylvester', in his *Christmas Carols*, 1861, was the first to publish the text in a collection; he took it from 'an old broadside, printed a century and a half since', i.e. *c.* 1710. Husk stated in 1868 that it was still retained in the broadsides printed at Birmingham. These two versions differ in the second line, 'Now are both well grown'. There is another carol of the Holly and the Ivy ('Holy berith beris') in Richard Hill's MS., another in the Harleian MS. ('Nay, Ivy, nay'), and others, for which Dyboski gives references. The subject is probably of pagan origin, and symbolized the masculine (holly) and the feminine (ivy) elements, as the tribal chorus developed into dialogue, all such songs being sung as a dance between the lads and the maids. 'The merry organ' occurs in Chaucer in the Nonne Preestes Tale: 'Chauntecleer's crowing had no peer— His voice was merrier than the merry organ/On mass-days that in the churche gon.'

39 THIS ENDRIS NIGHT

(NATIVITY)

15th century

Ibid.
(R.V.W.)

SOPRANO
ALTO

TENOR
BASS

1. This en - dris night I saw___ a sight, A
2. This love - ly la - dy sat___ and sung, And

star as bright___ as day;___ And e - ver a - mong, a
to her child___ did say:___ 'My son,___ my bro - ther,

mai - den sung, 'Lul - lay, by by, lul - - lay.'___
fa - ther, dear, Why liest thou thus in hay?___

FA-BURDEN

(M.S.)

S.
A.
T.
B.

3 'My sweetest bird, thus 'tis required,
Though thou be king veray;
But nevertheless I will not cease
To sing, By by, lullay.'

4 The child then spake in his talking,
And to his mother said:
'Yea, I am known as heaven-king,
In crib though I be laid;

(*Fa-Burden*)

5 'For angels bright down to me light:
Thou knowest 'tis no nay:
And for that sight thou may'st delight
To sing, By by, lullay.'

6 'Now, sweet son, since thou art a king,
Why art thou laid in stall?
Why dost not order thy bedding
In some great kingès hall?

7 'Methinks 'tis right that king or knight
Should lie in good array:
And then among, it were no wrong
To sing, By by, lullay.'

(*Fa-Burden*)

8 *'Mary mother, I am thy child,
Though I be laid in stall;
For lords and dukes shall worship me,
And so shall kingès all.

(*Fa-Burden*)

9*'Ye shall well see that kingès three
Shall come on this twelfth day.
For this behest give me thy breast,
And sing, By by, lullay.'

10 *'Now tell, sweet son, I thee do pray,
Thou art my love and dear—
How should I keep thee to thy pay,
And make thee glad of cheer?

11 *'For all thy will I would fulfil—
Thou knowest well, in fay;
And for all this I will thee kiss,
And sing, By by, lullay.'

(*Fa-Burden*)

12 *'My dear mother, when time it be,
Take thou me up on loft,
And set me then upon thy knee,
And handle me full soft;

(*Fa-Burden*)

13 *'And in thy arm thou hold me warm,
And keep me night and day,
And if I weep, and may not sleep,
Thou sing, By by, lullay.'

14 *'Now, sweet son, since it is come so,
That all is at thy will,
I pray thee grant to me a boon,
If it be right and skill,—

15 *'That child or man, who will or can
Be merry on my day,
To bliss thou bring—and I shall sing,
Lullay, by by, lullay.'

1. This endris—('thys ender' in the MS. Add. 31922, 'this endurs' in the MS., Advocates' Lib., Edinburgh), the other night, a few nights ago. ever among—every now and then. 3. veray—true. 5. light—alight. no nay—not to be denied. 10. pay—satisfaction. 11. fay—faith. 14. skill—reasonable.

Was not new when it was written out in the Bodleian MS., Eng. Poet., e. 1, which is dated between 1460 and 1490. It is in the MS. of Richard Hill, the grocer (cf. No. 36). Four versions are given by Dyboski in the Early English Text Society, Extra Series, c. 1, p. 174. Wright's version, from the Sloane MS. 2593 (see nos. 174, 182), Percy Society, 1841, is reprinted in Julian's *Dictionary of Hymnology* (p. 209) by Helmore. Two of the versions are in Chambers and Sidgwick, pp. 119 and 121. The tune is used in the *English Hymnal* (20) and *Songs of Praise* (72): it is in the fifteenth or sixteenth century MS., B.M., Royal Appendix 58, set for three voices, with melody in the tenor.

40 WONDER TIDINGS
(NATIVITY)

15th century

Ibid.
(School of J. Dunstable)
(M.S.)

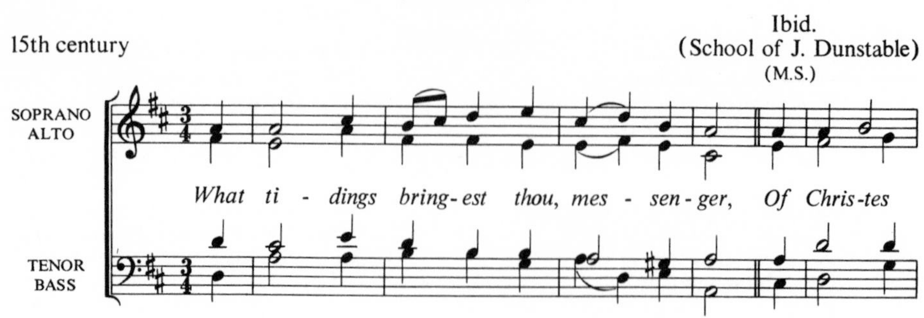

SOPRANO
ALTO
TENOR
BASS
What ti - dings bring-est thou, mes - sen-ger, Of Chris-tes

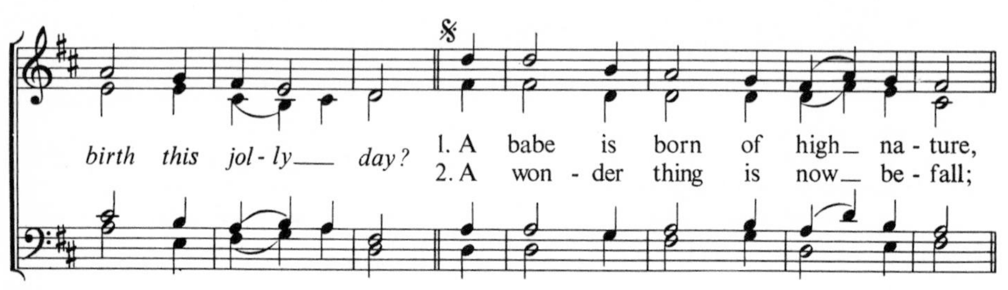

birth this jol-ly___ day?
1. A babe is born of high_ na-ture,
2. A won - der thing is now_ be-fall;

The Prince of peace that e-ver shall be; Of heav'n and earth he
That King that form-ed star_ and sun, Hea-ven and earth and

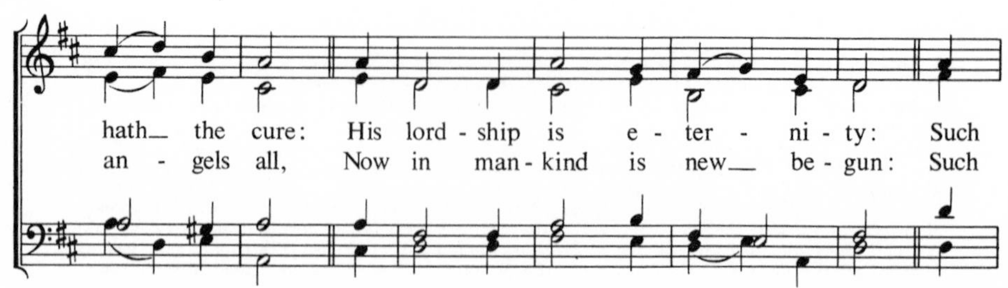

hath_ the cure: His lord-ship is e - ter - ni - ty: Such
an - gels all, Now in man-kind is new_ be-gun: Such

*
won - der ti - dings ye — may hear,
won - der ti - dings ye — may hear,
That man is made now
An in - fant now of
*

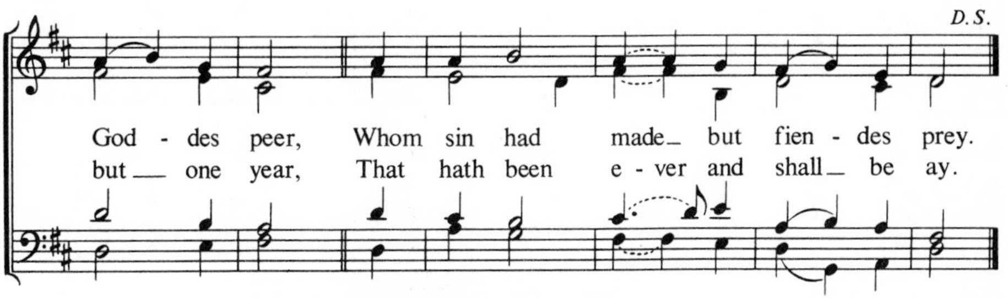
D. S.
God - des peer,
but — one year,
Whom sin had made — but fien - des prey.
That hath been e - ver and shall — be ay.

3 That seemeth strange to us to see,
   This bird that hath this babe yborn
  And Lord conceived of high degree
   A maiden is, as was beforn:
     Such wonder tidings ye may hear,
     That maiden and mother is one in fere,
       And she a lady of great array.

4 That loveliest gan greet her child,
   'Hail, son! Hail, brother! Hail, father dear!'
  'Hail, daughter! Hail, sister! Hail, mother mild!'
   This hailing was on quaint mannere:
     Such wonder tidings ye may hear,
     That hailing was of so good cheer
       That mannés pain is turned to play.

1. cure—charge. 3. bird—girl. beforn—before. in fere—together. 4. quaint—(from 'coint', 'cognitus', 'known'), had several shades of meaning in the fifteenth century—'strange', 'curiously wrought', 'dainty', 'graceful'.
Words and tune from a MS. at Cambridge (T.C.C., O.3.58). Another version from a Bodleian MS. is printed in Stainer's *Early Bodleian Music*, vol. 2, p. 125. Accurate transcriptions of both versions are to be found in *Medieval Carols*, Nos. 11 and 27, (Greene, No. 117); in both cases the chorus repeat the opening phrase 'What tidings bringest thou, messenger' at the point marked *. There is no evidence for the ascription to Dunstable. In this carol an opening challenge is preserved, both in words and music. We can imagine, with Sir Edmund Chambers, how 'the chanted question comes nearer and nearer along the crooked medieval street': or we can picture a company singing in a hall round the crackling yule logs; the door opens, and the Messenger enters; the company sings 'What tidings . . .', and the Messenger answers with the first stanza, and a choir perhaps takes up the refrain, which changes as the tidings are told out. The same might be done today in a parish hall; or in church, the Messenger, wearing a gown and carrying a staff, like a verger, might walk up the middle alley, the choir beginning 'What tidings' as he approaches the chancel. He would proceed as far as the midst of the chancel, and then, turning west, would sing his verses.

41 RIGHTEOUS JOSEPH
(NATIVITY: ADVENT)

Cornish

Ibid.
(M.S.)

SOPRANO
ALTO
TENOR
BASS
1. When right - eous Jo - seph wed - ded was To Is - rael's He - brew maid, The an - gel Gab - riel came from heav'n, And to the Vir - gin said:
'Hail, bless - ed Ma - ry, full of grace, The Lord re - main on thee; Thou shalt con - ceive and bear a son, Our Sa - viour for to be':
CHORUS: Then sing you all, both great and small, No - well, No - well, No - well! We may re - joice to hear the voice Of the an - gel Gab - ri - el.

2 *Then Joseph thought to shun all shame
And Mary to forsake;
But God's dear angel in a dream
His mind did undertake:
'Fear not, old Joseph, she's thy wife,
She's still a spotless maid;
There's no conceit or sin at all
Against her can be laid':

Then sing etc.

3 Thus Mary and her husband kind
Together did remain,
Until the time of Jesus' birth,
As scripture doth make plain.
As mother, wife, and virtuous maid,
Our Saviour sweet conceived;
And in due time to bring us him,
Of whom we were bereaved:

Then sing etc.

4 Sing praises all, both young and old,
To him that wrought such things;
And all without the means of man,
Sent us the King of kings,
Who is of such a spirit blest,
That with his might did quell
The world, the flesh, and by his death
Did conquer death and hell:

Then sing etc.

As in Davies Gilbert, 1822 (with seven verses); but v. 2 from the less corrupt version of Miss Hocking. The tune has been kindly communicated by the Rev. G. H. Doble, who noted it from Elizabeth Hocking, at Redruth, Cornwall. Miss Hocking was then 84 (1920), and had learnt it from her mother as a very small child, i.e. *c.* 1840.

42 REMEMBER
(LENT: CHRISTMAS)

Melismata, 1611

Ibid.
(Thomas Ravenscroft, 1611)

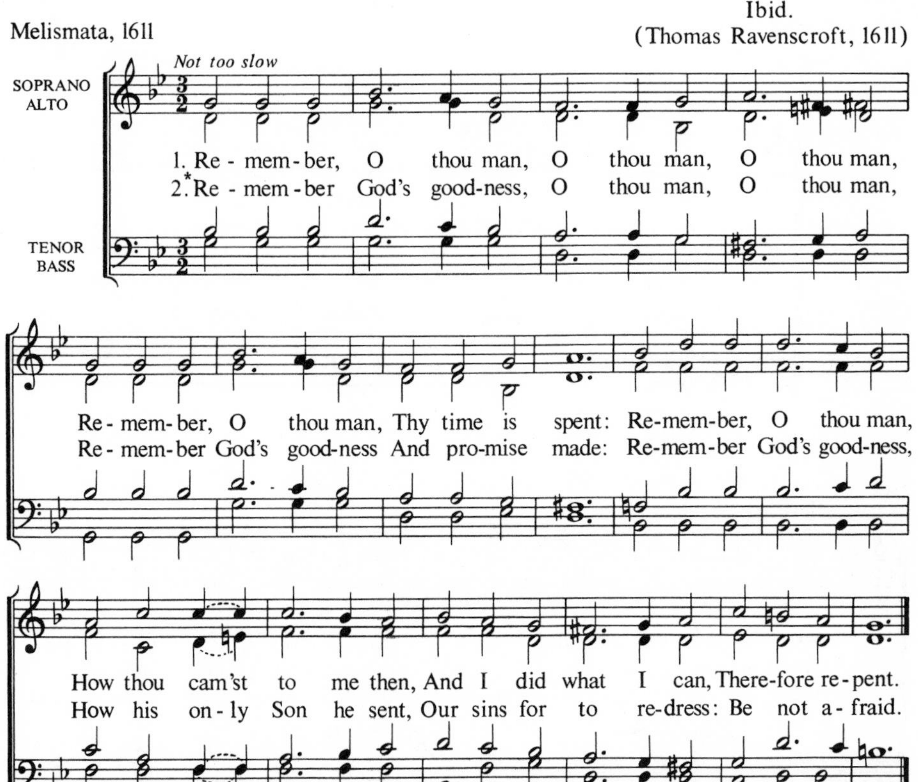

SOPRANO
ALTO
TENOR
BASS
Not too slow
1. Re - mem - ber, O thou man, O thou man, O thou man,
2.* Re - mem - ber God's good-ness, O thou man, O thou man,
Re - mem - ber, O thou man, Thy time is spent: Re-mem-ber, O thou man,
Re - mem - ber God's good-ness And pro-mise made: Re-mem-ber God's good-ness,
How thou cam'st to me then, And I did what I can, There-fore re - pent.
How his on - ly Son he sent, Our sins for to re-dress: Be not a - fraid.

3 The angels all did sing,
  O thou man, O thou man,
The angels all did sing,
  On Sion hill:
The angels all did sing
Praises to our heavenly King,
And peace to man living,
  With right good will.

4 To Bethlem did they go,
  O thou man, O thou man,
To Bethlem did they go,
  This thing to see:
To Bethlem did they go,
To see whether it was so,
Whether Christ was born or no
  To set us free.

5 In Bethlem was he born,
  O thou man, O thou man,
In Bethlem was he born,
  For mankind dear:
In Bethlem was he born
For us that were forlorn,
And therefore took no scorn,
  Our sins to bear,

6 Give thanks to God always,
  O thou man, O thou man,
Give thanks to God always,
  With hearts most jolly:
Give thanks to God always
Upon this blessèd day;
Let all men sing and say,
  Holy, holy.

The words, which are probably of the sixteenth century, are set to music in Ravenscroft's *Melismata*. Four verses omitted will be found in Bullen. Mr. Thomas Hardy gives another version in *Under the Greenwood Tree*. For Lent, vv. 1, 2, 3, 5 are suitable.

43 THE SEVEN VIRGINS
(THE PASSION)

Traditional

Ibid.
(R. V. W.)

(Omit in v. 12)
SOPRANO
ALTO
1. All un - der the leaves, the leaves of life, I
2. 'O what are you seek - ing, you sev - en fair maids, All
3. 'We're seek - ing for no leaves, Tho - mas, But
TENOR
BASS

met with vir - gins sev'n, And one of them was
un - der the leaves of life? Come tell, come tell me
for a friend of thine; We're seek - ing for sweet

Ma - ry mild, Our Lord's mo - ther from heav'n.
what seek you All un - der the leaves of life.'
Je - sus Christ, To be our guide and thine.'

4 'Go you down, go you down to yonder town,
And sit in the gallery;
And there you'll find sweet Jesus Christ,
Nailed to a big yew-tree.'

5 So down they went to yonder town,
As fast as foot could fall,
And many a grievous bitter tear,
From the virgins' eyes did fall.

6 'O peace, mother, O peace, mother,
Your weeping doth me grieve;
O I must suffer this,' he said,
'For Adam and for Eve.'

7 'O how can I my weeping leave,
Or my sorrows undergo,
Whilst I do see my own Son die,
When sons I have no mo'?'

8 'Dear mother, dear mother, you must take John,
All for to be your son,
And he will comfort you sometimes,
Mother, as I have done.'

9 'O, come, thou John Evangelist,
Thou'rt welcome unto me,
But more welcome my own dear son,
That I nursed upon my knee.'

10 Then he laid his head on his right shoulder,
Seeing death it struck him nigh:
'The Holy Ghost be with your soul,—
I die, mother dear, I die.'

11 Oh the rose, the rose, the gentle rose,
And the fennel that grows so green!
God give us grace in every place,
To pray for our king and queen.

12 Furthermore for our enemies all
Our prayers they should be strong.
Amen, Good Lord! your charity
Is the ending of my song.

Melody and a version of text from Mrs. Whatton and Mrs. Loveridge, The Homme, Dilwyn. From *Twelve Traditional Carols from Herefordshire* (Leather and Vaughan Williams), Stainer & Bell. Cf. *Popular Carols*, by F. Sidgwick (Sidgwick & Jackson). This fine example of the way in which a mystical vision is created by the best folk-poetry appeared in the Staffordshire *A Good Christmas Box*, 1847. Sylvester (1861) printed a version of it from an 'old Birmingham broadside'. Sir A. Quiller-Couch included it in the *Oxford Book of English Verse*, and Walter de la Mare in *Come Hither*.

44 THE LAMB OF GOD
(THE PASSION: EASTER: NEW YEAR)

Traditional
Ibid.
(M.S.)
SOPRANO
ALTO
TENOR
BASS
1. A - wake, a - wake, ye drow - sy souls, And hear what I shall tell; Re - mem - ber Christ, the Lamb of God, Re - deem'd our souls from hell. He's crowned with thorns, spit on with scorn, His friends have hid them- - selves:
2. They bound Christ's bo - dy to a tree, And woun - ded him full sore; From ev - 'ry wound the blood ran down, Till Christ could bleed no more; His dy - ing wounds, all rent and tore, Were co-vered with pear - ly gore:
CHORUS
So God send you all much joy in the year, in the

year, So God send you all— much– joy—— in— the year.

3 And when his foes had murdered Christ
And shown their cruel spite,
The sun and moon did hide their heads
And went in mourning straight;
The heavens stood amazed, and angels gazed,
And the earth was darkened quite:

So God send you etc.

4 *And when Christ's soul departed
And from his body fled,
The rocks did rend, the graves did ope,
And then appeared the dead;
All they that were there did quake for fear–
''Twas the Son of God', they said:

So God send you etc.

PART 2 (EASTER, ETC.)

5 It was early in the morning
That Mary did him seek;
She saw two angels sitting
At Jesus' head and feet:
Mary shed tears while Christ appeared,
And he said: 'Why dost thou weep?'

So God send you etc.

6 Then Christ he called Thomas,
And bid him: 'Come and see,
And put thy fingers in the wounds
That are in my body;
And be not faithless, but believe,
And happy shalt thou be':

So God send you etc.

7 Then Christ called his disciples,
Divided by his death,
And said: 'All powers are given to you
In heaven and on earth;
Go forth and teach all nations;
Despise them not,' he saith:

So God send you etc.

8 *'Go seek you every wandering sheep
That doth on earth remain,
Till I myself have paid your debts
And turned you back again;
Come all ye heavy laden,
I'll ease you of your pain':

So God send you etc.

PART 3 (GOOD WISHES)

9 *God bless the ruler of this house
And send him long to reign;
Let many a good and happy year
Go over his head again,
And all his godly family
That serveth the Lord so dear:

So God send you etc.

10 *God bless the mistress of this house,
With peace unto her breast,
And, let her body be asleep or awake,
Lord, send her soul to rest,
And all her godly family
That serveth the Lord so dear:

So God send you etc.

The melody and the first and last verses were taken down by Cecil Sharp at Donnington Wood, Shropshire; the refrain as noted was 'So God send you all a joyful New Year', and v. 5 comes after v. 8. We have substituted 'friends' in v. 1 and 'foes' in v. 3 for 'Jews'; vv. 4 and 7 seem to be corrupt in the original, and we have slightly amended them. The carol is printed in *A Good Christmas Box*, 1847, and in an undated chap-book printed by J. Bates, New Town, Bilston. It is given in Cecil Sharp's *English Folk-Carols*, and is evidently a Passiontide and Easter carol, not perfectly remembered, and adapted to the Christmas-Epiphany season to which carol-singing came to be restricted.

45 SUSSEX MUMMERS' CAROL
(LENT: THE PASSION)

Traditional | Ibid. (L.E.B.)

Slow
SOPRANO
ALTO
TENOR
BASS
1. O mortal man, remember well, When Christ our Lord was born, He was crucified between two thieves, And crowned with the thorn, And crown-ed with the thorn.
2. O mortal man, remember well, When Christ died on the rood, 'Twas for our sins and wicked ways Christ shed his precious blood, Christ shed his precious blood.

3 O mortal man, remember well,
When Christ was wrapped in clay,
He was taken to a sepulchre
Where no man ever lay.

4 *God bless the mistress of this house
With gold chain round her breast;
Where'er her body sleeps or wakes,
Lord, send her soul to rest.

5 *God bless the master of this house
With happiness beside;
Where'er his body rides or walks
Lord Jesus be his guide.

6 God bless your house, your children too,
Your cattle and your store;
The Lord increase you day by day,
And send you more and more.

Sung by Christmas Mummers from the neighbourhood of Horsham, c. 1876-81. Collected by Lucy E. Broadwood. See Broadwood's *Sussex Songs* (Stanley Lucas and Weber, later Leonard & Co.); L. E. Broadwood's *English Traditional Songs and Carols* (Boosey & Co.) and her *Christmas Carols for Children* (A. and C. Black), in all of which the original opening verse, describing the Annunciation, is retained.

45—Sussex Mummers' Carol

(R.V.W.)

ALTERNATIVE HARMONIZATION
1. O— mor - tal man, re - - mem - ber well, When—
2. O— mor - tal man, re - - mem - ber well, When—
Christ our Lord was— born,— He was cru - ci - fied— be -
Christ died on the— rood,— 'Twas— for our sins— and—
-tween two— thieves, And crown - ed with the— thorn,— And
wick - ed— ways— Christ shed his pre - cious— blood,— Christ
crown - - - ed— with the thorn.
shed— his— pre - - - - cious blood.

For unison setting of last verse see overleaf.

45—Sussex Mummers' Carol

UNISON SETTING FOR LAST VERSE
(R.V.W.)
ff
ff ORGAN
3
6. God bless your house, your children too, Your cattle and your store;
The Lord increase you day by day, And send you more and more,
And send you more and more.

46 THE BELLMAN'S SONG
(GENERAL: THE PASSION)

FIRST TUNE

Traditional

Ibid.
(M.S.)

VERSES 1, 2
SOPRANO
ALTO
1. The moon shines bright, and the stars give a light: A
2. A - wake, a - wake, good_ peo - ple_ all; A - -
TENOR
BASS

lit - tle be - fore it was day Our_ Lord, our_ God, he
- wake,_ and you shall_ hear, Our_ Lord, our_ God, died

called on us, And_ bid us a - wake_ and_ pray.
on the cross For_ us whom he loved_ so_ dear.

VERSES 3, 5
3. O fair, O fair Je - - ru - sa - lem, When
5. And for the sav - ing of our souls Christ

shall I come to thee? When shall my sor - rows
died up - on the cross; We ne'er shall do for
TENOR When We
[Bass: words as for S. and A.]

have an end, Thy joy that I may see?
Je - sus Christ As he hath done for us.
shall my sor - rows end, that I may see.
ne'er shall do for Christ as he for us.

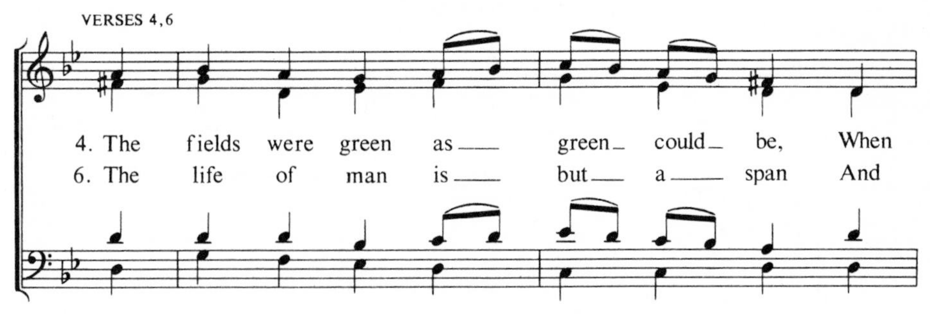
VERSES 4, 6
4. The fields were green as green could be, When
6. The life of man is but a span And

from his glo - rious seat Our Lord, our God, he
cut down in its flower; We are here to - day, and to-

wa - tered us, With his heav'n - ly dew so sweet.
-mor-row are gone, The crea - tures of an hour.

This carol is common in the old broadsides, and some of its verses have strayed into other folk-carols (e.g. into the May Carol from Hertfordshire, printed in Hone's *Every-day Book*, 1821, cf. No. 47). The longer version, in ten verses, is printed by Sandys, Husk, Bullen and others; it includes the 'With one turf' verse, and concludes with New Year wishes (like those of No. 47, with 'here' and 'Year' instead of 'stay' and 'May'); but the song is clearly a Passion carol or Atonement carol, of the type that became common in the later carol era. We have used Husk's form of v. 6. V. 3 is a variant of the first verse of 'Jerusalem, my happy home' (see No. 132), the twenty-six verses of which are in the *English Hymnal* and *Songs of Praise*. The first tune has been familiar since its publication by Bramley & Stainer in 1871. It might perhaps be some version of this carol to which Shakespeare refers in the page's song, 'It was a lover and his lass', in *As You Like It*—

> This carol they began that hour,
> With a hey, and a ho, and a hey nonino,
> How that a life was but a flower,
> In the spring time, the only pretty ring time.

46 THE BELLMAN'S SONG
(GENERAL: THE PASSION)

SECOND TUNE

Traditional

Ibid. (R.V.W.)

VOICES IN UNISON
ORGAN or PIANO
1. The moon shines bright, and the stars give a light: A little before it was day Our Lord, our God, he called on us, And bid us a-wake and pray.
2. A-wake, a-wake, good people all; A-wake, and you shall hear, Our Lord, our God, died on the cross For us whom he loved so dear.

3 O fair, O fair Jerusalem,
When shall I come to thee?
When shall my sorrows have an end,
Thy joy that I may see?

4 The fields were green as green could be,
When from his glorious seat
Our Lord, our God, he watered us,
With his heavenly dew so sweet.

5 And for the saving of our souls
Christ died upon the cross;
We ne'er shall do for Jesus Christ
As he hath done for us.

6 The life of man is but a span
And cut down in its flower;
We are here to-day, and to-morrow are gone,
The creatures of an hour.

Tune noted by Miss Lucy Broadwood, in Surrey, in 1894. Printed in the *Journal of the Folk Song Society*, vol. i, p. 176.

46 THE BELLMAN'S SONG

(GENERAL: THE PASSION)

THIRD TUNE

Traditional

Ibid. (R.V.W.)

SOPRANO
ALTO
TENOR
BASS
1. The moon shines bright, and the stars give a light: A lit - tle be-fore it was day Our Lord, our God, he called on us, And bid us a - wake and pray.
2. A - wake, a - wake, good peo - ple all; A - wake, and you shall hear, Our Lord, our God, died on the cross For us whom he loved so dear.

3 O fair, O fair Jerusalem,
When shall I come to thee?
When shall my sorrows have an end,
Thy joy that I may see?

4 The fields were green as green could be,
When from his glorious seat
Our Lord, our God, he watered us,
With his heavenly dew so sweet.

5 And for the saving of our souls
Christ died upon the cross;
We ne'er shall do for Jesus Christ
As he hath done for us.

6 The life of man is but a span
And cut down in its flower;
We are here to-day, and to-morrow are gone,
The creatures of an hour.

Tune noted at Kingsclere, Hants, by the late Godfrey Arkwright, in 1897, and printed in the *Journal of the Folk Song Society*, vol. i, p. 178. Harmonies from the *English Hymnal*, where the tune is called 'Newbury' and set to hymn 16.

47 MAY CAROL

Traditional

Ibid.
(R.V.W.)

Slow
VOICES IN UNISON
PIANO or ORGAN
(all verses)
p
1. A - wake, a - wake, good peo - ple all, A - - wake! and you shall hear That Christ has di - ed for our sins For he lov - ed us so dear.
1st time
Last time
2. So
3.*The
4. A
5.Now my
pp

47—May Carol

Melody (vv. 2-5)
2. So dear - ly, so dear - ly has Christ_ lov-ed us, And_
3. *The ear - ly___ cock so___ ear - - ly___ crows, That is

(v. 3)
for our___ sins was_ slain; Christ bids us leave off our___
pass - ing the night a - - way, For the trum - pet shall sound and the

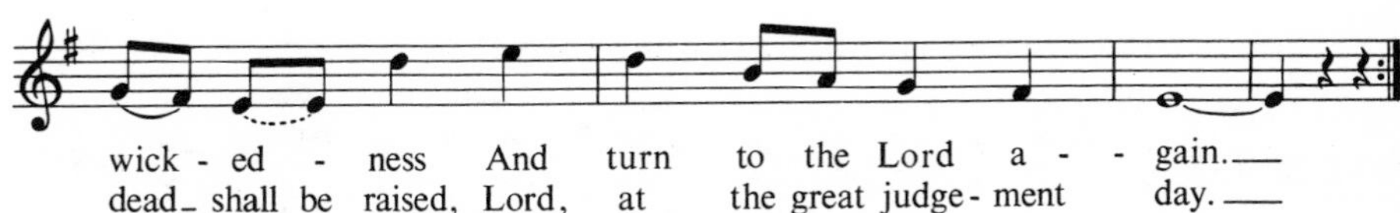
wick - ed - ness And turn to the Lord a - - gain.___
dead_ shall be raised, Lord, at the great judge - ment day.___

4. A branch of_may I have brought to_you, And at your door it stands; It

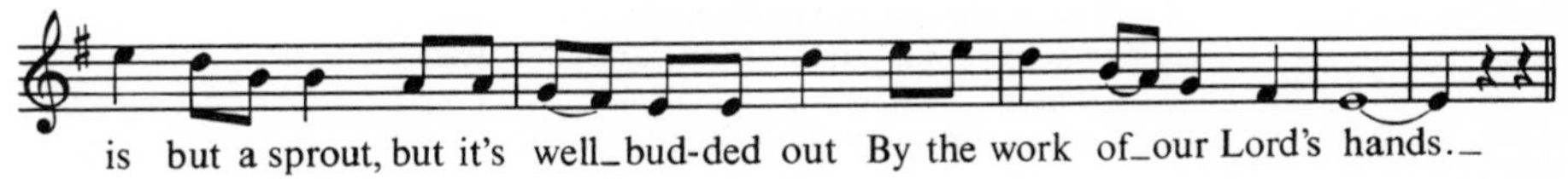
is but a sprout, but it's well_bud-ded out By the work of_our Lord's hands._

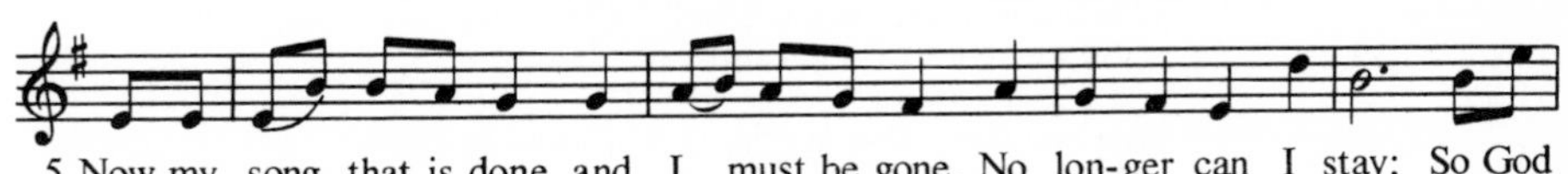
5. Now my song, that is done, and I_must be gone, No lon-ger can I stay; So God

bless you all, both great_and small, And I wish you a joy-ful May._

For version for unaccompanied singing see overleaf.

47—May Carol

VERSION FOR UNACCOMPANIED SINGING

(Sopranos should sing melody in vv. 2-5 as on page 97)

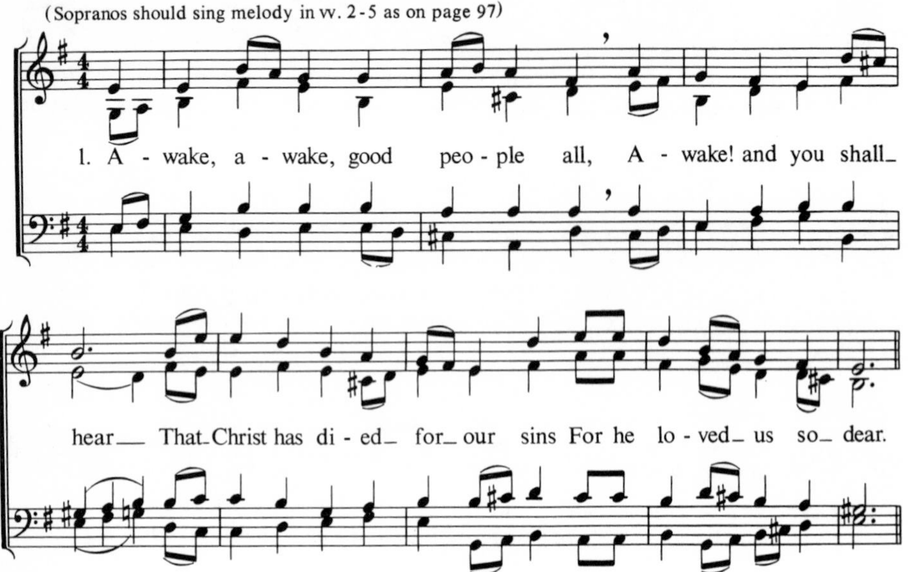
1. A - wake, a - wake, good peo - ple all, A - wake! and you shall_
hear__ That_Christ has di - ed_ for_ our sins For he lo - ved_ us so_ dear.

2 So dearly, so dearly has Christ lovèd us,
And for our sins was slain;
Christ bids us leave off our wickedness
And turn to the Lord again.

3 *The early cock so early crows,
That is passing the night away,
For the trumpet shall sound and the dead shall be raised,
Lord, at the great judgement day.

4 A branch of may I have brought to you,
And at your door it stands;
It is but a sprout, but it's well budded out
By the work of our Lord's hands.

5 Now my song, that is done, and I must be gone,
No longer can I stay;
So God bless you all, both great and small,
And I wish you a joyful May.

The melody and the text (exactly as here, except that 'was' has been put instead of 'were' in v. 2, and 'but' added in v. 4) were taken from Mr. Flack, Fowlmere, Cambs., and printed in *Eight Traditional English Carols* (Vaughan Williams), Stainer & Bell. Cecil Sharp and Miss Broadwood have collected other versions. V. 1 is a variant of the second verse in the Bellman's Song, 'The moon shines bright', No. 46. (See also *English County Songs*, and the *Journal of the Folk Song Society*, i. 180.) The Worcestershire version collected by Sharp has the 'fields were green' verse of the Bellman's Song.

47—May Carol

Melody (vv. 2-5)
2. So dear - ly, so dear - ly has Christ_ lov- ed us, And_
3. *The ear - ly___ cock so___ ear - - ly___ crows, That is

(v. 3)
for our___ sins was_ slain; Christ bids us leave off our___
pass - ing the night a - - way, For the trum - pet shall sound and the

wick - ed - ness And turn to the Lord a - - gain.___
dead_ shall be raised, Lord, at the great judge - ment day.___

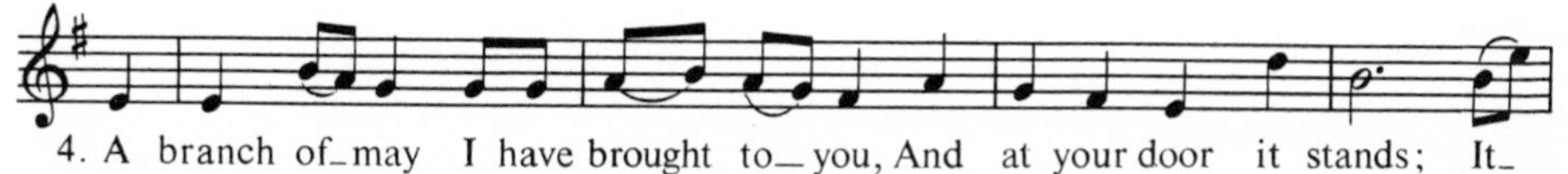
4. A branch of_may I have brought to_you, And at your door it stands; It_

is but a sprout, but it's well_bud-ded out By the work of_our Lord's hands._

5. Now my song, that is done, and I_must be gone, No lon-ger can I stay; So God

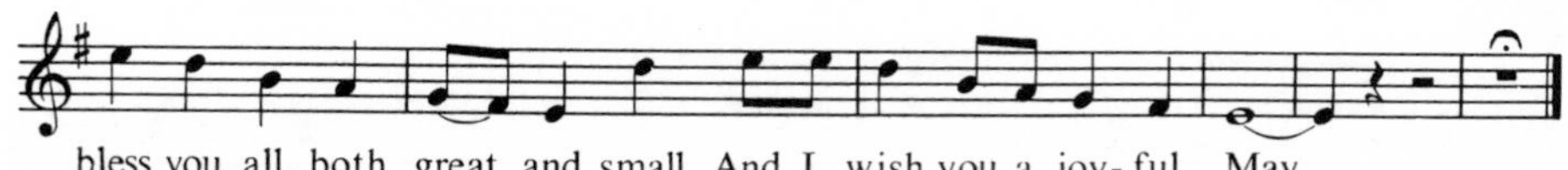
bless you all, both great_and small, And I wish you a joy- ful May._

48 MAY-DAY GARLAND
(MAY)

Traditional

Ibid. (M.S.)

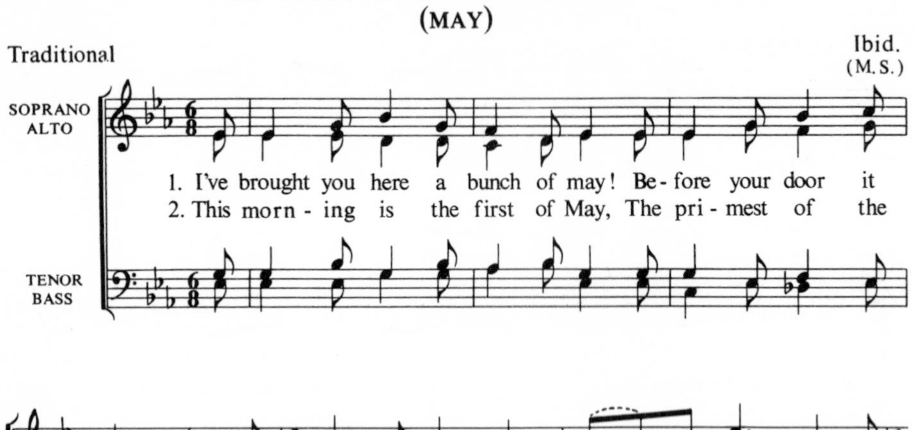
SOPRANO
ALTO
1. I've brought you here a bunch of may! Be-fore your door it
2. This morn-ing is the first of May, The pri-mest of the
TENOR
BASS

stands: It's well set out, and well spread a-bout, By the
year: So la-dies all, both great and small, I wish

work of our Lord's hands: It's well set out, and
you a joy-ful cheer: So la-dies all, both

well spread a-bout, By the work of our Lord's hands.
great and small, I wish you a joy-ful cheer.

3 Then take your bible in your hand,
And read the scriptures through;
And when the day of judgement comes,
The Lord will remember you:
And when the day, &c.

4 The clock's struck one! I must be gone!
No longer can I stay.
If I should live to carry again,
I'll call another May:
If I should live, &c.

This (or 46, or 47) might be sung in church at May-time, when Evensong is over, by one or two girls carrying a branch of may.

The words and tune were taken by Geoffrey and Martin Shaw from an English girl (now Mrs. Betambeau), in the Boro' Polytechnic, London, c. 1917; she had brought them from Northamptonshire.

A May carol from Hitchin is printed by Robert Bell in *Songs of the Peasantry*, 1857, of which verses 1 and 2 are the 1 and 2 of the Furry Day Carol; v. 3 is v. 4 of our May Carol and 1 of our Garland; and verses 4, 6, 7 are 4, 6 and 1 of the Bellman's Song.

49 FURRY DAY CAROL
(MAY)

Traditional

Ibid.
(M.S.)

SOPRANO
ALTO
TENOR
BASS
1. Re-mem-ber_ us poor_ May-ers_ all! And_ thus we do_ be-gin - - a To lead our_ lives in_ right-eous-ness, Or_ else we die_ in_ sin - - a:
2.*We have been ram-bling_ half the_ night, And_ al-most all_ the_ day - - a, And now, re-turn-ed_ back a-gain, We've brought you a branch of_ may - - a:
With Ho-lan-to, sing_ mer-ry,_ O, With_ Ho-lan-to, Ho-lan-to,_ sing_ mer - - ry, With
Ho-lan-to,

Ho - lan - to, sing_ mer - ry,_ O, With_ Ho - lan - to,_ sing_ mer - ry!

3 O, we were up as soon as day,
To fetch the summer home-a;
The summer is a-coming on,
And winter is a-gone-a:

With Holan-to, etc.

4 Then let us all most merry be,
And sing with cheerful voice-a;
For we have good occasion now
This time for to rejoice-a:

With Holan-to, etc.

5 *Saint George he next shall be our song:
Saint George, he was a knight-a;
Of all the men in Christendom
Saint George he was the right-a:

With Holan-to, etc.

6 God bless our land with power and might,
God send us peace in England;
Pray send us peace both day and night,
For ever in merry England:

With Holan-to, etc.

This Furry Day Carol is distinct, both in words and tune, from the Furry Day Song, annually sung at the Spring festival in Helston in Cornwall (the tune of which is given by Gilbert), though there is some resemblance. We are indebted to Mr. Henry Jenner, F.S.A., for much kind information about the Helston festivities, and about the Furry Day Song, which includes references to Robin Hood and the Spaniards—doubtless of the Armada period. The tune of the Carol is given in Duncan's *Story of the Carol*, where he includes also a Robin Hood verse. (For the May verses cf. No. 48, *n.*). The tendency to confine carols to Christmas led to a Christmas version, which must be later. *Furry* is a corruption of the Latin *feria*, holiday (though in its ecclesiastical use it came to mean an unoccupied day and not a holy day). In Chaucer it is (through the Old French *feire, foire*) 'faire', and hence our 'village fair'.

50 NOS GALAN
(WINTER)

Pr. K.E. Roberts
Welsh (M.S.)
SOPRANO ALTO
TENOR BASS
1. Now the joy - ful bells a - ring - ing, All_ ye_ moun - tains, praise the Lord! Lift our hearts, like_ birds a - wing - ing, All_ ye_ moun - tains, praise the Lord! Now our fes - tal sea - son, bring-ing Kins - men_ all,_ to bide and_ board,
2. Dear our home as dear none_ o - ther; Where the_ moun - tains praise the Lord! Glad - ly here our_ care we_ smo - ther; Where_ the_ moun - tains praise the Lord! Here we know that Christ our bro - ther Binds_ us_ all_ as by a_ cord:
3. Cold the year, new white - ness_wear - ing, All_ ye_ moun - tains, praise the Lord! Peace, good-will to_ us a - bear - ing, All_ ye_ moun - tains, praise the Lord! Now we all God's good - ness shar - ing Break_ the_ bread_ and sheathe the_ sword:

Sets our chee - ry voi - ces_ sing-ing: All__ ye_ moun-tains, praise the Lord!
He was born of Ma - ry_ mo-ther Where_ the_ moun-tains praise the Lord!
Bright our hearths the sig - nal_ fla-ring, All__ ye_ moun-tains, praise the Lord!

Words based on the Welsh New Year's Eve secular Carol, Nos Galan.
On New Year's Eve or Day v. 3, l. 5 may be 'Now we all the New Year sharing'.

ALTERNATIVE WORDS

(*Secular*)

DECK the hall with boughs of holly,
Fa la la la la la la la la,
'Tis the season to be jolly,
Fa la, *&c.*
Fill the mead cup, drain the barrel,
Fa la, *&c.*
Troll the ancient Christmas carol,
Fa la, *&c.*

2 See the flowing bowl before us,
Fa la la la la la la la la,
Strike the harp and join the chorus,
Fa la, *&c.*
Follow me in merry measure,
Fa la, *&c.*
While I sing of beauty's treasure,
Fa la, *&c.*

3 Fast away the old year passes,
Fa la la la la la la la la,
Hail the new, ye lads and lassies,
Fa la, *&c.*
Laughing, quaffing, all together,
Fa la, *&c.*
Heedless of the wind and weather,
Fa la, *&c.*

Traditional

51 THE SINNERS' REDEMPTION
(GENERAL)

17th century

Traditional
(R.V.W.)

SOPRANO
ALTO
TENOR
BASS
1. All you that are to mirth in-clined, Con-si-der well and bear in mind What our good God for us hath done, In send-ing his be-lo-ved Son.
2. Let all our songs and prai-ses be Un-to his heav'n-ly maj-es-ty; And e-ver-more a-mongst our mirth, Re-mem-ber Christ our Sa-viour's birth.

3 Moreover, let us every one
Call unto mind and think upon
His righteous life, and how he died,
To have poor sinners justified.

4 He in the Temple daily taught,
And many wonders strange he wrought.
He gave the blind their perfect sight,
And made the lame to walk upright.

5 He raisèd Lazarus from the grave,
And to the sick their health he gave,
But yet for all these wonders wrought,
The priests his dire destruction sought:

6 With vile reproachful taunts and scorns
They crowned him with a wreath of thorns:
Then to the cross through hands and feet
They nailed our blest Redeemer sweet;

7 Thus have you seen and heard aright,
The love of Christ, the Lord of might;
And how he shed his precious blood,
Only to do us sinners good.

One of the most popular carols; some verses of it used to be reprinted annually on the broadsides. The tune was noted from Mr. Hall of Castleton, Derbyshire, with the first verse only. The late Rev. W. H. Shawcross published other verses in his *Old Castleton Christmas Carols*, but these are nearly identical with those in Husk, who notes the appearance of the carol on a music-sheet of 1775. Gilbert, 1822, prints a west-country version—some of the opening Christmas verses, but with a refrain and a different tune. Our tune is from *Eight Traditional Carols* (Vaughan Williams), Stainer & Bell. Cecil Sharp prints a different text and tune in his *English Folk-Carols*, VIII.

We have gone back to the earliest known original, and have selected from the twenty-eight verses in '*The Garland of Good-Will*, containing many Pleasant Songs and Poems—T——D—— London: Printed for *G. Conyers* at the Sign of the *Golden-Ring* in *Little-Britain*' (not dated, except in pencil, 'printed about 1699'). Thomas Deloney was a famous ballad-writer and poet of the people, and one of the earliest of story-writers in English (his works were published by the Clarendon Press, ed. F. O. Mann, 1912). He first published in 1583 and died *c.* 1600. The *Garland* was first published in 1593, but without our carol. To all editions of later date new poems, not by Deloney, were added (this among them, some time after 1631) down to 1709, or later.

52 ANGELUS AD VIRGINEM

(GENERAL, Medieval: ANNUNCIATION)

14th century
Ibid.
(John A. Parkinson)
vv. 1, 2 Voices in unison
1. An - ge - lus ad vir - gi - nem Sub - in - trans in — con - cla - ve,
Vir - gi - nis for - mi - di - nem De - mul - cens, in - quit, 'A - ve!
2. 'Quo - mo - do con - ci - pe - rem Quae vi - rum non — co - gno - vi?
Qua - li - ter in - frin - ge - rem Quod fir - ma men - te vo - vi?'
A - ve, re - gi - na vir - gi - num; Coe - li ter - rae - que Do - mi-
'Spi - ri - tus Sanc - ti gra - ti - a Per - fi - ci - et haec om - ni-
-num Con - ci - pi - es Et pa - ri - es — In - ta - cta Sa - lu - tem ho - mi-
-a; Ne — ti - me - as, Sed gau - de - as, — Se - cu - ra Quod cas - ti - mo - ni-
-num; Tu — por - ta coe - li fac - ta, Me - de - la cri - mi - num'.
-a Ma - ne - bit in — te pu - ra De - i po - ten - ti - a'.
vv. 3, 4 S. S. A. or T. T. B. (Melody in middle voice)
3. *Ad haec vir - go no - bi - lis Re - spon - dens in - quit e - - - i:
'An - cil - la sum hu - mi - lis Om - ni - po - ten - tis De - - - i.
4. *E - ia ma - ter Do - mi - ni, Quae pa - cem red - di - di - - - sti
An - ge - lis et ho - mi - ni, Cum Chris - tum ge - nu - i - - - sti;
3. *Ad haec vir - go no - bi - lis Re - spon - dens in - quit e - - - i:
'An - cil - la sum hu - mi - lis Om - ni - po - ten - tis De - - - i.
4. *E - ia ma - ter Do - mi - ni, Quae pa - cem red - di - di - - - sti
An - ge - lis et ho - mi - ni, Cum Chris - tum ge - nu - i - - - sti;

For editorial notes see p. 108.

(3.) Ti - bi coe - le - sti nun - ti - o, Tan - ti se - cre - ti con - sci-
(4.) Tu - um ex - o - ra fi - li - um Ut se no - bis pro-pi - ti-
(3.)Ti - bi coe - le - sti nun - ti - o, Tan - ti se - cre - ti con - sci-
(4.)Tu - um ex - o - ra fi - li - um Ut se no - bis pro-pi - ti-
-o, Con - sen - ti - ens, Et cu - pi - ens Vi - de - re Fac - tum quod au - di-
-um Ex - hi - be - at, Et de - le - at Pec - ca - ta: Prae - stans aux - i - li-
-o, Con - sen - ti - ens, Et cu - pi - ens Vi - de - re Fac - tum quod au - di-
-um Ex - hi - be - at, Et de - le - at Pec - ca - ta: Prae - stans aux - i - li-
-o; Pa - ra - ta sum pa - re - re, De - i con - si - li - o'.
-um Vi - ta fru - i be - a - ta Post hoc ex - i - li - um.
-o; Pa - ra - ta sum pa - re - re, De - i con - si - li - o'.
-um Vi - ta fru - i be - a - ta Post hoc ex - i - li - um.

52—Angelus ad Virginem

Sources: (a) B. M. Cotton Fragm. XXIX, *c.* 1250, a fragmentary two-part conductus setting, with the melody in the upper voice. (b) *The Dublin Troper* of *c.* 1360, now at Cambridge University Library, (Add. MS. 710) gives two differing three-part versions, with the melody in the middle voice. (c) B.M. Arundel 248, an early 14th-century MS., gives the melody only, but with Latin and English words. Facsimiles of (b) and (c) are given in Wooldridge's *Early English Harmony*, pl. 34, 46, 47. The three-part version given here is taken from (b) where the original pitch is a fifth lower for A.T.B.

Chaucer mentions this early carol, or rather sequence, in the *Milleres Tale*: Nicholas, the Clerk of Oxenford, sang it in the evening to the accompaniment of his 'gay sautrye',—

> 'On which he made a nightes melodye
> So swetely, that al the chambre rong,
> And *Angelus ad virginem* he song.'

We suggest that it is best sung in the original Latin, and even thus, one verse is here omitted. There is a modern rendering by Gabriel Gillett in *The English Carol Book* (Mowbray). The 14th-century translation in (c) is more difficult; here is the first verse:

> 'Gabriel from evene King, Sent to the maide swete, Broute hire blisful tiding, And faire he gan hire greten: Heil be thu ful of grace arith, For godes sone this evene lith For mannes loven Wile man becomen And taken Fles of the maiden brith, Maken fre for to maken Of sene and deules mith.'

Another Middle English version by the blind monk, John Audlay, is quoted by John Stevens in *Music and Poetry in the Early Tudor Court*, p. 40.

53 THE CARNAL AND THE CRANE

(GENERAL, Legendary)

Traditional

Ibid.
(R.V.W.)

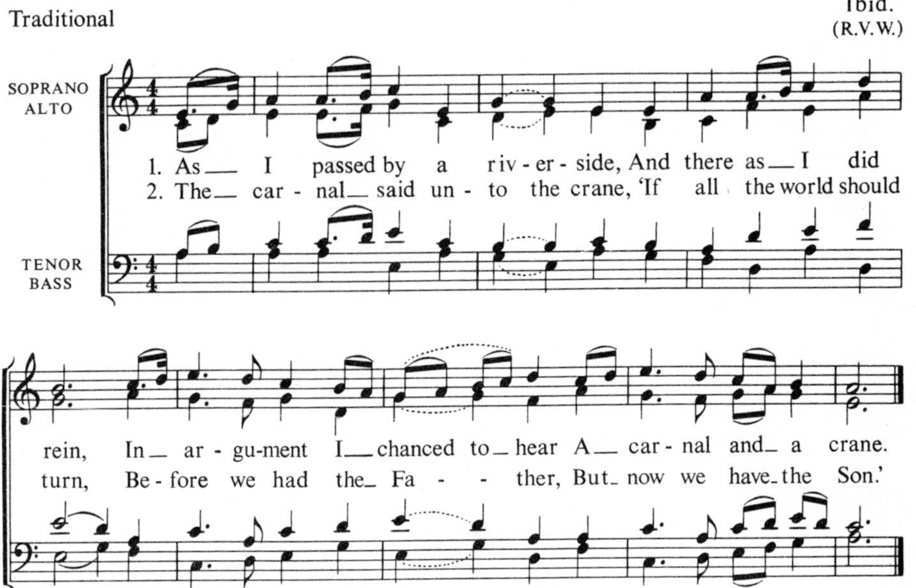
SOPRANO
ALTO
TENOR
BASS
1. As — I passed by a riv - er - side, And there as — I did rein, In — ar - gu-ment I — chanced to — hear A — car - nal and — a crane.
2. The — car - nal — said un - to the crane, 'If all the world should turn, Be - fore we had the — Fa - - ther, But — now we have — the Son.'

3 'From whence does the Son come?
From where and from what place?'
He said: 'In a manger,
Between an ox and ass.

4 'I pray thee,' said the carnal,
'Tell me before thou go,
Was not the mother of Jesus
Conceived by the Holy Ghost?'

5 'She was the purest virgin,
And the cleanest from sin;
She was the handmaid of our Lord,
And mother of our King.'

6 'Where is the golden cradle
That Christ was rockèd in?
Where are the silken sheets
That Jesus was wrapt in?'

7 'A manger was the cradle
That Christ was rockèd in;
The provender the asses left,
So sweetly he slept on.'

1. rein ('reign')—renne, run.

Cf. No. 54 and No. 55. The ballad of 'The Carnal and the Crane' (The Crow and the Crane) contains four subjects: (1) The conversation between the two birds; (2) The legend of Herod and the Cock (No. 54); (3) of The Lovely Lion (four verses); (4) of The Miraculous Harvest (No. 55). Imperfect versions of various portions have been taken down by Cecil Sharp, Miss Broadwood, and Vaughan Williams: these have been here collated with Sandys, and with Frank Sidgwick in *Popular Carols*. See F. C. Child's *Ballads*, ii, p. 7; and also *The Folk Song Society's Journal*, i. 183; iv. 22. *Carnal* seems to be from the French *corneille*, a crow, but *N.E.D.* leaves it with a query.

Melody and part of text from Mr. Hirons, Haven, Dilwyn, *Twelve Traditional Carols from Herefordshire* (Leather and Vaughan Williams), Stainer & Bell.

54 KING HEROD AND THE COCK

(GENERAL, Legendary)

Traditional

Ibid. (M.S.)

Not slow
SOPRANO
ALTO
TENOR
BASS
1. There was a star in — Da - vid's land, So — bright it did ap - pear In - to King He - rod's cham - - ber, And — bright - ly it — shined there.
2. The wise men soon es - pied — it, And — told the king on high, A — prince - ly babe was born that night No — king could e'er — de - stroy.

3 'If this be true,' King Herod said,
'As thou hast told to me,
This roasted cock that lies in the dish
Shall crow full fences three.'

4 The cock soon thrustened and feathered well,
By the work of God's own hand,
And he did crow full fences three,
In the dish where he did stand.

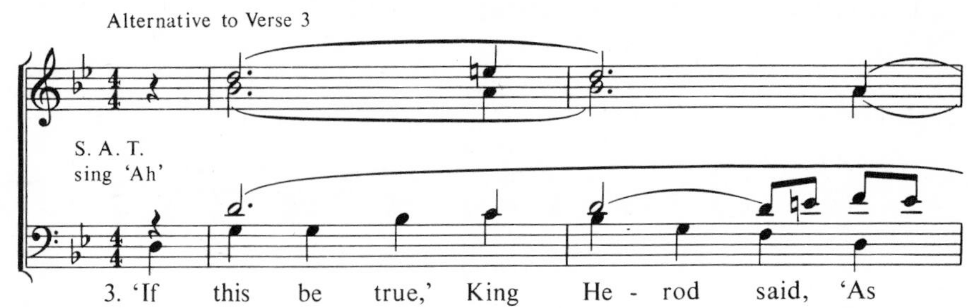
Alternative to Verse 3
S. A. T.
sing 'Ah'
3. 'If this be true,' King He - rod said, 'As

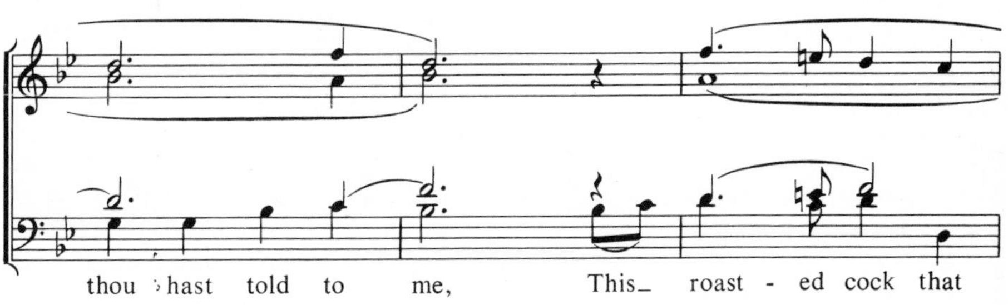
thou hast told to me, This roast - ed cock that

lies in the dish Shall crow full fen - ces three.'

3. fences or 'sences'—times. 4. thrustened—(Early Mid. Eng.), pressed, thrust out.
Cf. No. 53 and No. 55. Words and tune from Mrs. Plumb, Armscote, Worcestershire (*Cecil Sharp; by permission of Novello & Co., Ltd.*). The cock story is also in a ballad of St. Stephen, and is told of others: it has been traced to c. 1200 in Prior's *Ancient Danish Ballads*.

55 THE MIRACULOUS HARVEST

(GENERAL, Legendary)

Traditional

Ibid.
(R. V. W.)

SOPRANO
ALTO
1. 'Rise up, rise up, you mer - ry men all, See that you rea - dy be: All chil - dren un - der two years old Now slain they all shall be.'
2. Then Je - sus, aye, and Jo - - seph, And Ma - ry that was un - known, They tra - velled by a hus - band-man, Just while his seed was sown.
TENOR
BASS

3 'God speed your work,' said Jesus,
'Throw all your seed away,
And carry home as ripened corn
What you have sown this day;

4 'For to keep your wife and family
From sorrow, grief, and pain,
And keep Christ in remembrance
Till seed-time comes again.'

5 The husbandman fell on his knees,
Even upon his face;
'Long time hast thou been lookèd for,
But now thou'rt come at last.

6 *'And I myself do now believe
Thy name is Jesus called;
Redeemer of mankind thou art,
Though undeserving all.'

7 After that there came King Herod,
With his train so furiously,
Enquiring of the husbandman
Whether Jesus had passed by.

8 'Why, the truth it must be spoke,
And the truth it must be known,
For Jesus he passed by this way,
Just as my seed was sown.

9 'But now I have it reapen,
And some laid in my wain,
Ready to fetch and carry
Into my barn again.'

10 *'Turn back,' then says the Captain,
'Your labour and mine's in vain;
It's full three quarters of a year
Since he his seed has sown.'

11 *So Herod was deceivèd
By the work of God's own hand:
No further he proceeded
Into the Holy Land.

12 There's thousands of children young,
Which for his sake did die;
Do not forbid those little ones,
And do not them deny.

The tune here set to *The Miraculous Harvest* was noted by Miss Lucy Broadwood from some gypsies of the name of Goby in 1893. They sang it to the following words, which are an interesting example of the way old ballads become confused among illiterate singers. The illiterate, however, often preserve in their own way what the educated lose: King Pharim (Pharaoh), for instance, may go back to the apocryphal *Gospel of the Infancy* (the Holy Family 'went down to Memphis, and having seen Pharaoh, they stayed three years in Egypt, and the Lord Jesus wrought many miracles there'). These apocryphal legends seem to have got into ballads through the preaching Friars. See Miss Broadwood's *English Traditional Songs and Carols* (Boosey), and *Journal of the Folk Song Society* (1910), iv. 24, for further information.

King Pharim: 1. King Pharim sat a-musing, A-musing all alone; There came a blessed Saviour, And all to him unknown. 2. 'Say, where did you come from, good man, O where did you then pass?' 'It is out of the land Egypt, Between an ox and ass.' 3. 'O, if you come out of Egypt, man, One thing I fain I known, Whether a blessed Virgin Mary Sprung from an Holy Ghost? 4. For if this is true, is true, good man, That you've been telling to me, That the roasted cock do crow three times In the place where they did stand.' 5. O, it's straight away the cock did fetch, And feathered to your own hand, Three times a roasted cock did crow, On the place where they did stand. 6. Joseph, Jesus and Mary Were travelling for the West, When Mary grew a-tired She might sit down and rest. 7. They travelled further and further, The weather being so warm, Till they came unto some husbandman A-sowing of his corn. 8. 'Come, husbandman,' cried Jesus, 'From over speed and pride, And carry home your ripened corn That you've been sowing this day. 9. For to keep your wife and family From sorrow, grief and pain, And keep Christ in your remembrance Till the time comes round again.'

In the *English Hymnal* and *Songs of Praise* the tune is named 'Capel'.

56 THE HOLY WELL
(GENERAL, Legendary)

FIRST TUNE

Traditional

Ibid.
(E.M.)

SOPRANO
ALTO
TENOR
BASS
it fell
1. As it fell out one May morn-ing, And up-on a bright ho-li-day, Sweet Je-sus asked of his dear mo-ther If he might go to play. 'To play, to play, sweet Je-sus shall go, And to play now get you gone; And
2. Sweet Je-sus went down to yon-der town, As far as the Ho-ly Well, And there did see as fine chil-dren As a-ny tongue can tell. He said, 'God bless you ev-'ry one, And your bodies Christ save and see! And

let me— hear— of no com-plaint At night when you come home.'
now, lit-tle chil-dren, I'll play with you, And you shall play with me.'

3 But they made answer to him, 'No!
  Thou art meaner than us all;
Thou art but a simple fair maid's child,
  Born in an ox's stall.'
Sweet Jesus turned him round about,
  Neither laughed, nor smiled, nor spoke;
But the tears came trickling from his eyes
  Like waters from the rock.

4 Sweet Jesus turned him round about,
  To his mother's dear home went he,
And said, 'I have been in yonder town,
  As after you may see:
I have been down in yonder town,
  As far as the Holy Well;
There did I meet with as fine childrén
  As any tongue can tell.

5 'I said, "God bless you every one,
  And your bodies Christ save and see!
And now, little children, I'll play with you,
  And you shall play with me."
But they made answer to me, "No";
  They were lords' and ladies' sons,
And I the meanest of them all,
  Born in an ox's stall.'

6 'Though you are but a maiden's child,
  Born in an ox's stall,
Thou art the Christ, the King of heaven,
  And the Saviour of them all!
Sweet Jesus, go down to yonder town,
  As far as the Holy Well,
And take away those sinful souls,
  And dip them deep in hell.'

7 'Nay, nay,' sweet Jesus smiled and said;
  'Nay, nay, that may not be,
For there are too many sinful souls
  Crying out for the help of me.'
Then up spoke the angel Gabriel,
  Upon a good set steven,
'Although you are but a maiden's child,
  You are the King of heaven!'

3. simple—*orig.* 'silly': see note to No. 2. 7. steven—voice, an Anglo-Saxon word; it occurs in Spenser and still survives in dialect. Sometimes corrupted to 'our good Saint Stephen'.
Two Herefordshire versions collated with Sandys, 1833, and with the fine version printed by Frank Sidgwick. Melody from Sandys.

56 THE HOLY WELL
(GENERAL, Legendary)

SECOND TUNE

Traditional
Ibid.
(R.V.W.)
SOPRANO
ALTO
TENOR
BASS
1. As it fell out one May morn - ing, And up - on a bright ho - li - day, Sweet Je - sus asked of his dear mo - ther If he might go to play, if he might go to play.
'To play, to play, sweet Je - sus shall go, And to play now get you gone; And let me hear of no com - plaint At night when you come home, at night when you come home.'

2 Sweet Jesus went down to yonder town,
As far as the Holy Well,
And there did see as fine childrén
As any tongue can tell.
He said, 'God bless you every one,
And your bodies Christ save and see!
And now, little children, I'll play with you,
And you shall play with me.'

3 But they made answer to him, 'No!
Thou art meaner than us all;
Thou art but a simple fair maid's child,
Born in an ox's stall.'
Sweet Jesus turned him round about,
Neither laughed, nor smiled, nor spoke;
But the tears came trickling from his eyes
Like waters from the rock.

4 Sweet Jesus turned him round about,
To his mother's dear home went he,
And said, 'I have been in yonder town,
As after you may see:
I have been down in yonder town,
As far as the Holy Well;
There did I meet with as fine childrén
As any tongue can tell.

5 'I said, "God bless you every one,
And your bodies Christ save and see!
And now, little children, I'll play with you,
And you shall play with me."
But they made answer to me, "No";
They were lords' and ladies' sons,
And I the meanest of them all,
Born in an ox's stall.'

6 'Though you are but a maiden's child,
Born in an ox's stall,
Thou art the Christ, the King of heaven,
And the Saviour of them all!
Sweet Jesus, go down to yonder town,
As far as the Holy Well,
And take away those sinful souls,
And dip them deep in hell.'

7 'Nay, nay,' sweet Jesus smiled and said;
'Nay, nay, that may not be,
For there are too many sinful souls
Crying out for the help of me.'
Then up spoke the angel Gabriel,
Upon a good set steven,
'Although you are but a maiden's child,
You are the King of heaven!'

3. simple—*orig.* 'silly': see note to No. 2. 7. steven—voice, an Anglo-Saxon word; it occurs in Spenser and still survives in dialect. Sometimes corrupted to 'our good Saint Stephen'.

Tune noted by Cecil Sharp, at Camborne, 1913.
Printed in the *Journal of the Folk Song Society*, vol. v, p. 4.

57 DIVES AND LAZARUS
(GENERAL)

FIRST TUNE

Traditional

Ibid.
(R.V.W.)

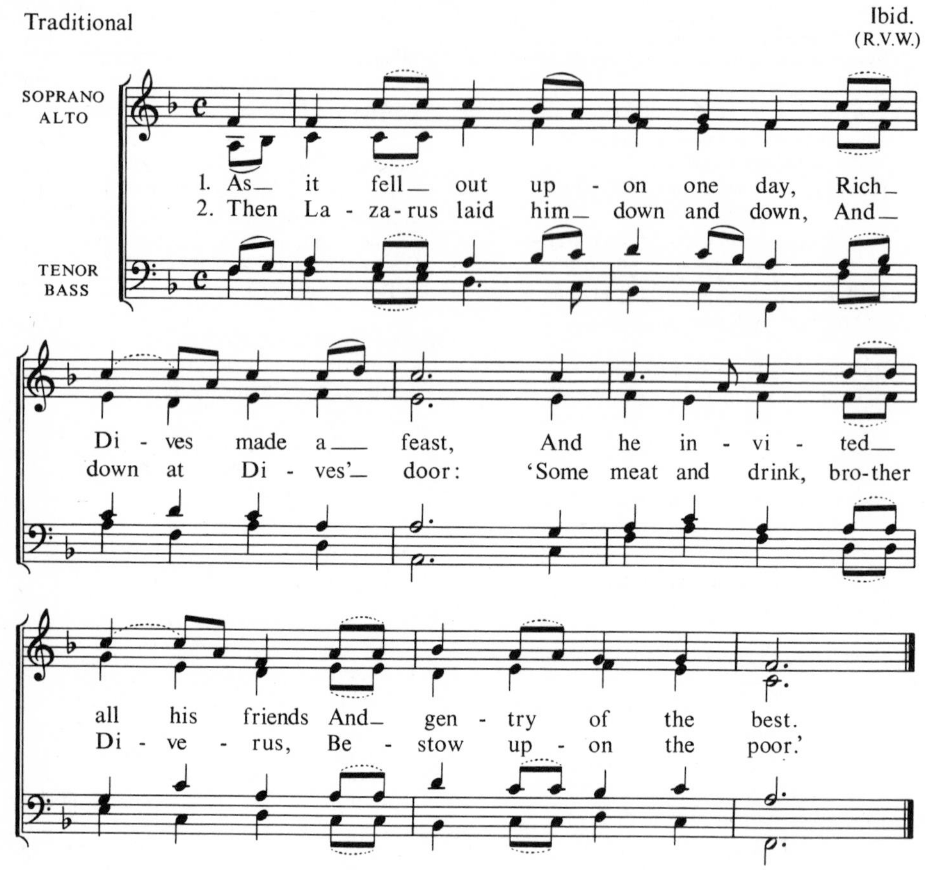

SOPRANO
ALTO
TENOR
BASS
1. As— it fell— out up - on one day, Rich— Di - ves made a— feast, And he in - vi - ted— all his friends And— gen - try of the best.
2. Then La - za - rus laid him— down and down, And— down at Di - ves'— door: 'Some meat and drink, bro-ther Di - ve - rus, Be - stow up - on the poor.'

3 'Thou'rt none of my brothers, Lazarus,
That liest begging at my door;
No meat, nor drink will I give thee,
Nor bestow upon the poor.'

4 *Then Lazarus laid him down and down,
All under Dives' wall:
'Some meat, some drink, brother Diverus,
For hunger starve I shall.'

5 *'Thou'rt none of my brothers, Lazarus,
That liest begging at my wall;
No meat, nor drink will I give thee,
For hunger starve you shall.'

6 *Then Lazarus laid him down and down,
And down at Dives' gate:
'Some meat! some drink! brother Diverus,
For Jesus Christ his sake.'

7 *'Thou'rt none of my brothers, Lazarus,
That liest begging at my gate;
No meat, no drink will I give thee,
For Jesus Christ his sake.'

8 *Then Dives sent out his hungry dogs,
To bite him as he lay;
They hadn't the power to bite one bite,
But licked his sores away.

9 *Then Dives sent to his merry men,
To worry poor Lazarus away;
They'd not the power to strike one stroke,
But flung their whips away.

10 As it fell out upon one day,
Poor Lazarus sickened and died;
There came two angels out of heaven,
His soul therein to guide.

11 'Rise up! rise up! brother Lazarus,
And go along with me;
For you've a place prepared in heaven,
To sit on an angel's knee.'

12 As it fell out upon one day,
Rich Dives sickened and died;
There came two serpents out of hell,
His soul therein to guide.

13 'Rise up! rise up! brother Diverus,
And come along with me;
There is a place provided in hell
For wicked men like thee.'

14 *Then Dives looked up with his eyes
And saw poor Lazarus blest;
'Give me one drop of water, brother Lazarus,
To quench my flaming thirst.

15 *'O, was I now but alive again
The space of one half hour!
O, that I had my peace again
Then the devil should have no power!'

V. 13, l. 4. In some versions 'To sit upon a serpent's knee', which is generally preferred by choirs. The text is the result of a collation of the two Herefordshire texts mentioned below with the help of other versions. A version of eighteen verses is given by Mr. F. Sidgwick in his *Popular Carols*. The various recurring words (such as 'Dives' (Divus), 'upon one day', &c.) have been made to conform with the version associated with the melody. The following verses are taken entirely from the other versions—2, 3, 11, 12, 13, 14, 15.

Melody from Mr. John Evans, Dilwyn. Text from Mr. John Evans and Mrs. Harris, Eardisley, &c. From *Twelve Traditional Carols from Herefordshire* (Leather and Vaughan Williams), Stainer & Bell.

The Elizabethan dramatist, Fletcher, mentions 'the merry ballad of Dives and Lazarus' in his *Monsieur Thomas*. Sylvester in 1861 claims to be the first to include it in a collection, giving it (but he was not a scrupulous transcriber) from an old Birmingham broadside. Hone includes it in his list, 1822; and Husk prints it from an eighteenth-century Worcester sheet. See also F. C. Child's *Ballads*, ii, p. 10.

This carol may be sung to the second tune of No. 60.

57 DIVES AND LAZARUS
(GENERAL)

SECOND TUNE

Traditional

Ibid.
(R.V.W.)

SOPRANO
ALTO
TENOR
BASS
1. As it fell out up - on one day, Rich Di - ves made a feast, And he in - vi - ted all his friends And gen - try of the best.
2. Then La - za - rus laid him down and down, And down at Di - ves' door: 'Some meat and drink, bro - ther Di - ve - rus, Be - stow up - on the poor.'

3 'Thou'rt none of my brothers, Lazarus,
That liest begging at my door;
No meat, nor drink will I give thee,
Nor bestow upon the poor.'

4 *Then Lazarus laid him down and down,
All under Dives' wall:
'Some meat, some drink, brother Diverus,
For hunger starve I shall.'

5 *'Thou'rt none of my brothers, Lazarus,
That liest begging at my wall;
No meat, nor drink will I give thee,
For hunger starve you shall.'

6 *Then Lazarus laid him down and down,
And down at Dives' gate:
'Some meat! some drink! brother Diverus,
For Jesus Christ his sake.'

7 *'Thou'rt none of my brothers, Lazarus,
That liest begging at my gate;
No meat, no drink will I give thee,
For Jesus Christ his sake.'

8 *Then Dives sent out his hungry dogs,
To bite him as he lay;
They hadn't the power to bite one bite,
But licked his sores away.

9 *Then Dives sent to his merry men,
To worry poor Lazarus away;
They'd not the power to strike one stroke,
But flung their whips away.

10 As it fell out upon one day,
Poor Lazarus sickened and died;
There came two angels out of heaven,
His soul therein to guide.

11 'Rise up! rise up! brother Lazarus,
And go along with me;
For you've a place prepared in heaven,
To sit on an angel's knee.'

12 As it fell out upon one day,
Rich Dives sickened and died;
There came two serpents out of hell,
His soul therein to guide.

13 'Rise up! rise up! brother Diverus,
And come along with me;
There is a place provided in hell
For wicked men like thee.'

14 *Then Dives looked up with his eyes
And saw poor Lazarus blest;
'Give me one drop of water, brother Lazarus,
To quench my flaming thirst.

15 *'O, was I now but alive again
The space of one half hour!
O, that I had my peace again
Then the devil should have no power!'

Tune noted for Mrs. Leather at Eardisley, Herefordshire, by Miss Andrews and Dr. Darling, in 1905. Harmonies from the *English Hymnal*, where the tune is called 'Eardisley', and is set to hymn 601. Also *Songs of Praise* No. 393.

This carol may be sung to the second tune of No. 60.

58 JACOB'S LADDER
(GENERAL)

Traditional

Ibid. (M.S.)

SEMI-CHORUS
SOPRANO
ALTO
TENOR
BASS
1. As Ja - cob with tra - vel was wea - ry one day, At night on a stone for a pil - low he lay; He saw in a vi - sion a lad - der so high, That its foot was on earth and its top in the sky:
2. This lad - der is long, it is strong and well-made, Has stood hun - dreds of years and is not yet de - cayed; Ma - ny mil - lions have climbed it and reached Si - on's hill, And thou - sands by faith are climb - ing it still:
FULL
Al - le - lu - ya to Je - sus, who

died on the tree,—And hath raised up a lad - der of mer - cy for
me, And hath raised up a lad - der of mer - cy for me.

3 Come, let us ascend! all may climb it who will;
For the angels of Jacob are guarding it still:
And remember, each step that by faith we pass o'er,
Some prophet or martyr hath trod it before:

Alleluya etc.

4 And when we arrive at the haven of rest,
We shall hear the glad words, 'Come up hither, ye blest,
Here are regions of light, here are mansions of bliss.'
O, who would not climb such a ladder as this?

Alleluya etc.

This is apparently a carol to which new words were fitted under the influence of the Methodist revival. It is printed here with its traditional melody, which Stainer made familiar in 1871.

59 WELSH CAROL
(GENERAL: WHITSUNTIDE)

Pr. K. E. Roberts
Welsh
(Dr. Caradog Roberts)
SOPRANO
ALTO
TENOR
BASS
1. A - wake were they on - ly, those shep-herds so lone - ly, On
2. May light now en - fold us, O Lord, for be - hold us Like
guard in that si - lence pro - found: — When co - lour had fa - ded, when
shep-herds, from tu - mult with - drawn, — Nor hear - ing, nor see - ing, all
night-time had sha - ded Their sen - ses from sight and from sound, Lo, —
oth - er care flee - ing, We wait the in - eff - a - ble dawn. O —
cresc.
f
then broke a won-der, then drif - ted a - sun-der The veils from the splen-dour of
Spi - rit all-know-ing, thou source o - ver-flow-ing, O move in the dark-ness a-

God,— When light from the Ho - ly came down to the low - ly, And
- round,— That sight may be in us, true hear - ing to win us Glad

1st time
2nd time
heav'n to the earth that they trod. Lo,— trod.—
ti - dings where Christ may be found. O— found.—

By permission of the Caniedydd Committee, Welsh Congregational Union.

A paraphrase of the Welsh Carol, 'Roedd yn y wlad honno'.

60 JOB
(GENERAL)

FIRST TUNE

Traditional

Ibid. (M.S.)

SOPRANO
ALTO
TENOR
BASS
1. Come all you wor - thy Christ - ian men That dwell up - on this land, Don't spend your time in ri - ot - ing; Re - mem - ber you're but man. Be watch - ful for your lat - ter end; Be
2. Now, Job he was a pa - tient man, The rich - est in the East: When he was brought to pov - er - - ty, His sor - rows soon in - creased. He bore them all most pa - tient - ly; From

rea - dy for your call. There are ma - ny chan - ges
sin he did re - frain; He al - ways trust - ed

in this world; Some rise while oth - ers fall.
in the Lord; He soon got rich a - gain.

3 Come all you worthy Christian men
That are so very poor,
Remember how poor Lazarus
Lay at the rich man's door,
While begging of the crumbs of bread
That from his table fell.
The scriptures do inform us all
That in heaven he doth dwell.

4 The time, alas, it soon will come
When parted we shall be;
But all the difference it will make
Is in joy and misery;
And we must give a strict account
Of great as well as small.
Believe me, now, dear Christian friends,
That God will judge us all.

Tune taken by Cecil Sharp from Mrs. Woodberry, Ash Priors, Somerset, *Folk Songs from Somerset*, No. 88 (*by permission of Novello & Co. Ltd.*).

60 JOB
(GENERAL)
SECOND TUNE

Traditional
Ibid.
(M.S.)
SOPRANO
ALTO
TENOR
BASS
1. Come all you wor - thy Christ - ian men That dwell up - on this land, Don't spend your time in ri - ot - ing; Re - mem - ber you're but man. Be watch - ful for your lat - ter end; Be rea - dy for your
2. Now, Job he was a pa - tient man, The rich - est in the East: When he was brought to pov - er - ty, His sor - rows soon in - creased. He bore them all most pa - tient - ly; From sin he did re -

call. There are ma - ny chan - ges in this world; Some
-frain; He al - ways trust - ed in the Lord; He

1st time
Last time
rise while oth - ers fall. Be fall.
soon got rich a - gain. He - gain.

3 Come all you worthy Christian men
That are so very poor,
Remember how poor Lazarus
Lay at the rich man's door,
While begging of the crumbs of bread
That from his table fell.
The scriptures do inform us all
That in heaven he doth dwell.

4 The time, alas, it soon will come
When parted we shall be;
But all the difference it will make
Is in joy and misery;
And we must give a strict account
Of great as well as small.
Believe me, now, dear Christian friends,
That God will judge us all.

Tune noted by the late A. J. Hipkins in Westminster and printed in *English County Songs* to the words of 'Dives and Lazarus', but it probably belongs to 'Job'. It belongs more properly, however, to the above words. (Cf. the hymn-tune 'Kingsfold', E.H. 574).

60 JOB
(GENERAL)
THIRD TUNE

Traditional
Ibid.
(R.V.W.)
Moderately slow
SOPRANO
ALTO
TENOR
BASS
1. Come all you wor - thy Christ - ian men_ That_ dwell up - on_ this_ land,_ Don't spend your time in_ ri - ot - ing; Re - mem - ber you're but man._ Be watch - ful for your lat - ter end; Be
2. Now, Job he was a pa - tient man,- The_ rich - est in_ the_ East:_ When he was brought to_ pov - er - ty, His_ sor - rows soon_ in - creased._ He bore them all most pa - tient - ly; From

rea - dy for your call. There are ma - ny chan - ges
sin he did re - frain; He al - ways trust - ed

in this world; Some rise while oth - ers fall.
in the Lord; He soon got rich a - - gain.

By permission of Novello & Co.

3 Come all you worthy Christian men
That are so very poor,
Remember how poor Lazarus
Lay at the rich man's door,
While begging of the crumbs of bread
That from his table fell.
The scriptures do inform us all
That in heaven he doth dwell.

4 The time, alas, it soon will come
When parted we shall be;
But all the difference it will make
Is in joy and misery;
And we must give a strict account
Of great as well as small.
Believe me, now, dear Christian friends,
That God will judge us all.

Tune noted by W. Percy Merrick and printed in the *Journal of the Folk Song Society*, vol. i, p. 74. Also published as a solo song in *Folk Songs from Sussex* (Novello).

60 JOB

(GENERAL)

FOURTH TUNE

Traditional

Ibid.
(R. V. W.)

Voices in unison
ACCPT
1. Come all you wor - thy Christ - ian men That dwell up - on this land, Don't spend your time in ri - ot - ing; Re - mem - ber you're but man. Be watch - ful for your lat - ter end; Be
2. Now, Job he was a pa - tient man, The rich - est in the East: When he was brought to pov - er - ty, His sor - rows soon in - creased. He bore them all most pa - tient - ly; From

rea - dy for your call. There are ma - ny chan - ges
sin he did re - frain; He al - ways trust - ed

in this world; Some rise while oth - ers fall.
in the Lord; He soon got rich a - gain.

3 Come all you worthy Christian men
That are so very poor,
Remember how poor Lazarus
Lay at the rich man's door,
While begging of the crumbs of bread
That from his table fell.
The scriptures do inform us all
That in heaven he doth dwell.

4 The time, alas, it soon will come
When parted we shall be;
But all the difference it will make
Is in joy and misery;
And we must give a strict account
Of great as well as small.
Believe me, now, dear Christian friends,
That God will judge us all.

Tune noted by R. Vaughan Williams, near Horsham, in 1904, and printed in the *Journal of the Folk Song Society*, vol. ii, p. 118.

61 DOWN IN YON FOREST
(GENERAL)

Traditional

Ibid.
(R.V.W.)

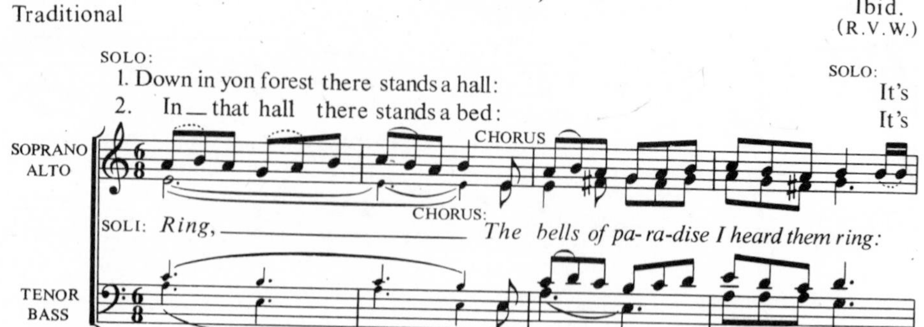

SOLO:
1. Down in yon forest there stands a hall:
2. In — that hall there stands a bed:
SOLO:
It's
It's
SOPRANO
ALTO
CHORUS
SOLI: Ring, ——
CHORUS: The bells of pa-ra-dise I heard them ring:
TENOR
BASS
The bells —— I heard them ring:

cov-er'd all o-ver with pur-ple and pall:
cov-er'd all o-ver with scar-let so red:
CHORUS
SOLI:
Ring, ——
CHORUS: And I love my Lord Je-sus a-bove a-ny-thing.
And I love Je-sus a-bove a-ny-thing.

NOTE. It is suggested that the solo portion be sung without harmony in the opening verses; also that the solo portion be divided among various voices (male and female).

3 At the bed-side there lies a stone:
Which the sweet Virgin Mary knelt upon:

4 Under that bed there runs a flood:
The one half runs water, the other runs blood:

5 At the bed's foot there grows a thorn:
Which ever blows blossom since he was born:

6 *Over that bed the moon shines bright:
Denoting our Saviour was born this night:

Melody and text taken from Mr. Hall, Castleton, Derbyshire, by R. Vaughan Williams (*Eight Traditional Carols*), Stainer & Bell. Text unaltered except for (4) *flood* for 'river', (5) *bed's foot* for 'foot of the bed'.

Cf. another folk version in No. 184. The earliest version is one only found in Richard Hill's MS. (cf. No. 36), and is printed below; it is in a different metre, but the hall, the bed, the knight of No. 184, the maid, and the stone are all there, and the words 'Corpus Christi' are written on the stone; the mystical meaning of the fifteenth-century original was therefore eucharistic, the altar and the sacrifice, while the thorn (not in the Hill MS.) and other allusions of this and the other two versions point to an interweaving of the legend of the Holy Grail. See F. Sidgwick, *Notes and Queries* (1905), iv. 181; *Folk Song Soc. J.* (1910), iv. 52; Greene, No. 322.

The text of the carol in the Hill MS. (c. 1500), printed by Dyboski and others is: *Lully, lulley, lully, lulley! The falcon hath borne my make away.* 1. He bare him up, he bare him down, He bare him in to an orchard brown [*Refrain*]. 2. In that orchard there was an hall, That was hanged with purple and pall. 3. And in that hall there was a bed, It was hanged with gold so red. 4. And in that bed there lieth a knight, His wounds bleeding day and night. 5. By that bed's side kneeleth a may, And she weepeth both night and day. 6. And by that bed's side there standeth a stone, 'Corpus Christi' written thereon.

62 ALL AND SOME

(GENERAL, Medieval)

c. 1450
Ibid. (M.S.)
SOPRANO
ALTO
TENOR
BASS
BURDEN
No - well sing we, both all — and some, Now Rex pa - ci - fi - cus is y - come.
Fine
VERSE
1. Ex - or - - tum est in love and lysse. Now Christ his gree he gan — us gysse, And with his bo - dy us brought to bliss,
2. De fruc - tu ven - tris of Ma - ry bright, Both God and man in her — a - light, Out of di - sease — he did us dight:
Both all — and some, both all and some.

The burden should be sung again after the last verse.

3 *Puer natus* to us was sent,
To bliss us bought, fro bale us blent,
And else to woe we had ywent:

4 *Lux fulgebit* with love and light,
In Mary mild his pennon pight,
In her took kind with manly might:

5 *Gloria tibi*, ay, and bliss,
God unto his grace he us wysse,
The rent of heaven that we not miss:

1. *Exortum est*—it is risen up. lysse—comfort, joy. gree (in MS. 'gre he')—favour. gysse—to prepare, attire (= guise). 2. *De fructu*, &c.—of the fruit of the womb. disease ('dysese')—dis-ease, discomfort, misery. dight—orig. dictate; prepare, hence make ready, array (revived by Walter Scott in the last sense). 3. *Puer natus*—a boy born. fro—from. bale—sorrow. blent—blenched, turned aside. ywent—gone. 4. *Lux*, &c.—the light will shine. pight—pitched. kind—nature. 5. *Gloria tibi*—glory to thee. wysse—guide. rent—tenure.

Source: Bodleian Library, Selden MS. b. 26, *c.* 1450, printed with transcription, in Stainer's *Early Bodleian Music*, and, more accurately, in *Medieval Carols*, No. 16 (Greene, No. 29). In the version above, spelling and harmony have been modernized.

63 GREEN GROW'TH THE HOLLY
(GENERAL)

O.B.C. version
16th century
(M.T.)
SOPRANO
ALTO
TENOR
1. Green grow'th the hol - ly, So doth the i - vy; Though win - ter blasts blow ne'er so high, Green grow'th the hol - - ly.
2. Gay are the flow - ers, Hedge - rows and plough-lands; The days grow long - er in the sun, Soft fall the show - - ers.
1. Green grow'th the hol - ly, So doth the i - vy; Though win - ter blasts blow ne'er so high, Green grow'th the hol - - ly.
2. Gay are the flow - ers, Hedge - rows and plough-lands; The days grow long - er in the sun, Soft fall the show - - ers.
1. Green grow'th the hol - ly, So doth the i - vy; Though win - ter blasts blow ne'er so high, Green grow'th the hol - - ly.
2. Gay are the flow - ers, Hedge-rows and plough-lands; The days grow long - er in the sun, Soft fall the show - - ers.

3 Full gold the harvest,
Grain for thy labour;
With God must work for daily bread,
Else, man, thou starvest.

4 Fast fall the shed leaves,
Russet and yellow;
But resting-buds are snug and safe
Where swung the dead leaves.

5 Green grow'th the holly,
So doth the ivy;
The God of life can never die.
Hope! saith the holly.

The music, one of the songs in B.M. Add. MS. 31922 (c. 1515) attributed to Henry VIII, has survived in this refrain, 'Green grow'th the holly', &c. (attached to a love-song in a different metre and with no tune extant); it has been transcribed by Lady Mary Trefusis, and other verses have been added in the metre of the old melody. The original version is given in Musica Britannica, vol. xviii.

64 A NEW DIAL
(GENERAL)

1625
Traditional
(M.S.)
SOPRANO
ALTO
TENOR
BASS
In those twelve days let us be glad, in those twelve days let us be glad, For God of his power hath all things made.
1. What are they that are but one? What are they that are but one? One God, one Bap - tism, and one Faith, One Truth there is, the scrip - ture saith:
2. What are they that are but two? What are they that are but two? Two Tes - ta - - ments, the old and new, We do ac - know - ledge to be true:

3 What are they that are but three?
Three Persons are in Trinity
Which make one God in unity:

4 What are they that are but four?
Four sweet Evangelists there are,
Christ's birth, life, death, which do declare:

5 *What are they that are but five?
Five Senses, like five kings, maintain
In every man a several reign:

6 *What are they that are but six?
Six Days to labour is not wrong,
For God himself did work so long:

7 *What are they that are but seven?
Seven Liberal Arts hath God sent down
With divine skill man's soul to crown:

8 *What are they that are but eight?
Eight Beatitudes are there given;
Use them aright and go to heaven:

9 *What are they that are but nine?
Nine Muses, like the heavens' nine spheres,
With sacred tunes entice our ears:

10 *What are they that are but ten?
Ten Statutes God to Moses gave,
Which, kept or broke, do spill or save:

11 *What are they that are but eleven?
Eleven thousand Virgins did partake,
And suffered death for Jesus' sake:

12 *What are they that are but twelve?
Twelve are attending on God's Son;
Twelve make our Creed. The dial's done:

In an almanack of 1625, in the Bagford collection. Gilbert (1822) prints a version too rough to be sung without constant mispronunciation and alteration of the music; this version is smoothed by Sandys, but is still almost unsingable. The refrain (from Gilbert) is not given in the almanack, but was probably then known. This 1625 version is evidently by a scholar working on a much older carol; and it is curious to see how the scholarly parts are absent from the folk-version of 1822. Two verses (and the tune) are from Sandys: v. 8 (Gilbert's singer gave 'Altitudes' instead of 'Beatitudes') where the Almanack has, 'Eight in Noah's Ark alive were found, When (in a word) the World lay drown'd'; and v. 11 (the same, but more confused, in Gilbert), where the Almanack rejects the Virgins of Cologne, only to give a duplicate Apostle verse, 'Eleven with Christ in Heaven do dwell, The Twelfth for ever burns in Hell'.

The Seven Liberal Arts (changed in Gilbert to 'Seven Days in week') and the Eleven Thousand Virgins point to a medieval origin for both verses. V. 5, We now know that there are more than five senses. V. 7, The Seven Liberal arts (the *Trivium* and *Quadrivium* of thirteenth-century schoolmen, and of St. Augustine, Boethius, and Cassiodorus) were: grammar, rhetoric, and dialectic, arithmetic, geometry, astronomy, and music. V. 9, The Nine Muses of the Greeks were: Calliope (epic song), Clio (history), Euterpe (lyric song), Thalia (comedy), Melpomene (tragedy), Terpsichore (dancing), Erato (erotic poetry), Polymnia (sacred songs), Urania (astronomy). V. 11, There are various explanations of the extravagant legend of St. Ursula and the Eleven Thousand Virgins (familiar through the paintings of Memlinc and Carpaccio): one is that it originated in an inscription to 'Ursula et Undecimilla, virgines', another that there were originally Ursula and eleven Martyrs, the MM. being read as 'thousand'. V. 12, The Twelve Apostles, and the twelve articles of the Apostles' Creed: each article is sometimes represented in art on a scroll held by an Apostle.

65 THE DECREE
(GENERAL)

FIRST TUNE
Traditional
Ibid.
(M.S.)
SOPRANO
ALTO
TENOR
BASS
1. Let Christ-ians all with one ac-cord re-joice, And prai-ses sing, with heart as well as voice, To God on high, for glo-rious things he's done, In send-ing us his best-be-lov-ed Son.
2. What pains and la-bours did not Christ en-dure To save our souls and hap-pi-ness se-cure! Was al-ways do-ing good, to let us see By his ex-am-ple what we ought to be.
FA-BURDEN (melody in the bass)
to see,
3. He made the blind to see, the lame to go, He raised the

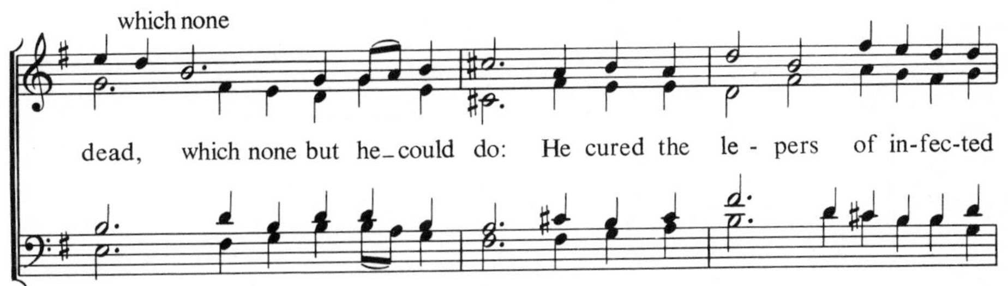
which none
dead, which none but he_could do: He cured the le - pers of in-fec-ted

e - vils, And by his migh - ty power he cast out de - vils.

4 But yet for all the wonders that he wrought,
Ungrateful men still his destruction sought:
Then to a cross the Saviour of mankind
Was led, an harmless Lamb, as was designed.

5 Thus blessèd Jesus freely did resign
His precious soul to save both thine and mine;
Then let us all his mercies highly prize,
Who for our sins was made a sacrifice.

Selected verses from the long carol of twenty-three, which takes its name 'The Black Decree' from three verses about the massacre of the Innocents, in the Dudley collection, *A Good Christmas Box*, 1847, which preserved the words. The verses were evidently written by one author, and not earlier than the eighteenth century, perhaps to replace some older folk-carol which had been associated with the tune. Stainer restored the second traditional melody; the first melody, also proper to the words, was noted by Cecil Sharp in an unpublished MS.

65 THE DECREE
(GENERAL)
SECOND TUNE

Traditional

Ibid.
(M.S.)

SOPRANO
ALTO
1. Let Christ-ians all with one ac-cord re-joice, And
2. What pains and la-bours did not Christ en-dure To
TENOR
BASS
prai-ses sing, with heart as well as voice, To God on high, for
save our souls and hap-pi-ness se-cure! Was al-ways do-ing
glo-rious things he's done, In send-ing us his best-be-lov-ed Son.
good, to let us see By his ex-am-ple what we ought to be.

3 He made the blind to see, the lame to go,
He raised the dead, which none but he could do:
He cured the lepers of infected evils,
And by his mighty power he cast out devils.

4 But yet for all the wonders that he wrought,
Ungrateful men still his destruction sought:
Then to a cross the Saviour of mankind
Was led, an harmless Lamb, as was designed.

5 Thus blessèd Jesus freely did resign
His precious soul to save both thine and mine;
Then let us all his mercies highly prize,
Who for our sins was made a sacrifice.

See footnote to first tune.

66 THE CHERRY TREE CAROL
PART 1 (GENERAL, Legendary)

FIRST TUNE

Traditional

Ibid. (M.S.)

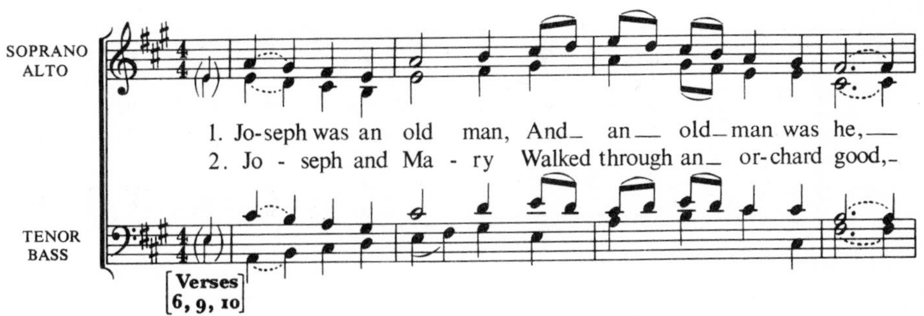
SOPRANO
ALTO
1. Jo-seph was an old man, And_ an_ old_man was he,_
2. Jo - seph and Ma - ry Walked through an_ or-chard good,_
TENOR
BASS
Verses 6, 9, 10

When he wed - ded_ Ma - ry In the land of Ga - li - lee.
Where was cher - ries and ber - - ries So_ red as an - y blood.

3 *Joseph and Mary
Walked through an orchard green,
Where was berries and cherries
As thick as might be seen.

4 O then bespoke Mary,
With words so meek and mild,
'Pluck me one cherry, Joseph,
For I am with child.'

5 *O then bespoke Joseph,
With answer most unkind,
'Let him pluck thee a cherry
That brought thee now with child.'

6 *O then bespoke the baby
Within his mother's womb—
'Bow down then the tallest tree
For my mother to have some.'

7 Then bowed down the highest tree,
Unto his mother's hand.
Then she cried, 'See, Joseph,
I have cherries at command.'

8 *O then bespoke Joseph—
'I have done Mary wrong;
But now cheer up, my dearest,
And do not be cast down.

9 'O eat your cherries, Mary,
O eat your cherries now,
O eat your cherries, Mary,
That grow upon the bough.'

10 *Then Mary plucked a cherry,
As red as any blood;
Then Mary she went homewards
All with her heavy load.

66 THE CHERRY TREE CAROL
PART 2 (CHRISTMAS EVE)

SECOND TUNE

Traditional

Ibid. (M.S.)

SOPRANO
ALTO
TENOR
BASS
11. As Joseph was a - walk - ing, He heard an an - gel
13. 'He nei - ther shall be clo - thed In pur - ple nor in
sing: 'This night there shall be born On earth our heav'n - ly
pall, But all in fair lin - en As wear the ba - bies
Last verse of Part II begins here.
King;
all.
12. 'He nei - ther shall be born In hou - sen nor in
14. 'He nei - ther shall be rock - ed In sil - ver nor in
15. 'He nei - ther shall be christ - en'd In white wine nor in
hall, Nor in the place of pa - ra - dise, But in an ox - 's stall.
gold, But in a wood - en cra - dle That rocks up - on the mould.
red, But with fair spring wa - ter As we were christ - en - ed.'

66 THE CHERRY TREE CAROL
PART 2 (CHRISTMAS EVE)

THIRD TUNE

Traditional

Ibid.
(M.S.)

SOPRANO
ALTO
TENOR
BASS
11. As Jo - seph was a - walk - ing, He heard an an - gel sing: 'This night there shall be born On earth our heav'n - ly King;
12. 'He nei - ther shall be born In hou - sen nor in hall, Nor in the place of pa - ra - dise, But in an ox - 's stall.

13 'He neither shall be clothèd
In purple nor in pall,
But all in fair linen
As wear the babies all.

14 'He neither shall be rockèd
In silver nor in gold,
But in a wooden cradle
That rocks upon the mould.

15 'He neither shall be christened
In white wine nor in red,
But with fair spring water
As we were christenèd.'

66 THE CHERRY TREE CAROL
Part 3 (Lent: Passiontide)

FOURTH TUNE

Traditional

Ibid.
(M.S.)

SOPRANO
ALTO
TENOR
BASS
16. Then Ma - ry took her young_ son, And set him on her knee: Say - ing, 'My dear son, tell__ me, Tell__ how this__ world shall be.'
17. 'O I shall be as dead, mo - ther, As stones are in the wall; O the stones in the__ streets, mo - ther, Shall__ sor - row__ for me all.
18. 'On Eas - ter Day, dear mo - ther, My ris - ing up shall be; O the sun and the__ moon, mo - ther, Shall__ both a - rise with me.'

This was one of the most popular carols, and was printed in broadsides in all parts of England. Hone gives a version, 1822, and Sandys another, 1833, identical down to v. 8 with Bullen's. The same legend, with a dialogue no less 'unkind', occurs in *The Coventry Mystery Plays*. Our first tune is from Husk, our second was preserved by Fyfe in his *Carols* of 1860, our third comes from Dr. E. F. Rimbault's *Old English Carols* 1865 and our fourth is also traditional. The whole story of carol-music is summed up in an incident related by Baring-Gould: about 1865 he was teaching carols to a party of mill-girls in the West Riding; 'and amongst them that by Dr. Gauntlett—"Saint Joseph was a-walking"—when they burst out with "Nay! we know one a great deal better nor yond"; and, lifting up their voices, they sang'.

67 SONG OF THE NUNS OF CHESTER

(CHRISTMAS, Medieval)

Chester MS., c. 1425
English words by Denis Stevens
and John A. Parkinson (vv. 4-5)

Ibid.
(arr. John A. Parkinson)

SOLO
CHORUS
1. Qui cre - a - vit coe - - lum,—
1. He who made the star - ry skies,—
Lul - ly, lul - ly,
2. Jo - seph e - mit pa - ni - cu - lum,—
2. Jo - seph brings a gar - ment there,—
By, by, by,— by,

SOLO
lu,—
Nas - ci - tur in sta - bu - lo,
Sleep - ing in a man - ger— lies,
by,—
Ma - ter in - vol - vit pu - e - - rum,
Ma - ry wraps up her child so— fair,

CHORUS
SOLO
By, by, by,— by, by,—
Rex qui re - git
Ru - ler of the
Lul - ly, lul - ly, lu,—
Et po - nit in prae -
Rests him while she

CHORUS
sae - cu - lum,—
cen - tu - ries,—
Lul - ly, lul - ly, lu.—
- se - pi - o,—
sings a prayer,
By, by, by,— by, by.—

67—Song of the Nuns of Chester

SOLO
CHORUS
3. In - ter a - ni - ma - li - a,
3. Hum - bly clad, the King of kings,
4. Lac - tat ma - ter Do - mi - ni,
4. On his mo - ther's breast he lies,
Lul - ly, lul - ly,
By, by, by, by,

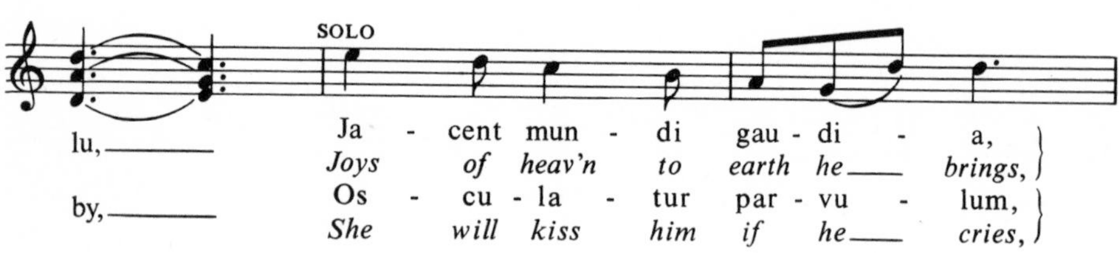
SOLO
lu,
by,
Ja - cent mun - di gau - di - a,
Joys of heav'n to earth he brings,
Os - cu - la - tur par - vu - lum,
She will kiss him if he cries,

CHORUS
SOLO
By, by, by, by, by,
Lul - ly, lul - ly, lu,
Dul - cis su - per
Sweet a - bove all
Et a - do - rat
Ru - ler of the

CHORUS
om - ni - a,
earth - ly things,
Do - mi - num,
earth and skies,
Lul - ly, lul - ly, lu.
By, by, by, by, by.

SOLO
CHORUS
5. Ro - ga ma - ter fi - li - um,—
5. Mo - ther, pray thy sweet child - ing,—
6. In sem - pi - ter - na sae - cu - la,—
6. Whilst we run this earth - ly race,—
Lul - ly, lul - ly,
By, by, by,— by,

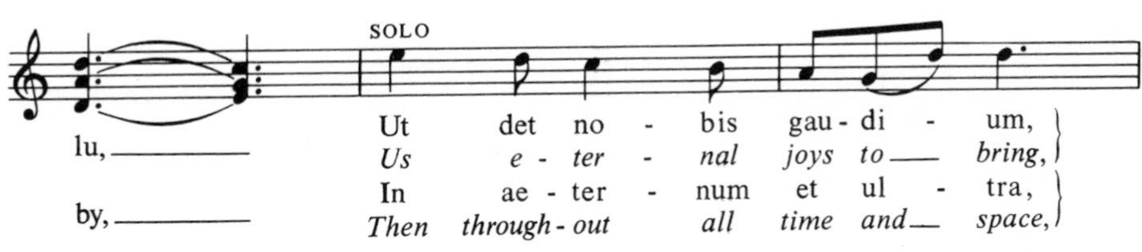
SOLO
lu,——
by,——
Ut det no - bis gau - di - um,
Us e - ter - nal joys to— bring,
In ae - ter - num et ul - tra,
Then through - out all time and— space,

CHORUS
SOLO
By, by, by,— by, by,——
Lul - ly, lul - ly, lu,——
In per - en - ni
That his prais - es
Det no - bis su - a
May he grant us

CHORUS
glo - ri - a,—
we may sing,—
gau - di - a,—
hope and grace,
Lul - ly, lul - ly, lu.——
By, by, by,— by, by.——

The manuscript processional of the nunnery of St. Mary, Chester, *c.* 1425, (formerly at Bridgewater House and now in the Huntingdon Library, San Marino, California) was printed in facsimile by the Henry Bradshaw Society, vol. xviii, 1899. The plainsong notation of the original lends itself to a variety of rhythmic interpretations. We are indebted to Mr. Denis Stevens for the suggestion of a faux-bourdon harmonization of the refrain.

68 THE TRUTH FROM ABOVE
(GENERAL)
FIRST VERSION

Traditional

Ibid. (R.V.W.)

Andante sostenuto
VOICES (UNISON)
ACCPT
1. This is the truth sent from a - bove, The
first thing which I do re - late
truth of God, the God of love, There-fore don't turn me
Is that God did man cre - ate; The next thing which to
from your door, But hearken all both rich and poor. 2. The
you I'll tell—Wo - man was made with man to dwell.
1st time
1st time

2nd time
3. Thus we were heirs_ to end - less woes, Till
at that sea - son of the year Our
2nd time
God the Lord did in-ter-pose; And so a pro - mise soon did run That he
blest Re - deem - er did ap-pear; He_ here did live, and_ here did preach, And_
1st time
would re - deem_ us___ by_ his Son. ___ 4. And
ma - ny thou_ sands_
1st time

2nd time
he did teach.
f
5. Thus he in love to
2nd time
cresc.
f
us be-haved, To show us how we must be saved; And
molto rall.
if you want to know the way, Be pleas'd to hear what he did say.
colla voce

68 THE TRUTH FROM ABOVE
(GENERAL)

SECOND VERSION

Traditional

Ibid.
(R.V.W.)

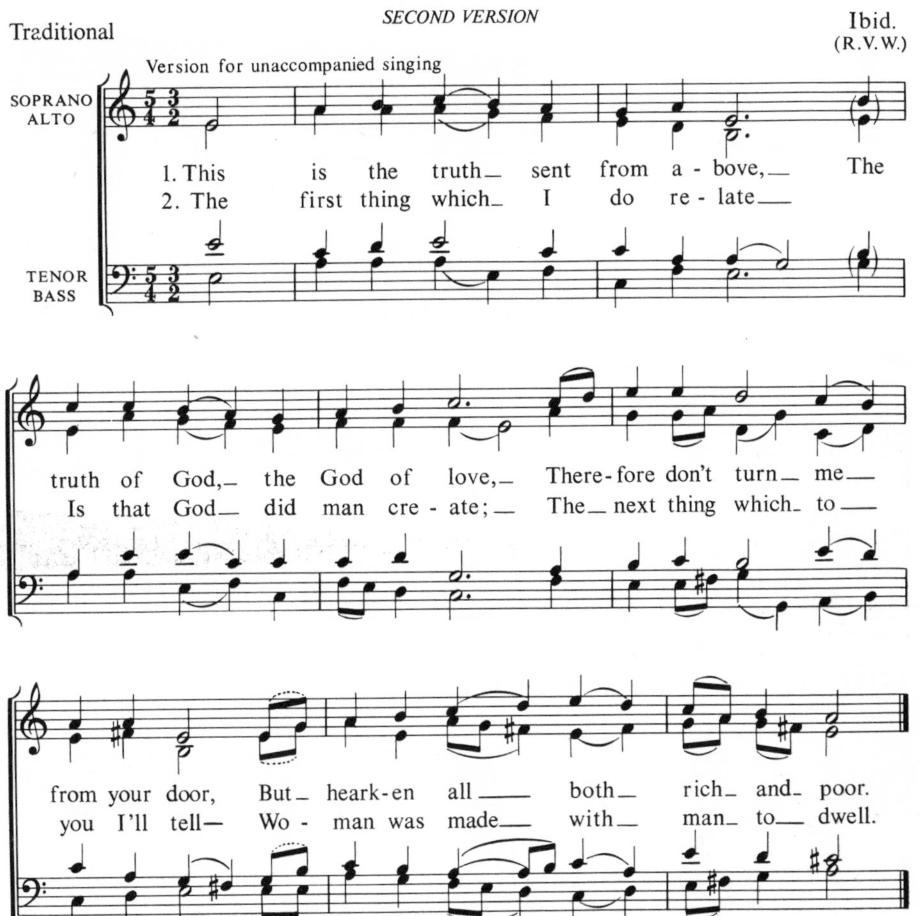

Version for unaccompanied singing
SOPRANO
ALTO
TENOR
BASS
1. This is the truth sent from a - bove, The truth of God, the God of love, There-fore don't turn me from your door, But heark-en all both rich and poor.
2. The first thing which I do re - late Is that God did man cre - ate; The next thing which to you I'll tell— Wo - man was made with man to dwell.

3 Thus we were heirs to endless woes,
Till God the Lord did interpose;
And so a promise soon did run
That he would redeem us by his Son.

4 And at that season of the year
Our blest Redeemer did appear;
He here did live, and here did preach,
And many thousands he did teach.

5 Thus he in love to us behaved,
To show us how we must be saved;
And if you want to know the way,
Be pleased to hear what he did say.

Melody and part of text from Mr. W. Jenkins, Kings Pyon, Herefordshire. Melody included by permission of Mrs. Leather. From *Eight Traditional English Carols* (Vaughan Williams), Stainer & Bell. For notes on the text and melody see the *Journal of the Folk Song Society*, iv. 17.

For another tune and different version of text see Sharp, *English Folk-Carols*, xviii. The version in *A Good Christmas Box* has sixteen verses.

69 THE SAVIOUR'S WORK
(GENERAL: NATIVITY)

Traditional

Ibid.
(E.M.)

SOPRANO
ALTO
TENOR
BASS
1. The babe in Beth-lem's man-ger laid In hum-ble form so low; By won-d'ring an-gels is sur-veyed Through all his scenes of woe:
2. A Sa-viour! sin-ners all a-round Sing, shout the won-drous word; Let ev-'ry bo-som hail the sound, A Sa-viour! Christ the Lord:
CHORUS
No-well, No-well, now sing a Sa-viour's birth, All

hail his_ com - ing down to earth Who_ rai - ses us to_ heav'n!

3 For not to sit on David's throne
With worldly pomp and joy,
He came on earth for sin to atone,
And Satan to destroy:

Nowell, etc.

4 To preach the word of life divine,
And feed with living bread,
To heal the sick with hand benign,
And raise to life the dead:

Nowell, etc.

5 *He preached, he suffered, bled and died,
Uplift 'twixt earth and skies;
In sinners' stead was crucified,
For sin a sacrifice:

Nowell, etc.

6 *Well may we sing a Saviour's birth,
Who need the grace so given,
And hail his coming down to earth,
Who raises us to heaven:

Nowell, etc.

In the Staffordshire *A Good Christmas Box*, 1847, without the chorus, which is given, with the tune, in Rimbault's *Old English Carols*, 1865.

70 JOYS SEVEN
(GENERAL)

Traditional
Ibid. (M.S.)
Solo or semi-chorus
SOPRANO ALTO
TENOR BASS
1. The first 2. The next good joy that Ma - ry had, It was the joy of
one; two;
To see the bless - ed Je - sus Christ When
To see her own son, Je - sus Christ, To
he was first her son:
make the lame to go:
CHORUS
When he was first her son,
To make the lame to go,
When
To
good man: And bless - ed may he be, Both
Fa - ther, Son, and Ho - ly Ghost, To all e - ter - ni - ty.

3 The next good joy that Mary had,
It was the joy of three;
To see her own son, Jesus Christ,
To make the blind to see:

4 The next good joy that Mary had,
It was the joy of four;
To see her own son, Jesus Christ,
To read the bible o'er:

5 The next good joy that Mary had,
It was the joy of five;
To see her own son, Jesus Christ,
To bring the dead alive:

6 The next good joy that Mary had,
It was the joy of six;
To see her own son, Jesus Christ,
Upon the crucifix:

7 The next good joy that Mary had,
It was the joy of seven;
To see her own son, Jesus Christ,
To wear the crown of heaven:

3. Adding 'To make the blind to see, good man', and so on in all verses.

Some versions have for v. 6 'to bear the crucifix'. The version in Hill's MS., in another metre, gives the seeing Jesus on the rood as the third joy: his five are the Annunciation, Nativity, Crucifixion, Harrowing of Hell, Ascension. The Sloane MS. 2593 of the fifteenth century also gives the witnessing of the Crucifixion as a 'joy of great might'. This carol was one of the most popular and was annually reprinted in eighteenth-century broadsides all over England. In late eighteenth-century and nineteenth-century sheets it is sometimes extended to twelve. A melody was noted by Cecil Sharp with a Ten Joy version (8, 'To bring the croked straight', 9, 'Turn water into wine', 10, 'Bring up ten gentlemen') from Mrs. Duddridge at Mark, Somerset—*Folk Songs from Somerset* (No. 125) and *English Folk Carols*. A Gloucestershire version gives Twelve Joys (10, 'To write with a golden pen', 11, 'To have the keys of heaven', 12, 'To have the keys of hell'); Husk gives Twelve from a Newcastle sheet, with many variants (e.g. 10, 'To write without a pen'). The Seven Joy versions are older and less corrupt descendants of the Seven Joys of the Sloane MS. Bramley & Stainer (1871) printed the traditional air here given. W. J. Phillips in *Carols* (*c.* 1890) stated that he remembered the unemployed, *c.* 1850, tramping with shovels through the London snow and singing to the tune, 'We've got no work to do-oo-oo'. We can corroborate this for a later period, *c.* 1890, only they sang, 'We're all froze out'.

71 MY DANCING DAY
PART 1 (GENERAL)

Traditional
Ibid. (M.S.)
SOPRANO ALTO
TENOR BASS
1. To-mor-row shall be my dan-cing day: I would my true love did so chance To see the le-gend of my play, To call my true love to my dance:
2. Then was I born of a vir-gin pure, Of her I took flesh-ly sub-stance; Thus was I knit to man's na-ture, To call my true love to my dance:
REFRAIN
Sing O my love, O my love, my love, my love; This have I done for my true love.

3 In a manger laid and wrapped I was,
So very poor, this was my chance,
Betwixt an ox and a silly poor ass,
To call my true love to my dance:

Sing O my love etc.

4 Then afterwards baptized I was;
The Holy Ghost on me did glance,
My Father's voice heard from above,
To call my true love to my dance:

Sing O my love etc.

Part 2 (Lent: Passiontide)

5 Into the desert I was led,
Where I fasted without substánce;
The devil bade me make stones my bread,
To have me break my true love's dance:

Sing O my love etc.

6 The Jews on me they made great suit,
And with me made great variance,
Because they loved darkness rather than light,
To call my true love to my dance:

Sing O my love etc.

7 For thirty pence Judas me sold,
His covetousness for to advance;
'Mark whom I kiss, the same do hold,'
The same is he shall lead the dance:

Sing O my love etc.

Part 3 (Passiontide: Easter: Ascension)

8 Before Pilate the Jews me brought,
Where Barabbas had deliveránce;
They scourgèd me and set me at nought,
Judged me to die to lead the dance:

Sing O my love etc.

9 Then on the cross hangèd I was,
Where a spear to my heart did glance;
There issued forth both water and blood,
To call my true love to my dance:

Sing O my love etc.

10 Then down to hell I took my way
For my true love's deliverance,
And rose again on the third day,
Up to my true love and the dance:

Sing O my love etc.

11 Then up to heaven I did ascend,
Where now I dwell in sure substánce
On the right hand of God, that man
May come unto the general dance:

Sing O my love etc.

Words and melody from Sandys, 1833. In many broadsides. This is probably based on a secular song, but the interweaving of the two love motives is as ancient and widespread as the association of religion with the dance. The text seems to go back earlier than the seventeenth century.

72 WONDROUS WORKS
PART 1 (GENERAL)

Traditional

Ibid. (M.S.)

SOPRANO ALTO
TENOR BASS
1. When Je - sus Christ was twelve years old, As ho - ly scrip - ture
2. At thir - ty years he then be - gan To preach the gos - pel
plain-ly told,
un - to man,
plain - ly told, He then dis - pu - ted brave and bold A -
un - to man, And all Ju - dae - a won - dered then To
- mongst the learn - ed doc - tors:
hear his heav'n - ly doc - trine:
REFRAIN
Then praise the Lord both high and low, 'Cause
works doth shew,
he his won - drous works doth shew, That
we at last to heav'n might go, Where Christ in glo - ry reign - eth.

3 The woman's son, that dead did lie,
When Christ our Saviour passèd by,
He rose to life immediately,
To her great joy and comfort:

Then praise the Lord etc.

4 Likewise he healed the lepers ten,
Whose bodies were full filthy then;
And there returnèd back but one
Him humble thanks to render:

Then praise the Lord etc.

5 *More of his heavenly might to shew,
Himself upon the sea did go;
And there was none that e'er did so,
But only Christ our Saviour:

Then praise the Lord etc.

PART 2 (PASSIONTIDE: EASTER: ASCENSION)

6 When they bereaved his life so good,
The moon was turnèd into blood,
The earth and Temple shaking stood,
And graves full wide did open:

Then praise the Lord etc.

7 Then some of them that stood thereby
With voices loud began to cry:
'This was the Son of God truly,'
♪ | ♩ ♩ ♩
Without any fear or doubting:

Then praise the Lord etc.

8 For, as he said, it came so plain,
That in three days he rose again;
Although he suffered bitter pain,
Both heaven and earth he conquered:

Then praise the Lord etc.

9 Then afterwards ascended he
To heaven in glorious majesty;
With him God grant us all to be
In heaven with him rejoicing:

Then praise the Lord etc.

As in Gilbert, 1822 (15 verses), with two corrections from Sandys (1833), who also gives the tune.

PART I (*CONTINUED*)

2. FOREIGN CAROLS

WITH THEIR TRADITIONAL WORDS TRANSLATED

73 DUTCH CAROL
(CHRISTMAS)

Tr. R.C. Trevelyan

Dutch, 1599
(arr. Julius Röntgen)

SOPRANO
ALTO
TENOR
BASS
mf
1. A child is born in Beth - le - hem: A - wait- eth him
2. The Son took up - on him hu - ma - ni - ty, That to the

f CHORUS
all Je - ru - sa - lem.
Fa - ther thus draws nigh:
A - mor, a - mor, a -
f

- mor, a - mor, a - mor! quam dul - cis est a - mor!

3 The angels above were singing then,
Below were rejoicing the shepherd men:

Amor, etc.

4 Now let us all with the angels sing,
Yea, now let our hearts for gladness spring:

Amor, etc.

1. Amor, &c.—Love! how sweet is love!
We owe the original of this carol, 'Een kint gheboren in Bethlehem' to the kindness of Professor Röntgen in Holland.

74 FLEMISH CAROL
(CHRISTMAS AND NEW YEAR)

Tr. R.C. Trevelyan

Old Flemish
(arr. Julius Röntgen)

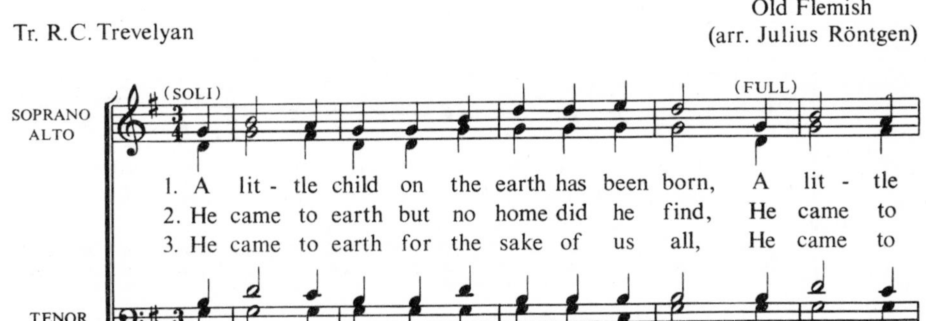

SOPRANO
ALTO
(SOLI)
(FULL)
1. A lit - tle child on the earth has been born, A lit - tle
2. He came to earth but no home did he find, He came to
3. He came to earth for the sake of us all, He came to
TENOR
BASS

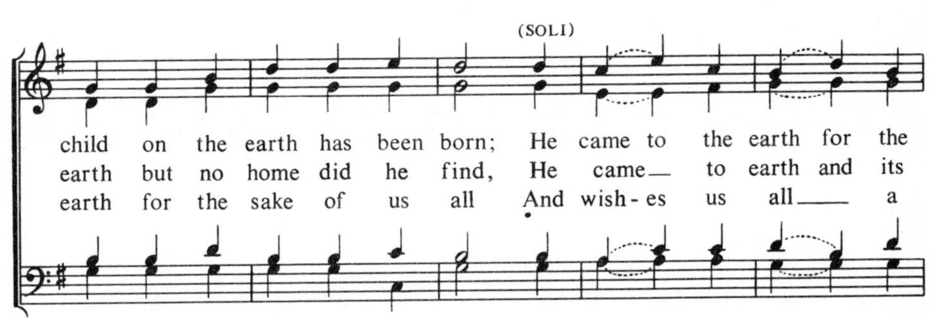

(SOLI)
child on the earth has been born; He came to the earth for the
earth but no home did he find, He came— to earth and its
earth for the sake of us all And wish - es us all— a

(FULL)
sake of us all, He came to the earth for the sake of us all!
cross did he bear, He came— to earth and its cross did he bear.
hap - py New Year, And wish-es us all— a hap - py New Year.

As in the case of No. 73, we owe the original,
'Er is een kindeken geboren op d'aard', to Professor Röntgen.

75 BETHLEHEM

DANS CETTE ETABLE

(CHRISTMAS)

Fléchier tr. Maurice F. Bell
French
(arr. Charles Gounod)
SOPRANO
ALTO
TENOR
BASS
1. In that poor sta - ble How charm - ing Je - sus lies, Words are not
2. See here God's pow - er In weak - ness for - ti - fies This in - fant
a - ble To fath - om his em - prise! No pal - ace of a
hour Of Love's e - pi - phan - ies! Our foe is now de -
king Can show so rare a thing In his - to - ry or
-spoiled, The wiles of hell are foiled: On earth there grows a
fa - ble As that of which we sing In that poor sta - ble.
Flow - er Pure, un - de-filed, un-soiled— See here God's pow - er!

3 Though far from knowing
The babe's divinity,
Mine eyes are growing
To see his majesty;
For lo! the new-born child
Upon me sweetly smiled,
The gift of faith bestowing;
Thus I my Lord descry,
Though far from knowing.

4 No more affliction!
For God endures our pains;
In crucifixion
The Son victorious reigns.
For us the sufferer brings
Salvation in his wings;
To win our souls' affection,
Could he, the King of kings,
Know more affliction?

DANS cette étable
Que Jésus est charmant,
Qu'il est aimable
Dans cet abaissement!
Que d'attraits à la fois!
Tous les palais des rois
N'ont rien de comparable
Aux charmes que je vois
Dans cette étable.

2 Que sa puissance
Paraît bien en ce jour,
Malgré l'enfance
Où l'a réduit l'amour!
Notre ennemi dompté,
L'enfer déconcerté,
Font voir qu'en sa naissance
Rien n'est si redouté
Que sa puissance.

3 Sans le connaître,
Dans sa divinité
Je vois paraître
Toute sa majesté;
Dans cet enfant qui naît,
À son aspect qui plaît,
Je découvre mon maître
Et je sens ce qu'il est
Sans le connaître.

4 *Plus de misère!
Un Dieu souffre pour nous
Et de son père
Appaise le courroux;
C'est en notre faveur
Qu'il naît dans la douleur;
Pouvait-il pour nous plaire
Unir à sa grandeur
Plus de misère?

We give the original as well as a translation of this French carol, which is often called Gounod's 'Bethlehem' because the traditional tune was arranged by C. F. Gounod (1818-93).

76 ES IST EIN' ROS'

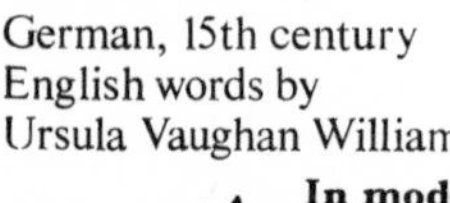

German, 15th century
English words by
Ursula Vaughan Williams

(*There is a flower*)

(CHRISTMAS)

Ibid.
(arr. Michael Praetorius)

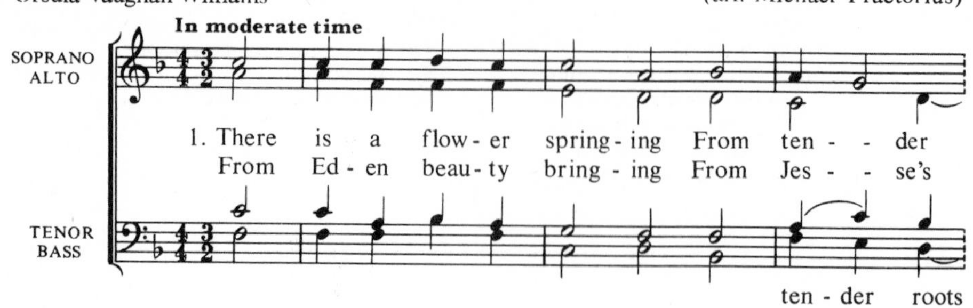
In moderate time
SOPRANO
ALTO
1. There is a flow - er spring - ing From ten - - der
From Ed - en beau - ty bring - ing From Jes - - se's
TENOR
BASS
ten - der roots
Jes - se's stem

roots it grows,
stem a rose.
On his green branch it blows: A
it grows,
a rose,

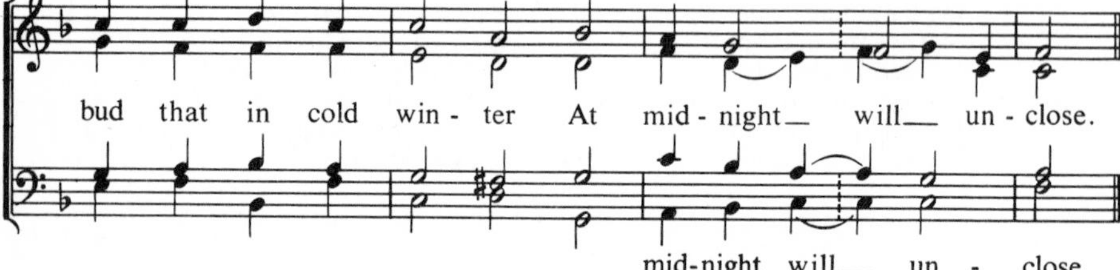
bud that in cold win - ter At mid - night will un - close.
mid-night will un - close.

The barring of this tune is necessarily irregular. But its performance will be found to be easy if it is remembered that the time-value of a crotchet is the same throughout.

2 Pure Mary, maiden holy,
The dream by prophets seen,
Who in a stable lowly
Above her child did lean
So gentle and serene:
This was Esaias' vision,
The tree of living green.

3 To Mary, rose of heaven,
With loving hearts we say
Let our sins be forgiven,
And grief be turned away
Upon this Christmas Day:
To Jesus, child of winter,
For grace and hope we pray.

Es ist ein' Ros' entsprungen
Aus einer Wurzel zart,
Als uns die Alten sungen:
Aus Jesse kam die Art;
Und hat ein Blümlein bracht,
Mitten im kalten Winter,
Wohl zu der halben Nacht.

2 Das Röslein das ich meine,
Davon Esaias sagt,
Hat uns gebracht alleine
Marie die reine Magd.
Aus Gottes ew'gem Rat
Hat sie ein Kind geboren,
Wohl zu der halben Nacht.

The fifteenth-century words and melody are in the *Speierschen Gesangbuch*, Cologne, 1600; the setting by Praetorius in *Musae Sioniae*, 1609.

77 SONG OF THE CRIB

JOSEPH LIEBER, JOSEPH MEIN

(CHRISTMAS)

Tr. N.S.T.

German, 15th century
(R.V.W.)

Moderately fast
VOICES IN UNISON
ACCPT.
1. Jo - seph dear - est, Jo - seph mine, Help me cra-dle the child di - vine; God re-ward thee and all that's thine In par - a - dise, So prays the mo - ther Ma - ry.
2. Glad - ly, dear one, la - dy mine, Help I cra-dle this child of thine; God's own light on us both shall shine In par - a - dise, As prays the mo - ther Ma - ry.
Servant(1) 3. Peace to all that have good-will! God, who heav-en and earth doth fill, Comes to turn us a - way from ill, And lies so still With - in the crib of Ma - ry.
Servant(2) 4. All shall come and bow the knee; Wise and hap-py their souls shall be, Lov - ing such a di - vin - i - ty, As all may see In Je - sus, Son of Ma - ry.
See overleaf for Chorus

77—Song of the Crib

CHORUS
He came a - mong us at Christ - mas - tide, At Christ - mas-tide, In
Beth - le - hem; Men shall bring him from far and wide Love's
di - a - dem: Je - - sus, Je - - sus,
Lo, he comes, and loves, and saves, and frees us!

Servant(3) 5. Now is born Em - man - u - el, Pro - phe - sied once by E - ze - ki - el, Pro - mis'd Ma - ry by Ga - bri - el— Ah, who can tell Thy prais - es, Son of Ma - - ry!
Servant(4) 6. Thou my la - zy heart hast stirred, Thou, the Fa - ther's e - ter - nal Word, Great-er than aught_ that ear hath heard, Thou ti - ny bird Of love, thou Son of Ma - - ry.
Servant(1) 7. Sweet and love - ly lit - tle one, Thou prince - ly, beau - ti - ful, God's own Son, With-out thee all of us were un - done; Our love is won By thine, O Son of Ma - - ry.
Servant(2) 8. Lit - tle man, and God in - deed, Lit - tle and poor, thou art all we need; We will fol - low where thou dost lead, And we will heed Our bro - ther, born of Ma - - ry.
(Chorus)

For German text and editorial note see overleaf.

77—Joseph lieber, Joseph mein

JOSEPH lieber, Joseph mein,
Hilf mir wiegen mein Kindelein;
Gott der will dein Lohner sein
Im Himmelreich, der Jungfrau Sohn Maria.

Er ist erschienen am heut'gen Tag,
Am heut'gen Tag in Israel:
Der Maria verkündigt ist
Durch Gabriel.
Eya, eya,
Jesum Christ hat uns geborn Maria.

2 Gerne, liebe Muhme mein,
Helf ich dir wiegen dein Kindelein
Dass Gott müsse mein Lohner sein
Im Himmelreich, der Jungfrau Sohn Maria.

Er ist erschienen usw.

3 Nun freu' dich, christenliche Schar
Der himmelische König klar
Nahm die Menschheit offenbar
Den uns gebar die reine Magd Maria.

Er ist erschienen usw.

4 O ew'gen Vaters ew'ges Wort
Wahr Gott, wahr Mensch, der Tugend Hort
In Himmel und Erde hie und dort
Der Sölden Pfort, die aufgetan Maria.

Er ist erschienen usw.

'Joseph lieber, Joseph mein, Hilf mir wiegen mein Kindelein' occurs in a MS. at Leipzig University, c. 1500, as part of a mystery play acted in church around the crib. It would make today a beautiful little Christmas play for children, Mary and Joseph singing vv. 1 and 2, and then the children singing the chorus. In the old arrangement the chorus was not sung after every verse; the remaining verses can be sung by one or more men and women (servants of the inn), each verse (or the alternate verses) being followed by the chorus. There are versions in German and Latin ('Resonet in laudibus'), some without the chorus, in Johann Walther's *Gesangbuch*, 1544, *Piae Cantiones* and elsewhere. The tune was used in polyphonic settings by Lassus, Handl, Praetorius and many others, and Brahms employs it as a viola obbligato in his song 'Geistliches Wiegenlied'. Our version is that of the *Mainzer Cantual*, 1605, the harmonies being those of *The English Hymnal* (612) and *Songs of Praise* (700), 'Resonet in laudibus' being there set to new words.

78 PERSONENT HODIE

SING ALOUD ON THIS DAY!

(CHRISTMAS: EPIPHANY)

Piae Cantiones, 1582
Tr. John A. Parkinson

German, 1360
(arr. Gustav Holst)

Moderato maestoso
VOICES IN UNISON
ACCPT.
1. Per - so - nent ho - di - e Vo - ces pu - - er - u - lae,
2. In mun - do nas - ci - tur, Pan - nis in - - vol - vi - tur,
3. Ma - gi tres ve - ne - runt, Par - vu - lum in - qui - runt,
4. Om - nes cle - - - ric - u - li, Par - i - ter pu - e - ri,
Lau - dan - tes ju - cun - de Qui no - bis est
Prae - se - pi po - ni - tur Sta - bu - lo bru -
Par - vu - lum in - qui - runt, Stel - lu - lam se -
Can - tent ut an - ge - li: Ad - ven - is - ti

78—Personent Hodie

na - - tus, Sum - mo De - o da - - tus,
-to - - rum, Rec - tor su - per - no - - rum.
-quen - - do, Ip - sum a - do - ran - - do,
mun - - do, Lau - des ti - bi fun - - do.
ff
Et de vir - vir - vir, Et de vir - vir - vir,
Per - di - dit, dit, dit, Per - di - dit, dit, dit,
Au - rum, thus, thus, thus, Au - rum, thus, thus, thus,
Id - e - o, o, o, Id - e - o, o, o,
R.H.
ff R.H. L.H.
sf
sf
Et de vir - gi - ne - o ven - tre pro - cre - a - tus.
Per - di - dit spo - li - a prin - ceps in - fer - no - rum.
Au - rum, thus, et myrr - ham e - i of - fe - ren - do.
Id - e - o glo - ri - a in ex - cel - sis De - o!
sf
sf

This carol is here printed with its original Latin words from *Piae Cantiones*, 1582, to make our book more complete. V. 1, in the original book, 'virgineo' is printed 'vir ij ij gineo' under the music to show the repetition at the end of each verse. For note on *Piae Cantiones* see No. 141.

78 *SING ALOUD ON THIS DAY!*

(English translation of PERSONENT HODIE)

Moderato maestoso
2
f
1. Sing a - loud on this day! Child - ren all raise the lay. Cheer - ful - ly we and they Hast - en to a - - dore thee, Sent from high - est glo - ry, For us born, born, born, For us born, born, born, For us born on this morn Of the Vir - gin Ma - ry.
2. Now a child he is born, Swath - ing bands him a - dorn, Man - ger bed he'll not scorn, Ox and ass are near him; We as Lord re - vere him, And the vain, vain, vain, And the vain, vain, vain, And the vain powers of hell Spoiled of prey now fear him.
3. From the far Or - i - ent Guid - ing star wise men sent; Him to seek their in - tent, Lord of all cre - - a - tion; Kneel in ad - or - a - tion. Gifts of gold, gold, gold, Gifts of gold, gold, gold, Gifts of gold, frank - in - cense, Myrrh for their ob - la - tion.
4. All must join him to praise; Men and boys voi - ces raise On this day of all days; An - gel voi - ces ring - ing, Christ - mas ti - dings bring - ing. Join we all, all, all, Join we all, all, all, Join we all, 'Glo - ri - a In ex - cel - sis' sing - ing.
ff

79 QUEM PASTORES

SHEPHERDS LEFT THEIR FLOCKS A-STRAYING

(CHRISTMAS: EPIPHANY)

German, 14th century
English words by Imogen Holst

Ibid.
(R.V.W.)

In moderate time ♩ = 144
SOPRANO
ALTO
1. Quem pas - to - res lau - da - ve - re, Qui - bus
1. Shep - herds left their flocks a - stray - ing, God's com-
TENOR
BASS

an - ge - li dix - e - re, Ab - sit vo - bis
-mand with joy o - bey - ing, When they heard the

jam ti - me - re, Na - tus est rex glo - ri - ae.
an - gel say - ing: 'Christ is born in Beth - le - hem.'

2 Ad quem magi ambulabant,
Aurum, thus, myrrham portabant,
Immolabant haec sincere
Nato regi gloriae.

3 Christo regi, Deo nato,
Per Mariam nobis dato,
Merito resonet vere
Laus, honor et gloria.

2 Wise Men came from far, and saw him:
Knelt in homage to adore him;
Precious gifts they laid before him:
Gold and frankincense and myrrh.

3 Let us now in every nation
Sing his praise with exultation.
All the world shall find salvation
In the birth of Mary's Son.

The carol occurs in V. Triller, 1555, *Leisentritt*, 1567, in Schein's *Cantional*, 1627, and elsewhere. According to tradition this carol was sung, line by line, by four separate groups of choir-boys.

80 THREE KINGS
(INNOCENTS: EPIPHANY)

Tr. Robert Graves

Flemish
(M.S.)

SOPRANO
ALTO
TENOR
BASS
1. Three kings are here, both weal-thy and wise, Come ri-ding far o - ver the
2. God's an - gel speaks Saint Jo-seph a - nigh: 'With Je - sus thy charge in-to
3. He - rod be-trays these in - no-cent lives Both young-er and el - der to
snow - co - vered ice; Roy - al in throng, No - ble in song,— They
far E - gypt fly. Stay not nor stand; He - rod's at hand.'— The
lan - ces and knives. Who can dare tell Mur-der so fell?— These
search for the child, the Re - deem-er of wrong; With tam-bours and drums they go
ass hast-ens pant-ing; the hot de-sert sand Has res-cued our Sa-viour from
pret - ty young chil-dren in an-guish of hell Were mar-tyred to - ge - ther his
sound-ing a - long, With tam - bours and drums they go sound- ing a - long.
He - rod's ill band, Has res - cued our Sa-viour from He - rod's ill band.
an - ger to quell, Were mar-tyred to - ge - ther his an - ger to quell.

A translation of 'De Drie Koningen', an old Flemish carol.

81 TORCHES
(CHRISTMAS)

Tr. J. B. Trend

Galician
(arr. from Pedrell)

Allegro moderato
SOPRANO
ALTO
1. Torch- es, torch - es, run with torch - es All the way to
2. Ah, ro - ro, ro - ro, my ba - by, Ah, ro - ro, my
3. Sing, my friends, and make you mer - ry, Joy and mirth and
TENOR
BASS

Beth - le - hem! Christ is born and now lies
love, ro - ro; Sleep you well, my heart's own
joy a - gain; Lo, he lives, the King of

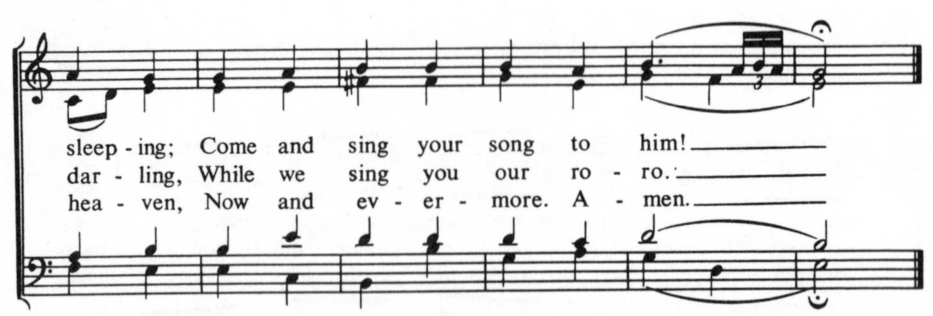
sleep - ing; Come and sing your song to him!
dar - ling, While we sing you our ro - ro.
hea - ven, Now and ev - er - more. A - men.

A Spanish carol from Galicia, 'Villancico de Navidad'. The melody is from Pedrell, *Cancionero musical;* the words are translated from the *Cancionero popular gallego* by J. Pérez Ballesteros. The second verse may be repeated at the end.

82 PATAPAN
(CHRISTMAS)

La Monnoye
Tr. O. B. C.

Burgundian
(M.S.)

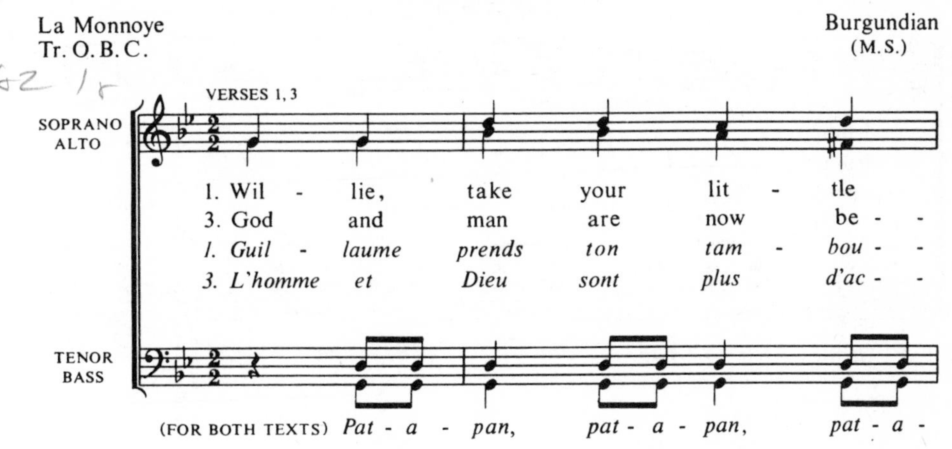
VERSES 1, 3
SOPRANO
ALTO
1. Wil - lie, take your lit - tle
3. God and man are now be - -
1. Guil - laume prends ton tam - bou - -
3. L'homme et Dieu sont plus d'ac - -
TENOR
BASS
(FOR BOTH TEXTS) Pat - a - pan, pat - a - pan, pat - a -

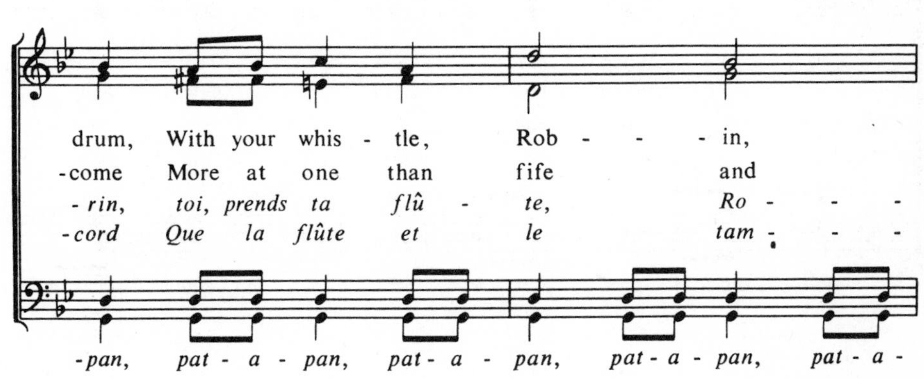
drum, With your whis - tle, Rob - - - in,
-come More at one than fife and
-rin, toi, prends ta flû - te, Ro - - -
-cord Que la flûte et le tam - - -
-pan, pat - a - pan, pat - a - pan, pat - a - pan, pat - a -

come! When we hear the fife and
drum. When you hear the fife and
-bin; Au son de ces in - stru -
-bour. Au son de ces in - stru -
-pan, pat - a - pan, pat - a - pan, pat - a - pan, pat - a -

drum,
drum,
- ments,
- ments,
Tu - re - lu - re - lu,
pat - a - pat - a -
Tu - re - lu - re - lu,
pat - a - pat - a -
-pan, pat - a - pan, pat - a - pan, pat - a - pan, pat - a -

-pan,
When we hear the fife and
When you hear the fife and
-pan,
Au son de ces in - stru -
Au son de ces in - stru -
-pan, pat- a - pan, pat - a - pan, pat - a - pan, pat - a -

drum, Christ-mas should be fro - lic - some.
drum, Dance, and make the vil - lage hum!
- ments, je di - rai No - ë gaî - ment.
- ments, chan - tons, dan - sons, sau - tons - en.
drum, tu - re - lu, tu - re - lu, tu - re - lu, lu, lu.
-pan, pat - a - pan, pat- a - pan, pat - a - pan, pan, pan.

VERSE 2

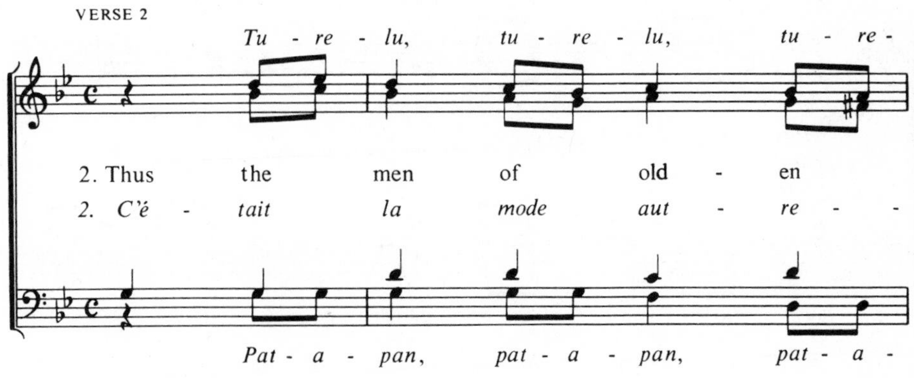
Tu - re - lu, tu - re - lu, tu - re -
2. Thus the men of old - en
2. C'é - tait la mode aut - re - -
Pat - a - pan, pat - a - pan, pat - a -

-lu, tu - re - lu, tu - re - lu, tu - re - lu, tu - re -
days Loved the King of kings to
-fois de lou - er le Roi des
-pan, pat - a - pan, pat- a - pan, pat - a - pan, pat - a -

-lu, tu - re - lu, tu - re - lu, tu - re - lu, tu - re
praise: When they hear the fife and
rois, Au son de ces in - stru -
-pan, pat - a - pan, pat - a - pan, pat - a - pan, pat - a -

-lu, tu - re - lu, tu - re - lu, tu - re - lu, lu,
drum,
-ments,
Tu - re - lu - re - lu, pat - a - pat - a -
-pan, pat - a - pan, pat - a - pan, pat - a - pan, pat - a -
lu, tu - re - lu, lu, lu, tu - re - lu, tu - re -
-pan,
When they hear the fife and
Au son de ces in - stru -
-pan, pat - a - pan, pat - a - pan, pat - a - pan, pat - a -
-lu, tu - re - lu, tu - re - lu, tu - re - lu, tu - re - lu.
drum, Sure our chil - dren won't be dumb!
-ments Il nous en faut faire au - - tant.
-pan, pat - a - pan, pat - a - pan, pat - a - pan, pan, pan.
D.C. for v. 3

(May be sung a semitone higher)

The French spelling has been modernized.

It may be worth while to print the first verse of the original dialect noël, which illustrates the genial nature of those old French carols that were not rewritten in an age of less spontaneous faith: 'Guillô, pran ton tamborin. | Toi, pran tai fleùte Rôbin; Au son de cés instruman, | *Turelurelu patapatapan;* Au son de cés instruman. | Je diron Noei gaiman. The carol is printed by F. Fertiault, *Noëls Bourgignons de Bernard de la Monnoye*, 1842. Bernard lived from 1641 to 1728.

The *tambourin* is a small elongated drum, hung from the shoulders, and played originally with the hands.

Sandys got hold of this carol a century ago; and the original words were reprinted, 1907, by H. J. L. Masse and C. Kennedy Scott in their first *Book of Old Carols*. As the tune runs quickly, it may be well to repeat one or more verses.

83 CONGAUDEAT
(CHRISTMAS: NEW YEAR: EPIPHANY)

Piae Cantiones, 1582
Tr. Maurice F. Bell

Ibid.
(harm. Geoffrey Shaw)

SOPRANO
ALTO
TENOR
BASS
1. With mer - - - - ry heart let all re - joice in one; The mo - ther-maid hath now brought forth her son
2. An an - - - - gel's voice de - clared the Sa - viour's birth, Glo - ry to God, good - will and peace on earth:
In Beth - le - hem.

3 The shepherds sped to see this wondrous thing
And found the babe, the which is Christ our King:
In Bethlehem.

4 Both ox and ass, adoring in the byre,
In mute acclaim pay homage to our Sire:
In Bethlehem.

5 As custom was, the babe when eight days old
Received his name of Jesus, long foretold:
In Bethlehem.

6 Three kings bowed low to infant majesty
And brought three gifts to hail the Trinity:
In Bethlehem.

7 Now bless we Christ, eternal glory's King,
And Christ bless us, as to his praise we sing:
In Bethlehem.

The words and melody of 'Congaudeat turba fidelium' occur in the Swedish *Piae Cantiones* (1582) (see note to No. 141); but the tune is much older than this; an early form of it is found in a twelfth-century MS., from Apt, near Avignon, printed in the *Revue du Chant Grégorien* for September 1902.

84 THE CRADLE

EIN KINDLEIN IN DER WIEGEN

(NATIVITY)

Austrian, 1649
Tr. Robert Graves
Ibid.
(M.S.)
SOPRANO
ALTO
TENOR
BASS
1. He smiles within his cradle, A babe with face so bright It beams most like a mirror Against a blaze of light: This babe so burning bright.
2. This babe we now declare to you Is Jesus Christ our Lord; He brings both peace and heartiness: Haste, haste with one accord To feast with Christ our Lord.
This babe
To feast

3 And who would rock the cradle
Wherein this infant lies,
Must rock with easy motion
And watch with humble eyes,
Like Mary pure and wise.

4 O Jesus, dearest babe of all
And dearest babe of mine,
Thy love is great, thy limbs are small.
O, flood this heart of mine
With overflow from thine!

Ein Kindlein in der Wiegen,
Ein kleines Kindelein,
Das gleisst gleich wie ein Spiegel
Nach Adelichem Schein,
Das kleine Kindelein.

2 Das Kindlein das wir meinen
Das heisst Herr Jesus Christ
Das verleih uns Fried und Innigkeit
Wohl heut zu dieser Frist,
Das geb Herr Jesus Christ.

3 Und wer das Kindlein will umtragen,
Das seelig Kindelein,
Der muss ein keusch Herz haben
Gleich wie ein Jungfrau rein,
Maria der Mutter sein.

4 Maria, wir wöllen dich bitten
Mit deinem Kindelein
Du wöllest uns nicht verlassen
Wöllest allzeit bei uns sein
Mit deinem Kindelein.

Translation of 'Ein Kindlein in der Wiegen'. Words and melody from D. G. Corner's *Geistliche Nachtigal*, Vienna, 1649. Wackernagel also gives it from an Augsburg print of 1590.

85 PUER NATUS
(NATIVITY)

Tr. N.S.T. German, 16th century (M.S.)

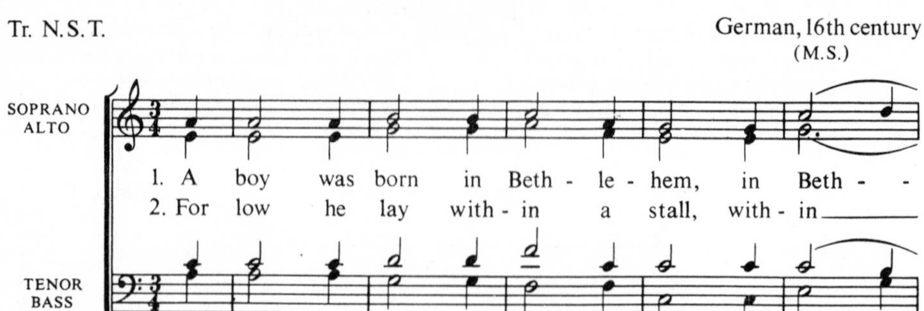
SOPRANO
ALTO
1. A boy was born in Beth - le - hem, in Beth - -
2. For low he lay with - in a stall, with - in
TENOR
BASS

- - - le - hem; Re - joice for that, Je - ru - sa -
a stall, Who rules for ev - er ov - er

- lem!
all:
Al - le - lu - ya, al - le - - - lu - ya.

3 He let himself a servant be,
a servant be,
That all mankind he might set free:
Alleluya.

4 Then praise the Word of God who came,
the Word of God who came,
To dwell within a human frame:
Alleluya.

5 And praised be God in threefold might,
And glory bright,
Eternal, good, and infinite!
Alleluya.

If both versions are used together it is suggested that the alternative be sung, slower, to the last verse.

This melody for 'Ein kind geborn zu Bethlehem' ('Puer natus in Bethlehem') is in L. Lossius's *Psalmodia*, 1553, the Ingolstadt *Obsequiale*, 1570, and in many German books of the seventeenth century: it is really the descant of an older melody which it has supplanted.

ALTERNATIVE VERSION (as harmonized by J. S. Bach)
SOPRANO
ALTO
TENOR
BASS
1. A boy was born in Beth - le - hem, in Beth - - - le - hem; Re - joice for that, Je - ru - sa - lem!
2. For low he lay with - in a stall, with - in a stall, Who rules for ev - er ov - er all:
5. And praised be God in three - fold might, And glo - - - ry bright, E - ter - nal, good, and in - fi - nite!
Al - le - lu - ya, al - le - - - lu - ya.

EIN Kind geborn zu Bethlehem, zu Bethlehem;
Des freuet sich Jerusalem!

Alleluya.

2 Hier liegt es in dem Krippelein, dem Krippelein
Ohn' Ende ist die Herrschaft sein,

Alleluya.

3 Gelobt seist du, Herr Jesu Christ, Herr Jesu Christ,
Der du als Mensch geboren bist.

Alleluya.

4 Zu dieser heiligen Weihnachtszeit, Weihnachtszeit
Sei Gott der Herr gebenedeit.

Alleluya.

86 IN DULCI JUBILO
(NATIVITY)

Tr. S.P.

German, 14th century
(harm. Bartholomew Gesius, 1601)

VERSES 1, 2, & 3
Allegro
SOPRANO
ALTO
1. *In dul- ci ju - bi - lo* Now sing with hearts a - glow!
2. *O Je - su, par- vu - le,* For thee I long al - way;
TENOR
BASS

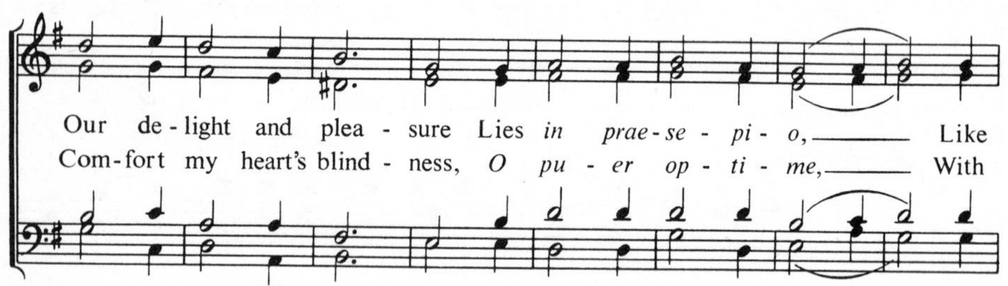

Our de - light and plea - sure Lies *in prae - se - pi - o,* Like
Com - fort my heart's blind - ness, *O pu - er op - ti - me,* With

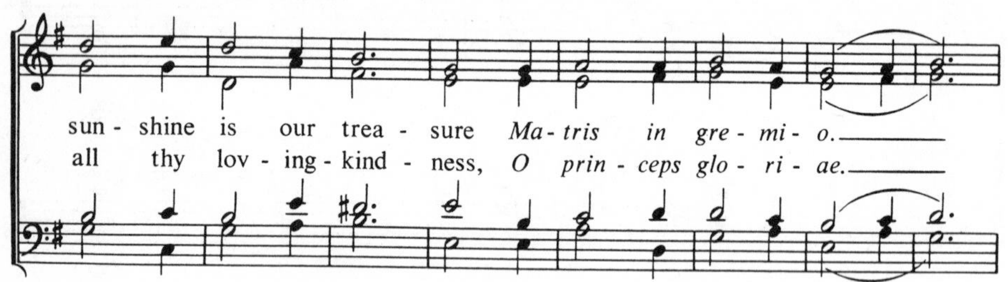

sun - shine is our trea - sure *Ma - tris in gre - mi - o.*
all thy lov - ing - kind - ness, *O prin - ceps glo - ri - ae.*

Al - pha es et O! Al - pha es et O!
Tra - he me post te! Tra - he me post te!

The small notes in the last two bars are added to preserve the usual version of the tune, and may be used if preferred.

3 *O Patris caritas!*
O Nati lenitas!
Deeply were we stainèd
Per nostra crimina;
But thou for us hast gainèd
Coelorum gaudia.
O that we were there!

4 *Ubi sunt gaudia*
In any place but there?
There are angels singing
Nova cantica,
And there the bells are ringing
In Regis curia.
O that we were there!

In dulci jubilo
Nun singet und seid froh!
Unsers Herzens Wonne
Leit *in praesepio,*
Und leuchtet als die Sonne
Matris in gremio.
Alpha es et O!

2 *O Jesu parvule*
Nach dir ist mir so weh!
Tröst mir mein Gemüte
O puer optime
Durch alle deine Güte
O princeps gloriae.
Trahe me post te!

3 *O Patris caritas!*
O Nati lenitas!
Wir wären all verloren
Per nostra crimina
So hat er uns erworben
Coelorum gaudia
Eia, wären wir da!

4 *Ubi sunt gaudia*
Nirgend mehr denn da!
Da die Engel singen
Nova cantica,
Und die Schellen klingen
In regis curia.
Eia, wären wir da!

Setting by J.S. BACH

VERSE 4
Maestoso
4. U - bi sunt gau - di - a In an - y place but there?
There are an - gels sing - - ing No - - va can - ti -
There are an - gels sing - ing

86—In Dulci Jubilo

-ca, And there the bells are ring - - ing In
Re - gis cu - ri - a. O that we were
Re-gis cu - ri - a. O that we were
Re - gis cu - ri - a. O that we were
there!
there! O that we were there!
there! O that we were there!
O that we were there!

1. *In dulci jubilo*—In sweet shouting, or jubilation. *In praesepio*—in a manger. *Matris*, &c.—In his mother's lap. *Alpha*, &c.—Thou art Alpha and Omega. 2. *O Jesu parvule*—O tiny Jesus. *O puer optime*—O best of boys. *O princeps gloriae*—O prince of glory. *Trahe*, &c.—Draw me after thee. 3. *O Patris*, &c.—O love of the Father. *O Nati*. &c.—O gentleness of the Son. *Per nostra*, &c.—Through our crimes. *Coelorum*, &c.—The joys of the heavens. 4. *Ubi sunt*, &c.—Where are joys? *Nova*, &c.—New songs. *In Regis*, &c.—In the court of the King.

This famous old German macaronic carol was first translated into English by John Wedderburn in his *Gude and Godly Ballates*, *c.* 1540, 'In dulci jubilo, Now let us sing with mirth and jo[y]', irregular, in three stanzas. Other translations are—*Lyra Davidica*, 1708, Sir J. Bowring, 1825, &c. R. L. de Pearsall (1795-1856) and G. R. Woodward in the *Cowley Carol Book* follow the tune correctly. The music only allows us to use three of Wedderburn's lines (21 and 28 in part, and 23) in this new rendering.

Because of the importance of this carol, we append the original old German lines: 1. Nu singet und seyt fro: Unsers herzens wonne Leyt: Und leuchtet als die sonne. 2. Nach dir ist mir so we: Tröst mir myn gemüte: Durch aller juncfrawen güte. 3. Wir weren all verloren: So hat er uns erworben: Eya, wär wir da! 4. Nirgend mer denn da: Da die engel singen: Und die schellen klingen: Eya, wär wir da! But there are many variants, old and new, e.g. in v. 2 the fifteenth-century line is modernized by Vehe to 'Durch alle deine Güte'.

The fourteenth-century melody occurs, with the words, in a MS. at Leipzig University Library, which belongs to the beginning of the fifteenth century. The developed form of the melody is in Michael Vehe's *Gesangbuch*, Leipzig, 1537, and in Witzel's *Psaltes Ecclesiasticus*, Cologne, 1550. In Babst's *Gesangbuch*, Leipzig, 1545, the last hymn-book produced for Luther and representing his final text-editorship, the third stanza, doubtless by Luther himself, 'O Patris caritas', is substituted for an earlier one. The melody and versions of the words occur in many other books, including *Piae Cantiones*, 1582, with a Swedish translation.

The original words are said by a fourteenth-century writer to have been sung by angels to Henry Suso (d. 1366), the mystic, who was drawn in thereby to dance with his celestial visitors.

87 ROCKING
(NATIVITY)

Tr. O.B.C. — Czech (M.S.)

Moderato
SOPRANO
ALTO
TENOR
BASS
1. Lit - tle Je - sus, sweet - ly — sleep, do not — stir;
2. Ma - ry's lit - tle ba - by, — sleep, sweet - ly — sleep,
We will — lend a — coat of — fur,
Sleep in — com - fort, — slum - ber — deep;
We will rock you,
rock you, rock you, We will rock you, rock you, rock you:
See the fur to keep you — warm, Snug - ly — round your — ti - ny — form.
We will serve you all we — can, Dar - ling, dar - ling — lit - tle — man.

Translation of the Czech carol, 'Hajej, nynjej'. This carol may well be sung twice.

88 WAKING-TIME

VOISIN, D'OU VENAIT?

(NATIVITY)

Pr. Eleanor Farjeon
French
(M.S.)
SOPRANO
ALTO
TENOR
BASS
1. Neigh-bour, what was the sound, I pray, That did a-wake me as I lay, And to their door-ways brought the peo - - - ple? Ev - 'ry - one heard it like a chime Peal - ing for joy with - in a stee - ple: 'Get up, good folk! Get up, good folk, 'tis wa - king - time! Get up, good folk, 'tis wa - king - time!'
2. Nay then, young Mar - tin, know you not That it is this our na - tive spot Sweet Love has cho - sen for his dwell - - - ing? In ev - 'ry quar - ter ru - mours hum, Ru - mours of news be - yond all tell - ing: 'Wake up, good folk! Wake up, good folk, for Christ is come, Wake up, good folk, for Christ is come.'

3 Neighbours, and is it really true,
True that the babe so small and new
Is lying even now among us?
What can we lay upon his knees—
He whose arrival angels sung us,
What can we give,
What can we give the child to please?

4 Dickon shall bring a ball of silk,
Peter his son a pot of milk,
And Tom a sparrow and a linnet,
Robin a cheese, and Ralph the half
Part of a cake with cherries in it,
And jolly Jack,
And jolly Jack a little calf.

5 I think this child will come to be
Some sort of workman such as we,
So he shall have my tools and chattels,
My well-set saw, my plane, my drill,
My hammer that so merry rattles,
And planks of wood,
And planks of wood to work at will.

6 When we have made our offerings,
Saying to him the little things
Whereof all babies born are witting,
Then we will take our leave and go,
Bidding goodnight in manner fitting—
Hush, hush, wee lamb,
Hush, hush, wee lamb, dream sweetly so.

7 And in a stable though he lies,
We in our hearts will soon devise
Such mansions as can never shame him:
There we will house and hold him dear,
And through the world to all proclaim him:
'Wake up, good folk!
Wake up, good folk, for Christ is here.'

VOISIN, d'où venait ce grand bruit
Qui m'a réveillé cette nuit
Et tous les gens du voisinage?
Vraiment, j'étais fort en courroux
D'entendre partout le village,
'Sus, sus, bergers!
Sus, sus, bergers réveillez-vous.'

2 Quoi donc, Colin, ne sais-tu pas
Qu'un Dieu vient de naître ici-bas;
Qu'il est logé dans une étable?
Il n'a ni langes ni drapeaux.
Et dans cet état misérable,
On ne peut voir
On ne peut voir rien de plus beau.

3 Qui t'a dit, voisin, qu'en ce lieu
Voudrait bien s'adresser un Dieu
Pour qui rien n'est trop magnifique?
Les anges nous l'ont fait savoir
Par une charmante musique,
Qui s'entendit,
Qui s'entendit hier tout le soir.

4 Sans plus tarder, allons donc tous,
Allons saluer à genoux
Notre Seigneur et notre maître:
Et dans cet aimable séjour,
Où pour nous l'amour l'a fait naître
Allons pour lui,
Allons pour lui mourir d'amour.

5 Partons de suite, cher Colin,
J'y veux être de bon matin
Pour lui offrir ma maisonette,
Où j'ai préparé, sur deux bancs,
Un lit en forme de couchette,
Et des linceuls,
Et des linceuls qui sont tout blancs.

6 Je vais faire tout de mon mieux
Pour le retenir dans ces lieux,
Ainsi que Joseph et Marie.
Quand ils seront tous trois chez-moi
Ma maison sera plus jolie
Que le palais,
Que le palais du plus grand roi.

7 Dès aujourd'hui, dans ce dessein,
Sans attendre jusqu'à demain,
Je veux quitter ma bergerie;
Et j'abandonne mon troupeau,
Pour mieux garder toute ma vie,
Dans ma maison,
Dans ma maison ce seul agneau.

The tune, with six verses, is in the *Grande Bible des Noëls Angevins*, 1766; there are many variants of the tune, in Anjou and elsewhere, and seven more verses are known of 'Voisin, d'où venait ce grand bruit?' which is here paraphrased.

89 SION'S DAUGHTER
(NATIVITY)

Tr. A.G.

Dutch (M.S.)

SOPRANO
ALTO
TENOR
BASS
1. O Si - on's daugh - ter, where art thou? Good news have I to tell thee, A great - er joy I bring thee now Than ev - er yet be - fell thee.
2. A maid - en hath brought forth a son; Great was the gift she gave us; In Beth - lem was that life be - gun Of him who came to save us.

3 As through a casement light will flood
That darkness may be ended,
So through her maiden motherhood
The child of God descended.

4 Upon her lap he lay so fair,
She kissed him and caressed him;
Great was the love she did him bear,
As to her heart she pressed him.

A translation of the old Netherland carol, 'Waer is die dochter van Syoen', from *Nederlandsch Volksliederenboek*, by Lange, Riemsdijk, and Kalff, 1896.

90 SONG OF THE SHIP

ES KOMMT EIN SCHIFF

(NATIVITY)

c. 1470, tr. O. B. C. German, 1608

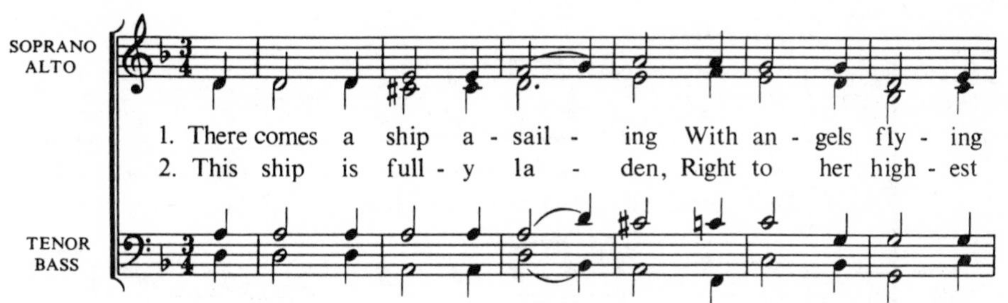
SOPRANO
ALTO
1. There comes a ship a - sail - ing With an - gels fly - ing
2. This ship is full - y la - den, Right to her high - est
TENOR
BASS

fast; She bears a splen - did car - - go And has a migh-ty mast.
board; She bears the Son from hea - - ven, God's high e - ter - nal Word.

3 Upon the sea unruffled
The ship moves in to shore,
To bring us all the riches
She has within her store.

4 And that ship's name is Mary,
Of flowers the rose is she,
And brings to us her baby
From sin to set us free.

5 The ship made in this fashion,
In which such store was cast,
Her sail is Love's sweet passion,
The Holy Ghost her mast.

Es kommt ein Schiff geladen
Bis an sein'n höchsten Bord,
Trägt Gottes Sohn voll Gnaden,
Des Vaters ewig's Wort.

2 Das Schiff geht still im Triebe,
Es trägt ein teure Last,
Das Segel ist die Liebe
Der Heilig Geist der Mast.

3 Der Anker haft auf Erden,
Und das Schiff ist am Land,
Gott's Wort tut uns Fleisch werden,
Der Sohn ist uns gesandt.

4 Zu Bethlehem geboren
Im Stall ein Kindelein,
Gibt sich für uns verloren,
Gelobet muss es sein.

The oldest text, in four stanzas (1 and 2 forming one stanza), is in a MS. 1470-80 (Royal Library, Berlin). Sudermann (*Gesänge*, 1626) gives what has become the better known text, and says that it was found among Tauler's writings. The melody is from the version ('Uns kompt ein Schiff gefahren') in the *Andernach Gesangbuch*, 1608. There is much doubt about Tauler's writings; and Sudermann seems to have rewritten the hymns in his collection. The last lines of the 1470 version are: Der segel is die minne, | Der heilig geist der mast.

91 IN THE TOWN

NOUS VOICI DANS LA VILLE

(NATIVITY)

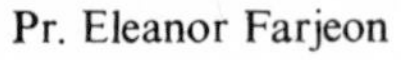
Pr. Eleanor Farjeon

French, 15th century
(M.S.)

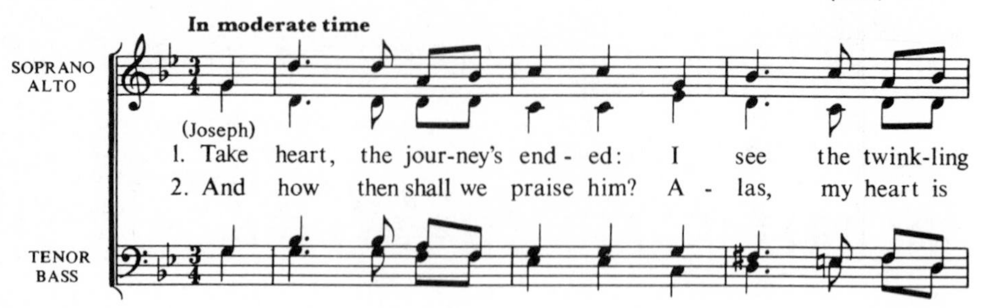

In moderate time
SOPRANO
ALTO
(Joseph)
1. Take heart, the jour-ney's end - ed: I see the twink-ling
2. And how then shall we praise him? A - las, my heart is
TENOR
BASS

lights, Where we shall be be - friend - ed On this the night of
sore That we no gifts can raise him Who are so ve - ry

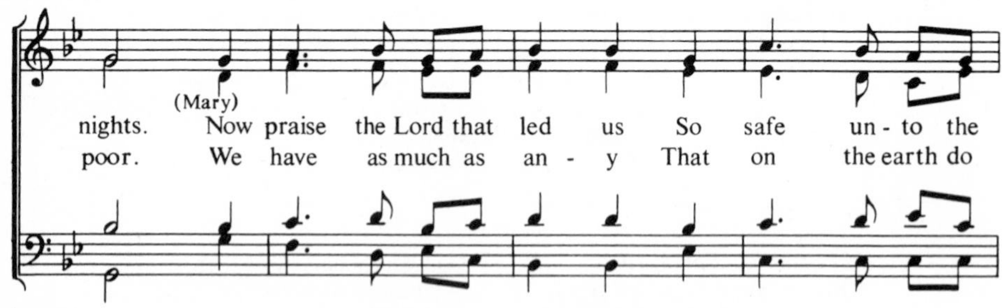

(Mary)
nights. Now praise the Lord that led us So safe un - to the
poor. We have as much as an - y That on the earth do

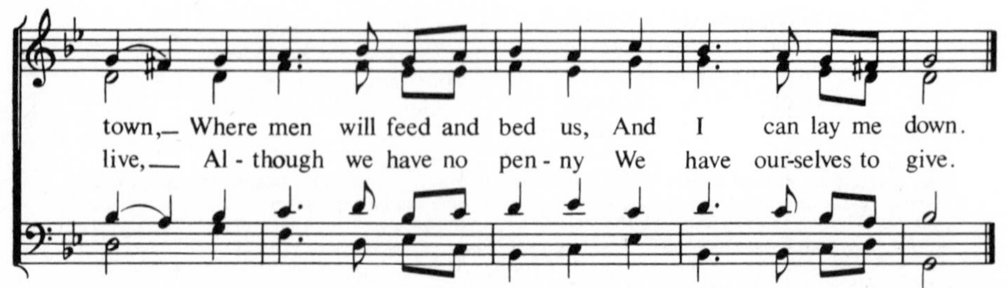

town,— Where men will feed and bed us, And I can lay me down.
live,— Al - though we have no pen - ny We have our-selves to give.

Joseph: 3 Look yonder, wife, look yonder!
An hostelry I see,
Where travellers that wander
Will very welcome be.

Mary: The house is tall and stately,
The door stands open thus;
Yet, husband, I fear greatly
That inn is not for us.

Joseph: 4 God save you, gentle master!
Your littlest room indeed
With plainest walls of plaster
Tonight will serve our need.

Host: For lordings and for ladies
I've lodging and to spare;
For you and yonder maid is
No closet anywhere.

Joseph: 5 Take heart, take heart, sweet Mary,
Another inn I spy,
Whose host will not be chary
To let us easy lie.

Mary: Oh, aid me, I am ailing,
My strength is nearly gone;
I feel my limbs are failing,
And yet we must go on.

Joseph: 6 God save you, Hostess, kindly!
I pray you, house my wife,
Who bears beside me blindly
The burden of her life.

Hostess: My guests are rich men's daughters
And sons, I'd have you know!
Seek out the poorer quarters
Where ragged people go.

Joseph: 7 Good sir, my wife's in labour,
Some corner let us keep.

Host: Not I: knock up my neighbour,
And as for me, I'll sleep.

Mary: In all the lighted city
Where rich men welcome win,
Will not one house for pity
Take two poor strangers in?

Joseph: 8 Good woman, I implore you
Afford my wife a bed.

Hostess: Nay, nay, I've nothing for you
Except the cattle-shed.

Mary: Then gladly in the manger
Our bodies we will house,
Since men tonight are stranger
Than asses are and cows.

Joseph: 9 Take heart, take heart, sweet Mary,
The cattle are our friends:
Lie down, lie down, sweet Mary,
For here the journey ends.

Mary: Now praise the Lord that found me
This shelter in the town,
Where I with friends around me
May lay my burden down.

For French words see overleaf.

A paraphrase of the touching old dialogue carol, 'Nous voici dans la ville'. The lovely tune is famous and widespread in France; the words set to it by Lucas Le Moigne ('Or, nous dites Marie') date it as at least not later than c. 1450, and the macaronic carol 'Célébrons la naissance' (which is given to the tune together with 'Nous voici' in the *Grande Bible des Noëls* of 1766) is clearly a fifteenth-century work. Other words (not all religious) have been sung to it, e.g. 'Hélas! je l'ai perdue', 'Voulez-vous plaire aux dames', 'Bergère que j'adore', and 'Chantons, je vous en prie'. In 1676 Le Bègue used the melody for an organ prelude; and its strains upon the organ are often heard creeping into the silence of the consecration at Christmas time in French churches.

We have arranged it in parts; and it can be sung thus in church, or else as a little play upon the stage.

Dr. Neale's words 'A day, a day of glory' are set to this tune in *The Cowley Carol Book*.

91—Nous voici dans la ville

Joseph: Nous voici dans la ville
Où naquit autrefois
Le roi le plus habile
Et le plus saint des rois.

Marie: Elevons la pensée
Vers le Dieu qui conduit
Nos pas cette journée,
Voici venir la nuit.

Joseph: 2 Quelle reconnaissance
Pouvons-nous rendre à Dieu?
De la sainte assistance
Qu'il nous donne en tout lieu?

Marie: Offrons nos corps, nos âmes
A notre créateur,
Allumons donc la flamme
De l'amour dans nos coeurs.

Joseph: 3 Allons, chère Marie,
De vers cet horloger.
C'est une hôtellerie;
Nous y pourrons loger.
Mon cher Monsieur, de grâce,
N'ayez vous point chez vous
Quelque petite place—
Quelque chambre pour nous?

L'Hôte: 4 Vous perdez votre peine
Vous venez un peu tard;
Ma maison est trop pleine,
Allez voir autre part.

Joseph: Passons à l'autre rue,
Laquelle est vis-à-vis
Tout devant notre rue,
Je vois d'autres logis.

Marie: 5 Joseph, ton bras, de grâce,
Je ne puis plus marcher
Je me trouve si lasse.
Il faut pourtant chercher.

Joseph: Patron des trois couronnes
Avez-vous logement
Chez vous, pour deux personnes?
Quelque trou seulement!

L'Hôte: 6 J'ai noble compagnie
Dont j'aurai du profit.
Je hais la gueuserie—
C'est tout dire, il suffit!

Marie: Salut, ma chère hôtesse,
Ayez pitié de nous.
Sensible à ma détresse,
Recevez-nous chez vous.

Joseph: 7 En attendant, madame,
Que j'ai un logement,
Permettez que ma femme
Se repose un moment.

L'Hôtesse: Très volontiers, m'amie,
Mettez-vous sur le banc.
Monsieur, voyez la Pie
Ou bien le Cheval Blanc.

8 Dans l'état déplorable
Où Joseph est réduit,
Il découvre une étable
Malgré la sombre nuit.
C'est la seule retraite
Qui reste à son espoir
Ainsi que le prophète
Avait su le prévoir.

92 PUER NOBIS
(NATIVITY)

15th century
Tr. O.B.C.
Piae Cantiones, 1582
(Geoffrey Shaw)
FULL
(VOICES IN UNISON)
1. Un - to us a boy is born! King of all cre - a - - tion, Came he to a world for - lorn, The Lord of ev - 'ry na - - - - - - - - - - - - tion.
1. Pu - er no - bis nas - ci - tur Rec - tor an - ge - lo - - rum, In hoc mun - do pas - ci - tur Do - mi - nus Do - mi - no - - - - - - - - - - - rum.
ORGAN
Ped.

92—Puer nobis

SOPRANOS
2. Cra - dled in a stall was he With sleep - y cows and
2. In prae - se - pe po - ni - tur Sub foe - no a - si -
Senza Ped.

ass - es; But the ve - ry beasts could see That
- no - rum. Cog - no - ve - runt Do - mi - num Chris-

he all men sur - pass - - - - - - - - - - - es.
- tum re - gem coe - lo - - - - - - - - - - - rum.

TENORS AND BASSES
3. He - rod then with fear was filled: 'A prince', he said, 'in
3. Hinc He - ro - des ti - mu - it Mag - no cum do -
Ped.
Jew - - ry!' All the lit - tle boys he killed At
-lo - - re, Et pu - e - ros oc - ci - dit, in -
Beth - lem in his fu - - - - - - - - - - ry.
-fan - tes cum li - vo - - - - - - - - - - re.

92—Puer nobis

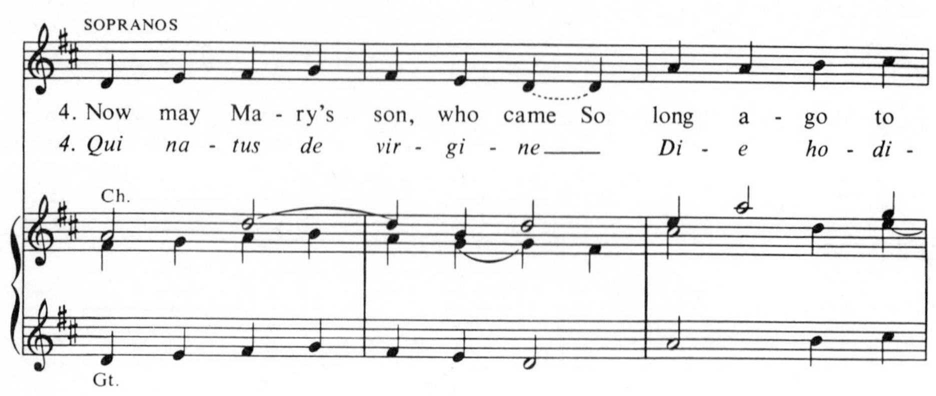
SOPRANOS
4. Now may Ma - ry's son, who came So long a - go to
4. Qui na - tus de vir - gi - ne Di - e ho - di -
Ch.
Gt.

love us, Lead us all with hearts a - flame Un -
- er - na Du - cat nos cum gra - ti - a Ad

- to the joys a - bove us.
gau - di - a su - per - na.

FULL
5. O - me - ga and Al - pha he! Let the org - an
5. O et A et A et O Cum can - ti - bus in
Gt. Trumpet
ff Swell
PEDALS
thun - - der, While the choir with peals of glee Doth
cho - - ro, Cum can - ti - cis et or - gan - o, Be -
Sw.
rend the air a - sun - - - - - - - - - - - - der.
-ne - di - ca - mus Do - - - - - - - - - - mi - no.
Gt. Trumpet
Sw.

The words and original melody of 'Puer nobis nascitur' are in a Trier MS. of the fifteenth century. There are many variants, given in Zahn, Dreves, and Baümker; a German translation ('Uns ist geborn ein Kindelein') is printed by Spangenberg, 1544, in the Mainz *Cantual*, 1605, and elsewhere. The melody in this form is in *Piae Cantiones*, 1582 (see note to No. 141), and the words are from the version of Mone (*Lateinische Hymnen*), who prints the Trier form.

93 MARY'S WANDERING

MARIAS WANDERSCHAFT

(THE PASSION)

Tr. A. F. D. German (M.S.)

Rather slowly
SOPRANO
ALTO
1. Once Ma - ry would go_wan-der-ing, To all the_lands would run,
2. Whom met she as she jour-neyed forth? Saint Pe - ter,_that good man,
TENOR
BASS
That she might find_ her_ son, that she_ might_find her son.
Who sad - ly did_ her_ scan, who sad - ly_ did her scan.
FA-BURDEN to verses 4 & 7
S.
A.
4.'Too well, too well, I've seen thy son; 'Twas by a pal - ace - gate,
7. 'Nay, Ma - ry, cease thy weep-ing, dear: The wounds they are but small;
T.
B.
Most griev - - ous was_ his_ state.'
But heav'n is won_ for_ all!'
Most griev - ous was_ his_ state.'
But heav'n is won_ for_ all!'
Most griev - ous was his state, most griev - ous_ was his state.'
But heav'n is won_ for_ all, but heav'n is_ won for all!'
Most griev - ous was his state, most griev - ous was his state.'
But heav'n is won for all, but heav'n is won for all!'

3 'O tell me have you seen him yet—
The one I love the most—
The son whom I have lost?'

4 'Too well, too well, I've seen thy son;
'Twas by a palace-gate,
Most grievous was his state.'

5 'O say, what wore he on his head?'
'A crown of thorns he wore;
A cross he also bore.'

6 'Ah me! and he must bear that cross,
Till he's brought to the hill,
For cruel men to kill.'

7 'Nay, Mary, cease thy weeping, dear:
The wounds they are but small;
But heaven is won for all!'

MARIA die wollt' wandern geh'n,
Wollt' alle Land ausgeh'n,
Wollt' suchen ihren Sohn.

2 Was begegnet ihr auf der Reise?
Sankt Petrus der heil'ge Mann,
Ganz traurig schaut s'ihn an.

3 'Habt ihr denn nicht gesehen
Mein allerliebsten Sohn,
Den ich verloren han?'

4 'Wohl hab' ich ihn gesehen
Vor einem Judenhaus;
Ganz traurig sah er aus.'

5 'Was trug er auf seinem Haupte?'
'Von Dornen eine Kron',
Das Kreuz, das trug er schon.'

6 'Das Kreuz, das musst' er tragen
Bis an dieselbige Stadt
Da er gemartert ward.'

7 'Maria, lass das Weinen;
Die Wunden, die sind klein,
Das Himmelreich ist mein!'

'Marias Wanderschaft' ('Maria die wollt' wandern geh'n') is one version of this legend, and to it belongs this folk-melody, which was published by Friedlaender. The third line of each verse is repeated.

See No. 179 for Brahms's tune to another version of the ballad.

94 EASTER EGGS

Tr. A.F.D.

Russian (M.S.)

Eas-ter eggs! Eas-ter eggs! Give to him that_ begs!
Those who hoard can't aff-ord– moth and rust their re-ward!
Eas-ter-tide, like a bride, comes, and won't be de-nied.
SOPRANO
ALTO
TENOR
BASS
'm
For
Christ the Lord is a-ris-en,— is a-ris-en.
To the
Those who
FINE
'm
poor, o-pen door, some-thing give from your store!
love free-ly give— long and well may they live!
For
Christ the Lord is a-ris-en,— is a-ris-en.

Words and melody from the traditional Easter song, 'Dalalin, Dalalin, po Yaichenku', in Rimsky-Korsakov's *Russian National Songs*, 1877.

95 NOW GLAD OF HEART

WIR WOLLEN ALLE FRÖHLICH SEIN

(EASTER: ASCENSION: TRINITY SUNDAY)

Tr. A.H. Fox-Strangways

German, 16th century
(Geoffrey Shaw)

SOPRANO
ALTO

1. Now glad of heart be ev - 'ry one! The fight is fought, the
2. Who on the rood was cru - ci - fied, Who rose a - gain,— as

TENOR
BASS

day— is won, The Christ— is set up - on his throne,
at— this tide, In glo - - ry to his Fa - ther's side,

3 Who baffled death and harrowed hell
And led the souls that loved him well
All in the light of lights to dwell;

4 To him we lift our heart and voice
And in his paradise rejoice
With harp and pipe and happy noise.

5 Then rise, all Christian folk, with me
And carol forth the One in Three
That was, and is, and is to be,

6 By faith, the shield of heart and mind,
Through love, which suffers and is kind,
In hope, that rides upon the wind.

WIR wollen alle fröhlich sein
In dieser osterlichen Zeit
Denn unser Heil an Gotte leit.

2 Es ist erstanden Jesu Christ
Der an dem Kreuz gestorben ist
Dem sei Lob, Ehr' zu aller Frist.

3 Er hat zerstört der Hellen Pfort
Und all die seinen herausgeführt
Und uns erlöst vom ewigen Tod.

4 Wir singen all Lob, Ehr' und Preis
Dem einigen Gottes Sohne weiss
Der uns erkauft das Paradeis.

5 Es freu' sich all die Christenheit
Und lob' die heilige Dreifaltigkeit
Von nun an bis in Ewigkeit.

In some versions of 'Wir wollen alle fröhlich sein', one or more stanzas of *Alleluya* (repeated) are added. This was 'an old song' already in Spangenberg's *Christlichs Gesangbüchlein*, 1568. It is also in the *Gesangbuch der Brüder in Behemen*, Nürnberg, 1544, and elsewhere.

96 HILARITER
(EASTER: SPRING: SUMMER)

Tr. O.B.C.

German, 1623 (M.S.)

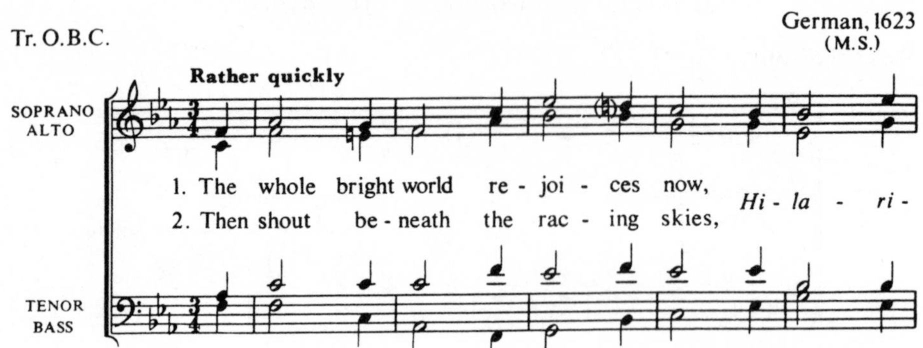

Rather quickly
SOPRANO
ALTO
1. The whole bright world re - joi - ces now,
2. Then shout be - neath the rac - ing skies,
Hi - la - ri -
TENOR
BASS

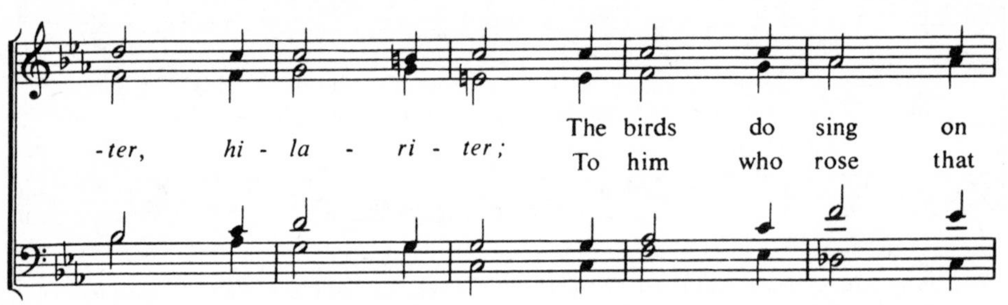

-ter, hi - la - ri - ter;
The birds do sing on
To him who rose that

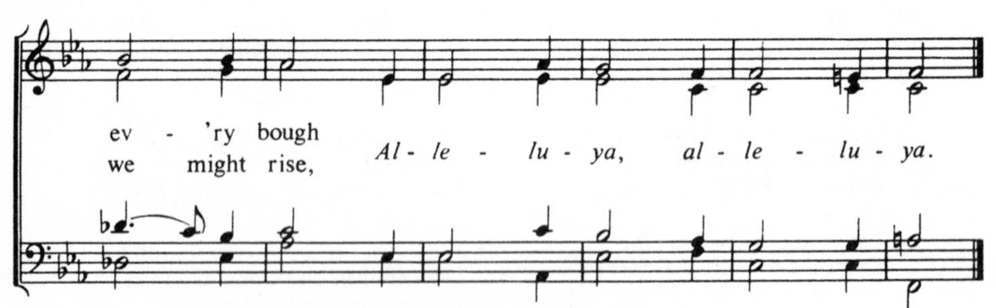

ev - 'ry bough
we might rise,
Al - le - lu - ya, al - le - lu - ya.

3 And all you living things make praise,
Hilariter, hilariter;
He guideth you on all your ways,
Alleluya, alleluya.

4 He, Father, Son, and Holy Ghost—
Hilariter, hilariter!—
Our God most high, our joy and boast.
Alleluya, alleluya.

DIE ganze Welt, Herr Jesu Christ,
Hilariter, hilariter,
In deiner Orstend fröhlich ist,
Alleluya, alleluya.

2 Das himmlisch Heer in Himmel singt
Hilariter, hilariter,
Die Christenheit auf Erden klingt,
Alleluya, alleluya.

3 Jetzt grünet was nur grünen kann
Hilariter, hilariter,
Die Baüm' zu blühen fangen an.
Alleluya, alleluya.

4 Es singen jetzt die Vögel all,
Hilariter, hilariter,
Jetzt singt und klingt die Nachtigall
Alleluya, alleluya.

5 Der Sonnenschein jetzt kommt herein
Hilariter, hilariter,
Und gibt der Welt ein neuen Schein.
Alleluya, alleluya.

The earliest appearance of 'Die ganze Welt' is in the Cologne *Kirchengesäng*, 1623; it appears later in several other books, e.g. at Mainz, 1628, Prague, 1655, and Strassburg, 1697.

97 THE SECRET FLOWER

GEBOR'N IST UNS EIN KINDELEIN

(EASTER: WHITSUNTIDE: SAINTS' DAYS)

German, 17th century
Pr. Eleanor Farjeon

German, 16th century
(M. S.)

SOPRANO
ALTO
TENOR
BASS
1. This child was born to men ___ of God:
2. He came the Word to man - - - - i - fest,
Love to the world ___ was giv - en;
Earth to the stars ___ he rais - es:
In him were
The teach - er's
truth ___ and beau - ty met,
err - - - ors are not his,
On him was set At
The Truth he is: No
birth the seal of hea - - - - - - - - - - ven.
man can speak his prais - - - - - - - - es.

3 He evil fought and overcame,
He took from death the power;
  To all that follow where he goes
  At last he shows
The kingdom's secret flower.

4 The secret flower shall bloom on earth
In them that have beholden;
  The heavenly spirit shall be plain
  In them again,
As first it was of olden.

5 The spirit like a light shall shine,
Evil himself dispelling,
  The spirit like a wind shall blow,
  And death shall go
Unfeared in her own dwelling.

6 And by the spirit shall be known
Heroes and saints and sages;
  Yea, they shall walk in all men's sight,
  Amid the light
God sent to crown the ages.

Gebor'n ist uns ein Kindelein
Von einer Jungfrau reine
  Gott Vater Sohn und heil'ger Geist
  Die sind gereist
Mit Maria alleine.

2 Wir woll'n Gott loben in Ewigkeit
Darzu das Kindelein klein
  Und Mariam die Mutter sein
  Die Jungfrau fein
Woll uns ihr Gnad' mitteilen.

3 Freu dich Maria in Ewigkeit!
Darum du hast empfangen
  Den Spiegel der Dreifaltigkeit
  Dein Lob ist bereit;
Zu dir haben wir Verlangen.

4 Das Kindlein ist der Gnaden voll;
Es gibt uns gute Lehre.
  Sein Lob niemand aussprechen kann;
  Ist sonder wann
Wir danken ihm seiner Lehre.

5 Er hat gelitten den bittern Tod
Für unser Sünden alle;
  Und gibt den Sündern guten Trost,
  Hat uns erlost
Wohl von dem ewigen Fall.

6 O Herz halt uns in deiner Hut
Das wir nicht mögen sterben
  In unser Sünd und Missetat,
  O ewiger Gott
Dein' Gnad' hilf uns erwerben.

A paraphrase of 'Gebor'n ist uns ein Kindelein'. Melody in the Mainz *Cantual*, 1605, but certainly of the sixteenth century, and perhaps earlier, says Riemann. Words and melody in the Cologne *Gesangbuch*, 1634.

98 SPRING HAS COME

(SPRING)

Piae Cantiones, 1582
Tr. Steuart Wilson

Ibid.
(G.S.)

SOPRANO
ALTO
TENOR
BASS
1. Now the spring has come a - gain,
Cold and wet are quite for - got,
1st time
2nd time
joy and warmth will fol - - low;
north - ward flies the swal - - low;
Ov - er sea and land and air spring's soft touch is
All our sin - ews feel new strung, hearts are light that
ev - 'ry - where And the world looks clean - - er;
once were wrung, Youth - ful zests are keen - - er.

2 All the woods are new in leaf, all the fruit is budding,
Bees are humming round the hive, done with winter's brooding;
Seas are calm and blue again, clouds no more foretell the rain,
Winds are soft and tender;
High above, the kingly sun laughs once more his course to run,
Shines in all his splendour.

3 God is in the midst of her, God commands her duty;
Earth does but reflect his light, mirrors back his beauty;
God's the fount whence all things flow, great and small, above, below,
God's their only maker:
We but poorest patterns are of that mind beyond compare,
God our great creator.

Neale turned this Spring carol, 'In vernali tempore', from *Piae Cantiones*, 1582 (see note to No. 141), into a Christmas carol in 1853 ('O'er the hill and o'er the vale'), as he did also with No. 99.

99 FLOWER CAROL
(SPRING)

Piae Cantiones, 1582
Tr. O. B. C.

Ibid.
(M. S.)

This harmonization may be used throughout if preferred
SOPRANO
ALTO
TENOR
BASS
1. Spring has now un-wrapped the flowers, Day is fast re - viv - ing,
Life in all her grow - ing powers Towards the light is striv - ing:
Gone the i - ron touch of cold, Win - ter time and frost time,
Seed-lings, work-ing through the mould, Now make up for lost___ time.

2 Herb and plant that, winter long,
Slumbered at their leisure,
Now bestirring, green and strong,
Find in growth their pleasure:
All the world with beauty fills,
Gold the green enhancing;
Flowers make glee among the hills,
And set the meadows dancing.

3 Through each wonder of fair days
God himself expresses;
Beauty follows all his ways,
As the world he blesses:
So, as he renews the earth,
Artist without rival,
In his grace of glad new birth
We must seek revival.

4 Earth puts on her dress of glee;
Flowers and grasses hide her;
We go forth in charity—
Brothers all beside her;
For, as man this glory sees
In the awakening season,
Reason learns the heart's decrees,
And hearts are led by reason.

5 Praise the Maker, all ye saints;
He with glory girt you,
He who skies and meadows paints
Fashioned all your virtue;
Praise him, seers, heroes, kings,
Heralds of perfection;
Brothers, praise him, for he brings
All to resurrection!

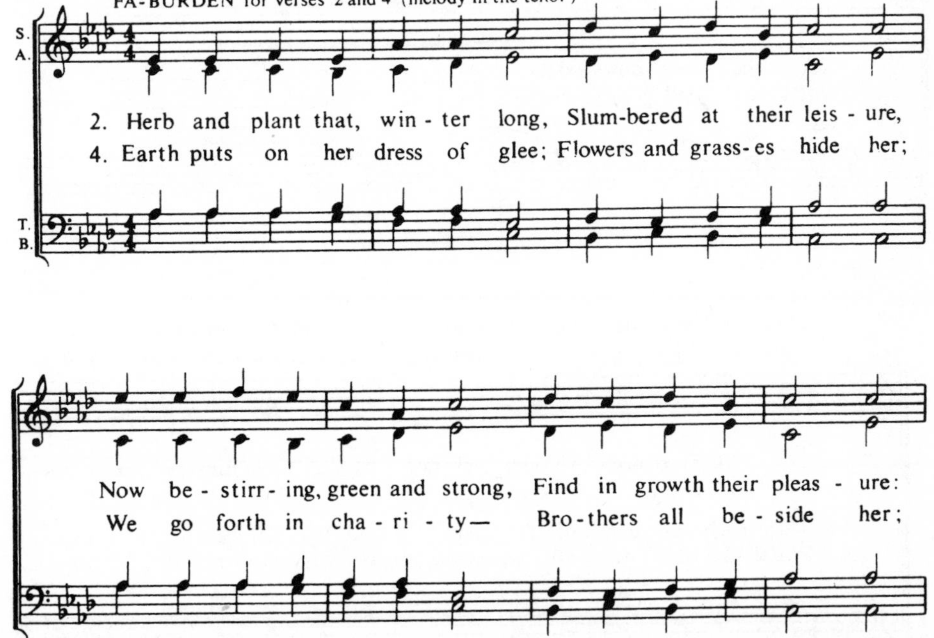
FA-BURDEN for verses 2 and 4 (melody in the tenor)
S.
A.
T.
B.
2. Herb and plant that, win - ter long, Slum-bered at their leis - ure,
4. Earth puts on her dress of glee; Flowers and grass-es hide her;
Now be - stirr - ing, green and strong, Find in growth their pleas - ure:
We go forth in cha - ri - ty— Bro-thers all be - side her;

99—Flower Carol

All the world with beau - ty fills, Gold the green en - hanc - - ing; Flowers make glee a - mong the hills, And set the mea - dows danc - - - ing.
For, as man this glo - ry sees In the a-wak'n - ing sea - - son, Rea - son learns the heart's de - crees, And hearts are led by rea - - - son.
set the mea - dows danc - - - ing.
hearts are led by rea - - - son.
danc - - - ing.
rea - - - son.
Verses 3 and 5
3. Thro' each won - der of fair days God him-self ex - press - es;
5. Praise the Mak - er, all ye saints; He with glo - ry girt you,
S.
A.
3. Thro' each won-der of fair days God him-self ex - press -
5. Praise the Mak-er, all ye saints; He with glo-ry girt
3. Thro' each won - der of fair days God him-self ex - press - es;
5. Praise the Mak - er, all ye saints; He with glo - ry girt you,
T.
B.

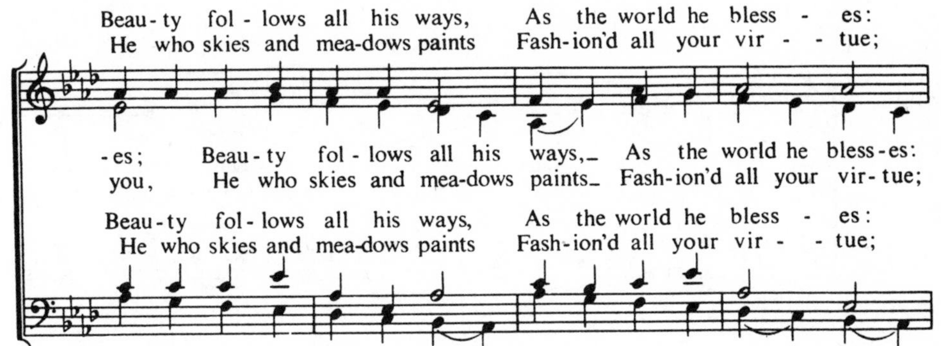
Beau-ty fol-lows all his ways, As the world he bless - - es:
He who skies and mea-dows paints Fash-ion'd all your vir - - tue;
-es; Beau-ty fol-lows all his ways,_ As the world he bless-es:
you, He who skies and mea-dows paints_ Fash-ion'd all your vir-tue;
Beau-ty fol-lows all his ways, As the world he bless - - es:
He who skies and mea-dows paints Fash-ion'd all your vir - - tue;

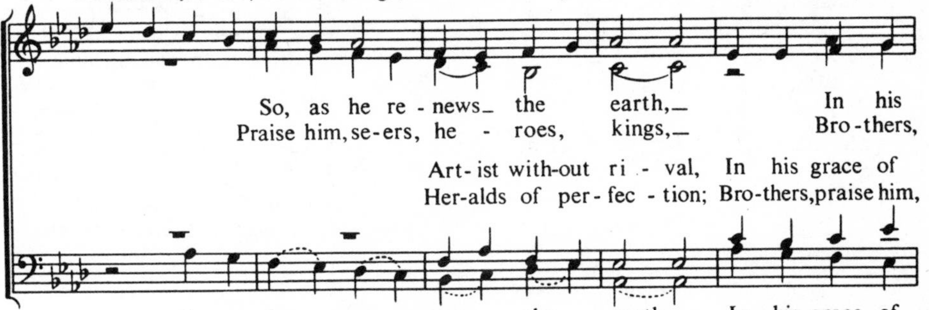
So, as he re-news the earth, Art-ist with-out ri - val, In his grace of
Praise him, se-ers, he-roes, kings, Her-alds of per-fec - tion; Bro-thers, praise him,
So, as he re - news_ the earth,_ In his
Praise him, se-ers, he - roes, kings,_ Bro-thers,
Art-ist with-out ri - val, In his grace of
Her-alds of per-fec - tion; Bro-thers, praise him,
So, as he_ re - news_ the_ earth,_ In his grace of
Praise him, se - ers, he-roes, Her-alds of per-fec - tion; Bro-thers, praise him,

glad new birth We must seek re - vi - - - - val.
for he brings All to re - sur - rec - - - - tion!
grace of glad new birth We must seek_ re - - vi - val.
praise him, for he brings All to re - - sur - - rec - tion!
glad new birth We must seek re - vi - - - - val.
for he brings All to re - sur - rec - - - - tion!
glad_ new_ birth_ We must seek re - vi - val.
for_ he_ brings_ All to re - sur - rec - tion!

This is a free translation, with a doxology, of the words proper to the melody of No. 136, 'Tempus adest floridum', the Spring carol which Neale turned into a Christmas carol by writing his rendering of the legend of 'Good King Wenceslas'. We have therefore reprinted the proper tune here, with the suggestion that it should be sung as a Spring carol.

100 THE MESSAGE
(GENERAL)

Pr. E. B. G.
Dutch
(M.S.)
SOPRANO
ALTO
TENOR
BASS
1. A mes - sage came to a mai - den young; The an - gel stood be - side her.
2. No great - er news could a mes - sen-ger bring; For 'twas from that young mo - ther
(Tenors) In shi - ning robes and with gold-en tongue, He told what should be - tide her: The
He came, who walked on the earth as a king, And yet was all men's bro - ther: His
In shi - ning robes and with gold - en tongue, He
He came, who walked on the earth as a king, And
maid was lost in won - der—Her world was
truth has spread like leav - en, 'Twill mar - ry

rent — a - sun - - der— Ah! how— could— she Christ's mo - ther
earth — to heav - - en, Till all — a - - gree In cha - ri -

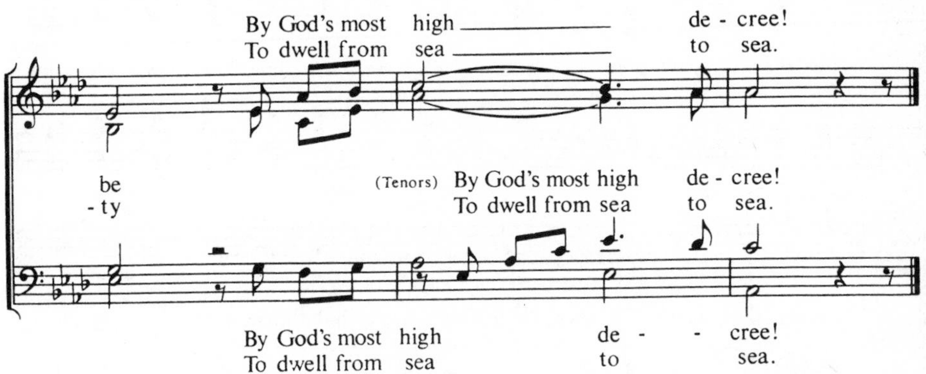
By God's most high — de - cree!
To dwell from sea — to sea.
be
- ty
(Tenors) By God's most high de - cree!
To dwell from sea to sea.
By God's most high de - - cree!
To dwell from sea to sea.

3 He came, God's Word to the world here below;
And round him there did gather
A band who found that this teacher to know
Was e'en to know the Father:
He healed the sick who sought him,
Forgave the foes who fought him;
Beside the sea
Of Galilee
He set the nations free.

4 And sometimes trumpets from Sion ring out,
And tramping comes, and drumming—
'Thy kingdom come,' so we cry; and they shout,
'It comes!' and still 'tis coming—
Far, far ahead, to win us,
Yet with us, nay within us;
Till all shall see
That King is he,
The Love from Galilee!

Melody and words of 'De Boodschap van Maria' (Er was een maagdetje) which is freely translated in the first verse. From the *Nederlandsch Volksliederenboek*, 1896.

101 GEMS OF DAY

LE VERMEIL DU SOLEIL

(GENERAL)

N. Denisot
Pr. Patrick R. Chalmers

French, 1553
(M.S.)

SOPRANO
ALTO
1. All the gay gems of day– Pearls the morn-ing sky a-dorn-ing,
Man-i-fold gems of gold, Gold-en get-ting now day's set-ting,
TENOR
BASS
Are the sun's pret-ty ones Of his shi-ning or de-cli-ning,
Are his joys, birth-day toys_These God's ve-ry babe make mer - - ry;

2 When Sir Sun his course done,
Westward stooping home's gone drooping,
It is naught, look! new wrought
Joy and beauty bear his duty—
Planets peep down night's deep,
Softly seeming gold and dreaming
Jasmine o'er heaven's door,
Lest God's only babe fall lonely.

3 Newly-born King of morn,
Noon and night time, dark and light time,
Be our light, day and night,
Ne'er withholden, greatlier golden
Than the boon sun at noon,
Than the garland sheen of starland;
Saviour small, light us all—
Light our blindness, of thy kindness!

Le vermeil du soleil
Quand l'aurore nous redore
Tous les cieux radieux
Ou quand même en l'extrême
De son jour fait séjour
Près la tente de sa tante
Chéant bas ne veut pas
Que sa roue plus on loue.

2 C'est bien peu que son feu
Aille arrière sa lumière
En égard au regard
De la voie qui flamboie
Cette nuit à minuit
Sous l'étoile qui au voile
Sombre et noir fait devoir
A son maître qui vient naître.

3 Mais oyez et voyez
La naissance l'Excellence
De la nuit qui nous luit
Précieuse, bienheureuse,
Nuit des nuits, nos ennuis
Dieu déchasse, Dieu nous trace
Ses saints pas, Dieu met bas
Toute outrance et puissance.

Paraphrased from 'Le vermeil du soleil', *Cantiques du Premier Advénement de Jésus-Christ*, par Le Comte d'Alsinois (Nicholas Denisot), Paris, 1553. There are twenty verses in the original; nine of them will be found in *A Book of Old Carols*, by H. J. L. J. Massé and Charles Kennedy Scott, 1907, No. 15, p. 24. The melody is stated to be by Marc-Antoine Muret in a MS. note, apparently of the sixteenth century, in the British Museum copy.

102 GABRIEL'S MESSAGE
(GENERAL: EASTER)

Piae Cantiones, 1582
Tr. J. M. Neale

Ibid.
(G. S.)

SOPRANO
ALTO
1. Ga-briel's mes-sage does a - way Sa-tan's curse and Sa-tan's sway, Out of
2. He that comes des-pised shall reign; He that can-not die, be slain; Death by
TENOR
BASS

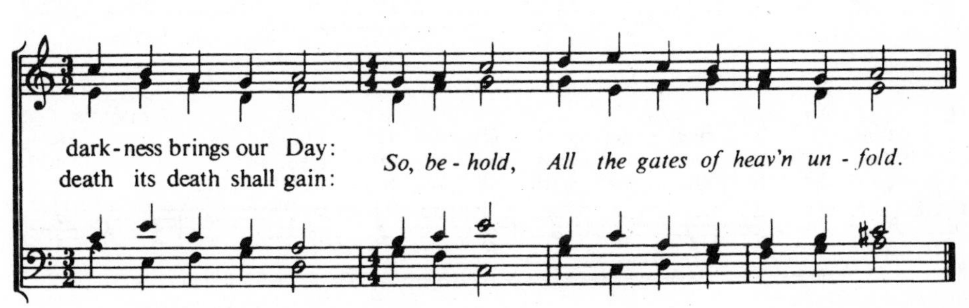
dark-ness brings our Day:
death its death shall gain:
So, be - hold, All the gates of heav'n un - fold.

3 Weakness shall the strong confound;
By the hands, in grave-clothes wound,
Adam's chains shall be unbound:

So, behold, etc.

4 By the sword that was his own,
By that sword, and that alone,
Shall Goliath be o'erthrown:

So, behold, etc.

5 Art by art shall be assailed;
To the cross shall Life be nailed;
From the grave shall Hope be hailed:

So, behold, etc.

The words, written by Neale in 1853, to this tune have been slightly altered, to bring them more in accordance with the original of 'Angelus emittitur' upon which they were based; the original refrain is 'Igitur Porta coeli panditur' and Neale's refrain runs 'Therefore sing,—Glory to the Infant King'. Two Christmas verses not in the original are omitted. The earliest known version is in *Piae Cantiones*, 1582 (see note to No. 141).

103 THE BIRDS
(GENERAL)

Tr. O.B.C.

Czech
(M.S.)

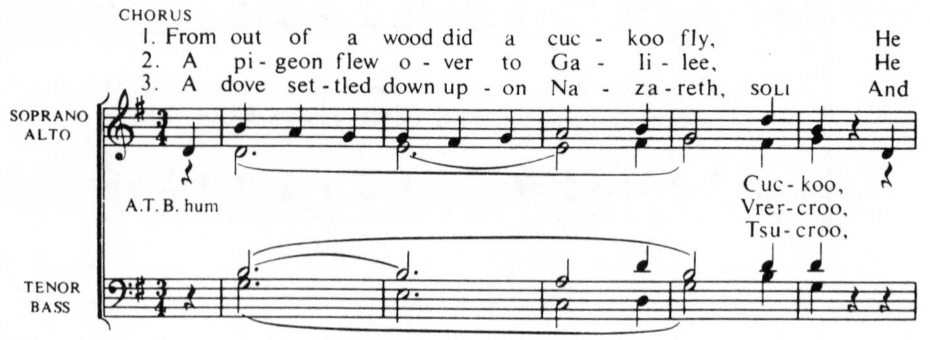

CHORUS
1. From out of a wood did a cuc - koo fly, He
2. A pi - geon flew o - ver to Ga - li - lee, He
3. A dove set - tled down up - on Na - za - reth, SOLI And
SOPRANO
ALTO
A.T.B. hum
Cuc - koo,
Vrer - croo,
Tsu - croo,
TENOR
BASS

came to a man - ger with joy - ful cry,
strut - ted and cooed, and was full of glee,
ten - der - ly chant - ed with all his breath SOLI
CHORUS
He
And
'O
(hum)
Cuc - koo;
Vrer - croo,
Tsu - croo:

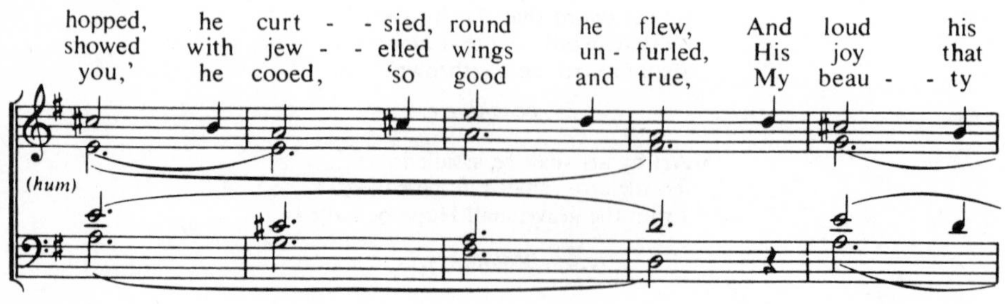

hopped, he curt - - sied, round he flew, And loud his
showed with jew - - elled wings un - furled, His joy that
you,' he cooed, 'so good and true, My beau - - ty
(hum)

ju - - bi - la - tion grew,
Christ was in the world,
do I give to you—
SOLI
Cuc - koo, cuc - koo, cuc - koo.
Vrer - croo, vrer - croo, vrer - croo.
Tsu - croo, tsu - croo, tsu - croo'.

A translation of an unpublished carol, 'Zezulka z lesa vylitla, kuku', which was taken down from a Czech peasant girl in the Christmas of 1921 at Policka, in the hills between Bohemia and Moravia, and kindly communicated by Miss Jakubičková.

104 HOW BRIGHTLY BEAMS

WIE SCHÖN LEUCHTET

(GENERAL: EPIPHANY: EASTER)

FIRST VERSION

Nicolai and Schlegel
Tr. C. Winkworth

German (P. Nicolai?)
(harm. J. S. Bach)

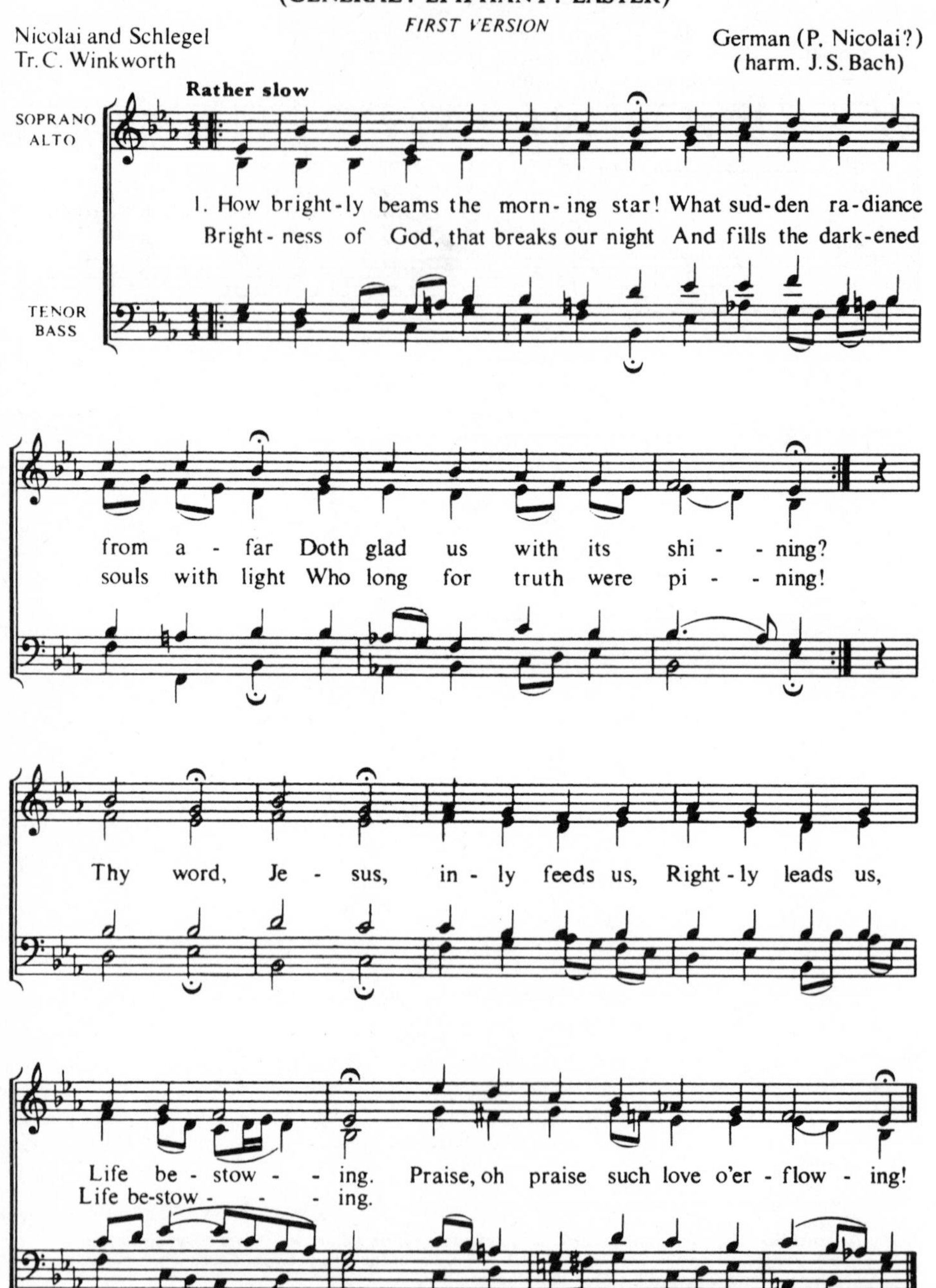

Rather slow
SOPRANO
ALTO
TENOR
BASS
1. How bright-ly beams the morn-ing star! What sud-den ra-diance from a - far Doth glad us with its shi - - ning?
Bright-ness of God, that breaks our night And fills the dark-ened souls with light Who long for truth were pi - - ning!
Thy word, Je - sus, in - ly feeds us, Right-ly leads us, Life be - stow - - ing.
Life be-stow - - - ing.
Praise, oh praise such love o'er - flow - ing!

2 Through thee alone can we be blest;
Then deep be on our hearts imprest
  The love that thou hast borne us;
So make us ready to fulfil
With burning zeal thy holy will,
  Though men may vex or scorn us;
Saviour, let us never lose thee,
    For we choose thee,
    Thirst to know thee;
All we are and have we owe thee!

3 O praise to him who came to save,
Who conquer'd death and burst the grave;
  Each day new praise resoundeth
To him the Lamb who once was slain,
The friend whom none shall trust in vain,
  Whose grace for ay aboundeth;
Sing, ye heavens, tell the story
    Of his glory,
    Till his praises
Flood with light earth's darkest places!

WIE schön leuchtet der Morgenstern
Voll Gnad' und Wahrheit von dem Herrn,
Die süsse Wurzel Jesse!
Du Sohn Davids aus Jacobs Stamm,
Mein König und mein Bräutigam,
Hast mir mein Herz besessen.
Lieblich, freundlich,
  Schön und herrlich,
  Gross und ehrlich,
Reich von Gaben,
Hoch und sehr prächtig erhaben.

2 Geuss sehr tief in mein Herz hinein
O du, mein Herr und Gott allein,
Die Flamme deiner Liebe,
Dass ich beständig in dir bleib'
Und mich kein Unfall von dir treib',
Nichts kränke noch betrübe.
In dir lass mir
  Ohn' Aufhören
  Sich vermehren
Lieb' und Freude,
Dass der Tod uns selbst nicht scheide.

3 Sing unserm Gott recht oft und viel
Und lasst andächtig Saitenspiel
Ganz freudenreich erschallen
Dem allerliebsten Jesulein,
Dem wunderschönen Braütigam mein,
Zu Ehren und Gefallen.
  Singet, springet,
  Jubilieret, triumphieret
Dankt dem Herrn!
Gross ist der König der Ehren.

Three verses of the seven in the recast by J. A. Schlegel (1721-93), 'Wie herrlich strahlt der Morgenstern', of 'Wie schön leuchtet der Morgenstern', which appeared with the tune in Nicolai's *Freudenspiegel*, 1599. The famous tune, to which very soon many city chimes in Germany were set, was published with Nicolai's hymn, and may therefore be by the author and composer of 'Wachet auf'. It may in part have been suggested by earlier melodies, especially by 'Resonet in Laudibus' (No. 77). The translation is almost entirely that of Miss C. Winkworth, 1863. See No. 193, where this tune is used as accompaniment to Cornelius's song 'The Kings'.

104 HOW BRIGHTLY BEAMS

WIE SCHÖN LEUCHTET

(GENERAL: EPIPHANY: EASTER)

SECOND VERSION

Nicolai and Schlegel
Tr. C. Winkworth
German (P. Nicolai?)
(harm. F. Mendelssohn-Bartholdy)
Rather slow
SOPRANO
ALTO
TENOR
BASS
1. How bright-ly beams the morn-ing star! What sud-den ra-diance from a - far Doth glad us with its shi - - ning?
Bright-ness of God, that breaks our night And fills the dark-ened souls with light Who long for truth were pi - - ning!
Thy word, Je - sus, in - ly feeds us, Right-ly leads us, Life be - stow - ing. Praise, oh praise such love o'er - flow - - ing!

2 Through thee alone can we be blest;
Then deep be on our hearts imprest
The love that thou hast borne us;
So make us ready to fulfil
With burning zeal thy holy will,
Though men may vex or scorn us;
Saviour, let us never lose thee,
For we choose thee,
Thirst to know thee;
All we are and have we owe thee!

3 O praise to him who came to save,
Who conquer'd death and burst the grave;
Each day new praise resoundeth
To him the Lamb who once was slain,
The friend whom none shall trust in vain,
Whose grace for ay aboundeth;
Sing, ye heavens, tell the story
Of his glory,
Till his praises
Flood with light earth's darkest places!

Wie schön leuchtet der Morgenstern
Voll Gnad' und Wahrheit von dem Herrn,
Die süsse Wurzel Jesse!
Du Sohn Davids aus Jacobs Stamm,
Mein König und mein Bräutigam,
Hast mir mein Herz besessen.
Lieblich, freundlich,
Schön und herrlich,
Gross und ehrlich,
Reich von Gaben,
Hoch und sehr prächtig erhaben.

2 Geuss sehr tief in mein Herz hinein
O du, mein Herr und Gott allein,
Die Flamme deiner Liebe,
Dass ich beständig in dir bleib'
Und mich kein Unfall von dir treib',
Nichts kränke noch betrübe.
In dir lass mir
Ohn' Aufhören
Sich vermehren
Lieb' und Freude,
Dass der Tod uns selbst nicht scheide.

3 Sing unserm Gott recht oft und viel
Und lasst andächtig Saitenspiel
Ganz freudenreich erschallen
Dem allerliebsten Jesulein,
Dem wunderschönen Braütigam mein,
Zu Ehren und Gefallen.
Singet, springet,
Jubilieret, triumphieret
Dankt dem Herrn!
Gross ist der König der Ehren.

Three verses of the seven in the recast by J. A. Schlegel (1721-93), 'Wie herrlich strahlt der Morgenstern', of 'Wie schön leuchtet der Morgenstern', which appeared with the tune in Nicolai's *Freudenspiegel*, 1599. The famous tune, to which very soon many city chimes in Germany were set, was published with Nicolai's hymn, and may therefore be by the author and composer of 'Wachet auf'. It may in part have been suggested by earlier melodies, especially by 'Resonet in Laudibus' (No. 77). The translation is almost entirely that of Miss C. Winkworth, 1863. See No. 193, where this tune is used as accompaniment to Cornelius's song 'The Kings'.

105 THE GARDEN OF JESUS

(GENERAL)

Tr. E. B. G.

Dutch, 1633
(Geoffrey Shaw)

SOPRANO
ALTO
TENOR
BASS
1. Lord Je - sus hath a gar-den, full of flow-ers gay, Where you and I can
2. There bloom-eth white the li - ly, flower of Pu - ri - ty: The fra-grant vio-let
ga - ther nose - gays all___the day:
hides there, sweet Hu - mi - li - ty:
There an-gels sing in ju- bi-lant ring, With
dul- ci-mers and lutes, And_harps, and cym-bals, trum-pets, pipes, And gen-tle, sooth-ing
flutes, And__ harps, and cym-bals, trum-pets, pipes, And gen-tle flutes.___

3 The rose's name is Patience, pruned to greater might;
The marigold's, Obedience, plentiful and bright:
There angels sing etc.

4 And Hope and Faith are there; but of these three the best
Is Love, whose crown-imperial spreads o'er all the rest:
There angels sing etc.

5 And one thing fairest is in all that lovely maze,
The gardener, Jesus Christ, whom all the flowers praise:
There angels sing etc.

6 O Jesus, all my good and all my bliss! Ah me!
Thy garden make my heart, which ready is for thee!
There angels sing etc.

The Dutch words and melody of 'Jesus' Bloemhof' (beginning 'Heer Jesus heeft een hofken waart vol bloemen staat') occur in *Geestlijke Harmonie* (1633), and were reprinted in *Oude en Nieuwere Kerst-Liederen* (1852). A translation ('Our Master hath a garden') by S. S. Greatheed was printed in *The Ecclesiologist* for February, 1856, and was included by E. Sedding in *Antient Christmas Carols*, 1860, and in *The People's Hymnal*, 1867. It does not, however, quite fit the melody; and therefore, while we have preserved the 'gentle, soothing' flutes, we give a new translation here.

106 SO, BROTHER
FESANS RAIJOUISSANCE
(GENERAL)

Père Christin Prost
Pr. A.A. Milne

Besançon
(M.S.)

Moderately quick
SOPRANO
ALTO
TENOR
BASS
1. Now, bro - thers, lift your voi - ces, And laugh and dance and sing,— For all the world re - joi - ces That Christ the Lord is King.— With joy in him to arm you The de - vil can not harm you: So, bro - ther! laugh and sing,
2. Poor Sa - tan, you can hear him, Is ra - ging down in hell,— For now there's none to fear him, And none to wish him well.— The fires that he was keep - ing Are on his foot - steps creep - ing: So, bro - ther! laugh and sing That Christ the Lord is King.—
3. And fierc - er now and fast - er The flames come roar - ing in — On him that was their mas - ter, On Sa - tan, prince of sin.— Then, bro - ther, as he lies there, Then, bro - ther, as he dies there, Come laugh and dance and sing—

A paraphrase of three verses (out of twelve) in the original carol 'Fesans raijouissance' (see overleaf) written by Père Christin Prost, a Capuchin friar who died in 1676. His carols were reprinted in *Recueil de Noëls anciens au patois de Besançon*, edited by Th. Belamy, 1842. The old air on which the carol was written was known as 'Je suis dans la tristesse' or 'De turlu turlutu'.

FESANS raijouissance,
Risans, dansans, chantans
Ca voicy ne naissance
Que tout le monde aitend.
In Prince ot né su tare
Que vint finir lai gare
Et tur-lu, tur-lu-tu
Tout perissa sans lu.

2 Lou Diable peste, enraige
D'être dedans l'Enfa;
Lou droule ouzé en caige,
Que lou peut Lucifa,
Qu'ot dedans ne chandére
D'huile ou d'autre maitére
Et tur-lu, tur-lu-tu
Y n'en soëthirct pu.

3 Pourquoi donc, peute béte,
Ai-te tanta Adam?
Qu'aivouë-te dans lai téte,
Dit, malheureux Satan?
Te nous crayon tous pâdre;
Main voici lou grand Matre
Et tur-lu, tur-lu-tu
Qu'ot pou nous daicendu.

107 PRAISE TO GOD
(GENERAL)

Tr. A. F. D.

Russian
(M. S.)

Moderato e maestoso

SOPRANO
ALTO

Praise to God in the high - est! Bless us, O
May the truth in its beau - ty flou - rish tri -
May the good be o - beyed, and e - vil be
Peace on earth, and good - will,— be ev - er a -

TENOR
BASS

(S.A.) Praise to God– in the
Fine
Fa - ther!
-um - phant:
con - quered:
- mongst us:
Praise– to— thee.
(T. B.)
Guide and pros - per the
May the mills bring us
Give us laugh - ter, and
Melody in tenor
Fine

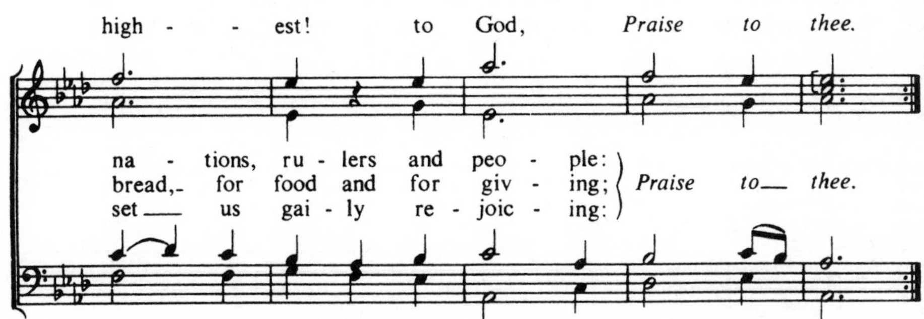

high - - est! to God, Praise to thee.
na - tions, ru - lers and peo - ple:
bread,– for food and for giv - ing;
set — us gai - ly re - joic - ing:
Praise to— thee.

'Slava Bogu na nebye' was printed by Yakushkin in 1815, and exists in many variants, as well as in Rimsky-Korsakov, who calls it a Christmas Song, though its many verses, from which we have selected, are all of general national application. The melody was used by Beethoven in his Quartet, Op. 59, No. 2; by Rimsky-Korsakov in his cantata 'Slava'; and by Mussorgsky in the Coronation Scene of 'Boris Godunov'.

108 THE KINGDOM

QUOI, MA VOISINE?

(GENERAL)

François Colletet (1675)
Pr. Patrick R. Chalmers
Angevin
(M.S.)
Rather quickly
SOPRANO
ALTO
TENOR
BASS
1. 'O, I have seen_ a king's new ba - by,' Su - san she said,
2. 'O the king's son_ he lies_ so spare - ly,' Su - san she told,
'Joy up-on his bright,_ dear birth - day be And on his bright head!'
'No_ lace to lap - pen him_ so fair - ly, No blue and gold.'
Cathe-rine, her kind - ly com - rade, then did Say, 'Show me too—
'Prince,–and he ne'er has fine a - dorn - ing?' Cath - er - ine cried,
Son of a king must lie so splen-did All gold_ and blue!'
'Prince, and the Sun, my giri, at morn-ing!' The maid_ re - plied.

3 'Where, then's his mighty kingdom, say
you?'
'Everywhere.'
'So! and how may I know it, pray you?'
'Kindness is there.'
'Kings have bright swords to follow after,
Bugles to ring?'
'Nay, here is only children's laughter,
Here thrushes sing.'

4 'Whom, say now, shall he rule anon? He
Coming to reign?'
'Both bird and beast and man, my bonny,
Mountain and plain.'
'These shall he hold and have securely—
How? Tell me, friend?'
'Only by being a servant, surely,
Unto the end.'

5 'Susan, who'll herald him, this stranger,
This kingly boy?'
'Just a lit star above a manger
Laughing for joy.'
'Still, gossip, I might doubt him, maybe,
Knowing no thing?'
'Dear my heart, would you doubt a baby
To be a King?'

Quoi, ma voisine, est-tu fâchée?
Dis-moi pourquoi.
Veux-tu venir voir l'accouchée
Avecque moi?
C'est une dame fort discrète,
Ce m'a-t-on dit,
Qui nous a produit le prophète
Souvent prédit.

2 Je le veux, allons, ma commère,
C'est mon désir.
Nous verrons l'enfant et sa mère
Tout à loisir.
Aurons-nous pas de la dragée
Et du gâteau?
La salle est-elle bien rangée,
Y fait-il beau?

3 Ah, ma bergère, tu te trompes
Bien lourdement;
Elle ne demande pas les pompes
Ni l'ornement.
Dedans une chétive étable
Se veut ranger,
Où n'y a ni buffet, ni table
Pour y manger.

4 Encore faut-il que l'accouchée
Ait un berceau,
Pour bercer, quand elle est couchée,
L'enfant nouveau:
N'a-t-elle pas garde et servante
Pour la servir?
N'est-elle pas assez puissante
D'y subvenir.

5 L'enfant a pour berceau la crèche
Pour sommeiller.
Et une botte d'herbe sèche
Pour oreiller;
Elle a pour boute compagnie
Son cher baron,
Elle a un boeuf pour sa mégnie
Et un ânon.

Words written for the older, modal, melody in Henri Lemeignen, *Vieux Noëls* (Nantes, 1876), and in Grimault, of the Angevin carol, 'Quoi ma voisine', a dialogue between two women, here freely paraphrased.

109 O LITTLE ONE

O JESULEIN SÜSS

(GENERAL)

FIRST VERSION

German, S. Scheidt, 1650
Tr. O. B. C.

Ibid.
(M.S.)

SOPRANO
ALTO
1. O lit - tle one sweet, O lit - tle one mild, Thy Fa-ther's pur-pose thou
2. O lit - tle one sweet, O lit - tle one mild, With joy thou hast___ the
TENOR
BASS

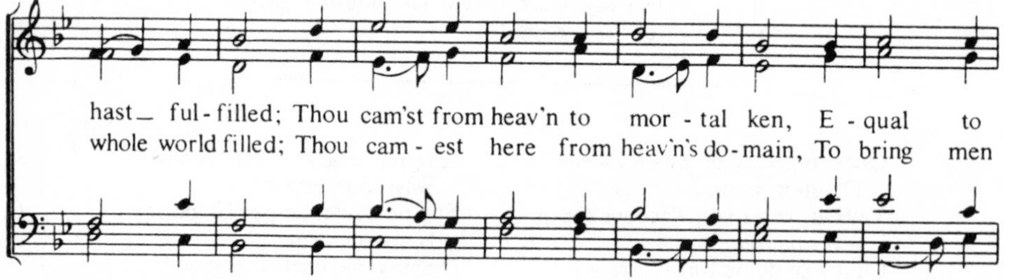

hast_ ful-filled; Thou cam'st from heav'n to mor - tal ken, E - qual to
whole world filled; Thou cam - est here from heav'n's do-main, To bring men

be___with us poor men, O lit - tle one sweet, O lit - tle one mild.
com- fort in their pain, O lit - tle one sweet, O lit - tle one mild.

3 O little one sweet, O little one mild,
In thee love's beauties are all distilled;
Then light in us thy love's bright flame,
That we may give thee back the same,
O little one sweet, O little one mild.

4 O little one sweet, O little one mild,
Help us to do as thou hast willed.
Lo, all we have belongs to thee!
Ah, keep us in our fealty!
O little one sweet, O little one mild.

109 O LITTLE ONE

O JESULEIN SÜSS

(GENERAL)

SECOND VERSION
German, S. Scheidt, 1650
Tr. O.B.C.
Ibid.
(harm. J. S. Bach)
Rather slowly
SOPRANO
ALTO
TENOR
BASS
*
1. O lit - tle one sweet, O lit - tle one mild, Thy Fa - ther's purpose thou hast ful - filled; Thou cam'st from heav'n to mor - tal ken, E - qual to be with us poor men, O lit - tle one sweet, O lit - tle one mild.
2. O lit - tle one sweet, O lit - tle one mild, With joy thou hast the whole world filled; Thou cam - est here from heav'n's do - main, To bring men com - fort in their pain, O lit - tle one sweet, O lit - tle one mild.

*If sung in conjunction with the first version the melody rhythm of this bar may be altered for the sake of consistency.

Scheidt's version, 'O Jesulein süss, O Jesulein mild, Des Vaters Will'n hast du erfüllt' (see overleaf), is in his *Tabulaturbuch*, 1650. Bach set it as a chorale melody with figured bass in Schemelli's *Gesangbuch*, 1736. The melody appears also in *Seelenharphe* (Halle, 1650) to the words 'Komm, heiliger Geist mit deiner Gnad'.

O Jesulein süss, O Jesulein mild,
Des Vaters Will'n hast du erfüllt,
Bist kommen aus dem Himmelreich
Uns armen Menschen worden gleich,
O Jesulein süss, O Jesulein mild.

2 O Jesulein süss, O Jesulein mild,
Des Vaters Zorn hast du gestillt.
Du zählst für uns all uns're Schuld
Und schaffst uns deines Vaters Huld,
O Jesulein süss, O Jesulein mild.

3 O Jesulein süss, O Jesulein mild,
Du bist der Lieb' ein Ebenbild.
Zünd an in uns der Liebe Flamm',
Dass wir dich lieben allzusamm,
O Jesulein süss, O Jesulein mild.

110 JESUS OF THE MANGER

(GENERAL)

Pr. Patrick R. Chalmers

Flemish
(M.S.)

SOPRANO
ALTO
TENOR
BASS
1. Sing, good com - pa-ny, frank and free! Je - sus, when so young was he, With the lit - tle calf shared the stall; Low he lay On a day, — on a day, With the lit - tle calf in the stall Low he lay, He lay there_ for us all, us all.
2. Rouse, good com - pa-ny, rouse you, rouse! All the earth to Je - sus bows; Yet the dwell - ing that he'd im - plore Poor must stay, By my fay, — by my fay, Still the dwell - ing that he'd im - -plore Poor must stay— Man's heart on - ly must serve there - for.
3. Sing, good com - pa-ny, glad and true! God may lodge with me and you; So let's love them— all beasts and men, Kind - li - ly, As doth he, — as doth he; If we love them— all beasts and men, Kind - li - ly, God will lodge_ with us then, ah then!
He lay there_ for us all.
Man's heart on - ly there - for.
God will lodge_ with us then!

Paraphrase of 'Jesus in den Stal', printed in *Chants Populaires Flamands*, by Lootens and Feys, reprinted by E. Duncan, *Story of the Carol*, and by H. J. L. J. Massé and C. Kennedy Scott, *Book of Old Carols*.

111 THE BUILDERS

(GENERAL: DEDICATION)

GRAND DIEU! QUE DE MERVEILLES

(CHRISTMAS)

Pr. Geoffrey Dearmer

Angevin (M.S.)

Moderately quick
SOPRANO
ALTO
TENOR
BASS
1. Sing, all good peo - ple ga-thered, Your voi-ces raise in song With-
2. Each rib from pil - lars spring-ing A froz-en foun-tain plays, A -
-in this church that fa - thered Our an - cient faith so strong, So
-bove the chan - cel sing - ing In har - mon - y of praise; Like
tried and wrought to fit - ness In scorn of fire and sword; Sing,
tall trees ev - er grow - ing The diff - ering col - umns stand To
as these stones bear wit - ness, Of men who praised the Lord.
bear the vault down - throw - ing The shad - ow of God's hand.

3 At all times and unceasing,
Work well and truly done,
In loveliness increasing,
Has mellowed here in one;
The towers and piers unshaken,
The vaulting finely groined,
Time in his span hath taken
And in one glory joined.

4 Of wealth and fame and power
These masons did not know:
'Let's build,' they said, 'a tower,
Square to the winds that blow;
We are not men of culture,
Yet we are here to build
Room for a king's sepulture
And worthy of our guild.'

5 So came each beam and rafter,
Each wingèd flight of stone.
Their deathless work lives after,
Their names were never known:
For beauty did they plead not,
Yet beauty they did win,
And, like a child you heed not,
The grace of heaven crept in.

6 Here, for a workman's wages,
This glass so surely stained
Down the long aisles of ages
In glory has remained.
As brother works with brother
The glaziers worked to paint
The blue robe of the Mother,
The red robe of a saint.

7 Proud heads lie here, disowning
All but a drooping Head;
Whole hands worked here, atoning
For open Hands that bled;
Full hearts and living voices
A broken Heart proclaim;
Life after death rejoices,
And after silence, fame.

GRAND Dieu! Que de merveilles
S'accomplissent pour moi!
Mes yeux et mes oreilles,
Rendez-vous à la foi!
La force et la faiblesse,
La justice et l'amour,
La gloire et la détresse
S'unissent en ce jour.

2 La lumière immuable
Est dans l'obscurité;
Je vois dans une étable
Le Dieu de majesté.
Son trône est une crèche,
Sa cour, des pastoureaux,
Son silence nous prèche,
Son mal guérit nos maux.

3 Son enfance sans armes
En fait un triomphant;
L'enfer est aux alarmes
Aux cris d'un tendre enfant.
Sa beauté l'épouvante,
Son nom le fait frémir,
Sa douceur le tourmente
Ses pleurs le font gémir.

4 Achevez le miracle,
Adorable vainqueur;
Si j'y mets un obstacle
Triomphez de mon coeur.
Echauffez-en la glace,
Brisez sa dureté
Afin qu'y prenne place
L'ardente charité.

Since the original twenty-two verses of 'Venez à Saint-Maurice' deal in great detail with the characteristics and treasures of Angers Cathedral, the English words have been written for the general idea rather than for the details of the original, and we claim the tune as proper to them only in this most generous and spiritual sense. Topical allusions in the original fix its date as earlier than 1699 and later than 1562. The gay melody has been always attributed to Urbain Renard, but the origin and date of folk-tunes is very doubtful. The carol (which is printed by Grimault in *Noëls Angevins*) very likely grew up from some humble fiddler seeking alms outside the Cathedral of Saint-Maurice. The alternative words 'Grand Dieu! que de merveilles' are given by Roques.

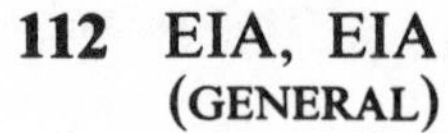

112 EIA, EIA

(GENERAL)

Cölner Psalter, 1638 — Ibid.
Pr. A. G. — (M.S.)

Moderately slow

SOPRANO
ALTO

TENOR
BASS

1. To us in Beth-lem ci - ty Was born a— lit - tle son; In him — all gen - tle gra - ces Were — ga - thered in - to — one, *Ei - a, ei - a,* Were — ga - thered in - to one.
2. And all our love and for-tune Lie in — his might-y hands; Our sor - rows, joys, and fail - ures, He — sees and un - der - stands, *Ei - a, ei - a,* He — sees and — un - der - stands.

3 O Shepherd, ever near us,
We'll go where thou dost lead;
No matter where the pasture,
With thee at hand to feed,
Eia, eia,
With thee at hand to feed.

4 No grief shall part us from thee,
However sharp the edge:
We'll serve, and do thy bidding—
O take our hearts in pledge!
Eia, eia,
Take thou our hearts in pledge!

Zu Bethlehem geboren
Ist uns ein Kindelein;
Das hab' ich auserkoren
Sein Eigen will ich sein,
Eia, eia,
Sein Eigen will ich sein.

2 In seine Lieb' versenken
Will ich mich ganz hinab.
Mein Herz will ich ihm schenken
Und alles, was ich hab',
Eia, eia,
Und alles, was ich hab'.

3 O Kindelein, von Herzen
Will ich dich lieben sehr
In Freuden und in Schmerzen
Je länger, mehr und mehr,
Eia, eia,
Je länger, mehr und mehr.

4 Dazu dein Gnad' mir gebe
Bitt' ich aus Herzensgrund,
Dass ich allein dir lebe
Jetzt und zu aller Stund',
Eia, eia,
Jetzt und zu aller Stund'.

The folk-carol here paraphrased, 'Zu Bethlehem geboren', appears first in print in the *Cölner Psalter*, 1638. Riemann reprinted this version from Nordstern's *Führer zur Seligkeit*, 1671.

113 SPANISH CAROL
(NATIVITY)

Galician
Tr. J. B. Trend
(arr. from Pedrell)
In moderate time
VOICES IN UNISON
1. Up now, lag-gard-ly lass - es, Up, a - wake and a - way!
2. See the tears in his eyes, now; (Sleep, my pret - ty one, sleep!)
Out and gone be-fore cock - crow, On the road be-fore day!
Let him dream when he can, now; (Sleep, my in - no-cent, sleep!)
Ma - ry meek and gen - tle, Rose of Je - ri - cho,
Ah, my pre - cious jew - el, Great the grief and pain,
Bore a babe and laid him In a man - ger low.
Suf - fered through the wide world For the sins___ of men!

'Panxoliña de Nadal', a Spanish carol from Galicia. The melody is from Pedrell, *Cancionero musical;* the words translated from the *Cancionero popular gallego* of J. Pérez Ballesteros. Cf. No. 81.

PART II
TRADITIONAL CAROL TUNES
SET TO OTHER TRADITIONAL OR OLD TEXTS

114 NO ROOM IN THE INN
(ADVENT)

Traditional

Traditional (M.S.)

In moderate time
SOPRANO
ALTO
TENOR
BASS
1. When Cae-sar Au-gust-us had raised a tax-a-tion, He as-sessed all the peo-ple that dwelt in the na-tion; The Jews at that time be-ing un-der Rome's sway Ap-peared in the ci-ty their tri-bute to pay:
2. Then Jo-seph and Ma-ry, who from Da-vid did spring, Went up to the ci-ty of Da-vid their king, And, there be-ing en-tered, cold wel-come they find: From the rich to the poor they are most-ly un-kind.

3 They sought entertainment, but none could they find,
Great numbers of strangers had fillèd the inn;
They knockèd and callèd all this at the door,
But found not a friend where in kind they had store;

4 Their kindred accounted they come were too soon;
'Too late,' said the innkeeper, 'here is no room.'
Amongst strangers and kinsfolk cold welcome they find —
From the rich to the poor they are mostly unkind.

5 Good Joseph was troubled, but most for his dear,
For her blessèd burden whose time now drew near;
His heart with true sorrow was sorely afflicted
That his virgin spouse was so rudely neglected.

6 He could get no house-room who houses did frame,
But Joseph and Mary must go as they came,
For little is the favour the poor man can find —
From the rich to the poor they are mostly unkind.

7 Whilst the great and the wealthy do frolic in hall,
Possess all the ground-rooms and chambers and all,
Poor Joseph and Mary are thrust in a stable
In Bethlehem city, ground inhospitáble,

8 And with their mean lodging contented they be:
For the minds of the just with their fortunes agree;
They bear all affronts with their meekness of mind,
And be not offended though the rich be unkind.

9 O Bethlehem, Bethlehem, welcome this stranger
That was born in a stable and laid in a manger;
For he is a physician to heal all our smarts—
Come welcome, sweet Jesus, and lodge in our hearts.

This simple and charming carol was probably sung to one of the traditional 'Virgin unspotted' tunes (cf. No. 4). We have chosen the one printed by Sandys in 1833. The text is also from Sandys, very slightly altered.

115 JOSEPH AND MARY
(ADVENT AND CHRISTMAS)

Traditional

English traditional
(R.V.W.)

Andante
VOICES IN UNISON
1. O, Jo - seph being an old man tru - ly, He married a vir - gin fair and free; A pur - er vir - gin could no man see Than he chose for his wife and his dear - est
- to the place where he was born, Un - - to the Em - per - or to be sworn, To pay a tri - bute that's du - ly known, Both for him - self and his dear - est
were they con - strain - ed pre - sent - ly With - in a sta - ble all night to lie, Where they did ox - en and as - ses tie, With his true love and his dear - est
ACCPT.
mf

Copyright, 1920, by Stainer & Bell Ltd.

dear. 2. They liv - - ed both in joy and bliss; But now a strict com-mand-ment is, In Jew - ry - land no man should miss To go a - - long with his dear - est dear,
dear. 4. And when they were to Beth - le-hem come, The inns were filled, both all and some; For Jo-seph en - treated them, ev - 'ry one, Both for him - self and his dear - est dear.
dear. 6. The king of all power was in Beth - le-hem born, Who wore for our sakes a crown of thorn. Then God pre-serve us both even and morn For Je - sus' sake, our dear - est dear!
pp
1st time
Last time
3. Un-
5. Then

ARRANGEMENT FOR UNACCOMPANIED VOICES

S.
A.
1. O, Jo - seph being an old man tru - ly, He
2. They liv - - ed both in joy and bliss; But
Melody
T.
B.

NOTE. The words to be sung by the tenors only, the other parts to vocalize.

mar-ried a vir - gin fair and free; A pur - - er vir - gin could
now a strict com - mand-ment is, In Jew - - ry - land no

no man see Than he chose for his wife and his dear - - est dear.
man should miss To go a - long with his dear - - est dear,

3 Unto the place where he was born,
Unto the Emperor to be sworn,
To pay a tribute that's duly known,
Both for himself and his dearest dear.

4 And when they were to Bethlehem come,
The inns were filled, both all and some;
For Joseph entreated them, every one,
Both for himself and his dearest dear.

5 Then were they constrainèd presently
Within a stable all night to lie,
Where they did oxen and asses tie,
With his true love and his dearest dear.

6 The king of all power was in Bethlehem born,
Who wore for our sakes a crown of thorn.
Then God preserve us both even and morn
For Jesus' sake, our dearest dear!

The original words ('There is a fountain') to which Mrs. Esther Smith sung this tune at Weobley were probably not traditional, and were moreover full of the rather unpleasant imagery which is characteristic of much of the eighteenth-century evangelistic verse. They are printed in the *Journal of the Folk-Song Society*, ii. 133 and iv. 21. Rather than omit such a fine tune, the Editors of *Twelve Traditional Carols from Herefordshire* decided to set other words to it—undoubtedly traditional, for which, as far as they know, no tune has been preserved, and we have done the same. These words are taken from Sandys. They seem to reach back to the seventeenth century; but the story of Joseph's doubts (here omitted from the sixteen verses of the original) was familiar in the fourteenth, and occurs in a different carol of the fifteenth century. See E. Rickert, *Ancient English Christmas Carols*, xix. 24-7.

116 A BABE IS BORN
(CHRISTMAS: EPIPHANY)

Nowell, el, el, el,
Now is well, that ever was woe.

15th century

English traditional
(M.S.)

SOPRANO
ALTO
TENOR
BASS
1. A babe is born all of a may, To bring sal - va - tion un - to us. To him we sing both night and day Ve - ni cre - a - tor Spi - ri - tus.
2. At Beth - le - hem, that bless - ed place, The child of bliss now born he was; And him to serve God give us grace, O lux be - a - ta Tri - ni - tas.

3 There came three kings out of the East,
 To worship the King that is so free,
With gold and myrrh and frankincense,
 A solis ortus cardine.

4 The shepherds heard an angel's cry,
 A merry song that night sung he.
'Why are ye so sore aghast?'
 Jam ortus solis cardine.

5 The angels came down with one cry,
 A fair song that night sung they
In the worship of that child:
 Gloria tibi Domine.

1. may—maid. *Veni creator*—Come, creator Spirit: the Whitsun hymns, *E.H.* 153, 154, 156. 2. *O lux beata*—O Trinity, blessed light: Evening hymn, *E.H.* 164. 3. *A solis ortus cardine*—Risen from the quarter of the sun: Christmas hymn, *E.H.* 18. 4. Orig. 'The herdes heardyn'. 5. *Gloria tibi Domine*—Glory to thee, O Lord.

Sloane MS. 2593, first half of the fifteenth century. Another version in Richard Hill's MS. (cf. No. 36), 'There is a child born of a may'. We have altered, in v. 1, 'In the savasyoun of us', with Bramley and Stainer, who preserved the tune, and in 4, 'A merye song then sungyn he', and similarly in 5. Greene: 122(b).

117 IMMORTAL BABE
(CHRISTMAS: EPIPHANY)

Bishop Joseph Hall

German, 16th century
(M.S.)

SOPRANO
ALTO
TENOR
BASS
1. Im - mor - tal babe, who this dear day Didst change thine hea - ven for our clay, And didst with flesh thy god - head veil, E - ter - nal Son of God, all hail!
2. Shine, hap - py star: ye an - gels sing Glo - ry on high to heav'n's King: Run, shep - herds, leave your night - ly watch, See heav'n come down to Beth - lem's cratch.

3 Worship, ye sages of the East,
The King of gods in meanness dressed:
O blessèd maid, smile and adore
The God thy womb and arms have bore.

4 Star, angels, shepherds, and wise sages,
Thou virgin glory of all ages,
Restorèd frame of heaven and earth,
Joy in your dear Redeemer's birth!

2. cratch—cradle.
From *The Shaking of the Olive Tree*, by Joseph Hall, Bishop of Exeter, 1660. The melody is a German traditional carol tune.

118 SUSANNI
(CHRISTMAS: EPIPHANY)

15th century

German (M.S.)

SOPRANO
ALTO
TENOR
BASS
1. A lit - tle child there is y - born, Ei - - a, ei - - - a, su - san - ni, su - san - ni, su - san - ni. And he sprang out of Jes - se's thorn, Al - le - lu - ya, al - le - - lu - ya, To save all us that were for - lorn.
2. Now Je - sus is the child - es name, Ei - - a, ei - - - a, su - san - ni, su - san - ni, su - san - ni. And Ma - ry mild she is his dame; Al - le - lu - ya, al - le - - lu - ya, And so our sor - row is turned to game.

3 It fell upon the high midnight,
Eia, eia, etc.
The stars they shone both fair and bright,
Alleluya, alleluya
The angels sang with all their might.

4 *Three kings there came with their presénts
Eia, eia, etc.
Of myrrh and gold and frankincense,
Alleluya, alleluya
As clerkès sing in their sequence.

5 Now sit we down upon our knee,
Eia, eia, etc.
And pray we to the Trinity,
Alleluya, alleluya,
Our help, our succour for to be.

VOM Himmel hoch, o Engel, kommt!
Eia, eia, susanni, susanni, susanni.
Kommt singt und klingt, kommt pfeift und trombt,
Alleluya, alleluya,
Von Jesus singt und Maria.

2 Kommt ohne Instrumenten nit,
Eia, eia, usw.
Bringt Lauten, Harfen, Geigen mit!
Alleluya, alleluya,
Von Jesus singt und Maria.

3 Lasst hören euer Stimmen viel
Eia, eia, usw.
Mit' Orgel und mit Saitenspiel!
Alleluya, alleluya,
Von Jesus singt und Maria.

4 Sehr süss muss sein der Orgel Klang,
Eia, eia, usw.
Süss über allen Vögelsang.
Alleluya, alleluya,
Von Jesus singt und Maria.

5 Das Lautenspiel muss lauten süss,
Eia, eia, usw.
Davon das Kindlein schlafen müss.
Alleluya, alleluya,
Von Jesus singt und Maria.

6 Singt Fried' den Menschen weit und breit,
Eia, eia, usw.
Gott Preis und Ehr' in Ewigkeit.
Alleluya, alleluya,
Von Jesus singt und Maria.

Ashmolean MS. 1393. Printed *Early Bodleian Music*, 1901, Greene, No. 35, and Chambers and Sidgwick; here collated with Richard Hill's MS. The proper tune is, however, unknown: we have therefore used the melody of a similar carol, 'Susanni, Susanni' (Vom Himmel hoch); the refrain is that of this German carol, which is given in Hölscher's *Niederdeutsche geistliche Lieder* (Berlin, 1854) from a source of 1588, but is of earlier origin.

119 ANGELS, FROM THE REALMS

LES ANGES DANS NOS CAMPAGNES

(CHRISTMAS: EPIPHANY)

J. Montgomery

French (M.S.)

SOPRANO
ALTO
TENOR
BASS
1. An-gels, from the realms of glo-ry, Wing your flight o'er all the earth;
2. Shep-herds in the field a-bid-ing, Watch-ing o'er your flocks by night,
Ye who sang cre-a-tion's sto-ry Now pro-claim Mes-si-ah's birth:
God with man is now re-sid-ing; Yon-der shines the in-fant Light:
p
Come and wor-ship
*Glo-ria
Come and wor-ship
*Glo-ria
Christ the new-born King,
in ex-cel-sis De-o,
f
Come
Glo-
Christ the new-born King,
in ex-cel-sis De-o,
Come
Glo-

* alternative refrain

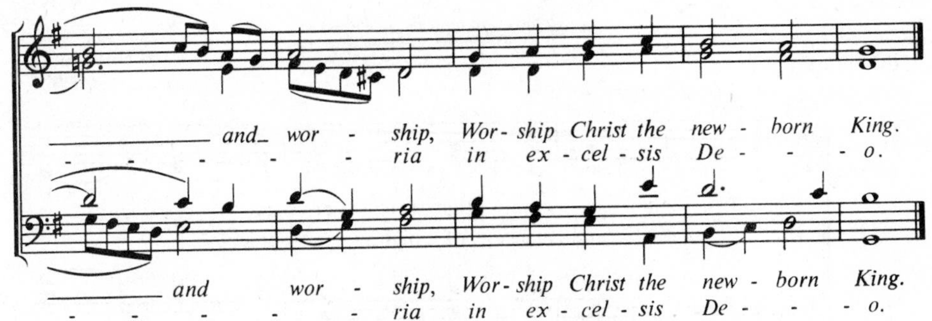
and wor - ship, Wor- ship Christ the new - born King.
- - - - - - ria in ex - cel - sis De - - - o.
and wor - ship, Wor- ship Christ the new - born King.
- - - - - - ria in ex - cel - sis De - - - o.

3 Sages, leave your contemplations;
Brighter visions beam afar;
Seek the great Desire of Nations;
Ye have seen his natal star:
Come and worship, etc.

4 Saints before the altar bending,
Watching long in hope and fear,
Suddenly the Lord, descending,
In his temple shall appear:
Come and worship, etc.

5 Though an infant now we view him,
He shall fill his Father's throne,
Gather all the nations to him;
Every knee shall then bow down:
Come and worship, etc.

LES anges dans nos campagnes
Ont entonné l'hymne des cieux;
Et l'écho de nos montagnes
Redit ce chant mélodieux:
Gloria in excelsis Deo.

2 Bergers, pour qui cette fête?
Quel est l'objet de tous ces chants?
Quel vainqueur, quelle conquête
Mérite ces cris triomphants?
Gloria in excelsis Deo.

3 Ils annoncent la naissance
Du libérateur d'Israël,
Et, pleins de reconnaissance,
Chantent en ce jour solennel:
Gloria in excelsis Deo.

4 Bergers, loin de vos retraites
Unissez-vous à leurs concerts
Et que vos tendres musettes
Fassent retentir dans les airs:
Gloria in excelsis Deo.

5 Cherchons tous l'heureux village
Qui l'a vu naître sous ses toits,
Offrons-lui le tendre hommage
Et de nos coeurs et nos voix!
Gloria in excelsis Deo.

Montgomery's well-known hymn, first printed in his newspaper *Iris*, December 24, 1816, and included among 'Three New Carols' in *The Christmas Box*, 1825 (the first complete book of the Religious Tract Society, and precursor of the popular 'Christmas Books'), reads almost like an early nineteenth-century translation of the opening verses of 'Les anges dans nos campagnes', the old French carol from which we take the tune. The fifth verse is taken from 'The Babe of Bethlehem', another carol in *The Christmas Box*. The refrain 'Gloria in excelsis Deo' may well be preferred in the English version also.

120 IN BETHLEHEM, THAT FAIR CITY

(CHRISTMAS: INNOCENTS' DAY)

To bliss God bring us, all and some.
Christe redemptor omnium.
15th century
14th century
(G.S.)
SOPRANO
ALTO
TENOR
BASS
1. In Beth - le - hem, that fair ci - ty, *Al - le - - - - lu - - - - ya,* Was born a child that was so free, *Al - le - - - - - - - - - - - - - lu - ya.*
2. Lord and prince of high de - gree, *Jam lu - - cis or - - to si - - de - -re.*
ALTERNATIVE VERSION (MELODY IN TENOR)
S.
A.
T.
B.
3. Je - su, for the love of thee,
4. In Beth - le - hem, that fair ci - ty, *Al - le - - -*

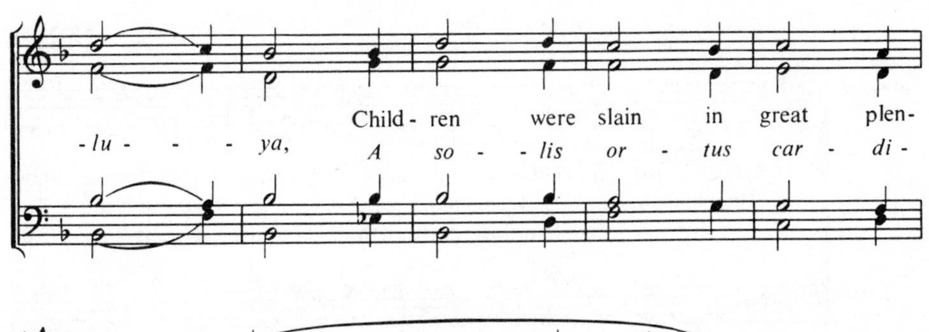
Child - ren were slain in great plen-
- lu - - - ya, A so - - lis or - tus car - di -

- ty,
- ne.
Al - le - - - - - - - - - - - lu - ya.

3 Jesu, for the love of thee,
Children were slain in great plenty,

4 In Bethlehem, that fair city,
A solis ortus cardine.

5 As the sun shineth through the glass,
So Jesu in her body was.

6 Then him to serve God give us grace,
O lux beata Trinitas.

7 Now is he born our Lord Jesus,
He that made merry all of us:

8 Then be all merry in this house,
Exultet coelum laudibus.

Christe, &c.—Christ, redeemer of all (Christmas Mattins hymn, *E.H.* 17). 2. *Jam lucis*, &c.—'Now that the daylight fills the sky' (Prime, *E.H.* 254). 4. *A solis*, &c. and 6. *O lux*, &c.—See No. 23. 8. *Exultet*, &c.—Let heaven exult with praises, *E.H.* 176.

There are different versions of this carol in the fifteenth-century Cambridge T.C.C. (O 3. 58) MS., in Richard Hill's MS., &c. These different versions are printed in Fuller Maitland, Wright, Chambers and Sidgwick, and Greene, No. 21. The refrain belongs to the fourteenth-century melody of 'Puer natus in Bethlehem', of which there are very many variants, the earliest (fifteenth century) MSS., being at Strassburg and Munich. Our version of the tune appears in *Piae Cantiones*, and was harmonized by Bach (1685-1750). Compare No. 85, which gives Bach's harmonization, and the original German words.

121 FALAN-TIDING
(EPIPHANY: CHRISTMAS)

c. 1610
Tyrolese
(M.S.)
SOPRANO
ALTO
TENOR
BASS
1. Out of the o - rient crys - tal_skies A blaz - ing star did shine, Show-
2. This shin - ing star three kings did_guide Even from the furth - est East, To
3. And for the joy of his great birth A thou - sand an - gels sing: 'Glo-
-ing the place where poor - ly_ lies A_ bless - ed babe di - vine, Born
Beth - le - hem where it be - tide This_ bless - ed babe did rest, Laid
-ry and peace un - to the_earth Where born is this new King!' The
of a maid of roy - al blood Who Ma - ry hight by name, A
in a sil - ly man - ger poor, Be - twixt an ox and ass, Whom
shep - herds dwell - ing there a - bout, When they this news did know, Came
sa - cred rose which once did_bud By grace of heav'n - ly flame.
these three kings did all a - dore As God's high plea - sure was.
sing - ing all even in a_rout, 'Fal - an - ti - ding - di - do!'

2. silly—simple.

ALTERNATIVE WORDS

THE wise may bring their learning,
  The rich may bring their wealth;
And some may bring their greatness,
  And some bring strength and health:
We too would bring our treasures
  To offer to the King;
We have no wealth or learning,
  What shall we pilgrims bring?

2 We'll bring him hearts that love him,
  We'll bring him thankful praise,
And mortals, daily striving
  To walk in holy ways:
And these shall be the treasures
  We offer to the King,
And these are gifts that even
  The humblest soul may bring.

3 We'll bring the many duties
  We have to do each day;
We'll try our best to please him,
  In all we do and say:
And better are these treasures
  To offer to our King
Than richest gifts without them;
  Yet these we all may bring.

In the B.M. Add. MS. 29401, with a contemporary five-part setting; as this is a motet we are not including it, but have used the tune of a Tyrolese carol, 'Ihr Hirten, stehet alle auf'. The alternative English words are from *Book of Praise for Children* (1881).

122 HERRICK'S CAROL
(CHRISTMAS)

Robert Herrick (1647)
German
(M.S.)
Rather quick
SOPRANO
ALTO
TENOR
BASS
1. What swee-ter mu - sic can we bring — Than a ca - rol,
2. Dark and dull night, fly hence a - way, And give the hon - our
The birth of this our
That sees De - cem - ber
for to — sing The birth of this our heav'n - ly — King? A -
to this — day, That sees De - cem - ber turned to — May, If
(Melody in Tenor)
A -
If
-wake the voice! A - wake the — string:
we may ask the rea - son, - say:
A - wake the voice! A - wake the string:
If we may ask the rea - son, say:
f (Melody)
We see him come,
-wake the voice!
we may ask
f
pp (echo)
f
pp (echo)
f
(see him come) and know him ours, (know him ours) Who with his sun-shine
pp
f
pp
f

p
and his showers Turns all the pa - tient ground to flowers.
p

3 The darling of the world is come,
And fit it is we find a room
To welcome him. The nobler part
Of all the house here is the heart:

We see him come, etc.

4 Which we will give him, and bequeath
This holly and this ivy wreath,
To do him honour who's our King,
And Lord of all this revelling:

We see him come, etc.

Herrick's *Hesperides*, from which these words are taken, was performed before Charles I, 'in the Presence, at Whitehall'. The words are here arranged for 'Als ich bei meinen Schafen wacht', a Christmas-play carol in the *Cölner Gesangbuch* (1623), and elsewhere, reprinted in Böhme. The original words do not fit this arrangement, but a literal translation ('As I was watching by my sheep') will be found in *Songs for all Seasons* (O.U.P.).

123 CHANTICLEER
(NATIVITY)

W. Austin

English traditional (M.S.)

Moderately quick
SOPRANO
ALTO
TENOR
BASS
1. All this night shrill chan-ti - cleer, Day's pro-claim-ing trum - pet-er,
2. Wake, O earth, wake ev - 'ry— thing! Wake and hear the joy I bring;
3. Hail, O Sun, O bless-ed— Light, Sent in-to the world by night!
Claps his wings and loud - ly cries, Mor-tals, mor - tals,– wake and rise!
Wake and joy; for all this night Heav'n and ev - 'ry— twink-ling light,
Let thy rays and heav'n-ly powers Shine in these dark– souls of ours;
See a won - der Heav'n is un - der; From the earth– is—
All a - maz - ing, Still stand gaz - ing. An - - gels, powers, and–
For most du - ly Thou art tru - ly God and man,– we—
Shines– all— night, though day be done.
Wake,– and– joy this Sun to see.
Hail,— O— Sun of Right - - - eous - ness!
risen a Sun Shines all night, though day be done.
all that be, Wake, and joy this Sun to see.
do con - fess: Hail, O Sun of Right-eous - ness!
Shines all night, though day be done.
Wake, and joy this Sun to see.
Hail, O Sun of Right - - eous - - ness!

From '*Devotionis Augustinianae Flamma* by William Austin, of Lincolnes Inne Esquier', who died 16 January 1633 (published, 1635). There is a monument to him in St. Saviour's, Southwark. The tune is adapted from an English traditional melody.

124 SUMMER IN WINTER
(NATIVITY)

R. Crashaw

Alsatian (M.S.)

In moderate time
SOPRANO ALTO
TENOR BASS
1. Gloo-my night em-braced the place Where the no-ble in-fant lay; The babe looked up and shewed his face, In spite of dark-ness it was day! It was thy day, sweet, and did rise, Not from the East, but from thine eyes.
2. Win-ter chid a-loud, and sent The an-gry North to wage his wars. The North for-got his fierce in-tent, And left per-fumes, in-stead of scars. By those sweet eyes' per-sua-sive powers Where he meant frost, he scat-tered flowers.

3 We saw thee in thy balmy nest,
Bright Dawn of our eternal day!
We saw thine eyes break from their east
And chase the trembling shades away;
We saw thee, and we blessed the sight,
We saw thee by thine own sweet light.

4 Welcome, all wonders in one sight,
Eternity shut in a span,
Summer in winter, day in night,
Heaven in earth, and God in man!
Great little one! whose all-embracing birth
Lifts earth to heaven, stoops heaven to earth.

From the eighteen stanzas of Crashaw's 'Hymn in the Holy Nativity', 1648. The melody is from *Cantiques de Strasbourg*, 1697.

125 RORATE
(NATIVITY)

William Dunbar

Scottish traditional

SOPRANO
ALTO
TENOR
BASS
1. *Ro - ra - te coe - li de - su - per!* Hea - vens, dis - til your bal - my showers; For now is risen the bright Day - star, From the rose Ma - ry, flower of flowers: The clear Sun, whom no cloud de - vours, Sur - mount - ing Phoe - bus in the east, Is
2. Sin - ners be glad, and pen - ance do, And thank your Ma - ker heart - ful - ly; For he that ye might not come to, To you is co - men full hum - bly, Your soul - es with his blood to buy, And loose you of the fiend's ar - rest, And

co - men of his heav'n-ly towers, Et no - bis pu - er na - tus est.
on - ly of his own mer - cy; Pro no - bis pu - er na - tus est

3 Celestial fowlès in the air,
Sing with your notès upon height,
In firthès and in forests fair
Be mirthful now at all your might;
For passèd is your dully night;
Aurora has the cloudès pierced,
The sun is risen with gladsome light,
Et nobis puer natus est.

4 Sing, heaven imperial, most of height,
Regions of air make harmony,
All fish in flood and fowl of flight
Be mirthful and make melody:
All *Gloria in excelsis* cry,
♪ | ♩
Heaven, earth, sea, man, bird, and beast;
He that is crowned above the sky
Pro nobis puer natus est.

1. *Rorate*, &c.—Drop down, ye heavens, from above (Is. 45, 8). *Et nobis*, &c.—And for us a boy is born.

On the eve of the 'Reformation, Dunbar, the Scottish diplomat, ex-Franciscan, and poet, still uses the sounded 'e' when he thinks fit; he is, as Palgrave says, 'the fine flower of expiring medievalism'. The verses are here set to a little-known Scottish melody.

126 CANDLEMAS EVE
(1 FEBRUARY, AND SPRING)

R. Herrick
Church-gallery book
(M.S.)
SOPRANO
ALTO
TENOR
BASS
1. Down with the rose-ma-ry and bays, Down with the mis-tle-toe; In-
3. Then youth-ful box, which now hath grace Your hou-ses to re-new, Grown
5. Green rush-es then, and sweet-est bents, With cool-er oak-en boughs, Come
-stead of hol-ly, now up-raise The green-er box, for show. 2. The
old, sur-ren-der must his place Un-to the crisp-ed yew. 4. When
in for come-ly or-na-ments, To re-a-dorn the house. 6. Thus
hol-ly hith-er-to did sway: Let box now dom-in-eer Un-
yew is out, then birch comes in, And ma-ny flowers be-side, Both
times do shift, thus times do shift; each thing his turn does hold; New
-til the dan-cing Eas-ter Day, Or Eas-ter's Eve ap-pear.
of a fresh and fra-grant kin, To hon-our Whit-sun-tide.
things suc-ceed, new things suc-ceed, as form-er things grow old.

The tune is from an old church-gallery book, discovered by the Rev. L. J. T. Darwall.

127 GOD IS ASCENDED

GEN HIMMEL AUFGEFAHREN IST

(ASCENSION)

Henry More

German, 16th century
(M.S.)

SOPRANO
ALTO
TENOR
BASS
1. God is as - cen - ded up on high,
2. And prince - ly seat - ed in the sky,
Al - le - lu-
-ya, *Al - le - lu - ya.*
With mer - ry noise of
Rules ov - er all the
trum - pet's sound,
world a - round.
Al - le - lu - ya, *Al - le - lu - ya.*

3 In human flesh and shape he went,
Alleluya.
Adornèd with his passion's scars,
Alleluya.

4 Which in heaven's sight he did present
Alleluya.
More glorious than the glittering stars.
Alleluya.

5 Lord, raise our sinking minds therefore
Alleluya.
Up to our proper country dear,
Alleluya.

6 And purify us evermore,
Alleluya.
To fit us for those regions clear.
Alleluya.

GEN Himmel aufgefahren ist, *Alleluya.*
Der König der Ehren, Jesus Christ, *Alleluya.*

2 Er sitzt zur rechten Gottes Hand, *Alleluya.*
Herrscht über Himmel und alle Land. *Alleluya.*

3 Zwei Engel sagten offenbar, *Alleluya.*
'Ihr Galiläer, nehmet wahr:' *Alleluya.*

4 'Jesus, der von euch ist genommen,' *Alleluya.*
Die Welt zu richten wird er kommen. *Alleluya.*

5 Der Gläubigen hat er bereit't, *Alleluya.*
Einen Weg zu der Seeligkeit. *Alleluya.*

6 Zu dieser freudenreicher Zeit, *Alleluya.*
Sei Gott gelobt in Ewigkeit. *Alleluya.*

The German text and melody of 'Gen Himmel aufgefahren ist' are in David Corner, 1631, as 'Ein altes Lobgesang von Christi Himmelfahrt'. More's first stanza almost exactly reproduces the short text of the original as reprinted in Riemann. Henry More, the saintly Cambridge Platonist, became Fellow of Christ's College in 1639.

128 WELCOME, SUMMER

Geoffrey Chaucer
Irish traditional (M.S.)
Moderately quick
SOPRANO ALTO
TENOR BASS
Solo: 1. Now wel-come, Sum - mer, with thy sun - ne soft,
Chorus: 2. Saint Val - en - tine that art full high on loft,
Solo: 3. Well have they cau - se for to glad - den oft,
Solo: 4. 'Now wel-come, Sum - mer, with thy sun - ne soft,
Chorus: Now wel - come, Sum - mer, with thy sun - ne soft,
Thus sing - en smal - le fowl - es for thy sake
Chorus: Well have they cau - se for to glad - den oft,
Chorus: Now wel - come, Sum - mer, with thy sun - ne soft,
That___ hast this win - ter's wea - thers o - ver - shake
'Now___ wel - come, Sum - mer, with thy sun - ne soft,
Since___ each of them re - - cov - ered hath his make;
That___ hast this win - ter's wea - thers o - ver - shake
And driven a - way the lon - ge night - es black.
That hast this win - ter's wea - thers o - ver - shake.'
Full bliss - ful may they sing - en when they wake—
And driven a - way the lon - ge night - es black.'

1. overshake—shaken off. 2. on loft—in the air. fowlès (foules)—birds. 3. gladden—rejoice. make—mate.

This roundel comes at the end of *The Parlement of Foules*. We have set it to an old Irish carol tune, slightly adapted.

129 PLEASURE IT IS
(SUMMER AND HARVEST)

William Cornish

B. Waldis (1553)
(M. S.)

In moderate time
SOPRANO
ALTO
TENOR
BASS
Plea - sure it is —— To hear, I wis, The bir - des
sing. The deer in the dale, The sheep in the vale, The corn – spring-ing;
God's pur-vey-ance For sus-te-nance It is for man. Then we al-ways To
him give praise, And thank – him then, and thank – him then.

William Cornish, or Cornysshe, was Master of the Chapel Royal under Henry VII and Henry VIII, for whom he composed music and acted in court pageants; in 1518 he forced Wolsey to give up one of his choristers to the Chapel Royal. The words occur in a book of which only one copy is known to exist (B.M., K. 1, e. 1), '*Bassus.* In this boke ar cōteynyd XX sōgs, IX of IIII partes and XI of thre partes', printed in 1530, not by Wynkyn de Worde, as was formerly assumed, but by an unknown printer, whose colophon, together with the title-leaf of the missing Medius part, was discovered in a binding at Westminster Abbey. The melody is lost, only the bass part being given in *Bassus*: the words are here set to B. Waldis's tune for Ps. 124 (1553), printed by Zahn, no. 5571.

130 WATTS'S CRADLE SONG
(GENERAL)

Isaac Watts

Northumbrian
(Freely arr. M.S.)

Rather slowly, but with flowing movement
1. Hush! my dear, lie still and slum-ber; Ho-ly an-gels guard thy bed!
Heav'n-ly bless-ings with-out num-ber Gent-ly fall-ing on thy head.
2. Sleep, my babe; thy food and rai-ment, House and home, thy friends pro-vide;
All with-out thy care and pay-ment, All thy wants are well sup-plied.
SOPRANO
ALTO
VERSES 1 & 2
Verse 1 sung as a soprano solo unaccompanied.
Verse 2, the words sung by sopranos, other parts hum accompaniment.
TENOR
BASS
VERSE 3 (all sing words)
3. How much bet-ter thou'rt at-ten-ded Than the Son of God could be
When from hea-ven he de-scend-ed, And be-came a child like thee.
VERSE 4
(S. & A.) Hush! my dear, lie still and slum-ber;
Melody in Tenor:
4. Soft and ea-sy is thy cra-dle; Coarse and hard thy Sa-viour lay,
When his birth-place was a sta-ble And his soft-est bed was hay.

VERSE 5
5. See the love-ly babe ad-dress-ing: Love-ly in-fant, how he smiled!
When he wept, the mo-ther's bless-ing Soothed and hushed the ho-ly— child.
rit. e dim.
VERSE 6 a tempo
Hush! my dear, lie still and slum-ber;
Melody in Alto
6. Lo, he slum-bers in his man-ger, Where the horn-ed ox-en fed;
Peace, my dar-ling! here's no dan-ger; Here's no ox a-near thy bed.
Hush! my dear, lie still and slum-ber;
VERSE 7
7. Mayst thou live to know and fear him, Trust and love him all thy days:
Then go dwell for ev-er near him, See his face and sing his praise, and sing his praise.

Watts's words are here set to a traditional carol tune, sung to these words, and noted in Northumberland by R. Vaughan Williams.

131 COVERDALE'S CAROL
(GENERAL)

Miles Coverdale
English traditional
(R.V.W.)
Lento (In free rhythm)
VOICES IN UNISON
ACCPT.
p
1. Now bless - ed be thou, Christ Je - su, Thou
2. E - ter - nal light doth now ap - pear Un-
5. All this did he for us free - ly, For
art man born, and this is true: With
-to the world both far and near; It
to de - clare his great mer - cy. All
our poor flesh and our poor blood, Was
shin - eth clear even at mid - night, Mak -
Christ - en - dom be mer-ry there - fore, And

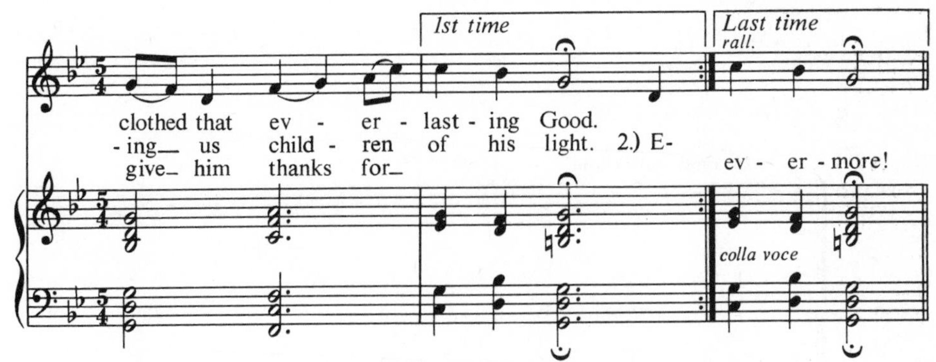

1st time
Last time
rall.
clothed that ev - er - last - ing Good.
- ing us child - ren of his light. 2.) E-
give him thanks for
ev - er - more!
colla voce

ARRANGEMENT FOR UNACCOMPANIED VOICES

(The words to be sung by sopranos only; the other parts to vocalize)

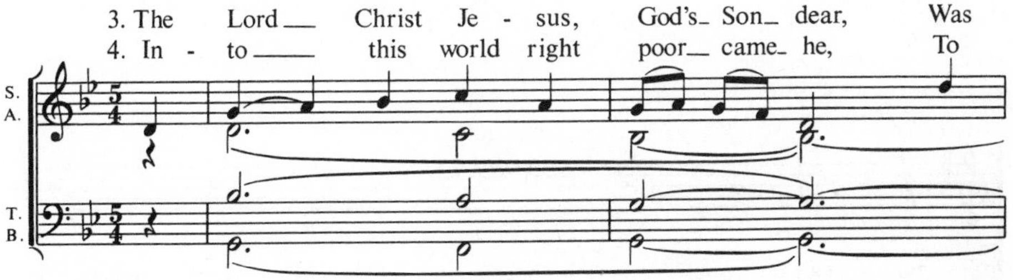

3. The Lord Christ Je - sus, God's Son dear, Was
4. In - to this world right poor came he, To

S.
A.
T.
B.

once a guest and stran - ger here, Us for to bring from
make us rich in his mer - cy; There - fore would he our

mi - se - ry, That we might live e - ter - nal - ly.
sins for - give, That we with him in heav'n might live.

The melody was noted from Mrs. Esther Smith, Dilwyn, sung by her to the strange carol or song about the farmer who ploughed on Christmas Day—see *Twelve Traditional Carols from Herefordshire*, E. M. Leather and R. Vaughan Williams (Stainer & Bell). The words (slightly altered) are a translation of 'Gelobet seist du Jesu Christ' from Coverdale's *Goostly Psalmes and Spiritualle Songes*, 1546: the unique copy is at Queen's College, Oxford, reprinted by the Parker Society.

132 PSALM OF SION
(GENERAL)

W. Prid (1585)

English traditional
(R. V. W.)

In moderate time
SOPRANO
ALTO
1. O mo - ther dear, Je - ru - - sa - lem, Je -
2. O come - ly queen, in glo - - ry clad, In
TENOR
BASS

- ho - vah's throne on high,
hon - our and de - gree;
O sa - cred ci - ty,
All fair thou art, ex -

queen, and wife Of Christ e - ter - nal - ly!
- ceed - ing bright, No spot there is in thee.

3 Thy part, thy shape, thy stately grace,
Thy favour fair in deed,
Thy pleasant hue and countenance,
All others doth exceed.

4 O then thrice happy, should my state
In happiness remain,
If I might once thy glorious seat
And princely place attain,

5 And view thy gallant gates, thy walls,
Thy streets and dwellings wide,
Thy noble troop of citizens
And mighty King beside.

6 He is the King of kings, beset
Amidst his servants' right;
And they his happy household all
Do serve him day and night.

7 O mother dear, Jerusalem,
The comfort of us all,
How sweet thou art and delicate;
No thing shall thee befall!

Versions of the New Jerusalem Hymn formed part of English folk-carol singing from the end of the sixteenth century onwards, and sometimes fragments strayed into other carols (as in No. 46). There are two originals, that by Prid in *The Glasse of vaine-glorie: Faithfully translated (out of S. Augustine his booke intituled Speculum peccatoris)*, by W. Prid, Doctor of the Laws, printed by J. Windel, London, 1585; and the less close paraphrase of Augustine in the British Museum MS., by 'F. B. P.', beginning 'Jerusalem, my happy home', about the same date. Versions appeared in the broadsides: Julian describes an English one of *c.* 1660, and a Scottish one of the eighteenth century, which latter combines Prid with 'F. B. P.' The version of 1801 attributed to Montgomery in the *Oxford Hymn Book* is probably by Joseph Bromehead.

'F. B. P.'s' version was sung to the tune 'Diana', of which one part only has been discovered. The *c.* 1660 version was sung to 'O man in desperation'. We have used the old carol tune, 'Saint Austin' ('In Pescod time', Chappell), which is set in the *English Hymnal* (638) and *Songs of Praise* (395) to the 'F. B. P.' version.

PART III
MODERN TEXTS
WRITTEN FOR OR ADAPTED TO TRADITIONAL TUNES

133 CAROL OF THE ADVENT
(NOVEMBER AND DECEMBER)

SHEPHERDS, SHAKE OFF YOUR DROWSY SLEEP
(CHRISTMAS)

Eleanor Farjeon
(alternative words: Anon.)

Besançon
(M.S.)

SOLO OR SEMI-CHORUS
SOPRANO
ALTO
1. Peo-ple, look East. The time is near Of the
TENOR
BASS

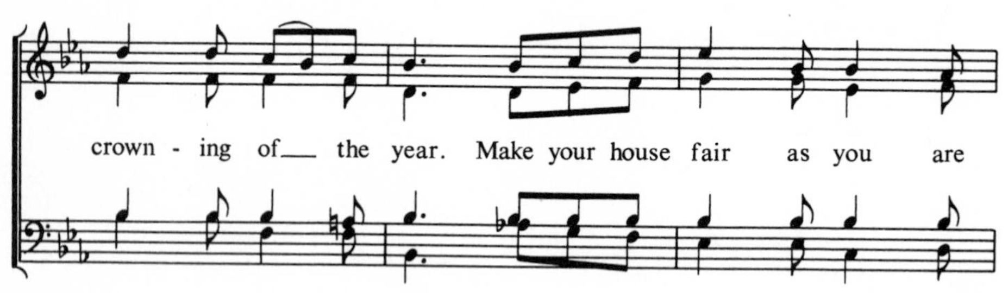
crown - ing of __ the year. Make your house fair as you are

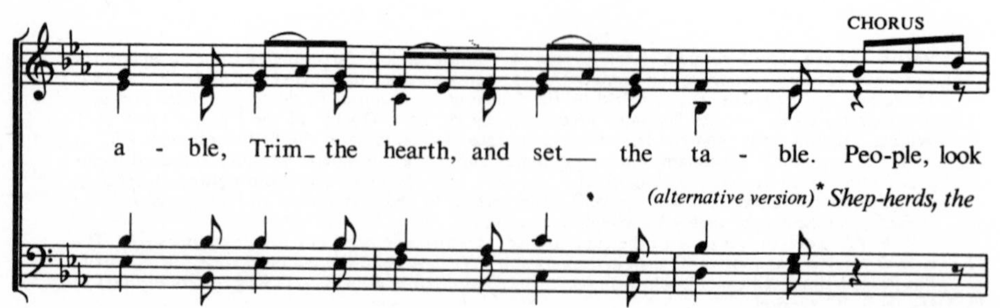
CHORUS
a - ble, Trim _ the hearth, and set __ the ta - ble. Peo-ple, look
(alternative version)* Shep-herds, the

* for use with alternative words only

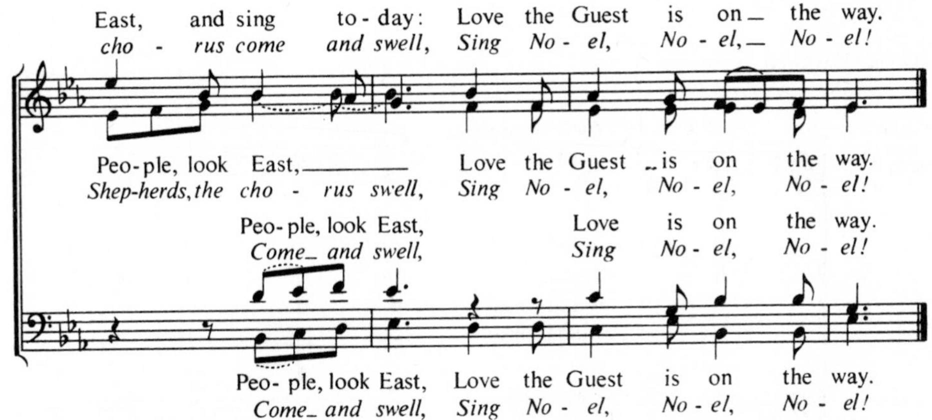
East, and sing to-day: Love the Guest is on the way.
cho - rus come and swell, Sing No - el, No - el, No - el!
Peo-ple, look East, Love the Guest is on the way.
Shep-herds, the cho - rus swell, Sing No - el, No - el, No - el!
Peo-ple, look East, Love is on the way.
Come and swell, Sing No - el, No - el!
Peo- ple, look East, Love the Guest is on the way.
Come and swell, Sing No - el, No - el, No - el!

2 Furrows, be glad. Though earth is bare,
One more seed is planted there:
Give up your strength the seed to nourish,
That in course the flower may flourish.
People, look East, and sing today:
Love the Rose is on the way.

3 Birds, though ye long have ceased to build,
Guard the nest that must be filled.
Even the hour when wings are frozen
He for fledging-time has chosen.
People, look East, and sing today:
Love the Bird is on the way.

4 Stars, keep the watch. When night is dim
One more light the bowl shall brim,
Shining beyond the frosty weather,
Bright as sun and moon together.
People, look East, and sing today:
Love the Star is on the way.

5 Angels, announce to man and beast
Him who cometh from the East.
Set every peak and valley humming
With the word, the Lord is coming.
People, look East, and sing today:
Love the Lord is on the way.

ALTERNATIVE WORDS

SHEPHERDS, shake off your drowsy sleep,
Rise, and leave your silly sheep;
Angels from heaven around are singing,
Tidings of great joy are bringing.
Shepherds, the chorus come and swell,
Sing Noel, Noel, Noel!

2 Hark! even now the bells ring round,
Listen to their merry sound;
Hark! how the birds new songs are making,
As if winter's chains were breaking.
Shepherds, the chorus etc.

3 See how the flowers all burst anew,
Thinking snow is summer dew;
See how the stars afresh are glowing,
All their brightest beams bestowing.
Shepherds, the chorus etc.

4 Cometh at length the age of peace,
Strife and sorrow now shall cease;
Prophets foretold the wondrous story
Of this heaven-born Prince of glory.
Shepherds, the chorus etc.

5 Shepherds! then up and quick away,
Seek the babe ere break of day;
He is the hope of every nation,
All in him shall find salvation.
Shepherds, the chorus etc.

The tune is an old Besançon carol tune, 'Chantons, bargiés, Noué, Noué' (cf. No. 106) which appeared with the words 'Shepherds, shake off your drowsy sleep' in Bramley and Stainer's collection.

Michel Corrette uses this melody in his XVIth Concerto Comique (1733) under the title 'V'la ce que c'est que d'aller au bois'.

134 IF YE WOULD HEAR
(ADVENT: CHRISTMAS EVE)

Dora Greenwell

Dutch
(Adapted R.V.W. and M.S.)

VERSES 1, 2, 4, & 6 With movement
SOPRANO
ALTO
TENOR
BASS
1. If ye would hear the an - - gels sing
2. If ye would hear the an - - gels sing,
4. If ye would hear the an - - gels sing,
6. If ye would hear the an - - gels sing,

'Peace on earth and mer - cy mild',___ Think_ of him who was
Rise, and spread your Christ - mas fare; 'Tis merr - ier still___ the
Rise, and light your Christ - mas fire; And see that ye pile___ the
Christ - ians! See ye let each door Stand wid - - er than it e'er

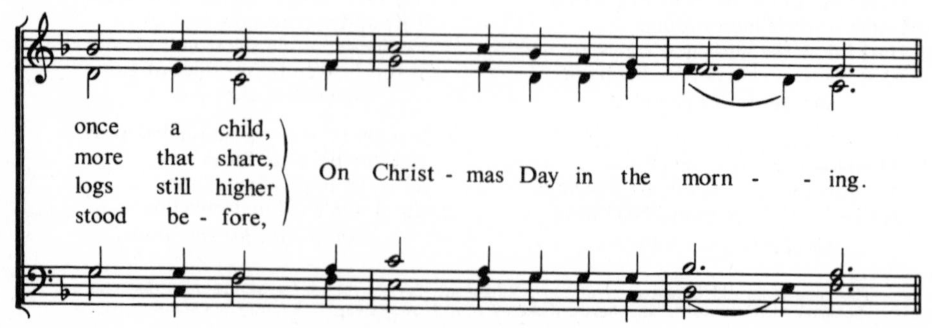
once a child,
more that share,
logs still higher
stood be - fore,
On Christ - mas Day in the morn - - ing.

VERSES 3, 5, & 7
3. Rise, and bake your Christ - mas bread: Christ - ians, rise! The
5. Rise, and light your Christ - mas fire; Christ - ians, rise! The
7. Rise, and o - pen wide the door; Christ - ians, rise! The
Rise, and bake your Christ - mas bread: the
Rise, and light your Christ - mas fire; the
Rise, and o - pen wide the door; the
3. Rise, and bake your Christ - mas bread: Christ - ians, rise! The
5. Rise, and light your Christ - mas fire; Christ - ians, rise! The
7. Rise, and o - pen wide the door; Christ - ians, rise! The
world is bare, And blank, and dark with
world is old, And Time is wea - ry, and
world is wide, And ma - ny there be that
want and care,
worn, and cold,
stand out - side,
Yet Christ - mas comes in the morn - ing.

A Dutch melody, from *Souter Liedekens Ghemaect ter Eeren Gods*, Antwerp, 1539, has been adapted to these words.

135 EARTHLY FRIENDS
(CHRISTMAS)

J. M. Neale

German, 16th century
(Geoffrey Shaw)

SOPRANO
ALTO
1. Earth - ly friends will change and fal - ter, Earth-ly hearts will va - ry:
He is born that can - not al - ter, Of the Vir - gin Ma - ry.
TENOR
BASS
Born to - day, Raise the lay! Born to - day, Twine the bay!
2. Je - sus Christ is born to suf - fer, Born for you, Born for you,
Hol - ly strew! 3. Je - sus Christ was born to con - quer, Born to save,

Born to save, Lau - rel wave! 4. Je - sus Christ was born to gov - ern,
Born a King, Born a King, Bay wreaths bring! 5. Je - sus Christ was
born of Ma - ry, Born for all. Well be - fall Hearth and hall!
Je - sus Christ was born at Christ - mas, Born for all.

Words written in 1853 by Dr. Neale for the melody in *Piae Cantiones* (cf. No. 141) of 'Omnis mundus jucundetur'. The tune is printed in Quentel, *Alte Catholische Geistliche Kirchengeseng*, 1599, the *Constanzer Gesangbuch*, 1600, and in many German books of the seventeenth century.

136 GOOD KING WENCESLAS

(ST. STEPHEN, 26 DECEMBER)

J. M. Neale

Piae Cantiones (M. S.)

SOPRANO
ALTO
TENOR
BASS
1. Good King Wen-ces - las looked out, On the Feast of Ste - phen,
2. 'Hi - ther, page, and stand by me, If thou know'st it, tell - ing,
When the snow lay round a - bout, Deep, and crisp, and ev - en:
Yon - der pea - sant, who is he? Where and what his dwell - ing?'
Bright-ly shone the moon that night, Though the frost was cru - el,
'Sire, he lives a good league hence, Un - der-neath the moun - tain,
When a poor man came in sight,_Gath'-ring win-ter fu - - el.
Right a-gainst the for - est fence,_ By Saint Ag-nes' foun - tain.'

3 'Bring me flesh, and bring me wine,
Bring me pine-logs hither:
Thou and I will see him dine,
When we bear them thither.'
Page and monarch, forth they went,
Forth they went together;
Through the rude wind's wild lament
And the bitter weather.

4 'Sire, the night is darker now,
And the wind blows stronger;
Fails my heart, I know not how;
I can go no longer.'
'Mark my footsteps, good my page;
Tread thou in them boldly:
Thou shalt find the winter's rage
Freeze thy blood less coldly.'

5 In his master's steps he trod,
Where the snow lay dinted;
Heat was in the very sod
Which the saint had printed.
Therefore, Christian men, be sure,
Wealth or rank possessing,
Ye who now will bless the poor,
Shall yourselves find blessing.

This rather confused narrative owes its popularity to the delightful tune, which is that of a Spring carol, 'Tempus adest floridum', No. 99. Unfortunately Neale in 1853 substituted for the Spring carol this 'Good King Wenceslas', one of his less happy pieces, which E. Duncan goes so far as to call 'doggerel', and Bullen condemns as 'poor and commonplace to the last degree'. The time has not yet come for a comprehensive book to discard it; but we reprint the tune in its proper setting ('Spring has now unwrapped the flowers'), not without hope that, with the present wealth of carols for Christmas, 'Good King Wenceslas' may gradually pass into disuse, and the tune be restored to spring-time. Neale did the same kind of thing to another Spring carol, 'In vernali tempore' (No. 98; cf. No. 102); but this was not popularized by Bramley & Stainer.

137 MASTERS IN THIS HALL
(CHRISTMAS)

William Morris

French
(arr. Gustav Holst)

Allegro moderato
p
First verse Full
Subsequent verses soprano voices only
VOICES
ACCPT.
f
p
1. Mas - ters in this hall, Hear ye news to - day Brought from ov - er sea, And ev - er I you pray:
3. *Shep - herds ma - ny an one Sat a - mong the sheep, No man spake more word Than they had been a - sleep:
5.*'Shep - herds should of right Leap and dance and sing, Thus to see ye sit, Is a right strange thing':
7.*'How name ye this lord, Shep-herds?' then said I, 'Ve - ry God,' they said, 'Come from heav - en high':
9. There - in did we see A sweet and good - ly may And a fair old man, Up - on the straw she lay:
11. *Ox and ass him know, Kneel - ing on their knee, Won - drous joy had I This lit - tle babe to see:
cresc.
Now - ell! Now - ell! Now - ell!
cresc.

Now - ell sing we clear! Holp - en are all folk on earth,– Born–
is God's Son so dear:
f Tutti
Now - ell! Now - ell! Now - ell!
ff
Now - ell sing we loud! God to - day hath poor folk raised– And–
cast a - down the proud.

(Men's voices only until last verse. Last verse Tutti)
2. *Go - ing o'er the hills, Through the milk - white snow,
4.*Quoth I, 'Fel - lows mine, Why this guise sit ye?
6 *Quoth these fel - lows then, 'To Beth - lem town we go, To
8. Then to Beth - lem town We went two and two, And
10. And a lit - tle child On her arm had she,
12. *This is Christ the Lord, Mas - ters, be ye glad!
Heard I ewes bleat While the wind did blow:
Mak - ing but dull cheer, Shep - herds though ye be?'
see a might - y lord Lie in man - ger low':
in a sor - ry place Heard the ox - en low:
'Wot ye who this is?' Said the hinds to me:
Christ - mas is come in, And no folk should be sad:
cresc.
Now - ell! Now - ell! Now - ell! Now - ell sing we clear! Holp - en

are all folk on earth,— Born— is God's Son so dear:
ff Tutti
Now - ell! Now - ell! Now - ell! Now - ell sing we loud! God to-
ff
-day hath poor folk raised— And— cast a - down the proud.

The words were written for the old French carol tune shortly before 1860 by Morris, who was in Street's office with Edmund Sedding (architect and compiler of carols, brother of the more famous J. D. Sedding; he died early, in 1868). Sedding had obtained the tune from the organist at Chartres Cathedral, and he published the words and tune in his *Antient Christmas Carols*, 1860. The melody is here reharmonized. The starred verses can be omitted (the chorus gives the answer to v. 10); but a long carol is useful sometimes for processions, both in and out of church. This one should be popular with children. The characters can be distinguished in the singing, and the chorus sung by all.

138 O LITTLE TOWN
(CHRISTMAS EVE: CHRISTMAS)

Bishop Phillips Brooks

English traditional (R.V.W.)

In moderate time
SOPRANO
ALTO
TENOR
BASS
1. O lit - tle town of Beth - le - hem, How
A - bove thy deep and dream - less sleep The
2. O morn - ing stars, to - ge - - - ther Pro -
And prais - es sing to God the King, And
still we see thee lie!
si - lent stars go by. (1.) Yet in thy dark streets
-claim the ho - ly birth, (2.) For Christ is born of
peace to men on earth;
shi - - neth The ev - er - last - ing light; The
Ma - - ry; And, gath - ered all a - - bove, While
hopes and fears of all the years Are met in thee to - night.
mor - tals sleep, the ang - els keep Their watch of wond-'ring love.

3 How silently, how silently,
The wondrous gift is given!
So God imparts to human hearts
The blessings of his heaven.
No ear may hear his coming;
But in this world of sin,
Where meek souls will receive him, still
The dear Christ enters in.

4 Where children pure and happy
Pray to the blessèd child,
Where misery cries out to thee,
Son of the mother mild;
Where charity stands watching
And faith holds wide the door,
The dark night wakes, the glory breaks,
And Christmas comes once more.

5 O holy child of Bethlehem,
Descend to us, we pray;
Cast out our sin, and enter in,
Be born in us to-day.
We hear the Christmas angels
The great glad tidings tell:
O come to us, abide with us,
Our Lord Emmanuel.

This hymn, with its tune ('The Ploughboy's Dream') from the *English Hymnal* (15), and *Songs of Praise* (79), is so much a carol that we feel bound to include it in this book also.

139 INFINITE LIGHT
(EPIPHANY: LENT: GENERAL: MISSIONARY)

B. M. G.
English traditional
(M.S.)
SEMI-CHORUS
SOPRANO
ALTO
TENOR
BASS
1. The great-ness of God in his love has been shown, The
2. He rolls the grim dark-ness and sor-row a-way, And
light of his life on the na-tions is thrown; And
brings all our fears to the light of the day; The
that which the Jews and the Greeks did di-vine Is
i-dols are fall-en of an-ger and blood, And
come in the full-ness of Je-sus to shine:
God is re-vealed as the lov-ing and good:
CHORUS
The

Light of— the World- in— the— dark - ness has— shone, And—

grows— in— our— sight as— the— a - ges flow on.

3 And, though we have sinned like the prodigal son,
His love to our succour and welcome will run.
His gospel of pardon, of love and accord,
Will master oppression and shatter the sword:

The Light of the World etc.

4 The Light of the World is more clear to our sight
As errors disperse and men see him aright:
In lands long in shadow, his churches arise
And blaze for their neighbours the way of the wise:

The Light of the World etc.

This carol has been written to carry another traditional 'Virgin unspotted' tune, which has been familiar for many years. Cf. Nos. 4 and 114.

140 THE BAND OF CHILDREN

(INNOCENTS' DAY: EPIPHANY TO LENT)

LAISSEZ PAITRE VOS BETES

(CHRISTMAS)

Frank Kendon French (M.S.)

Moderately quick
SOPRANO
ALTO
TENOR
BASS
The stars shall light your jour - ney; Your mo - ther holds you
close and warm; The don- key's pace shall rock you: Sleep, ba - by; dream no harm.
1. What songs are these, faint heard and far? The
2. What songs are these, faint heard and far? 'Tis
wind, may-be, in palm trees tall, Or run-ning stream, or night- bird's call; The
nei - ther wind in palm trees tall, Nor wa - ter-brook, nor night- bird's call, It
dark lies deep on de - sert, Where Jo-seph walked and Ma - ry rode, The
is the voice of child - ren Where Jo-seph walked and Ma - ry rode, The

dark lies deep on de - sert— Sleep well, thou child of God:
fierce wild beasts are friend - ly— Sleep well, thou child of God:

3 What forms are these, clear on the dark,
That shine, and yet are flesh and blood,
That laugh and sing along the road?
It is a crowd of children
Where Joseph walked and Mary rode,
A singing crowd of children—
Sleep well, thou child of God:

4 Never was seen so strange a guard:
About the footsore travellers they
In lovely circles moved, till day,
Until the baby wakened,
While Joseph trudged and Mary rode!
Such lullaby be all men's,
Sleep well, thou child of God:

Laissez paître vos bêtes,
Pastoureaux, par monts et par vaux,
Laissez paître vos bêtes
Et venez chanter Nau.

J'ai ouï chanter le rossignol
Qui chantait un chant si nouveau,
Si haut, si beau,
Si resonneau,
Il me rompait la tête,
Tant il prèchait
Et caquetait.
A-donc prins ma houlette
Pour aller voir Naulet.

2 Je m'enquis au berger Naulet;
As-tu ouï le rossignolet
Tant joliet,
Qui gringotait
Là-haut sur une épine?
Oui, dit-il, oui,
Je l'ai ouï;
J'en ai pris ma buccine
Et m'en suis réjoui.

3 Nous courûmes avec roideur
Pour voir notre doux rédempteur,
Et Créateur
Et formateur:
Il avait, Dieu le sçaiche,
Assez besoin
De plus de soin;
Il gisait dans la crèche
Sur un botteau de foin.

4 Sa mère avec lui se trouvait;
Un vieillard si leur éclairait.
Point à l'enfant
Ne ressemblant;
Il n'était pas son père,
Ce qu'au museau
J'aperçus tôt;
Il ressemble à sa mère,
Encore est-il plus beau.

5 Or prions l'enfant, Roi du ciel
Qu'il nous donne à tous bon noël,
Et bonne paix
De nos méfaits,
Ne veuille avoir mémoire
De nos péchés,
Mais pardonner
A ceux du purgatoire
Et leurs maux soulager.

The words have been written for this tune, which is given as a 'noël ancien' by the Abbé Pellegrin (1663-1745) early in the eighteenth century, and is reprinted in the *Grande Bible des Noëls angevins* in 1766. The tune is still sung in the west of France to 'Laissez paître vos bêtes'; another and earlier carol, 'Laisse-qu'y tes affaires', is also associated with it. Roques prints yet another version, 'Venez, divin Messie'. The refrain may be sung at the end of each verse, as well as at the beginning.

141 JANUARY CAROL
(JANUARY AND FEBRUARY)

J. M. Neale

Piae Cantiones (G.S.)

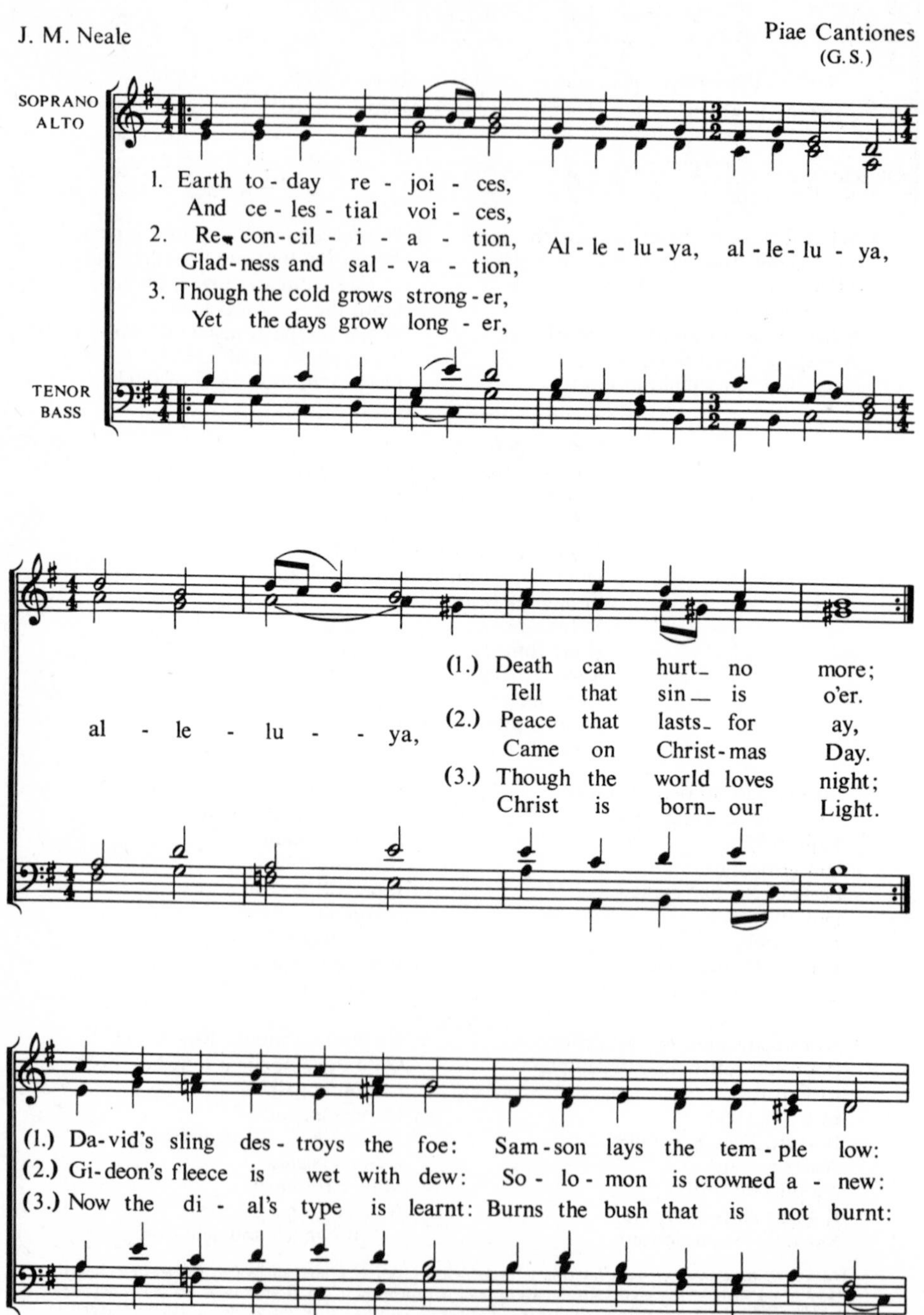

SOPRANO
ALTO
1. Earth to-day re-joi-ces,
And ce-les-tial voi-ces,
2. Re-con-cil-i-a-tion,
Glad-ness and sal-va-tion,
3. Though the cold grows strong-er,
Yet the days grow long-er,
Al-le-lu-ya, al-le-lu-ya,
TENOR
BASS
al-le-lu-ya,
(1.) Death can hurt no more;
Tell that sin is o'er.
(2.) Peace that lasts for ay,
Came on Christ-mas Day.
(3.) Though the world loves night;
Christ is born our Light.
(1.) Da-vid's sling des-troys the foe: Sam-son lays the tem-ple low:
(2.) Gi-deon's fleece is wet with dew: So-lo-mon is crowned a-new:
(3.) Now the di-al's type is learnt: Burns the bush that is not burnt:

War_ and strife_ are done; God and man are_ one.

Written by Dr. Neale in 1853 for the tune 'Ave maris stella lucens' in *Piae Cantiones* (1582).

The now famous *Piae Cantiones* was compiled by Theodoricus Petrus of Nyland in Finland, in 1582, when he was a student at Rostock near Lübeck: he was still alive in 1625. The songs spread in the reformed Church of Sweden and Finland, and were still sung in Swedish schools in 1700, and in Finland late in the nineteenth century. Peter of Nyland's *Piae Cantiones* (perhaps the unique copy) was brought over by the British Minister at Stockholm, who gave it to Dr. Neale, *c.* 1852. Neale gave it to Helmore; and together they published from it *Carols for Christmastide* (1853) and *Carols for Eastertide* (1854), from which collections Neale's carols are taken. An edition of *Piae Cantiones* (altered) was published by Dr. G. R. Woodward in 1910. The original copy is now in the British Museum. See preface.

142 CHILDREN'S SONG OF THE NATIVITY

Frances Chesterton
English traditional
(R.V.W.)
In moderate time
VOICES IN UNISON
1. How far is it to Beth - le - hem? Not ve - ry far. Shall_
3. May we stroke the crea - tures there, Ox, ass, or sheep? May_
5. __ Great kings have pre - cious gifts, And we have naught, __
ACCPT.
(Omit in v. 5)
(Omit in v. 5)
we find the sta - ble - room Lit by a star? 2. Can we see the
we peep like them and see Je - sus a - sleep? 4. If we touch his
Lit-tle smiles and lit - tle tears Are all__ we brought. 6. For all wea - ry
7. __ God in his
(Omit in v. 7)
lit - tle child, Is he with - in? If__ we lift the wood-en latch May we go in?
ti - ny hand Will he a - wake? Will he know we've come so far Just for his sake?
chil - dren Ma - ry must weep. __ Here, on his bed of straw Sleep, chil-dren, sleep.
mo-ther's arms, Babes in the byre, __ Sleep, as they sleep who find Their heart's de-sire.
(Omit in vv. 6 & 7)

This folk-tune 'Stowey' appears in *Songs of Praise* (377) where it is set to other words.

143 THE WORLD'S DESIRE
(NATIVITY)

G. K. Chesterton
Traditional (M.S.)
In moderate time
SOPRANO ALTO
TENOR BASS
1. The Christ-child lay_ on Ma-ry's lap, His hair was like a_ light._ (O_ wea-ry, wea-ry, were the world, But here is all a-right.)
3. The Christ-child lay_ on Ma-ry's heart, His hair was like a_ fire._ (O_ wea-ry, wea-ry, is the world, But here the world's de-sire.)
O wea-ry,
2. The Christ-child lay_ on Ma-ry's_ breast, His_ hair_ was like_ a star. (O stern and cun-ning are the kings, But here the true hearts are.)
4. The Christ-child stood_ at Ma-ry's_ knee, His_ hair_ was like_ a crown, And all the flowers looked up at him And all the stars looked down.

Set to a tune kindly communicated by the Rev. J. R. Van Pelt, Theological Seminary, Atlanta, Georgia, U.S.A.

144 WHITE LENT

(ASH WEDNESDAY TO THE EVE OF PASSION SUNDAY)

QUITTEZ, PASTEURS

(CHRISTMAS)

L. M.

Angevin (M.S.)

Sopranos and altos sing the words. Tenors and basses hum the accompaniment.

In moderate time
SOPRANO
ALTO
TENOR
BASS
1. Now quit your_ care And an - xious fear and wor - ry; For schemes are vain And frett - ing brings no gain. To prayer, to prayer! Bells call and clash and hur - ry, In Lent the bells do cry, 'Come buy,___ come buy,___ Come buy with love the love most high, Come buy,___ come buy,___ Come buy with love the love most high!'
2. Lent comes in the spring, And spring is pied with bright-ness; The sweet - est flowers, Keen winds, and sun, and showers, Their health do bring To make Lent's chas-tened white-ness; For life to men brings light And might,__ and might,__ And might to those whose hearts are right, And might,__ and might,__ And might to those whose hearts are right.

3 To bow the head
In sackcloth and in ashes,
* Or rend the soul,
Such grief is not Lent's goal;
But to be led
To where God's glory flashes,
His beauty to come nigh,
To fly, to fly,
To fly where truth and light do lie.

4 For is not this
The fast that I have chosen?—
The prophet spoke—
To shatter every yoke,
Of wickedness
The grievous bands to loosen,
Oppression put to flight,
To fight, to fight,
To fight till every wrong's set right.

5 For righteousness
And peace will show their faces
To those who feed
The hungry in their need,
And wrongs redress,
Who build the old waste places,
And in the darkness shine.
Divine, divine,
Divine it is when all combine!

6 Then shall your light
Break forth as doth the morning;
Your health shall spring,
The friends you make shall bring
God's glory bright,
Your way through life adorning;
And love shall be the prize.
Arise, arise,
Arise! and make a paradise!

Rather quick
The last verse and any other selected verses. (All sing the words)
S.
A.
T.
B.
6. Then shall your light Break forth as doth the morn-ing; Your health shall spring, The
friends you make shall bring God's glo - ry bright, Your way through life a - dorn - ing; And
A - rise, a - rise, A - rise! and make a par - a -
love shall be the prize. A-rise, a-rise, A - rise, a-rise, a-
A-rise! and make a par - a-
- dise! A - rise, a - rise,
- rise, a - rise, A - rise, a - rise, A - rise! and make a par - a - dise!
- dise!

For French words and footnote see overleaf.

* *Or to afflict the soul,* in some editions

QUITTEZ, pasteurs,
Vos brebis, vos houlettes,
Votre hameau
Et le soin du troupeau;
Changez vos pleurs
En une joie parfaite;
Allez tous adorer
Un Dieu, un Dieu,
Un Dieu qui vient vous consoler.

2 Vous le verrez
Couché dans une étable
Comme un enfant
Nu, pauvre, languissant;
Reconnaissez
Son amour ineffable
Pour nous venir chercher
Il est, il est,
Il est le fidèle berger!

3 Rois d'Orient
L'étoile vous éclaire;
A ce grand roi
Rendez hommage et foi.
L'astre brillant
Vous mène à la lumière
De ce soleil naissant;
Offrez, offrez,
Offrez l'or, la myrrhe et l'encens.

4 Esprit divin
A qui tout est possible
Percez nos coeurs
De vos douces ardeurs;
Notre destin
Par vous devient paisible;
Dieu prétend nous donner
Le ciel, le ciel,
Le ciel en venant s'incarner.

The English words are in part a paraphrase of the Lent Lesson, Isaiah lviii. The tune is printed in L. Roques, *Noëls Anciens* (nineteenth century, undated); there is a slightly different version in L. Eugène Grimault, *Noëls Angevins*, 1878.

145 MOTHERING SUNDAY

(MID-LENT)

ICH WEISS EIN LIEBLICH ENGELSPIEL

(GENERAL)

George Hare Leonard

German, 14th century
(M.S.)

Sopranos sing words, other parts hum accompaniment

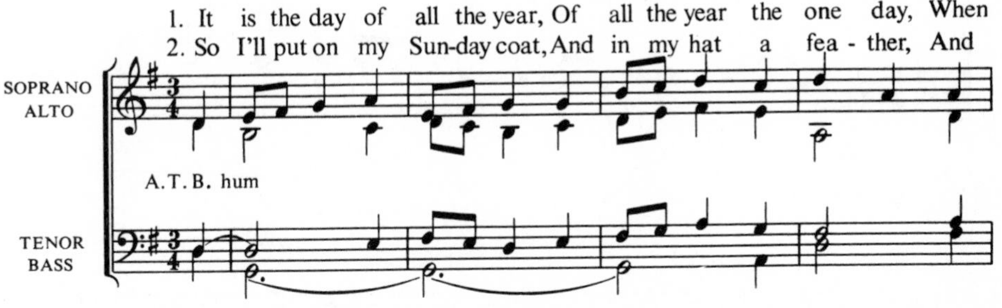
1. It is the day of all the year, Of all the year the one day, When
2. So I'll put on my Sun-day coat, And in my hat a fea - ther, And
SOPRANO
ALTO
A.T.B. hum
TENOR
BASS

I shall see my mo-ther dear And bring her cheer, A - mo-ther-ing on Sun- day.
get the lines I writ by rote, With many a note, That I've a-strung to - ge - ther.

3 And now to fetch my wheaten cake,
To fetch it from the baker,
He promised me, for mother's sake,
The best he'd bake
For me to fetch and take her.

4 Well have I known, as I went by
One hollow lane, that none day
I'd fail to find—for all they're shy—
Where violets lie,
As I went home on Sunday.

5 *My sister Jane is waiting-maid
Along with Squire's lady;
And year by year her part she's played,
And home she stayed,
To get the dinner ready.

6 *For mother'll come to church, you'll see—
Of all the year it's the day—
'The one,' she'll say, 'that's made for me.'
And so it be:
It's every mother's free day.

7 *The boys will all come home from town,
Not one will miss that one day;
And every maid will bustle down
To show her gown,
A-mothering on Sunday.

8 It is the day of all the year,
Of all the year the one day;
And here come I, my mother dear,
To bring you cheer,
A-mothering on Sunday.

For alternative harmonizations see overleaf.

145—Mothering Sunday

FAUX BOURDON Version (for choice of verses)
Tenors sing words, other parts hum accompaniment

It is the day of all the year,
Of all the year the one day,
When I shall see my mother dear
And bring her cheer,
A-mothering on Sunday.

2 So I'll put on my Sunday coat,
And in my hat a feather,
And get the lines I writ by rote,
With many a note,
That I've a-strung together.

3 And now to fetch my wheaten cake,
To fetch it from the baker,
He promised me, for mother's sake,
The best he'd bake
For me to fetch and take her.

4 Well have I known, as I went by
One hollow lane, that none day
I'd fail to find—for all they're shy—
Where violets lie,
As I went home on Sunday.

5 *My sister Jane is waiting-maid
Along with Squire's lady;
And year by year her part she's played,
And home she stayed,
To get the dinner ready.

6 *For mother'll come to church, you'll see—
Of all the year it's the day—
'The one,' she'll say, 'that's made for me.'
And so it be:
It's every mother's free day.

7 *The boys will all come home from town,
Not one will miss that one day;
And every maid will bustle down
To show her gown,
A-mothering on Sunday.

8 It is the day of all the year,
Of all the year the one day;
And here come I, my mother dear,
To bring you cheer,
A-mothering on Sunday.

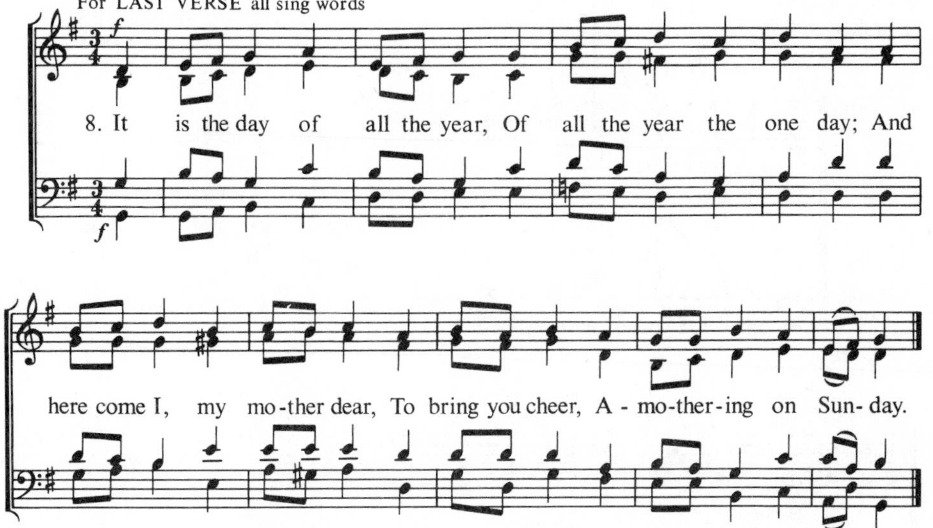
For LAST VERSE all sing words
8. It is the day of all the year, Of all the year the one day; And
here come I, my mo-ther dear, To bring you cheer, A - mo-ther-ing on Sun- day.

ICH weiss ein lieblich Engelspiel
Da ist all's Leid zergangen:
Im Himmelreich ist Freuden viel
Ohn' Endes Ziel;
Dahin soll uns verlangen.

2 Weil Gott uns durch die Gnade sein
Wollt lieblich dahin weisen,
So steh' auf, edle Seele mein,
Und walle herein
Sein Lob sollst ewig preisen.

3 Gott spricht: Nun leb' in Seeligkeit;
Von dir will ich nicht scheiden.
Dies Reich hab' ich dich zubereit
Von Ewigkeit
In Wonn und allen Freuden.

Heinrich von Laufenberg, 1421

'He who goes a-mothering finds violets in the lane.' In many parts of the country it was the custom for the children of the family who had left the old home to come back to visit their mother on the 4th Sunday in Lent (Mid-Lent Sunday). The eldest son would bring a wheaten cake—in modern times a plum cake with an icing of sugar, or a simnel-cake. Sometimes cinnamon comfits ('lambs'-tails'), or little white sugar-plums with a carraway seed, or some morsel of spice, within—such as may still be found at country fairs—were brought for an offering. One of the children home for the day would stay in and mind the house, so that the mother should be free for once to attend morning service at the church.

A folk-tune of the fourteenth century, made into a carol ('Ich weiss ein lieblich Engelspiel'), c. 1450. In a fifteenth-century Strassburg MS. (which was burnt in the war of 1870), printed by Wackernagel and others.

A translation of the artless German words is given below (and may be sung when a carol of more general character is wanted):

I know a lovely angel-game,
Where sorrow has its ending;
And heaven is there with joy aflame,
And endless fame:
'Tis there we would be wending.

2 May God through his abounding grace
Us there in love be leading!
Now stand up, noble soul, and face
That happy place
To which thou would'st be speeding!

3 Then God a ring from off his hand
Will place upon thy finger,
And pledge thee,—' 'Mid this happy band
Within this land
For ever shalt thou linger.'

146 THE MERCHANTS' CAROL
(PALM SUNDAY: HOLY WEEK)

Frank Kendon
English traditional
(M.S.)
Rather quick
SOPRANO
ALTO
TENOR
BASS
1. As we rode down the steep hill-side, Twelve mer-chants with our
2. Be-neath the o - lives fast we rode, And lou - der came the
fair - - ing, A shout a - cross the hol - low land Came
shout - - ing: 'So great a noise must mean,' said we, 'A
loud up - on our hear - - ing, A shout, a song, a
king, be - yond all doubt- - ing!' Spurred on, did we, this
thou - sand strong, A thou - sand lus - ty voi - ces: 'Make
king to see, And left the mules to fol - low; And

haste,' said I, I knew not why, 'Je - ru - sa - lem re - joi - ces!'
near - er, clear - er rang the noise A - long the Ki - dron hol - low.

3 Behold, a many-coloured crowd
About the gate we found there;
But one among them all, we marked,
One man who made no sound there;
Still louder ever rose the crowd's
'Hosanna in the highest!'
'O King,' thought I, 'I know not why
In all this joy thou sighest.'

4 *A Merchant:*
'Then he looked up, he looked at me;
But whether he spoke I doubted:
How could I hear so calm a speech
While all the rabble shouted?
And yet these words, it seems, I heard:
"I shall be crowned tomorrow."
They struck my heart with sudden smart,
And filled my bones with sorrow.'

5 We followed far, we traded not,
But long we could not find him.
The very folk that called him king
Let robbers go and bind him.
We found him then, the sport of men,
Still calm among their crying;
And well we knew his words were true—
He was most kingly dying.

The words written for the traditional tune, which we have distinguished by the name of 'Golden'; cf. Nos. 165 and 173. It can also be sung to the words of No. 165.

147 EASTER CAROL

(EASTER)

NOUS ALLONS, MA MIE

(CHRISTMAS)

N.S.T.

French (M.S.)

Moderately quick
SOPRANO
ALTO
TENOR
BASS
1. Cheer up, friends and neigh - bours, Now it's East - er - tide;
2. Out from snow- drifts chill - y, Roused from drow-sy hours,
Stop from end - less la - bours, Wor - ries put a - - side:
Blue - bell wakes, and li - ly; God calls up the flowers!
Men should rise from sad - ness, E - - vil, fol - ly, strife,
In - - to life he rais - es All the sleep - ing buds;
When God's might - y glad - ness Brings the earth to life.
Mea - dows weave his prais - es, And the spang - led woods.

3 All his truth and beauty,
   All his righteousness,
Are our joy and duty,
   Bearing his impress:
Look! the earth waits breathless
   After winter's strife:
Easter shows man deathless,
   Spring leads death to life.

4 Ours the more and less is;
   But, changeless all the days,
God revives and blesses,
   Like the sunlight rays.
'All mankind is risen,'
   The Easter bells do ring,
While from out their prison
   Creep the flowers of spring!

Nous allons, ma mie,
   Voir un nouveau-né;
C'est notre Messie
   Qui nous est donné:
Nous verrons la mère
   De ce bel enfant,
Nous verrons le père—
   Ah, que Dieu est grand!

2 Dieu, quelle nouvelle!
   Qu'est-ce que j'entends!
Le croyant fidèle
   Sait bien qu'en ce temps
Nous verrons paraître
   Le Sauveur promis.
Il vient donc de naître,
   Cet aimable fils.

3 Allons, mes compagnes,
   Voir le fils de Dieu.
Est-ce en ces campagnes,
   Autour de ce lieu
Qu'il a pris naissance?
   Quels sont ses parents?
Ayons connaissance
   De ces bonnes gens.

4 Ne soyez en peine
   De savoir ce lieu;
C'est en cette plaine
   Que le fils de Dieu
Pour nous vient de naître:
   O bienheureux jour
Qui voit notre maître
   Bénir ce séjour!

Words written for the French carol tune,
'Nous allons, ma mie', printed by Grimault, Roques, and others.

148 CHRIST THE LORD IS RISEN

(EASTER)

I. Watts (1709)

German
(arr. Geoffrey Shaw)

SOPRANO
ALTO
1. Christ the Lord is ri - - sen! Now
2. Christ the Lord is ri - - sen! 'Twas
3. Christ the Lord is ri - - sen! Re-
TENOR
BASS

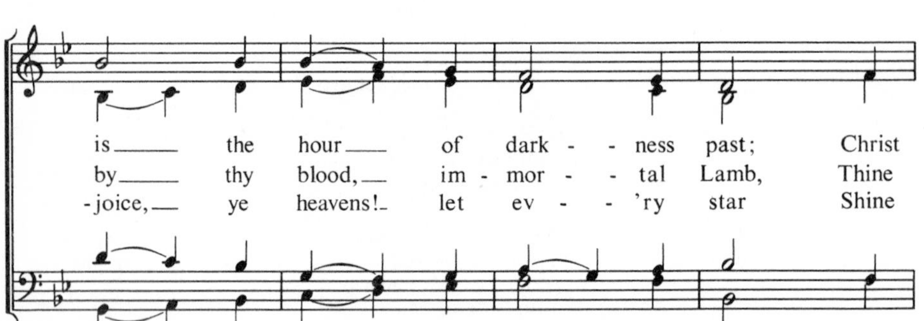

is the hour of dark - - ness past; Christ
by thy blood, im - mor - - tal Lamb, Thine
-joice, ye heavens! let ev - - 'ry star Shine

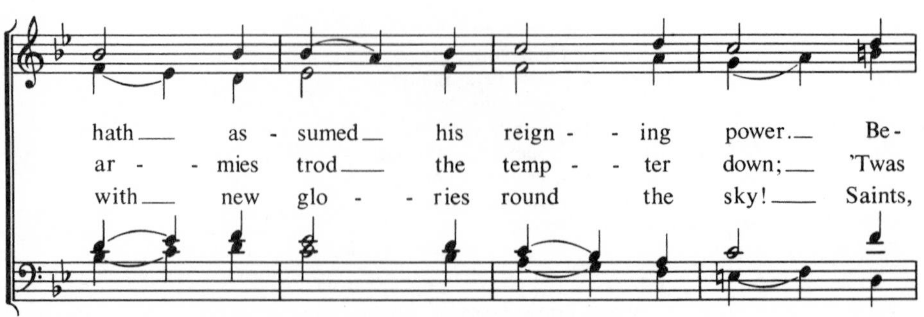

hath as - sumed his reign - - ing power. Bear - - mies trod the temp - - ter down; 'Twas
with new glo - - ries round the sky! Saints,

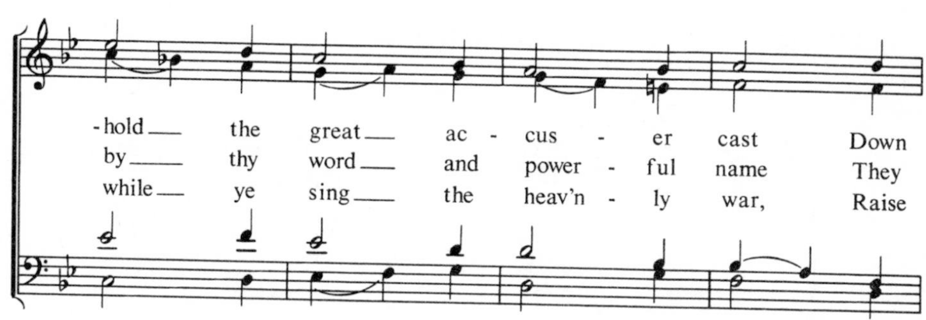
-hold the great ac - cus - er cast Down
by thy word and power - ful name They
while ye sing the heav'n - ly war, Raise

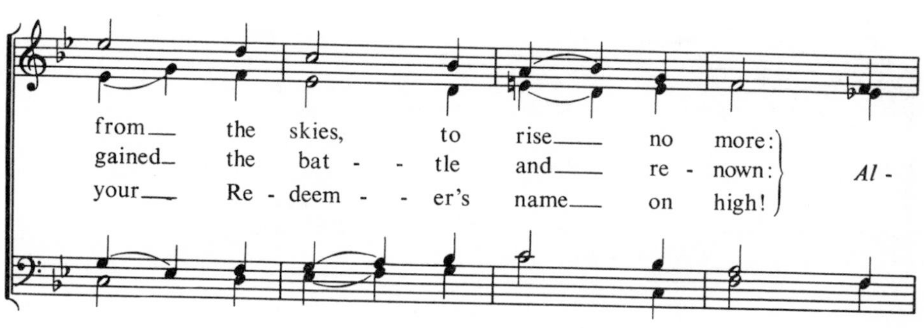
from the skies, to rise no more:
gained the bat - tle and re - nown:
your Re - deem - er's name on high!
Al -

-le - - lu - ya, al - le - - lu - ya.

Verses by Isaac Watts (1674-1748), with refrains added, to fit an old German melody reprinted in the *Gesang- und Gebetbuch für die Diöcese Trier*, 1871.

149 LOVE IS COME AGAIN

(EASTER)

NOEL NOUVELET

(CHRISTMAS)

J. M. C. Crum

French (M.S.)

In moderate time
SOPRANO
ALTO
TENOR
BASS
1. Now the green blade ris - eth from the bur - ied grain,
2. In the grave they laid him, Love whom men had slain,
Wheat that in dark earth ma - ny days has lain;
Think - ing that nev - er he would wake a - gain,
Love lives a - gain, that with the dead has been:
Laid in the earth like grain that sleeps un - seen:
Love is come a - gain, Like wheat that spring - eth green.
Love is come a - gain, Like wheat that spring - eth green.

3 Forth he came at Easter, like the risen grain,
He that for three days in the grave had lain,
Quick from the dead my risen Lord is seen:

Love is come again, etc.

4 When our hearts are wintry, grieving, or in pain,
Thy touch can call us back to life again,
Fields of our hearts that dead and bare have been:

Love is come again, etc.

NOEL nouvelet, Noël chantons ici.
Dévotes gens, crions à Dieu merci!
Chantons Noël pour le roi nouvelet.

Noël nouvelet, Noël chantons ici.

2 L'ange disait; pasteurs, partez d'ici
L'âme en repos et le coeur réjoui;
En Bethléem trouverez l'agnelet;

Noël nouvelet, etc.

3 En Bethléem, étant tous réunis,
Trouvent l'enfant, Joseph, Marie aussi.
La crèche était au lieu d'un bercelet,

Noël nouvelet, etc.

4 Bientôt les rois, par l'ëtoile éclaircis
De l'orient dont ils étaient sortis
A Bethléem vinrent un matinet.

Noël nouvelet, etc.

5 L'un portait l'or, l'autre l'encens béni;
Un autre encore à Jésus myrrhe offrit.
L'étable alors au paradis semblait.

Noël nouvelet, etc.

6 Voici mon Dieu, mon Sauveur Jésus-Christ,
Par qui sera le prodige accompli
De nous sauver par son sang vermeillet!

Noël nouvelet, etc.

Words written for the old French tune associated with 'Noël nouvelet'.

150 THE WORLD ITSELF
(EASTER)

J. M. Neale
Piae Cantiones
(G. S.)
SOPRANO
ALTO
TENOR
BASS
1. The world it - self keeps Eas - ter Day, And Eas - ter larks are sing - ing; And Eas - ter flowers are bloom - ing gay, And Eas - ter buds are spring - ing: Al - le - lu - ya, al - le - lu - ya: The Lord of all things lives a - new, And all his works are
2. There stood three Ma - ries by the tomb, On Eas - ter morn - ing ear - ly; When day had scarce - ly chased the gloom, And dew was white and pearl - y: Al - le - lu - ya, al - le - lu - ya: With lov - ing but with err - ing mind, They came the Prince of

ris - ing too: Ho - san - na in ex - cel - - sis.
life__ to find: Ho - san - na in ex - cel - - sis.

3 But earlier still the angel sped,
His news of comfort giving;
And 'Why', he said, 'among the dead
Thus seek ye for the Living?'
Alleluya, alleluya:
'Go, tell them all, and make them blest;
Tell Peter first, and then the rest':

Hosanna etc.

4 But one, and one alone remained
With love that could not vary;
And thus a joy past joy she gained,
That sometime sinner, Mary,
Alleluya, alleluya:
The first the dear, dear form to see
Of him that hung upon the tree:

Hosanna etc.

5 The world itself keeps Easter Day,
Saint Joseph's star is beaming,
Saint Alice has her primrose gay,
Saint George's bells are gleaming:
Alleluya, alleluya:
The Lord hath risen, as all things tell:
Good Christians, see ye rise as well!

Hosanna etc.

The words were written by Neale (*Carols for Eastertide*, 1854) for the tune 'O Christe, rex piissime' in *Piae Cantiones* (cf. No. 141) with the Alleluyas repeated for the concluding refrain. As this does not fit the melody, 'Hosanna in excelsis' has been substituted.

151 ATHENS
(EASTER)

J. M. Neale

Piae Cantiones
(Geoffrey Shaw)

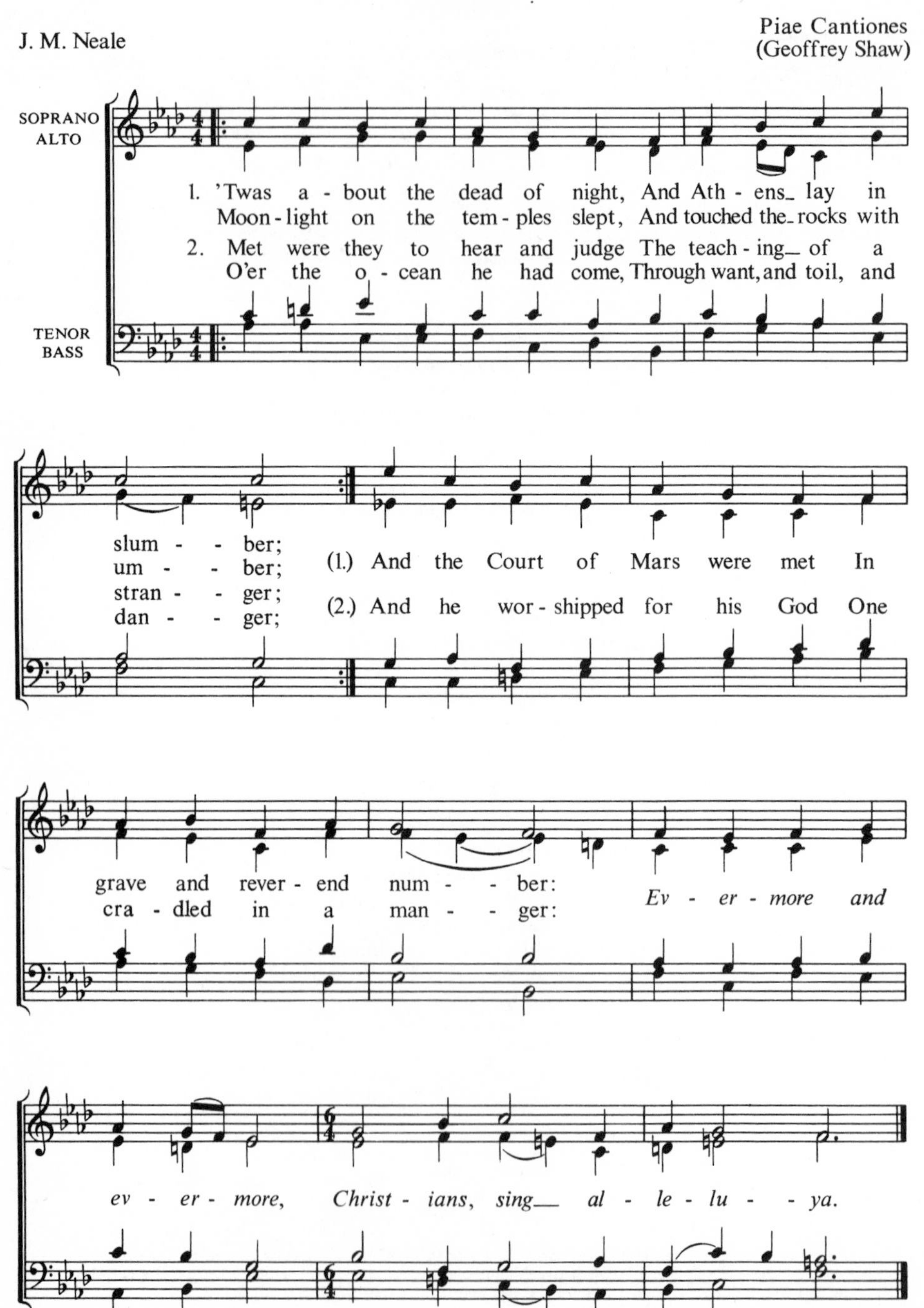
SOPRANO
ALTO
TENOR
BASS
1. 'Twas a - bout the dead of night, And Ath - ens_ lay in
Moon - light on the tem - ples slept, And touched the_ rocks with
2. Met were they to hear and judge The teach - ing_ of a
O'er the o - cean he had come, Through want, and toil, and
slum - - ber;
um - - ber;
stran - - ger;
dan - - ger;
(1.) And the Court of Mars were met In
(2.) And he wor - shipped for his God One
grave and rever - end num - - ber:
cra - dled in a man - - ger:
Ev - er - more and
ev - er - more, Christ - ians, sing_ al - le - lu - - ya.

3 While he spake against their gods,
And temples' vain erection,
Patiently they gave him ear,
And granted him protection;
Till with bolder voice and mien
He preached the resurrection:

Evermore etc.

4 Some they scoffed, and some they spake
Of blasphemy and treason;
Some replied with laughter loud,
And some replied with reason;
Others put it off until
A more convenient season:

Evermore etc.

5 Athens heard and scorned it then,
Now Europe hath received it,
Wise men mocked and jeered it once,
Now children have believed it;
This, good Christians, was the day
That gloriously achieved it:

Evermore etc.

Written by Neale in 1853 for a tune ('Scribere proposui') in *Piae Cantiones* (cf. No. 141).

152 FESTIVAL CAROL
(EASTER TO TRINITY SUNDAY, ETC.)

S. P.
Dutch
(Geoffrey Shaw)
SOPRANO
ALTO
TENOR
BASS
1. How great the har - vest is Of him who came to save us!
The hearts of men are his, Our law the love he gave us.
2. And though the news did seem Too good for man's be - liev - ing,
'Tis not an emp - ty dream Too high for our a - chiev - ing.
(1.) The world lay cru - el, blind, Nought hold - ing, nought di - vin - ing; He came to hu - man kind, And now the light is shi - ning, is shi - ning, is
(2.) He tri - umphed in the strife, O'er all his foes he tow - ered; They killed the Prince of life, But he hath death o'er - pow - ered, o'er - pow - ered, o'er -

shi - ning, is shi - - - - - - - - ning.
-pow - ered, o'er - pow - - - - - - - ered.

3 Then came the Father's call;
His work on earth was ended;
That he might light on all,
To heaven the Lord ascended.
To heaven so near to earth,
Our hearts we do surrender:
There all things find their worth
And human life its splendour, its splendour.

4 The power by which there came
The Word of God among us
Was love's eternal flame,
Whose light and heat are flung us;
That Spirit sent from God,
Within our hearts abiding,
Hath brought us on our road
And still the world is guiding, is guiding.

5 In Three made manifest,
Thou source of all our being,
Thou loveliest, truest, best,
Beyond our power of seeing;
Thou power of light and love,
Thou life that never diest—
To thee in whom all move
Be glory in the highest, the highest!

Words written for the Dutch tune, 'De Liefde Voortgebracht', a very popular song in the seventeenth century, which was set to 'Hoe groot de Vruechten zijn' in the Amsterdam Psalter of J. Oudaen.

153 SONG OF THE SPIRIT
(WHITSUNTIDE, ETC.)

O.B.C.
Dutch
(M.S.)
SOLO
Now sing we of the Par- a-clete, The Light, the Beam of God, to greet.
CHORUS
SOPRANO
ALTO
1. When Christ blessed his dis - ci - ples, 'Ye are my friends,' he
2. Long af - ter, rose a pro - phet Who hailed the Spi - rit's
TENOR
BASS
said, 'Let not your_ heart be trou - bled, And be ye not a -
day, And said, 'Men_ first in ter - ror As slaves did God o -
Bass
(1.) 'Let not your heart_ be_ trou - bled, And be ye not a -
(2.) And said, 'Men first_ in_ ter - ror As slaves did God o -
-fraid; When_ he the Breath of Truth is come, To_ all the truth he'll
-bey. Then_came the age when man as son Could serve, and so God's
Tenor
(1.) When he is come, To_
(2.) Then came the age, Could
(3.) The power of fraud, Vain_
(4.) He_ sci - ence finds, And_
-fraid; When he the Breath of Truth is come, To all the truth he'll
-bey. Then came the age when man as son Could serve, and so God's

bring you home, Tho' now ye can - not bear it.' So spoke he un - to
grace be won: A third— and we are near it— Will be of love, all
all the truth, tho' now ye can - not bear it.' (1.) So spoke he un - to
serve, and so, a third— and we are near it–(2.) Will be of love, all
forms, and fear, love's crown is ours to wear it;
he the light, and his the he - ro's mer - it;
bring you home, Tho' now ye can - not bear it.' So
grace be won: A third–and we are near it— Will

And prom-ised us the Spi - - rit.
The free - dom of the Spi - - rit.'
Christ - en - dom,
blind - ness gone,
And prom-ised us the Spi - rit.
The free - dom of the Spi - rit.'

3 From slavery and childhood
   Man grows to noble youth,
And free the Spirit makes us
   To follow after truth:
The power of fraud, and dull pretence,
Vain forms, and fear, is banished hence;
   Love's crown is ours to wear it;
Through all our faithless impotence
   The light shines from the Spirit.

4 Brave thinkers saw the vision,
   The story poets wove,
Of truth and grace unhindered,
   The eternal Spirit's love:
For he the knowledge science finds,
And he the light in artists' minds,
   And his the hero's merit;
All lovely things of all the kinds
   Are planets of the Spirit.

The words have been written for an old Dutch carol tune, given by J. A. Thijm to E. Sedding, who published it in England in 1864. The reference in v. 2 is to the twelfth-century mystic, Joachim of Floris, Dante's:

Il Calavrese abate Giovacchino
Di spirito profetico dotato,

(*Paradiso*, xii) who was the precursor of Francis of Assisi.

154 THE SPIRIT

(WHITSUNTIDE: GENERAL)

COURONS A LA FETE

(CHRISTMAS)

Geoffrey Dearmer

Angevin (M.S.)

In moderate time
SOPRANO ALTO
TENOR BASS
1. Winds of God un - fail - ing fill the sun - lit sails Of a
2. If ye then per - ceive and if the heart de - sire, Shall the
great ship sail - ing where con - jec - ture fails: Seek - ers
mind a - chieve, and spi - rit shall as - pire; Then shall
Seek - ers
Then shall
we, and we must dis - co - ver, Doubt we not tho' the chart is hid– Chart we
man see him, and shall praise him In the fern, in the sea and cloud; Ev - 'ry
we, seek - ers we, Doubt we not, doubt we not.
man, then shall man, In the fern, in the fern,
may not see, Plot - ted by the world's great Lo - ver Down in
flower and tree In the sap of life must raise him, As in

Ga - li - lee; Cap - tain, Prince and Pi - lot he.
Ga - li - lee In the form of man rose he.

3 His is each profession, every man his priest
Who in work's expression finds his joy increased:
In his church are the ploughman, sailor,
Merchant, prince, artisan, and clerk,
All whoe'er they be,
Craftsman, thinker, tinker, tailor,
Come to Galilee,
Find a plan, and that is he.

4 Those who love him wholly need not him confess,
Since their lives must solely him in them express;
He's the goal that man ever searches,
How should man see that goal afar?
Each in his degree
That doth love him, of his church is.
Down in Galilee
Founder of our church was he.

COURONS à la fête, ne différons pas,
Que chacun s'apprête à suivre mes pas.
Venez donc, bergers, bergères,
Hâtez-vous, redoublez vos pas!
Un Dieu plein d'appas
Mérite que l'on s'empresse;
Un Dieu plein d'appas
Vient nous sauver du trépas.

2 Quittons nos houlettes, laissons nos troupeaux,
Prenons nos musettes et nos chalumeaux,
Pour chanter mille chansonnettes,
Pour jouer nos beaux airs nouveaux,
Oublions nos maux,
Ne craignons plus la disette;
Le fils du Très-Haut
Nous donnera ce qu'il faut.

3 Cet enfant aimable et plein de douceur
Demande en partage l'amour de nos coeurs.
Offrons-lui d'un amour sincère,
Aimons-bien ce doux rédempteur;
Ce divin sauveur
Prend pitié de nos misères;
Ce divin sauveur
Vient nous combler de bonheur.

4 Il voit notre crime et sa charité
Le rend la victime d'un père irrité.
Quel excès d'amour le plus tendre!
Nos péchés nous sont effacés;
Cessons de pleurer.
Réjouis-toi, berger Sylvandre;
Cessons de pleurer,
Oublions nos maux passés.

Words written for the melody 'Courons à la fête', in the *Grande Bible des Noëls Angevins*, 1766, republished by Grimault in 1878. Cf. Legeay, *Noëls Anciens*, 1875.

155 APRIL

Geoffrey Dearmer
Welsh
(M.S.)
Rather quick
SOPRANO
ALTO
TENOR
BASS
1. Now A - pril has come, The coun-try grows sweet here, The chiff-chaff and
2. A touch of her wand— The buds rise to meet her, And birds' eyes all
wheat - ear, Be - hold, from the land of ripe o - ran - ges come! And
greet her— Why ev - en the gar - ru - lous ducks on the pond See
cher - ry and plum, With white blos - som gleam - ing, The hill - sides are
signs of her wand! As if the Ma - gi - cian Sent ducks on a
seam - ing. Too long have been dumb The woods and the wold: With
miss - ion With news from be - yond, With ti - dings which they Through

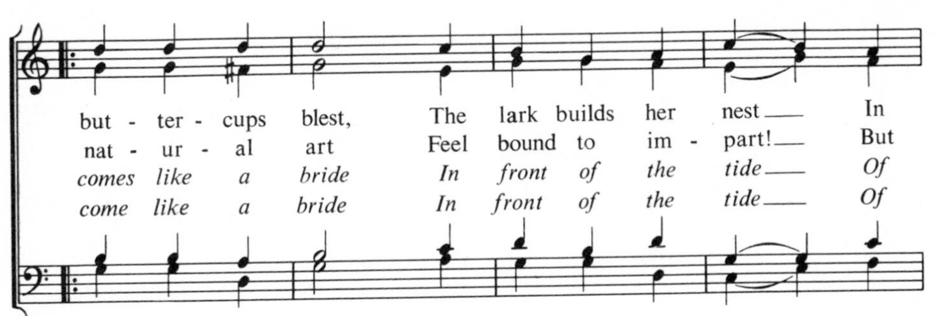
but - ter - cups blest, The lark builds her nest In
nat - ur - al art Feel bound to im - part! But
comes like a bride In front of the tide Of
come like a bride In front of the tide Of

green and in gold. There's cov - er for all birds, For
A - pril and May Them - selves are their voi - ces, And
em - er - ald mist. No keen wea - ther stays her; No
em - er - ald mist. No keen wea - ther stays them; No

Fine
CHORUS
large birds and small birds, Where furled leaves un - fold. She
no bird re - joi - ces Su - perb - ly as they. They
bird dis - o - beys her; No bud can re - sist.
bird dis - o - beys them; No bud can re - sist.
Fine

Words written for the Welsh traditional carol tune, 'Hir Oes i Fair'

156 SUMMER TIME

(SUMMER)

UNE VAINE CRAINTE

(CHRISTMAS)

Rose Fyleman

French (M.S.)

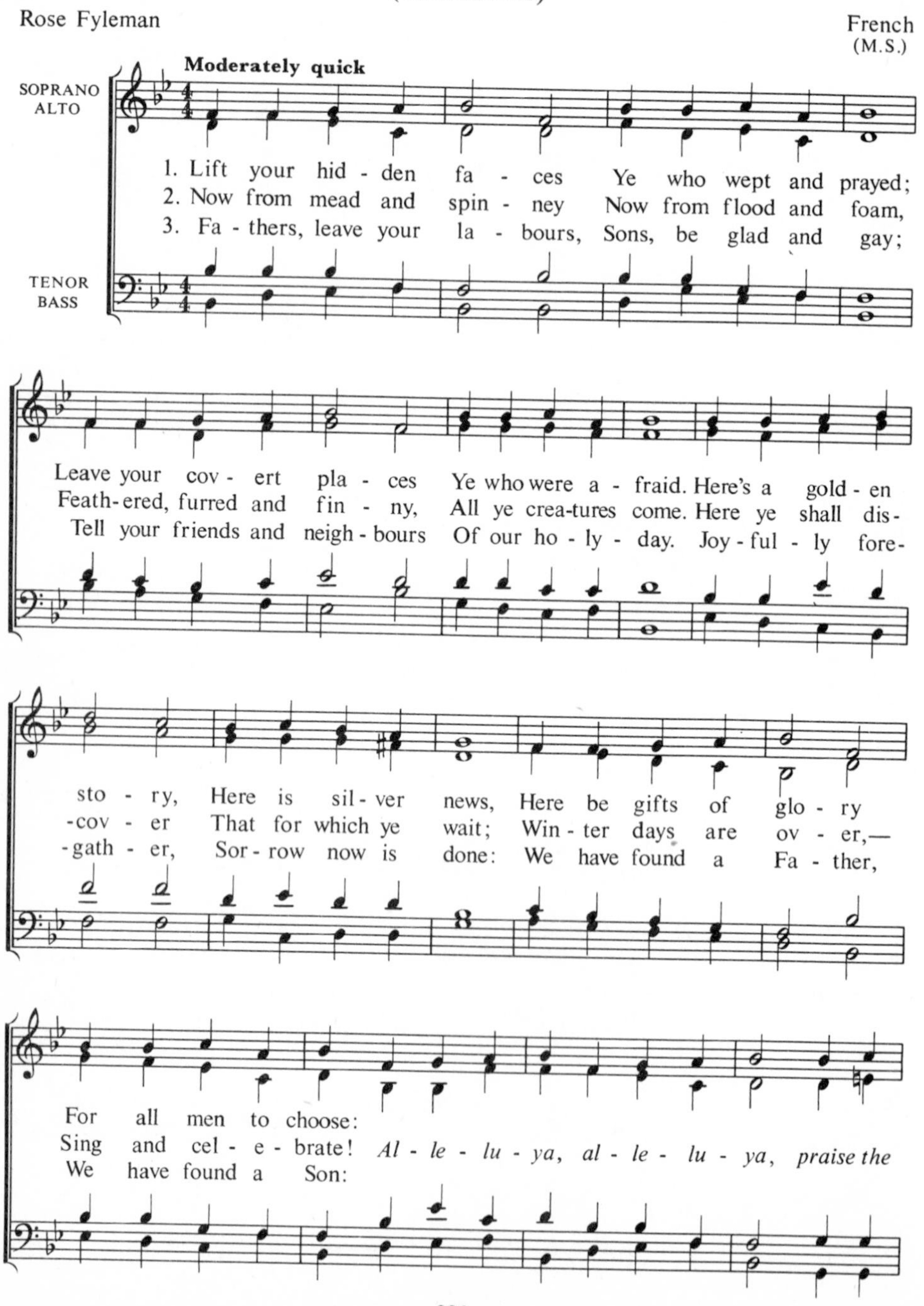

SOPRANO
ALTO
TENOR
BASS
Moderately quick
1. Lift your hid - den fa - ces Ye who wept and prayed;
2. Now from mead and spin - ney Now from flood and foam,
3. Fa - thers, leave your la - bours, Sons, be glad and gay;
Leave your cov - ert pla - ces Ye who were a - fraid. Here's a gold - en
Feath-ered, furred and fin - ny, All ye crea-tures come. Here ye shall dis-
Tell your friends and neigh - bours Of our ho - ly - day. Joy - ful - ly fore-
sto - ry, Here is sil - ver news, Here be gifts of glo - ry
-cov - er That for which ye wait; Win - ter days are ov - er,—
-gath - er, Sor - row now is done: We have found a Fa - ther,
For all men to choose:
Sing and cel - e - brate! Al - le - lu - ya, al - le - lu - ya, praise the
We have found a Son:

Lord with thanks - giv - ing : prais - es sing to God.

UNE vaine crainte trouble vos esprits.
L'âme en est atteinte, vous êtes surpris;
Chassez la tristesse qui règne en ces lieux
Que votre allégresse vole jusqu'aux cieux.
Alleluya, alleluya
Kyrie, Christe, Kyrie eleison.

2 La bonne nouvelle vient en ce grand jour,
Cher peuple fidèle, chercher ton amour.
C'est Dieu qui m'envoie ici t'annoncer
La plus grande joie qui puisse arriver.
Alleluya, etc.

3 Prêtez donc l'oreille attentivement
A cette merveille, car en ce moment
Une vierge mère vous donne le fils
Dont Dieu est le père, Oui, je vous le dis.
Alleluya, etc.

4 Rendez-lui visite, redoublez le pas,
Allez donc bien vite et ne craignez pas.
De vos bergeries, s'il en est besoin,
Et de ces prairies nous prendrons le soin.
Alleluya, etc.

5 Ce maître des Anges, Dieu de majesté,
Dans de pauvres langes est emmailloté.
C'est là le Messie, roi de l'univers,
Qui vous rend la vie en brisant vos fers.
Alleluya, etc.

Based on the French carol, 'Une vaine crainte', with last part of the refrain from Ps. 147. Roques prints the melody, and also Grimault (to the words 'Grâce soit rendue') who says there are many variants in Champagne, Burgundy, and Anjou.

Summer carols seem to have been more common in Wales than in England. Hone, analysing the *Blodeugerdd Cymru*, an Anthology for Wales, in his *Ancient Mysteries*, at the beginning of the nineteenth century, says that it contains '48 Christmas carols, 9 summer carols, 3 May carols, one winter carol, one nightingale carol, and a carol to Cupid'.

157 SUMMER CAROL

Geoffrey Dearmer

Béarnais
(M.S.)

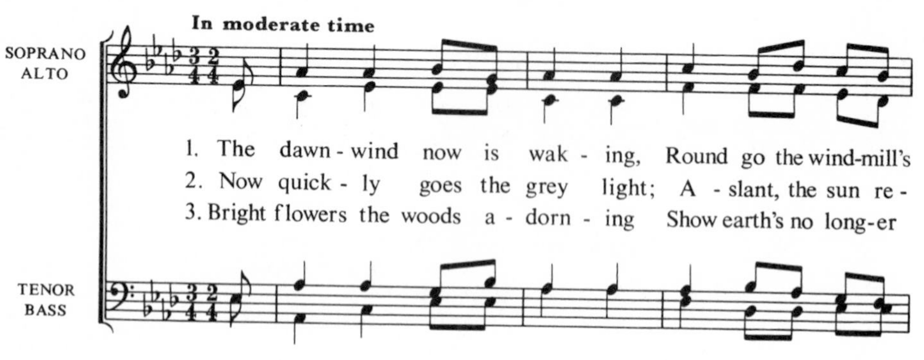

In moderate time
SOPRANO
ALTO
1. The dawn-wind now is wak - ing, Round go the wind-mill's
2. Now quick - ly goes the grey light; A - slant, the sun re -
3. Bright flowers the woods a - dorn - ing Show earth's no long-er
TENOR
BASS

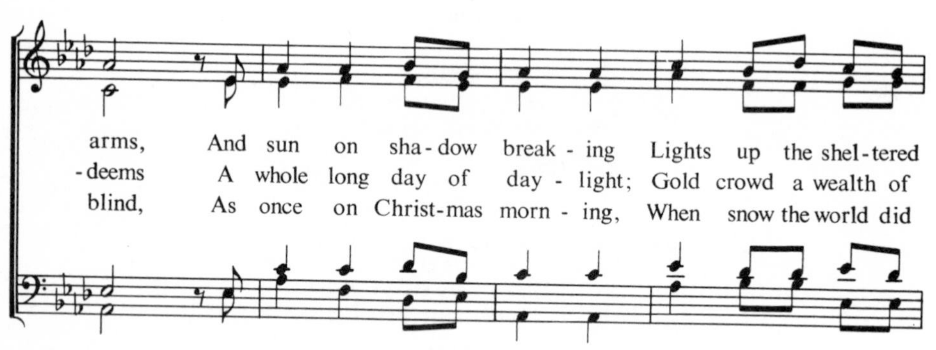

arms, And sun on sha-dow break - ing Lights up the shel-tered
-deems A whole long day of day - light; Gold crowd a wealth of
blind, As once on Christ-mas morn - ing, When snow the world did

farms.— Un-der cows the milk-maids crouch-ing In the
beams.— Chick-ens flut - ter, strut and bab - ble; Run-ning
bind,— When the shep - herds and the sa - ges And the

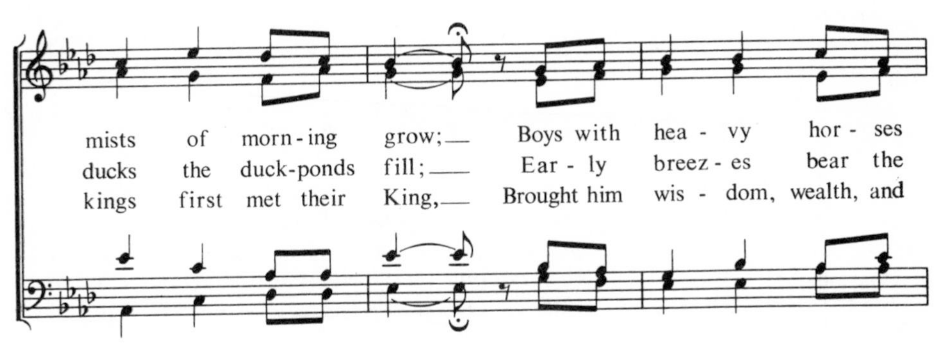
mists of morn-ing grow; — Boys with hea - vy hor - ses
ducks the duck-ponds fill; — Ear - ly breez - es bear the
kings first met their King, — Brought him wis - dom, wealth, and

slouch - ing Down to wa - ter lum - ber slow; — Grey as
gab - ble, And the light in - creas - es till — Soon it
wag - es, Though he was the lit - tlest thing; — Sud-den-

rocks the strag - gling sha-dowy flocks With si - lent shep - herds go.
finds be-yond the rab - ble The black-bird's yel - low bill.
-ly the ir - on ag - es Had yield-ed to the spring.

Written for the Béarnais carol-tune, 'Haut! haut! Pierrot', printed by P. Darricades, in *Noëls Béarnais*, 1877.

158 THANKSGIVING CAROL
(HARVEST: AUTUMN)

Eleanor Farjeon

German, 15th century
(Geoffrey Shaw)

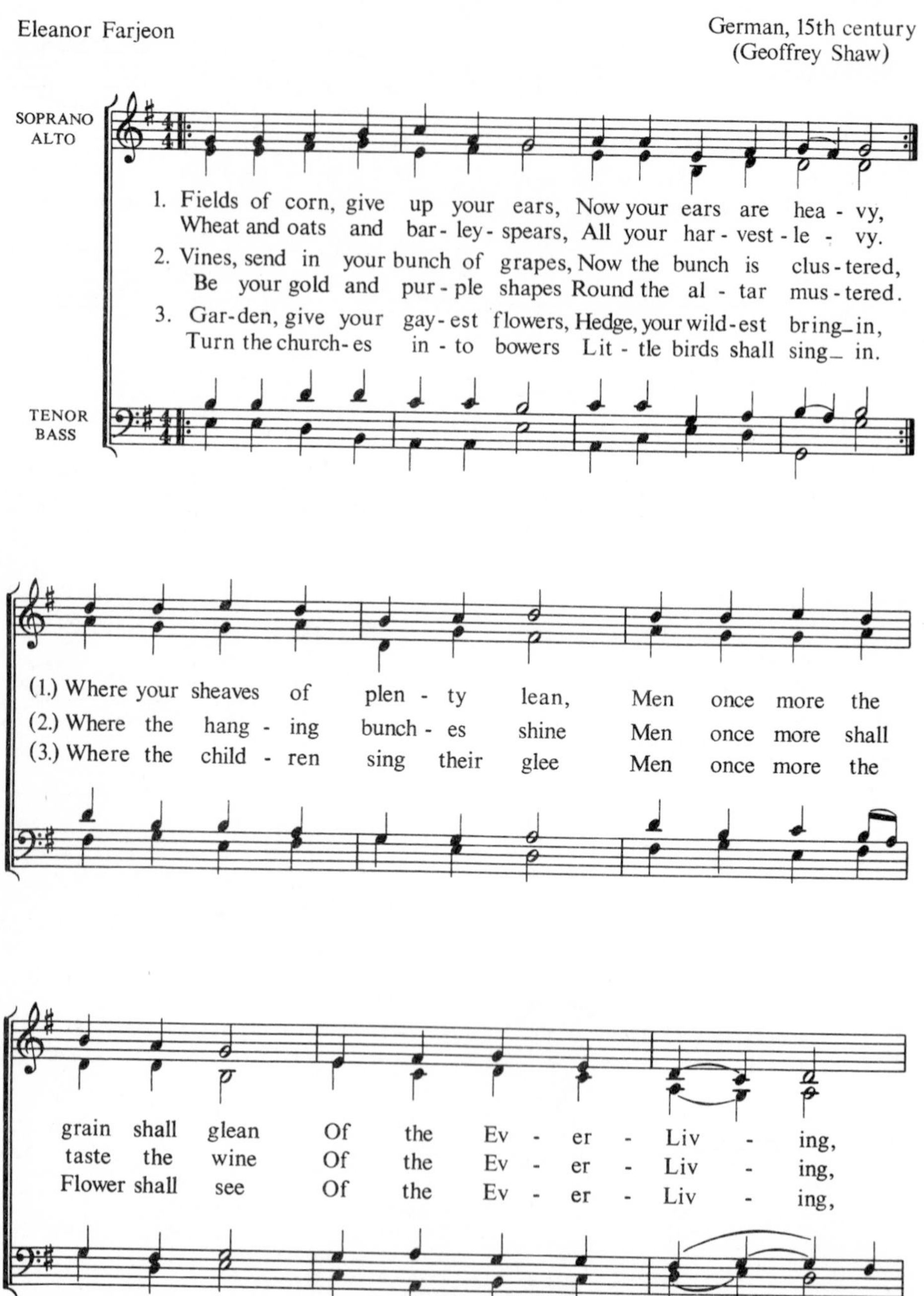
SOPRANO
ALTO
1. Fields of corn, give up your ears, Now your ears are hea - vy,
Wheat and oats and bar - ley - spears, All your har - vest - le - vy.
2. Vines, send in your bunch of grapes, Now the bunch is clus - tered,
Be your gold and pur - ple shapes Round the al - tar mus - tered.
3. Gar - den, give your gay - est flowers, Hedge, your wild - est bring_in,
Turn the church - es in - to bowers Lit - tle birds shall sing_ in.
TENOR
BASS
(1.) Where your sheaves of plen - ty lean, Men once more the
(2.) Where the hang - ing bunch - es shine Men once more shall
(3.) Where the child - ren sing their glee Men once more the
grain shall glean Of the Ev - er - Liv - ing,
taste the wine Of the Ev - er - Liv - ing,
Flower shall see Of the Ev - er - Liv - ing,

God the Lord will bless the field,— Bring - ing in its
God the Lord will bless the root,— Bring - ing in its
God the Lord will bless the throng,— Lift - ing up its

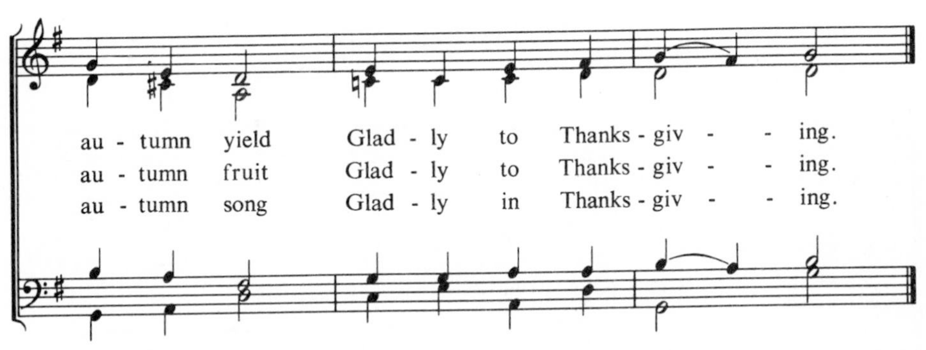
au - tumn yield Glad - ly to Thanks - giv - - ing.
au - tumn fruit Glad - ly to Thanks - giv - - ing.
au - tumn song Glad - ly in Thanks - giv - - ing.

Words based upon 'Der Tag der ist so freudenreich'; with melody in M. Vehe's *Gesangbuch*, 1537, Strassburg, *Gros-Kirchengesangbuch*, 1560, Corner, 1631, &c. A melody, says Riemann, at latest of the fifteenth century; set by J. S. Bach in the eighteenth century. Mone gives the Latin words ('Dies est laetitiae) from a fifteenth-century MS.; but there are many versions of the German words, and several melodies are given by Baümker.

Neale's version 'Royal day that chasest gloom' also appears in the *Cowley Carol Book*.

159 GOLDEN SHEAVES
(HARVEST)

J. S. B. Monsell

Basque (M.S.)

Moderately quick
1. Sing to the Lord of har - vest,
2. By him the clouds drop fat - ness,
3. Heap on his sa - cred al - tar
SOPRANO ALTO
1, 2, 3. Sing to the Lord,
(1.) Sing songs of love and
(2.) The des - erts bloom and
(3.) The gifts his good - ness
TENOR BASS
1, 2, 3. Sing to the Lord,

praise; With joy - ful hearts and voi - - ces Your
spring, The hills leap up in glad - - ness, The
gave, The gold - en sheaves of har - - vest, The

al - le - lu - yas raise: By him the roll - ing
val - leys laugh and sing: He fill - eth with his
souls he died to save: Your hearts lay down be -

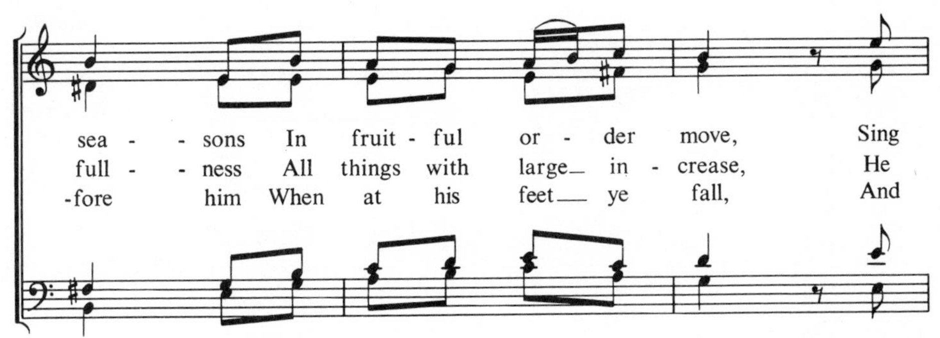
sea - - sons In fruit - ful or - der move, Sing
full - - ness All things with large_ in - crease, He
-fore him When at his feet__ ye fall, And

to the Lord of har - vest A song of hap - py love.
crowns the year with good - ness, With plen - ty and with peace.
with your lives a - dore__ him, Who gave his life for all.
(♯)
C♯ for last verse

Monsell's words set to 'Khanta zagun', as given in C. Bordes, *Archives de la Tradition Basque*, and *Noëls Basques Anciens*, 1897.

160 ANGELS HOLY

(GENERAL: PRAISE)

John Stuart Blackie

Flemish
(M.S.)

In moderate time
SOPRANO
ALTO
TENOR
BASS
1. An - gels ho- ly, high- and- low-ly, Sing the prais- es of— the— Lord; Earth and sky, all liv - ing na - ture, Star - ry tem- ples a - zure- -floored, Man, the stamp of thy— Cre - a - tor, Praise ye, praise ye, God— the— Lord:
2. O - cean hoar- y, tell— his— glo - ry, Cliffs, where tum-bling seas- have- roared, Might - y moun-tains, pur - ple- breast - ed, Crag where ea - gle's pride hath soared, Peaks cloud-cleav- ing, snow-y - crest-ed, Praise ye, praise ye, God— the— Lord:
Praise ye, praise ye, God the Lord, Praise ye, praise ye, God the Lord.

3 Rolling river, praise him ever,
From the mountain's deep vein poured,
Silver fountain, clearly gushing,
Sing the praises of the Lord,
Troubled torrent, madly rushing,
Praise ye, praise ye, God the Lord:
Praise ye, etc.

4 Youth, whose morning smiles at warning,
Age, in counsel deeply stored,
Each glad soul its free course winging,
Praise him, Father, Friend, and Lord,
Each glad voice its free song singing,
Praise the great and mighty Lord:
Praise ye, etc.

Professor Blackie published this rendering of the *Benedicite* in the London *Inquirer* in 1840. By the omission of some lines we have adapted it to the fine Flemish melody, 'De Dryvoudige Geboorte'.

161 THE SHEPHERD
(GENERAL)

Laurence Binyon

Austrian
(M.S.)

In moderate time
SOPRANO
ALTO
1. Down in the val - ley where sum - mer's laugh - ing_ beam
2. Ah, how they strug - gle, and pant, the_ sil - ly_ sheep,
3. Eve - ning is o - ver the land, with_ peace and_ light,
TENOR
BASS
hum
Un - der the wil - low - tree lights a - long the_ stream,
Fear - ing the hands that dip, fear - ing_ w - ter_ deep.
Now sits the shep - herd a - lone in_ eve - ning_ bright,
Shep - herds come driv - ing their flocks and seek_ the_ pool,
Ten - der - ly lift - ed up, glad - ly, one_ by_ one,
Now has he joy with - in, where he pi - peth_ low,
Plung - ing their sheep in the sun - ny_ wa - ter_ cool.
White in the green of the mea - dow,_ lo, they_ run.
See - ing his flock ga - thered round him_ white as_ snow.

The words written for the Austrian dialect folk-carol *Hirtenlied*, 'Schteff'l, du Schlafhaub'n geh' heb' dich aus dai'm Nest', printed by F. Tschischka and J. M. Schottky in *Oesterreichische Volkslieder mit ihren Singweisen*, Buda-Pesth, 1844.

162 BELL CAROL

(GENERAL)

JE SAIS, VIERGE MARIE

(CHRISTMAS)

Steuart Wilson
French
(M.S.)
In moderate time
SOPRANO
ALTO
TENOR
BASS
1. In ev - 'ry town and vil - lage The bells do ring,
2. Then pull your ropes with vi - gour, And watch your ways
3. And we who hear the bells ring With all their might,
ring, do ring, O'er woods and grass and till - age, Hey ding - a - ding,
ways, your ways To thread with strict - est ri - gour The noi - sy maze;
might, their might, As they do say the an - gels sing Both day and night,
ring,
ways
might,
Ring - ing for joy to start the week a - gain, And
Keep in your heart the fire of youth a - light, That
Praise we the men who built our bel - fries high That
call all Christ - ian men To pray and praise and sing.
he who rings a - right May ring in hap - py days.
mu - sic from the sky Might sound for our de - light.

Je sais, vierge Marie,
  Ce que je dois
Pour fêter le Messie
  Qu'ici je vois;
C'est mon Sauveur, dont Dieu seul est le père
  Et vous, Vierge, la mère
  Dont il a fait le choix.

2 Je vois en vous, Princesse,
  Tant de bonté,
D'amour et de tendresse,
  De charité
Que librement, aujourd'hui je demande,
  Une grâce bien grande
  Avec humilité.

3 Vierge sainte et parfaite
  Ah, dites-nous,
Quel fut le doux prophète
  Qui vint à vous,
Pour annoncer cet aimable mystère
  Que vous seriez la mère
  De cet enfant si doux?

4 C'était en Galilée,
  A Nazareth,
La ville où je suis née,
  Comme l'on sait
Dieu m'envoya le message authentique
  D'un esprit angélique
  Qu'on nomme Gabriel.

5 Il dit: 'Vierge Marie,
  Croyez ma voix!
Dieu qui vous a choisie
  Vers vous m'envoie.
Car le Seigneur connaît votre mérite;
  En votre âme il habite
  Et vous juge et vous voit'.

6 Donc à l'ange avec joie
  Je répondis:
Mon Dieu qui vous envoie
  Du paradis,
Sait que je suis sa très humble servante,
  Toujours obéissante
  Et que pour lui je vis.

163 THE THREE TRAITORS
(GENERAL)

Walter de la Mare

English traditional
(M.S.)

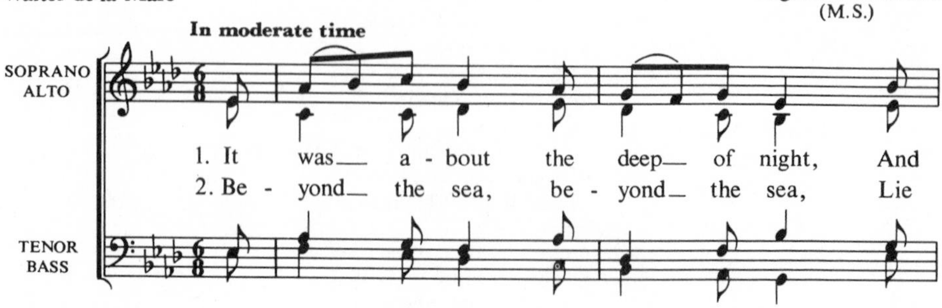

In moderate time

SOPRANO
ALTO

TENOR
BASS

1. It was — a - bout the deep — of night, And still — was earth and sky, — When 'neath — the moon - light dazz - ling bright, Three ghosts — came rid - ing by. —

2. Be - yond — the sea, be - yond — the sea, Lie king - doms for them all: — I wot — their steeds trod wea - ri - ly — The jour - ney was not small. —

ALTERNATIVE VERSION (may be used for verses 3, 6, 9, & 11, or for any other selection of verses if desired)

(Melody in Tenor)
3. By rock and des - ert, sand and stream, They foot-sore late — did go: — Now

like a sweet and bless - ed dream Their path was deep with snow.

4 Shining like hoar-frost, rode they on,
Three ghosts in earth's array:
It was about the hour when wan
Night turns at hint of day.

5 O, but their hearts with woe distraught
Hailed not the wane of night,
Only for Jesu still they sought
To wash them clean and white.

6 For bloody was each hand, and dark
With death each orbless eye;—
It was three Traitors mute and stark
Came riding silent by.

7 Silver their raiment and their spurs,
And silver-shod their feet,
And silver-pale each face that stares
Into the moonlight sweet.

8 And he upon the left that rode
Was Pilate, Prince of Rome,
Whose journey once lay far abroad,
And now was nearing home.

9 And he upon the right that rode
Herod of Salem sate,
Whose mantle dipped in children's blood
Shone clear as heaven's gate.

10 And he these twain betwixt that rode
Was clad as white as wool,
Dyed in the mercy of his God
White was he crown to sole.

11 Throned mid a myriad saints in bliss
Rise shall the Babe of heaven
To shine on these three ghosts, I wis,
Smit through with sorrows seven.

12 Babe of the blessèd Trinity
Shall smile their steeds to see:
Herod and Pilate riding by,
And Judas one of three.

The tune from Gilbert, 1823, 'The Three Knights'.

164 CAROL OF BEAUTY

(GENERAL: PRAISE)

QUELLE EST CETTE ODEUR AGREABLE?

(CHRISTMAS)

Steuart Wilson

French (M.S.)

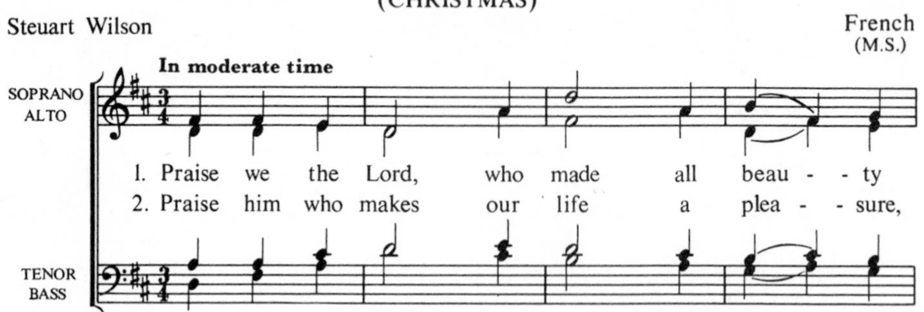
In moderate time
SOPRANO
ALTO
TENOR
BASS
1. Praise we the Lord, who made all beau - - ty
2. Praise him who makes our life a plea - - sure,

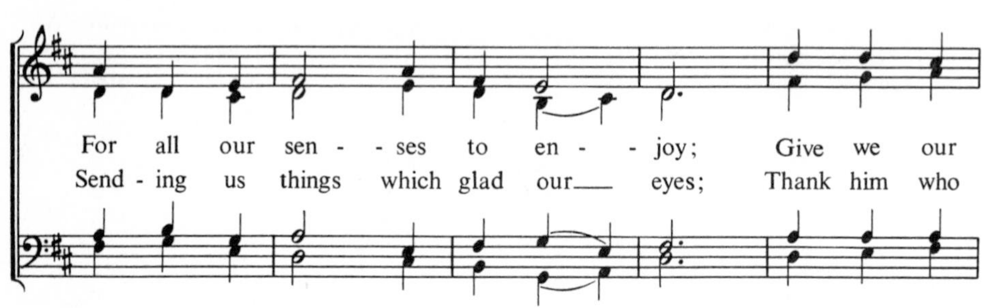
For all our sen - - ses to en - - joy; Give we our
Send - ing us things which glad our eyes; Thank him who

hum - ble thanks and du - ty That sim - ple plea - sures
gives us wel - come lei - sure, That in our heart sweet

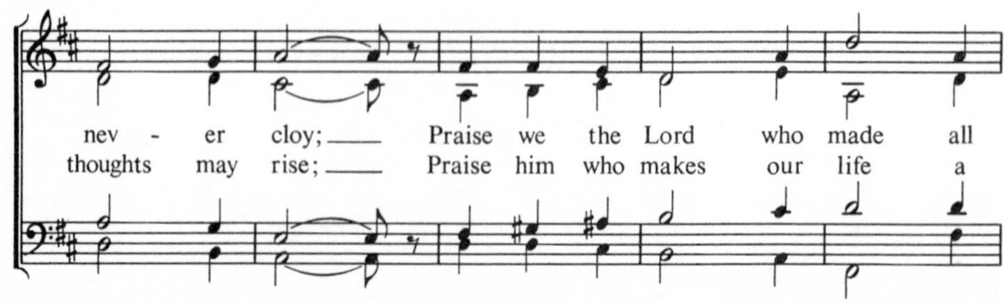
nev - er cloy; Praise we the Lord who made all
thoughts may rise; Praise him who makes our life a

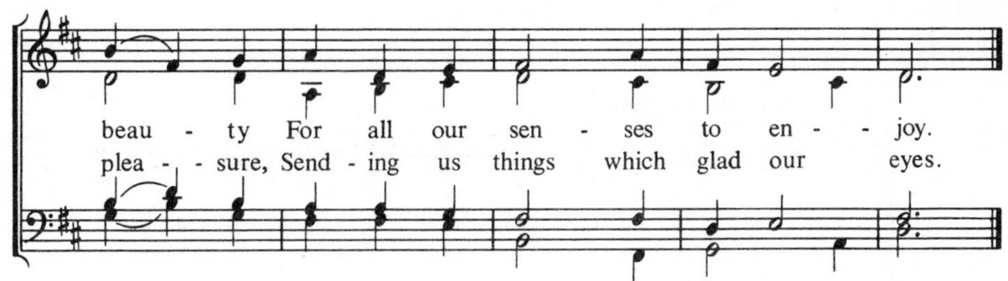
beau - ty For all our sen - ses to en - - joy.
plea - - sure, Send - ing us things which glad our eyes.

3 Praise him who loves to see young lovers,
  Fresh hearts that swell with youthful pride;
Thank him who sends the sun above us,
  As bridegroom fit to meet his bride;
Praise him who loves to see young lovers,
  Fresh hearts that swell with youthful pride.

4 Praise him who by a simple flower
  Lifts up our hearts to things above;
Thank him who gives to each one power
  To find a friend to know and love;
Praise him who by a simple flower
  Lifts up our hearts to things above.

5 Praise we the Lord who made all beauty
  For all our senses to enjoy;
Give we our humble thanks and duty
  That simple pleasures never cloy;
Praise we the Lord who made all beauty
  For all our senses to enjoy.

QUELLE est cette odeur agréable
  Bergers, qui ravit tous nos sens?
S'exhale-t-il rien de semblable
  Au milieu des fleurs du printemps?
Quelle est cette odeur agréable
  Bergers, qui ravit tous nos sens?

2 Mais quelle éclatante lumière
  Dans la nuit vient frapper nos yeux!
L'astre du jour, dans sa carrière,
  Fût-il jamais si radieux?
Mais quelle éclatante lumière
  Dans la nuit vient frapper nos yeux?

3 Ne craignez rien, peuple fidèle,
  Ecoutez l'ange du Seigneur;
Il vous annonce une nouvelle
  Qui va vous combler de bonheur,
Ne craignez rien, peuple fidèle,
  Ecoutez l'ange du Seigneur.

4 A Bethléem, dans une crèche,
  Il vient de vous naître un Sauveur;
Allons, que rien ne vous empêche
  D'adorer votre Rédempteur.
A Bethléem, dans une crèche,
  Il vient de vous naître un Sauveur.

5 Dieu tout-puissant, gloire éternelle
  Vous soit rendue jusqu'aux cieux;
Que la paix soit universelle,
  Que la grâce abonde en tous lieux.
Dieu tout-puissant, gloire éternelle
  Vous soit rendue jusqu'aux cieux.

Words written for the French carol, 'Quelle est cette odeur agréable'. The tune found its way to England so long ago as to appear in Gay's *Beggar's Opera*, 1728. Paul Arma, in *Noël, chantons noël*, gives two different versions: 'Bergers, écoutez la musique', and 'Viens vite, laisse ta houlette'.

165 GOLDEN MORNINGS
(GENERAL)

A.F.D. English traditional (M.S.)

In moderate time
SOPRANO
ALTO
TENOR
BASS
1. They saw the light shine out a - far On Christ-mas in the morn - ing; And straight they knew it was the star That came to give them warn - ing: Then did they fall on bend - ed knee, The light their heads a - dorn - ing, And praised the
2. For three short years he went a - broad And set men's hearts a - burn - ing; That mis - sion turned the world to God And brought the night to morn - ing: He bore for man re - pulse and pain, In - gra - ti - tude, and scorn - ing; He suf - fered,

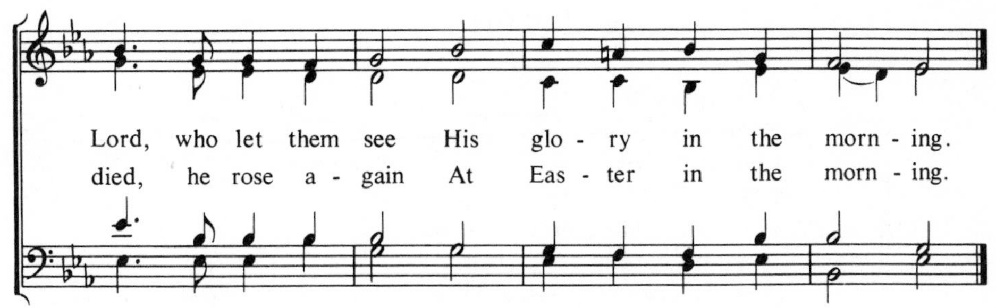
Lord, who let them see His glo - ry in the morn - ing.
died, he rose a - gain At Eas - ter in the morn - ing.

3 O every thought be of his grace,
On each day in the morning;
And for his kingdom's loveliness
Our souls be ever yearning:
So may we live, to heaven our hearts
In hope for ever turning;
Then may we die, as each departs,
In joy at our new morning.

Part 2

Paean

Lift up your heads, rejoice and dance,
Forget the days of mourning!
The waves of light advance, advance,
The fire of love is burning.
Farewell to hate and stupid fears,
To ignorance and sorrow!
He who was with us through the years
Shall bring us to the morrow!

There are two tunes (this, from Fyfe's *Carols*, 1860, and No. 146) to which the name of 'Golden Carol' is found attached, with a pair of indifferent verses, in some publications of about ninety years ago. The name 'Golden Carol' was loosely used and was sometimes applied to 'The First Nowell'; but the real text of the Golden Carol is in a different metre, fifteenth century in its earlier form, and its tune is lost (see No. 173). The two tunes, which we are calling 'Golden Mornings' (No. 165) and 'Golden' (No. 146) are, however, fine and distinct traditional tunes; and the verses attached to them seem to contain phrases of an original which may have been sung to them. These phrases have therefore been retained in this new text, which may be sung equally well to No. 146.

Part 2 has been supplied for occasions when one concluding verse is needed for a carol recital or service (cf. No. 16); it can also be treated as a fourth verse to this carol.

166 CAROL OF SERVICE

(GENERAL)

PROMPTEMENT LEVEZ-VOUS

(CHRISTMAS)

Steuart Wilson — French (M.S.)

Moderately quick
SOPRANO
ALTO
TENOR
BASS
1. Up, my neigh-bour, come a - way, See the work for us to-day, The hands to help, the mouths to feed, The sights to see, the books to read:
2. Up, my neigh-bour, see the plough For our hands lies wait-ing now; Grasp well the stilt, yoke up the team, Stride out to meet the morn-ing beam:
Up and get us gone, to help the world a-long, Up and get us gone, my neigh-bour.

3 Up, my neighbour, see the land
Ready for the sower's hand;
The plough has made an even tilth,
The furrows wait the golden spilth:

Up and get etc.

4 Up, my neighbour, now the corn
Ripens at the harvest morn;
Then let it to our sickle yield,
And pile with sheaves the golden field:

Up and get etc.

5 Up, my neighbour, let us pray,
Thank our Maker every day,
Who gave us work our strength to test
And made us proud to do our best:

Up and get etc.

PROMPTEMENT levez-vous, mon voisin,
Le Sauveur de la terre
Est enfin parmi nous, mon voisin,
Envoyé par son père, mon voisin.

Allez, mon voisin, à la crèche, mon voisin,
Courez, mon voisin, à la crèche.

2 Veillant sur mon troupeau, mon voisin,
Autour de ce village
J'entends un air nouveau, mon voisin,
Et du plus beau langage, mon voisin.

Allez, etc.

3 Rempli d'étonnement, mon voisin,
Je laisse ma houlette
Pour voir ce Dieu naissant, mon voisin,
Accomplir le prophète, mon voisin.

Allez, etc.

4 Je ne suis pas trompeur, mon voisin,
Les choses sont certaines;
Notre divin Sauveur, mon voisin,
Finit toutes nos peines, mon voisin.

Allez, etc.

5 Choisissez le meilleur, mon voisin,
De votre bergerie,
Donnez-le de bon coeur, mon voisin,
A Joseph, à Marie, mon voisin.

Allez, etc.

6 L'enfer est confondu, mon voisin,
Le ciel a la victoire;
Le Messie attendu, mon voisin,
Chantons, chantons sa gloire, mon voisin.

Allez, etc.

'Promptement levez-vous, mon voisin', upon which the English words are based, is an example of a carol made up for a familiar folk-tune, in this case an old ritournelle, 'C'est de nos moutons l'allure, mon cousin'. The carol is sung in many parts of France, and is printed by Grimault and by Legeay.

167 CAROL OF THE KINGDOM
(GENERAL)

Steuart Wilson

Manx (M.S.)

SOPRANO
ALTO
TENOR
BASS
ba - by
car-pen-ter,
1. When Je - sus was a ba - by And born of mor-tal men, The first who asked to see him Came straight from their sheep-pen: So let each one re - mem - ber, When he his off-'ring brings, That Je - sus loved the shep - herds As well as the three kings.
2. When Je - sus was a car-pen-ter, He held the saw and adze, And learned a trade to fol - low Like oth - er sim - ple lads: So let us not be sha - med Of hon - est work and sweat, Re-mem-b'ring that a bet - ter brow Than ours was of - ten wet.

3 When Jesus was a-dying
Upon the cruel tree,
Two thieves upon each hand of him
He had for company:
So look not upon any man
With vain or scornful eyes,
For one poor thief was called by him
To dwell in paradise.

4 Now Jesus has gone up on high,
And truth and justice reign.
Let tenderness and kindliness
Dwell in the hearts of men:
So, when we have to leave this earth,
If only we can know
We leave it better than we found,
We shall be glad to go.

The tune is a traditional Manx carol-tune 'Ny Drogh Vraane', noted by the late Dr. John Clague, apparently from T. Cowell, Marown.

PART IV

TRADITIONAL CAROLS

(*together with some by old writers*)

SET TO TUNES BY MODERN COMPOSERS

168 BEN JONSON'S CAROL
(CHRISTMAS EVE: CHRISTMAS)

Ben Jonson

Rutland Boughton

SOPRANO
ALTO
TENOR
BASS
1. I sing the birth was born_to-night, The au-thor both of life_and light; The an-gels so_did sound_it, And, like the_ra-vished shep-herds said, Who_saw the light,_and_ were_a-fraid, Yet searched, and true_they found it.
2. The Son of God, th'e-ter-nal King, That did_us all sal-va-tion bring, And freed our soul_from dan-ger, He whom the_whole world could_not take, The_Word, which heav'n_and_ earth_did_make, Was now_laid in_a man-ger.

3 The Father's wisdom willed it so,
The Son's obedience knew no No;
Both wills were in one stature,
And, as that wisdom had decreed,
The Word was now made flesh indeed,
And took on him our nature.

4 What comfort by him we do win,
Who made himself the price of sin,
To make us heirs of glory!
To see this babe, all innocence,
A martyr born in our defence,
Can man forget the story?

169 TYRLEY, TYRLOW
(CHRISTMAS)

c. 1450

Peter Warlock

Fast and gay
TENORS
VOICES
ACCPT.
1. A-
f Ob. & fag.
Horns & violas
-bout the field they piped full right, So mer-ri-ly the shep-herds be-
mp Strings
-gan to blow; A-down from heav'n they
Fl.
f
Cl. & horns
mf Strings

CHORUS (lightly)
S.
A.
saw__ a light:
*Tyr - ley, tyr - - low, tyr - ley, tyr - -
T.
B.
-low, tyr - ley, tyr - low!
Ob., cl. & fag.
f Strings sustain
Female voices in unison
2. Of an - gels there came a
mp Strings

* Pronunciation nearer to *tyrol-y* than *turl-y*.

com - pa - ny, With mer - ry songs and mel - o - - dy,
Fl. & cl. ob.
cresc.
f
Horns
Male voices in unison
The shep-herds a - non gan them a - spy:
Strings mf
SOPRANOS
Tyr - ley, tyr - low, tyr - ley, tyr - low, tyr - ley, tyr -
Cl.
p Fag. +Strings pizz.
-low!
Fl.
Clar.
Fl.
f Strings sustain
Ped.

169—Tyrley, Tyrlow

CHORUS
mf
3. The shep - herds hied them to Beth-lem, To
mf
Fl. & clar.
mf W-W & horns
*
see — that bless - ed sun - nes beam; And
f
f
Strings
there they found — that glo - rious stream: — Tyr -
p
Full, without trombones
p
Clar.

-ley, tyr - low, tyr - ley, tyr - low, tyr - ley, tyr - low!
Fl.
+Ob.
Fl. & cl.
Ob. & fag.
+pizz.
+Horns
Horns
Soprano solo (or soprano semi-chorus)
4. Now
Fl. & cl.
Ob. & fag.
Fl. & cl.
Violins
pray we to that me - ke child, And to his mo - ther that
mp Strings
is so mild, The which was nev - er de - filed:
+ Horns

169—Tyrley, Tyrlow

CHORUS (lightly)
mf
Tyr - ley, tyr - low, tyr - ley, tyr - low, tyr - ley,
mf
mp
pizz.
Fag. + celli pizz.
Fl.
tyr - low!
(TENORS) 5. That
Ob.
Clar.
Fl.
Strings sustain
we may come un - to his bliss, Where joy shall
Fl.
p subito
Cl. & viola
Str., w-w, & horns
cresc. molto

BASSES
nev - er miss,
Then may we sing in
f
ff
W-W, horns, trumpets, glock.
mf Strings
par - a - dise:
SOPRANOS
mf (lightly)
Tyr - -
Fl.
+Clar. & fag.
p
Strings
Clar.
mf legato
-ley, tyr - low, tyr - ley, tyr - low, tyr - ley, tyr - low!
Ob., cl., & fag.
f Strings
Ped.

6. I pray you all that be here,
For to sing and make good cheer,
In the
f
ff
Fl.
Brass alone
+Fag.
+pizz.
Allargando molto
W-W & horns
*

a tempo

wor - ship of God this year: ________

ff Full orchestra

Ob. + fag. *a tempo* Clar.

lunga *Presto*

Tyr - ley, tyr - low, tyr - ley, tyr - low,

lunga

Fl. *lunga* *Presto*

lunga Horns + *pizz.*

lunga

tyr - - ley, tyr - - low!

lunga

lunga

W-W & horns

fff *sffz* Trombones, cl., fag. + *pizz.*

+ D. Bass

From the *Commonplace Book* of Richard Hill (cf. No. 36), c. 1500, and the Bodleian MS. (Engl. Poet. e. 1), 1460-90, the latter printed by Wright, *Songs and Carols* (Percy Society), 1847, and Greene, No. 79.

170 NEW PRINCE, NEW POMP
(CHRISTMAS)

Robert Southwell — John Ireland

Not slowly
SOPRANO
ALTO
TENOR
BASS
No - well, No - well, No - well, sing we with mirth!
Christ is come well, with us to dwell, By his most
no - ble birth.
1. Be - hold a sim - ple ten - der
2. The inns are full; no man will
babe, In freez - ing win - - ter night, In home - ly
yield This lit - tle pil - - grim bed; But forced he

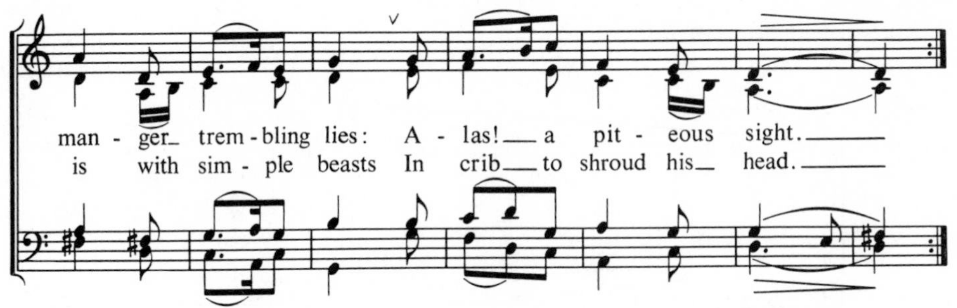
man - ger_ trem - bling lies: A - las! __ a pit - eous sight. ____
is with sim - ple beasts In crib __ to shroud his_ head. ____

3 Despise him not for lying there;
First what he is inquire:
An orient pearl is often found
In depth of dirty mire.

4 Weigh not his crib, his wooden dish,
Nor beasts that by him feed;
Weigh not his mother's poor attire,
Nor Joseph's simple weed.

5 This stable is a prince's court,
This crib his chair of state,
The beasts are parcel of his pomp,
The wooden dish his plate;

6 The persons in that poor attire
His royal liveries wear;
The Prince himself is come from heaven.
This pomp is prizèd there.

7 With joy approach, O Christian wight,
Do homage to thy King;
And highly praise this humble pomp,
Which he from heaven doth bring.

1 and 2. We have altered 'silly' to its modern equivalent 'simple'. 5. *Parcel* in the old sense of 'part' (from 'particella', 'parcelle').
The prelude 'Nowell', &c., is an old prelude, but not by Southwell.
Robert Southwell was the good Jesuit, executed for treason under Elizabeth.

171 SHAKESPEARE'S CAROL

(CHRISTMAS, Secular)

FIRST TUNE

Dr. Arne
(arr. M.S.)

Moderato
VOICES IN UNISON
mf
1. Blow, blow,_ thou_ win - ter
freeze, thou_ bit - ter
ACCPT.
mf

wind,_ Thou art_ not_ so un - kind,_ Thou art not so un -
sky,_ That dost_ not_ bite so nigh_ As ben - e - fits for -

-kind As man's in - gra - - ti - tude; Thy tooth is not so
-got, As ben - e - fits ___ for - got: Though thou the wa - ters

keen, Be - cause thou art not seen, Thy
warp, Thy sting is not so sharp, Though
tooth is not so keen, Be - cause thou art not seen, Al-
thou the wa - ters warp, Thy sting is not so sharp As
-though thy breath be rude, Al- though thy breath be rude, Al-
friend re - mem - ber'd not, As friend re - mem - ber'd not, As
-though thy breath be rude.
friend re - mem - ber'd not.
2. Freeze,
Fine

171 SHAKESPEARE'S CAROL

(**CHRISTMAS**, Secular)

SECOND TUNE

R. J. S. Stevens

Andante
SOPRANO
ALTO
TENOR
BASS
Blow, blow, thou win - ter_ wind, Thou_ art_ not_ so un -
-kind_ As man's in - gra - ti - tude, as man's in - gra - - ti - tude;
Thy_ tooth is_ not so_ keen, Be - cause_ thou_ art not_
seen,_ Al - though thy breath be rude,_ al - -
-though thy_ breath be rude. Heigh - ho! Sing, heigh - ho! un -
Allegretto moderato

cresc.
-to the green hol-ly: Most friend - ship is feign - ing, most
cresc.
f
p
f
lov-ing mere fol-ly: Then, heigh - ho, the hol-ly, the hol-ly! This
f
p
f
life is most jol - ly, most jol - ly, this life is most
jol - ly, most jol - ly, this life is most jol - ly!
Fine
Fine
Tempo Imo
mf
p
2. Freeze, freeze, thou bit - ter sky, That dost not
mf
p

171—Shakespeare's Carol

bite so nigh As ben-e-fits for-got, as ben-e-fits for-
for-got, as ben-e-fits for-
-got: Though thou the wa-ters warp, Thy sting is not so
-got: Though thou the wa-ters warp, Thy
sharp As friend re-mem-ber'd
sharp, is not so sharp As friend re-mem-ber'd
sting's not so sharp As friend re-mem-ber'd
sting is not so sharp As friend re-mem-ber'd
not, as friend re-mem-ber'd not.
not, as friend re-mem-ber'd not.
not, as friend re-mem-ber'd not.
dim.
D.S.

From *As You Like It*, Act II. Dr. Arne does not include the chorus, as Stevens does.

172 MAKE WE MERRY

(CHRISTMAS, Secular)

c. 1500

Martin Shaw

Allegro con spirito (♩. = about 100)
VOICES IN UNISON
ACCPT.
f
1. Make we mer-ry, both more and less, For
now is the time of Chris-te-mas, of Chris-te-mas, of Chris-te-mas.
mf
2. Let no man come in-to this hall, Nor
groom, nor page, nor yet mar-shall, But that some sport he bring with-al.

3. If that he say he can-not sing, Some
o-ther sport then let him bring, That it may please at this feast-ing.
4. If he say he naught can do,
Then, for my love, ask him no mo' But to the stocks then let him

f
go.
5. Make we mer-ry, both more and less, For
f
now is the time of Chris-te-mas, of Christ - mas, of Christ - mas, of
Christ - - - - - - - - mas.
Ped.
*

1. more and less—in the old sense, 'great and small'. 4. mo'—more. stocks—The Lord of Misrule at Christmas often had stocks, pillory, and gibbet.

From the *Commonplace Book* of Richard Hill (cf. No. 36), and Balliol MS. 354. See Greene, No. 11.

173 THE GOLDEN CAROL
(CHRISTMAS: EPIPHANY)

15th century
R. Vaughan Williams
Allegro vivace
VOICES IN UNISON
1. — Now is Chris - te - mas y - come, Fa-ther and Son_ to-
3. Three king - es came fro Ga - li - lee To Beth - le - hem, that
5. 'From whence come ye, you king - es three?' 'Out of the East, as
7. — When they came in - to the place, Where Je - sus with_ his
8. — Kneel we now___ here a - down; Pray we in good de-
ACCPT.
Marcato
-ge - ther in one, Ho - ly Ghost, as ye__ be one,__ In
fair__ ci - ty, For__ to of - fer and__ to see,__ By
ye__ may see, To__ seek him that ev - er shall be,__ By
mo - ther was, Of-fer'd they up with great_ so - lace,__ In
-vo - ti - oun, To__ that King of great_ re - nown,_ For
fere - a, God send___ us good new year - a.
night - a, It was___ a full fair sight - a.
right - a,___ Lord___ and king and knight - a.'
fere - a,___ Gold,___ in - cense, and myrrh - a.
grace - a, In heav'n___ to have a place - a.

173—The Golden Carol

2. I will you sing with all my might, Of a child— so
4. As they came forth with their offer-ing, They met with Her-od, that
6. They took their leave, both eld and ying, Of Her-od,— that
fair in sight, A maid-en bare on Christ-mas night,— So
mood-y king, He ask-ed them of their com-ing,— That
mood-y king, And forth they went with their offer-ing— By
still-a,— As— it was his will-a.
tide-a, And thus— to them he said-a:
light-a, By the star— that shone so bright-a.

6. eld and ying—old and young. 7. Where—orig. MS., 'There' with this meaning.

This, which has most right to the name, 'Golden Carol', was printed by T. Wright from the Bodleian MS. Eng. Poet. e. I (*c.* 1460-90) in his *Songs and Carols* (Percy Society), 1847; also by Sandys in his *Christmas Tide*, 1852; A. H. Bullen (*Carols and Poems*, 1885) prints another version from *Notes and Queries*. Miss E. Rickert (*Ancient English Christmas Carols*, 1910) gives two versions, one in sixteen verses and without the tag. We have used that by Mr. F. Sidgwick in *Ancient Carols*, 1908. Greene, No. 125, gives a version from B. M. Harley 541. No tune has survived. Cf. Nos. 146 and 165.

174 WELCOME YULE
(CHRISTMAS, ST. STEPHEN, ETC.: CANDLEMAS)

15th century
Sydney H. Nicholson
SOLO VOICE
Wel-come Yule, thou merry man, In wor-ship of this ho - ly day!
With vigour
SOPRANO
ALTO
TENOR
BASS
rit.
tempo
Wel-come Yule, wel - - come Yule.
1. Wel-come be thou,
2, 3, 4, 5, Wel-come be ye,
(1.) hea - - ven-king, Wel - come born in one morn - ing,
(2.) Ste - phen and John, Wel - come Inno - cents ev - 'ry one,
(3.) good New Year, Wel - come Twelfth Day, both in fere,
(4.) Can - dle-mas, Wel - come be ye, queen of bliss,
(5.) that are here, Wel - come all, and make good cheer,
Wel - come for whom we shall sing
Wel - come Tho-mas, mar - - tyr one:
Wel - come saint-es lief and dear:
Wel - come both to more and less:
Wel - come all an - o - - - ther year!
Wel - come Yule,
VERSES 1 - 4
wel - - - come Yule.
LAST VERSE
wel - - - come Yule.

3. in fere—together lief—beloved

Sloane MS. 2593 (cf. No. 36), of the beginning of the fifteenth century or *temp.* Henry VI. Another version in the Bodleian Douce MS. 302, the collection of John Audlay, the blind chaplain, *c.* 1430, printed in Sandys' *Christmastide*, 1852. See Preface. Greene, No. 7.

175 THE VIRGIN'S CRADLE HYMN
(NATIVITY)

Pr. S.T. Coleridge

Edmund Rubbra

Andante moderato (flowing)
mp
SOPRANO
Dor - mi, Je - su! Ma - ter ri - det
Sleep, sweet babe! my cares be- guil - ing:
ALTO
Dor - mi, Je - su! Ma - ter ri - det
Sleep, sweet babe! my cares be - guil - ing:
TENOR
Dor - mi, Je - su! Ma - ter ri - det
Sleep, sweet babe! my cares be - guil - ing:
BASS
Dor - mi, Je - su! Ma - ter ri - det
Sleep, sweet babe! my cares be - guil - ing:
Andante moderato (flowing)
(for practice only)

175—The Virgin's Cradle Hymn

Quae tam dul - cem som - num vi - det, Dor - mi, Je - su!
Mo - ther sits be - side thee smi - ling; Sleep, my dar - ling,
rall.
mf a tempo
blan - du - le! Si non dor - mis,
ten - der - ly! If thou sleep not,

ma - - ter plo - - rat, In - ter fil - a can - tans o - rat,
mo - - ther mourn - eth, Sing - ing as her wheel she turn - eth:

ma - - ter plo - - rat In - ter fil - a can - tans o - rat,
mo - - ther mourn - eth, Sing - ing as her wheel she turn - eth:

ma - - ter plo - - rat In - ter fil - a can - tans o - rat,
mo - - ther mourn - eth, Sing - ing as her wheel_ she turn - eth:

ma - ter plo - - rat In - ter fil - a can - tans o - rat,
mo - ther mourn - eth, Sing - ing as her wheel she turn - eth:

Blan - - de, ven - - i, som - nu - le.
Come, soft slum - - ber, balm - i - ly!

Blan - - de, ven - - i, som - nu - le.
Come, soft slum - - ber, balm - i - ly!

Blan - - de, ven - - i, som - - - - - nu - le.
Come,_ soft_ slum - - ber, balm - - - - - i - ly!

Blan - - de, ven - - i, som - nu - le.
Come,_ soft_ slum - - ber, balm - i - ly!

Coleridge copied the Latin words from a print in a German village, and paraphrased them as printed, under the title 'The Virgin's Cradle Hymn'. These verses are therefore akin to such Cradle Hymns as the Chester Nuns' Song (No. 67), 'Lullay, my liking' (No. 182), and the Lute Book Lullaby (No. 30).

176 HERRICK'S ODE
(NATIVITY)

Robert Herrick — Armstrong Gibbs

SOPRANO
ALTO
TENOR
BASS
1. In num - bers, and but these_ few, I sing thy birth,_ O
2. In - stead of neat en - clo - sures Of in - ter - wo - ven
Je - su, Thou pret - ty ba - by, born_ here, With su - pera - bun - dant
o - siers; In - stead of fra - grant po - sies Of daf - fo - dils_ and
scorn_ here, Who for thy prince - ly_ port_ here, Hadst
ro - - - ses, Thy cra - dle, king - ly_ stran - ger, As
for thy place Of birth, a base Out - sta - ble for_ thy_ court_ here.
gos - pel tells, Was no - thing else But here a home - ly_ man - ger.

3 But we with silks, not crewels,
With sundry precious jewels,
And lily-work will dress thee;
And, as we dispossess thee
Of clouts, we'll make a chamber,
Sweet babe, for thee,
Of ivory,
And plastered round with amber.

4 The Jews, they did disdain thee,
But we will entertain thee
With glories to await here
Upon thy princely state here,
And, more for love than pity,
From year to year
We'll make thee here
A free-born of our city.

177 OUT OF YOUR SLEEP
(NATIVITY)

15th century

Martin Shaw

Rather slowly

SOPRANO
ALTO

1. Out of_ your sleep a - rise and wake, For God_ man-
2. And through a maid - e fair and wise Now man_ is
4. That ev-er was thrall, now is he free; That ev-er was
6. Now, bless - ed Broth - er, grant us grace, At doom - es

TENOR
BASS

-kind_ now hath y - take All of a maid with-out a - ny
made_ of full great price; Now an-gels kne - len to man's ser-
small,_ now great is she; Now shall God deem_ both thee_ and
day_ to see thy face, And in thy court_ to have_ a

make; Of all_ wo - men she bear-eth the bell,_ the bell.
-vice, And at_ this time all this_ be - fell,_ be - fell.
me Un - to his bliss,_ if we_ do well,_ do well.
place, That we_ may_ there sing thee no - well,_ no - well.

the bell._
be - fell._
do well._
no - well._

Of all_ wo - men she bear-eth the bell.
And at_ this_ time all this be - fell.
Un - to his bliss,_ if we_ do well.
That we_ may_ there sing thee no - well.

For fa-burden to vv. 3 and 5 see overleaf.

3 Now man is brighter than the sun;
Now man in heaven on high shall won;
Blessèd be God this game is begun
And his mother empress of hell.

5 Now man he may to heaven wend;
Now heaven and earth to him they bend;
He that was foe now is our friend. 5
This is no nay that I you tell.

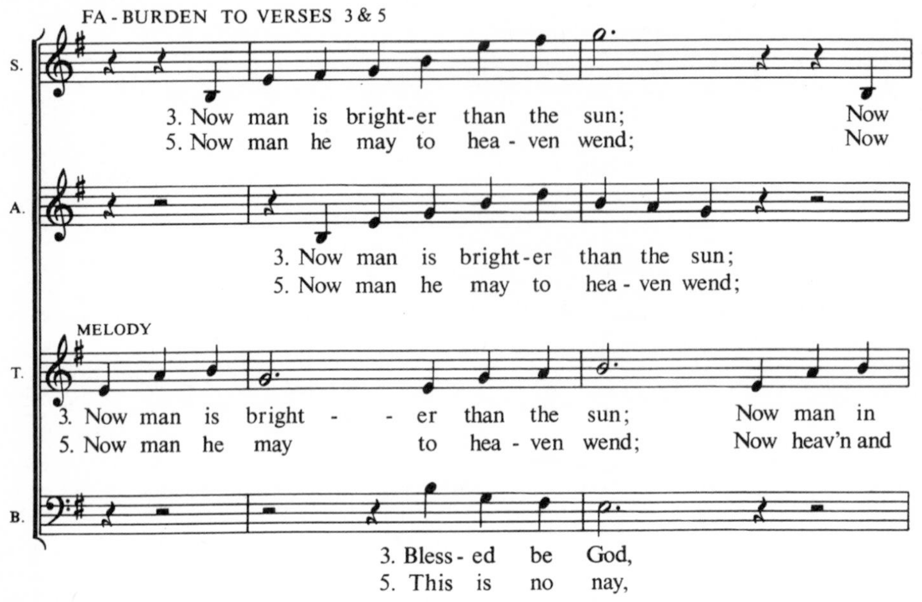
FA-BURDEN TO VERSES 3 & 5
S.
3. Now man is bright-er than the sun; Now
5. Now man he may to hea-ven wend; Now
A.
3. Now man is bright-er than the sun;
5. Now man he may to hea-ven wend;
MELODY
T.
3. Now man is bright - - er than the sun; Now man in
5. Now man he may to hea-ven wend; Now heav'n and
B.
3. Bless-ed be God,
5. This is no nay,

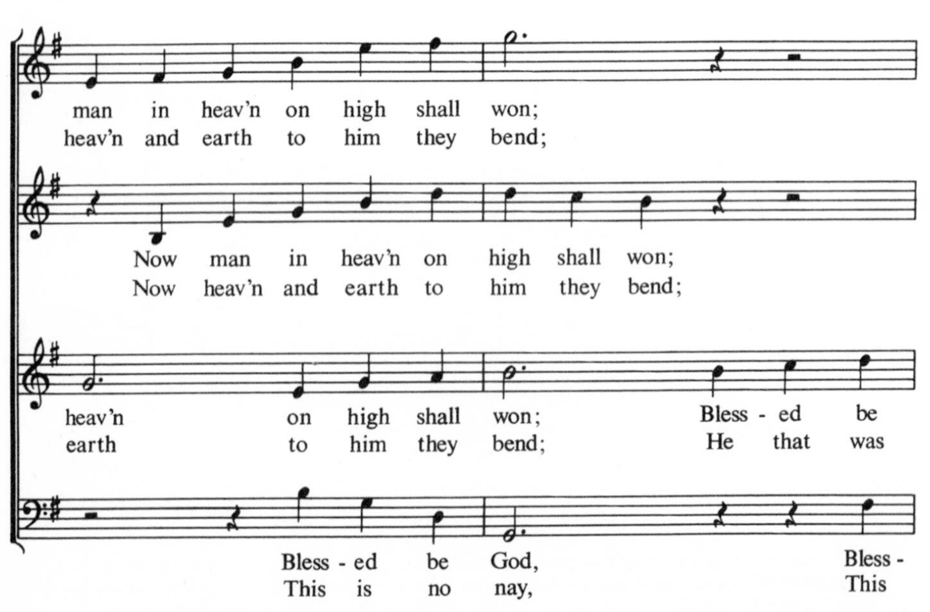
man in heav'n on high shall won;
heav'n and earth to him they bend;
Now man in heav'n on high shall won;
Now heav'n and earth to him they bend;
heav'n on high shall won; Bless-ed be
earth to him they bend; He that was
Bless-ed be God, Bless-
This is no nay, This

Bless - ed be God this game is be - gun
He that was foe now is our friend.
Bless - ed be God, And his
This is no nay, This is
God this game is be - gun And his
foe now is our friend. This is
-ed be God, be God,
is no nay, no nay,

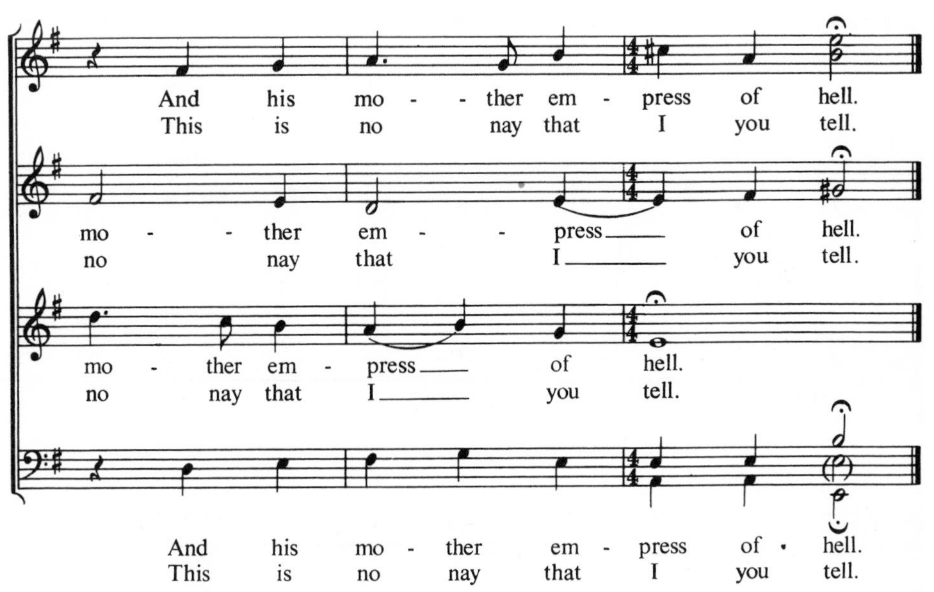
And his mo - - ther em - press of hell.
This is no nay that I you tell.
mo - - ther em - - press of hell.
no nay that I you tell.
mo - ther em - press of hell.
no nay that I you tell.
And his mo - ther em - press of hell.
This is no nay that I you tell.

3. won—dwell. 4. deem—judge. 5. no nay—not to be denied.
This fine carol is from the Selden MS. at Oxford, *c.* 1450, printed in Greene, No. 30, and in *Mediaeval Carols*, No. 25, with the original words. This setting is founded on a Danish chime.

178 IN EXCELSIS GLORIA
(NATIVITY)

FIRST TUNE

1456 A. H. Brown

OPTIONAL INTRODUCTION
mf
S.
A.
T.
B.
f
1. When Christ was born of Ma - ry free, In
3. This King is come to save his kind,
Beth - lem in that fair ci - ty, An - gels sung e'er with
In the script - ure as we find; There - fore this song have
mirth and glee,
we in mind:
p
In ex - cel - sis glo - ri - a,
p

CHORUS

In ex-cel - sis glo - ri - a, In ex-cel - sis glo - ri - a,

In ex - cel - sis glo - ri - a, In ex - cel - sis glo - ri - a.

VERSES 2 & 4
2. Herd - men be - held these an - gels bright— To them ap - pear - ed with great light, And said, 'God's Son is
4. Then, dear Lord, for thy great grace, Grant us in bliss to see thy face, Where we may sing to

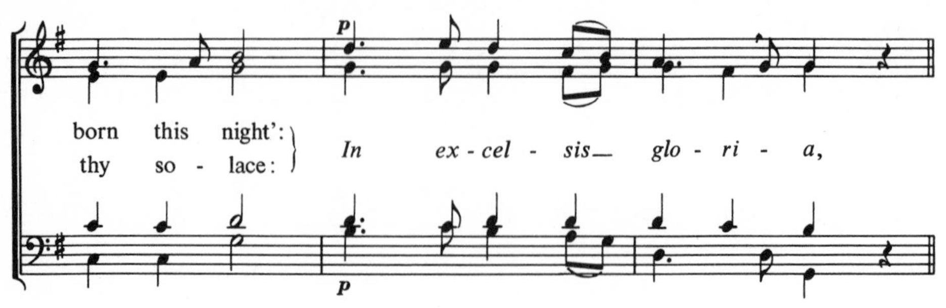
p
born this night':
thy so - lace:
In ex - cel - sis— glo - ri - a,
p

CHORUS
ff
In ex-cel - sis glo - ri - a, In ex-cel - sis glo - ri - a,
ff

D.S.
In ex - cel - sis— glo - ri - a, In— ex - cel - sis glo - ri - a.
D.S.

See footnote to second tune.

178 IN EXCELSIS GLORIA
(NATIVITY)

SECOND TUNE

1456 Martin Shaw

SOLO VOICE
Christ-o pa-re-mus can-ti-ca, In ex-cel-sis glo-ri-a.

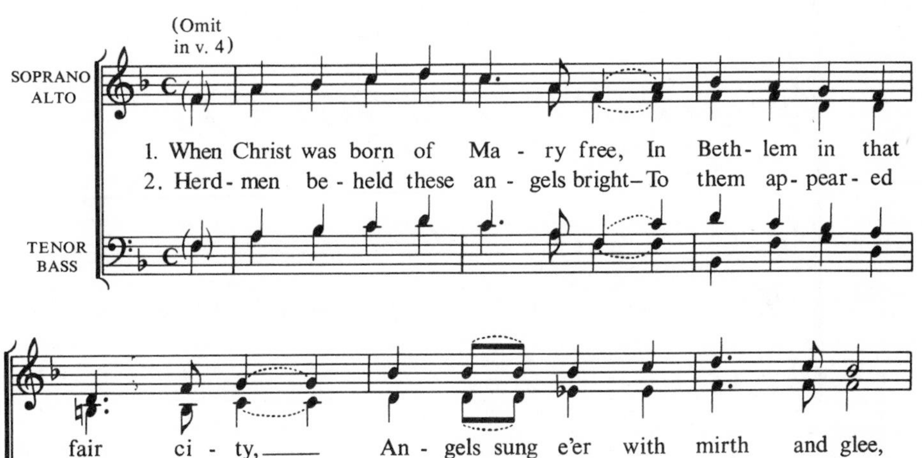
(Omit in v. 4)
SOPRANO ALTO
TENOR BASS
1. When Christ was born of Ma-ry free, In Beth-lem in that
2. Herd-men be-held these an-gels bright—To them ap-pear-ed

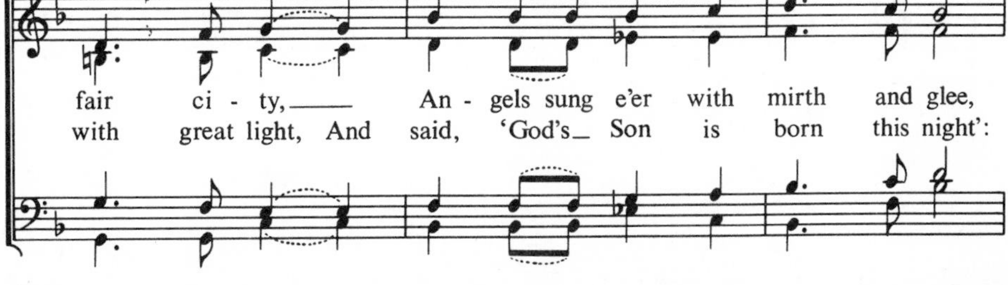
fair ci-ty, An-gels sung e'er with mirth and glee,
with great light, And said, 'God's Son is born this night':

In ex-cel-sis glo-ri-a.
In ex-cel-sis glo-ri-a.

3 This King is come to save his kind,
In the scripture as we find;
Therefore this song have we in mind:

In excelsis gloria.

4 Then, dear Lord, for thy great grace,
Grant us in bliss to see thy face,
Where we may sing to thy solace:

In excelsis gloria.

Harleian MS. 5396 (c. 1450). Printed Wright, &c., and Chambers and Sidgwick, and Greene, No. 80. Original tune lost; A. H. Brown's tune appeared in Bramley & Stainer, 1871. Beyond the modernizing of the spelling, the following lines of the original only are altered: v. 1. 'Angellis songen with mirth and glee', v. 3. 'This king is comen to save kinde', v. 4. 'Then Lord, for thy gret grace'.

179 THE QUEST

MARIAS WALLFAHRT

(THE PASSION)

Traditional, tr. H. T. Wade-Gery

J. Brahms

Con moto
SOPRANO
1. Saint Ma - ry goes a - seek - ing Through Jew - ry up and
2. O look, for she has found him; By He - rod's house stood
ALTO
1. Saint Ma - ry goes a - seek - ing Through Jew - ry up and
2. O look, for she has found him; By He-rod's house stood
TENOR
1. Saint Ma - ry goes a - seek - ing Through Jew - ry up and
2. O look, for she has found him; By He - rod's house stood
BASS
1. Saint Ma - ry goes a - seek - ing Through Jew - ry up and
2. O look, for she has found him; By He-rod's house stood

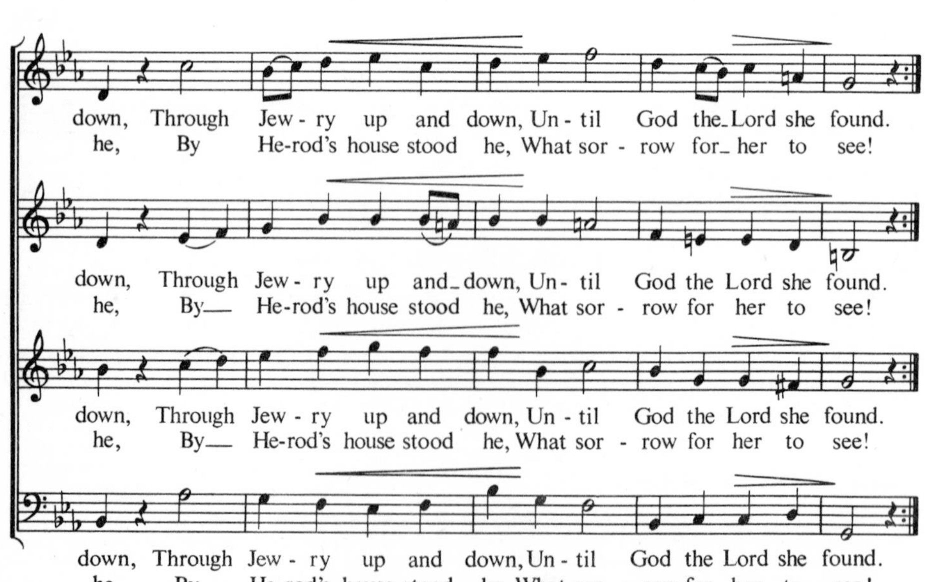
down, Through Jew - ry up and down, Un - til God the Lord she found.
he, By He-rod's house stood he, What sor - row for her to see!
down, Through Jew - ry up and down, Un - til God the Lord she found.
he, By He-rod's house stood he, What sor - row for her to see!
down, Through Jew - ry up and down, Un - til God the Lord she found.
he, By He-rod's house stood he, What sor - row for her to see!
down, Through Jew - ry up and down, Un - til God the Lord she found.
he, By He-rod's house stood he, What sor - row for her to see!

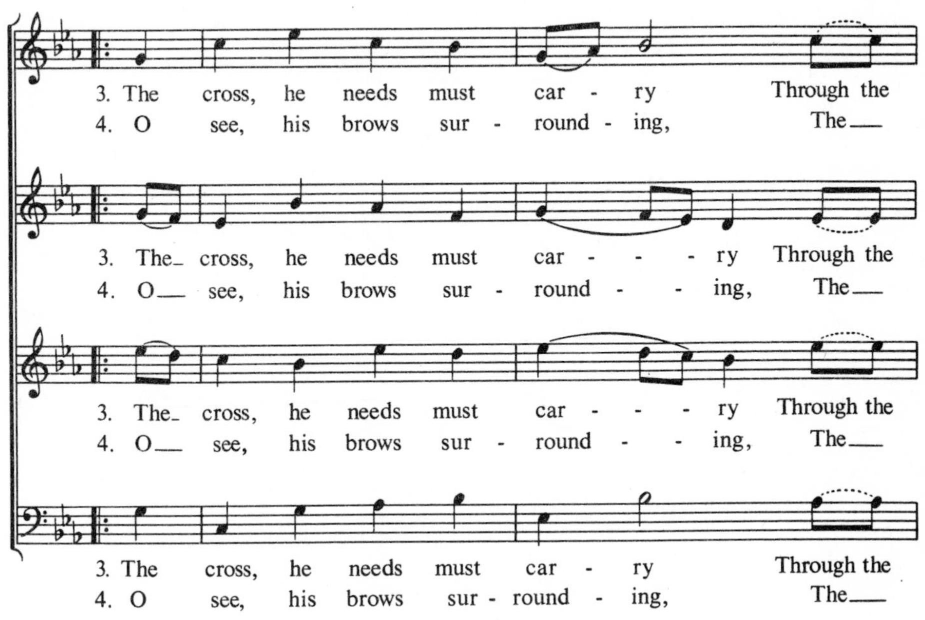
3. The cross, he needs must car - ry Through the
4. O see, his brows sur - round - ing, The
3. The cross, he needs must car - - - ry Through the
4. O see, his brows sur - round - - ing, The
3. The cross, he needs must car - - - ry Through the
4. O see, his brows sur - round - - ing, The
3. The cross, he needs must car - ry Through the
4. O see, his brows sur - round - ing, The

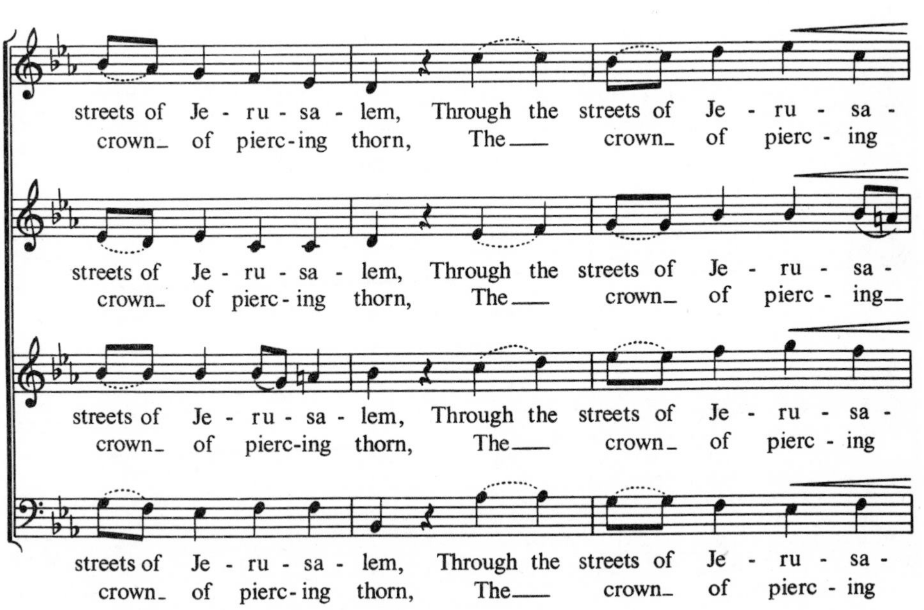
streets of Je - ru - sa - lem, Through the streets of Je - ru - sa -
crown of pierc-ing thorn, The crown of pierc - ing
streets of Je - ru - sa - lem, Through the streets of Je - ru - sa -
crown of pierc - ing thorn, The crown of pierc - ing
streets of Je - ru - sa - lem, Through the streets of Je - ru - sa -
crown of pierc-ing thorn, The crown of pierc - ing
streets of Je - ru - sa - lem, Through the streets of Je - ru - sa -
crown of pierc - ing thorn, The crown of pierc - ing

-lem, To where he will_ suf - fer shame.
thorn, The cross___ on_shoul - der borne!
5. O young and old, look

-lem, To where he will suf - fer shame.
thorn, The cross___ on shoul - der borne!
5. O young and old, look

-lem, To where he will suf - fer shame.
thorn, The cross___ on shoul - der borne!
5. O young and old, look

- lem, To where he will suf - fer shame.
thorn, The cross___ on shoul - der borne!
5. O young and old, look

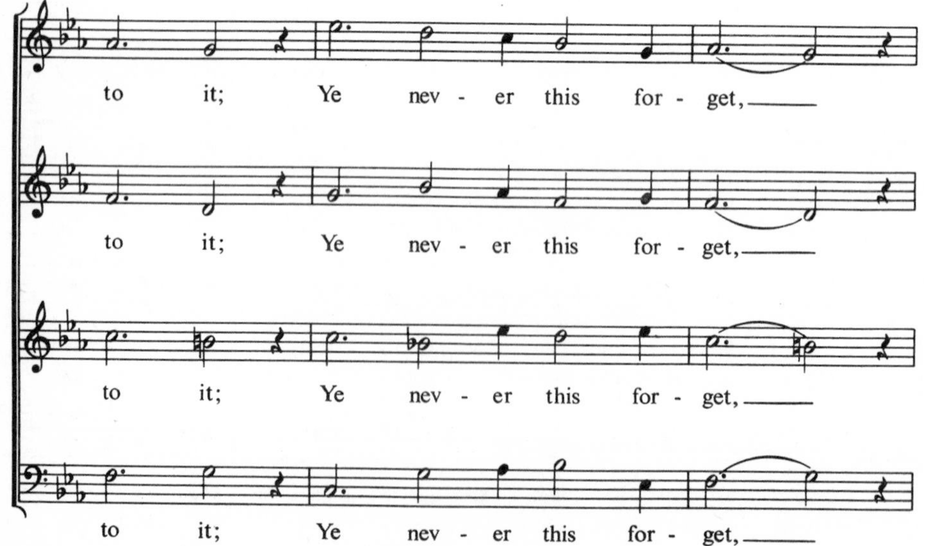
to it; Ye nev - er this for - get,___
to it; Ye nev - er this for - get,___
to it; Ye nev - er this for - get,___
to it; Ye nev - er this for - get,___

f
That his wounds set wide high hea - ven's gate!
f
That his wounds set wide high hea - ven's gate!
f
That his wounds set wide high hea - ven's gate!
f
That his wounds set wide high hea - ven's gate!

MARIA ging aus wandern
  So fern ins fremde Land
Bis sie Gott den Herren fand.

2 Sie hat ihn schon gefunden
  Wohl vor des Herodes Haus,
Er sah so betrüblich aus.

3 Das Kreuz, das musst' er tragen
  Nach Jerusalem vor die Stadt
Wo er gemartert ward.

4 Was trug er auf seinem Haupte?
  Ein' scharfe Dornenkron,
Das Kreuz, das trug er schon.

5 Daran soll man bedenken,
  Ein jeder, jung or alt,
Dass das Himmelreich leidet Gewalt.

'Marias Wallfahrt' ('Maria ging aus wandern') is given here as it was set by Brahms in his *Marienlieder*, with a new translation of the words. The second line in each verse is repeated. Cf. No. 93.

180 ADAM LAY YBOUNDEN
(GENERAL, Medieval)

c. 15th century

Peter Warlock

Allegretto
VOICE(S)
ACCPT.
mp
mf
mp
1. A - dam lay y-
-boun - den, Boun-den in a bond; Four thou-sand win - ter
Thought he not too long. 2. And all was for an ap-ple, An ap-ple that he
took, As clerk - es find - en writ-ten In their book. 3. Ne
p

Rather slower
a tempo
had the ap-ple tak-en been, The ap-ple tak-en been, Ne had nev-er our
Rather slower
p
a tempo
la - dy A - been heavenè queen. 4. Bless - ed be the
mf
pochiss. rit.
a tempo
p
mf
time That ap-ple tak-en was. There - fore we moun sing - en
f cresc.
f cresc.
ff allargando
De - o gra - ci - - as!
ff allargando

From the Sloane MS. 2593 (fifteenth century). Printed Wright, &c., and Chambers and Sidgwick.

181 BALULALOW
(GENERAL)

Wedderburn, 1567

Peter Warlock

SOPRANO SOLO
Slow and very quiet throughout
VOICE
ACCPT.
p
1. O
muted strings
p legato e tranquillo
con Ped.
poco rit.
pp
my dear heart, young Je - sus sweet, Pre - pare thy
a tempo
cra - dle in my spreit, And I sall rock thee
in my heart, And ne - ver mair from thee de -

SOLO
S.
A.
CHORUS
T.
B.
poco rit.
-part.
(closed lips) Mm
poco rit.
Chorus alone
mf a tempo
2. But I sall praise thee ev - - er -
(still closed) Mm
(open) Ah
(open) Ah
sempre legato
(open) Ah
(Very slight aspiration every 3rd beat of the bar)
a tempo
cantabile
muted
strings
pp
CHORUS

-more, With sang - is sweet un - to thy
Mm
Ah
Ah
Ah
gloir; The knees of my heart sall I
quasi 4/4
Mm
Ah
Ah
espressivo
Ah

poco rit. al fine
bow, And sing that richt ba - lu - - la -
Mm (open) Ah
Ah
Ah
Ah
poco rit. al fine
- low.
Ah (closed lips) Mm
pp morendo
Ah (closed lips) Mm
Ah (closed lips) Mm
Ah (closed lips) Mm
pppp
Chorus alone

1. spreit—spirit. sall—shall. 2. sangis—songs. gloir—glory.

From 'Ane Sang of the birth of Christ' ('I come from heaven to tell'), a piece of fifteen stanzas, from *Ane Compendious Buik of Godly and Spirituall Sangis*, 1567, by the brothers James, John, and Robert Wedderburn. The whole poem is a translation of the Christmas Eve Carol which Luther wrote for his son Hans, 'Vom Himmel hoch', first published in *Geistliche Lieder*, 1535. Luther's tune is in *Songs of Praise*, No. 80.

182 LULLAY MY LIKING

(GENERAL, Medieval)

15th century

Gustav Holst

REFRAIN
Allegretto
SOPRANO
ALTO
TENOR
BASS
p
Lul - lay my lik - ing, my dear son, my sweet - ing;

p
pp
Lul - lay my dear heart, mine own dear dar - ling!

SOLO
p
1. I saw a fair maid - en Sit - ten and sing: She
lul - led a lit - tle child, A swee - te lord - ing:

REFRAIN
p
Lul - lay my lik - ing, my dear son, my sweet - ing;

p
pp
Lul - lay my dear heart, mine own dear dar - ling!
p
pp
SOLO
mf
2. That e - ter - nal Lord is he That made al - le thing; Of
al - le lord - es he is Lord, Of al - le king - es King:
REFRAIN
p
Lul - lay my lik - ing, my dear son, my sweet - ing;
p
p
pp
Lul - lay my dear heart, mine own dear dar - ling!
p
pp
SOLO
3. There was mic - kle mel - o - dy At that child - es birth: Al - though
they were in hea-ven's bliss They ma - de mic - kle mirth:

182—Lullay my Liking

REFRAIN
p
Lul - lay my lik - ing, my dear son, my sweet - ing;
p
Lul - lay my dear heart, mine own dear dar - ling!
p
pp
CHORUS
mf
4. An - gels bright they sang that night And said - en to that child 'Bless-ed be thou, and so be she That is both meek and mild':
f
REFRAIN
p
Lul - lay my lik - ing, my dear son, my sweet - ing;

Lul - lay my dear heart, mine own dear dar - ling!
SOLO
5. Pray we now to that child, And to his mo - ther dear, God
grant them all his bless - ing That now mak - en cheer:
REFRAIN
Lul - lay my lik - ing, my dear son, my sweet - ing;
Lul - lay my dear heart, mine own dear dar - ling!

2. eternal—*orig*. 'eche', with the same meaning. 3. mickle—much.
Words from the Sloane MS. (see Nos. 116, 174, 180, 183).
Greene (No. 143) calls this 'the masterpiece of the lullaby carols' and is inclined to attribute it to the same unknown author as the carol that follows.

183 I SING OF A MAIDEN
(GENERAL, Medieval)

15th century

Martin Shaw

SOLO VOICE
Rather slowly
p
1. I sing of a maid - en That is makè - less;
King of all kings To her son she ches.

CHORUS (VERSES 2, 3, & 4)
Slow
2. He came all so still Where his mo - ther was, As
3. He came all so still To his mo - ther's bowr, As
4. He came all so still Where his mo - ther lay, As
S.
A.
pp
2,3,4. He came all so still, so still, As
T.
B.
2,3,4. He came all so still, so still, As

dew in A - pril That fall - eth on the grass.
dew in A - pril That fall - eth on the flower.
dew in A - pril That fall - eth on the spray.

(VERSE 5)
pp Slow
5. Mo - ther and maid - en Was nev - er none but she;
pp

Well may such a la - dy God- es mo - ther be.

1. makèless—matchless. ches (pronounce to rhyme with 'less')—chose. 2, 4. Where —*orig*. MS. 'There,' with this meaning. all so—*orig*. 'also', as.

This famous little classic is also in the Sloane MS. Of its 'ineffable grace' Prof. Saintsbury says: 'In no previous verse had this Aeolian music—this "harp of Ariel"—that distinguishes English at its very best in this direction . . . been given to the world' (*Short History of English Literature*, 1913, p. 202). If ever there was a tune, it has been lost.

184 ALL BELLS IN PARADISE
(GENERAL)

Traditional

Martin Shaw

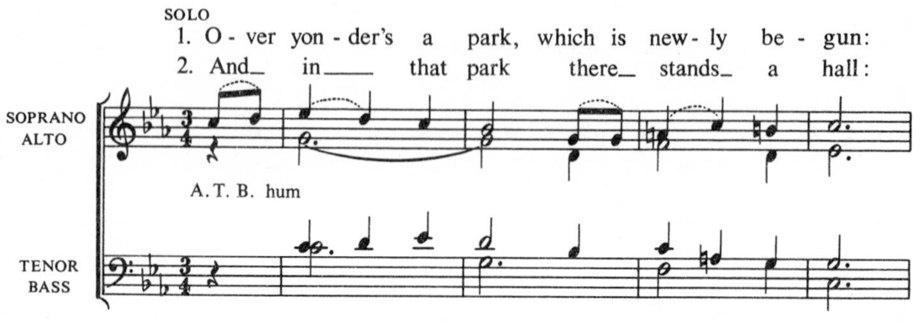
SOLO
1. O - ver yon - der's a park, which is new - ly be - gun:
2. And_ in___ that park there_ stands_ a hall:
SOPRANO
ALTO
A. T. B. hum
TENOR
BASS

SOLO
(1.) Which is
(2.) Which is
CHORUS (all sing words)
p
All bells in pa - ra - dise I heard them a - ring,
(A. T. B. hum)
p

sil - ver on the out - side and gold___ with - in:
cov - ered all___ o - ver with pur - ple and pall:
CHORUS
mf
And I
mf

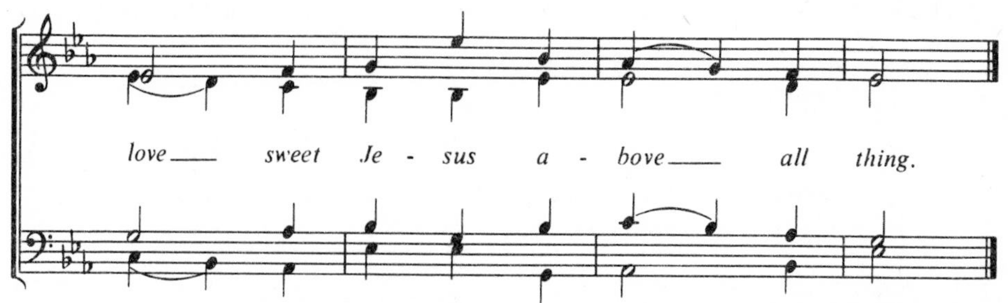
love — sweet Je - sus a - bove — all thing.

3 And in that hall there stands a bed:
Which is hung all round with silk curtains so red:

4 And in that bed there lies a knight:
Whose wounds they do bleed by day and by night:

5 At that bedside there lies a stone:
Which our blest Virgin Mary knelt upon:

6 At that bed's foot there lies a hound:
Which is licking the blood as it daily runs down:

7 At that bed's head there grows a thorn:
Which was never so blossomed since Christ was born:

See No. 61 for the version with its traditional tune. This version was recovered in the middle of the nineteenth century in North Staffordshire and contributed to *Notes and Queries* in 1862, but without its tune. The theme is still eucharistic: v. 3 describes the altar with dorsal and riddels; v. 7 the Glastonbury thorn. See Greene, No. 322.

185 WITHER'S ROCKING HYMN
(GENERAL)

George Wither

R. Vaughan Williams

SOLO
Lento con moto
p
VOICE
1. Sweet ba - by, sleep! What ails my dear?
2. Whilst thus thy lul - - la - by I sing,
ACCPT.
p
What ails my dar - ling thus to cry? Be still, my
For thee great bless - ings ripe - ning be; Thine el - dest
child, and lend thine ear To hear me sing thy
bro - ther is a King, And hath a king - dom

pp
lul - la - by. My pret - ty lamb, for - bear to weep;
bought for thee. Sweet ba - by, then, for - bear to weep;
S. pp Chorus unaccompanied
A.
Sweet ba - - - by,
T.
B.
pp
Be still, my dear; sweet ba - by, sleep.
Be still, my babe; sweet ba - by, sleep.
sleep, sweet ba - by, sleep.

3 When God with us was dwelling here,
In little babes he took delight:
Such innocents as thou, my dear,
Are ever precious in his sight.
Sweet baby, then, forbear to weep;
Be still, my babe; sweet baby, sleep.

4 A little infant once was he,
And strength in weakness then was laid
Upon his virgin mother's knee,
That power to thee might be conveyed.
Sweet baby, then, forbear to weep;
Be still, my babe; sweet baby, sleep.

5 The King of kings, when he was born,
Had not so much for outward ease;
By him such dressings were not worn,
Nor suchlike swaddling-clothes as these.
Sweet baby, then, forbear to weep;
Be still, my babe; sweet baby, sleep.

6 The wants that he did then sustain
Have purchased wealth, my babe, for thee;
And by his torments and his pain
Thy rest and ease securèd be.
My baby, then, forbear to weep;
Be still, my babe; sweet baby, sleep.

George Wither's most famous lyrics were early written, 'Shall I wasting in despair' in 1615. He became a Puritan in 1623, and was raising a troop of horse in 1642. The 'Rocking Hymn' was in *Halelujah*, 1641.

PART V

CAROLS BY MODERN WRITERS AND COMPOSERS

186 SNOW IN THE STREET
(CHRISTMAS)

William Morris | R. Vaughan Williams

Andante con moto (𝅗𝅥. = about 63)

VOICES IN UNISON

ORGAN (OR VOICES IN HARMONY)

1. From far a - way we come to you,
2. For as we wan - dered far and wide,

The snow in the street and the wind on the door,

To tell of great ti - dings strange— and true.
What hap do you deem there should us be - tide?

Min - strels and maids stand

forth on the floor: From far a - way we come to you, To
tell of great ti - dings strange and true.

3 Under a bent when the night was deep,
There lay three shepherds tending their sheep:

4 'O ye shepherds, what have ye seen,
To slay your sorrow and heal your teen?'

5 'In an ox-stall this night we saw
A babe and a maid without a flaw:

PART 2

6 'There was an old man there beside;
His hair was white, and his hood was wide:

7 'And as we gazed this thing upon,
Those twain knelt down to the little one.

8 'And a marvellous song we straight did hear,
That slew our sorrow and healed our care.'

9 News of a fair and a marvellous thing,
Nowell, Nowell, Nowell, we sing!

From William Morris's *The Earthly Paradise* (1868-70) in the poem, 'The Land East of the Sun and West of the Moon'. The carol begins 'Outlanders, whence came ye last', the first, second, and fourth verses being here omitted.

187 MID-WINTER
(CHRISTMAS)

Christina Rossetti
Gustav Holst
In moderate time
SOPRANO
ALTO
TENOR
BASS
1. In the bleak mid - win - ter Frost - y wind made moan,
2. Our God, heav'n can - not hold him Nor earth sus - tain;
3. E - nough for him, whom che - ru - bim Wor - ship night and day, A
4. An - gels and arch - an - gels May have ga - thered there,
5. What can I give him, Poor as I am?
Earth stood hard as i - - ron, Wa - ter like a stone;
Heav'n and earth shall flee a - way When he comes to reign:
breast - - ful of milk, And a man - ger - ful of hay; E -
Che - ru - bim and se - ra - phim Thronged the air: But
If I were a shep - herd I would bring a lamb;
Snow had fal - len, snow on snow, Snow on snow,
In the bleak mid - win - ter A sta - ble - place suf - ficed The
-nough for him, whom an - gels Fall down be - fore, The
on - ly his mo - ther In her maid - en bliss
If I were a wise man I would do my part; Yet
In the bleak mid - win - ter, Long a - - go.
Lord God Al - might - y Je - sus Christ.
ox and ass and ca - mel Which a - - dore.
Wor - shipped the Be - lov - ed With a kiss.
what I can I give him Give my heart.

This poem, with its tune from the *English Hymnal* and *Songs of Praise*, is so much a carol that we feel bound to include it here also.

188 OUR BROTHER IS BORN
(CHRISTMAS)

Eleanor Farjeon

Harry Farjeon

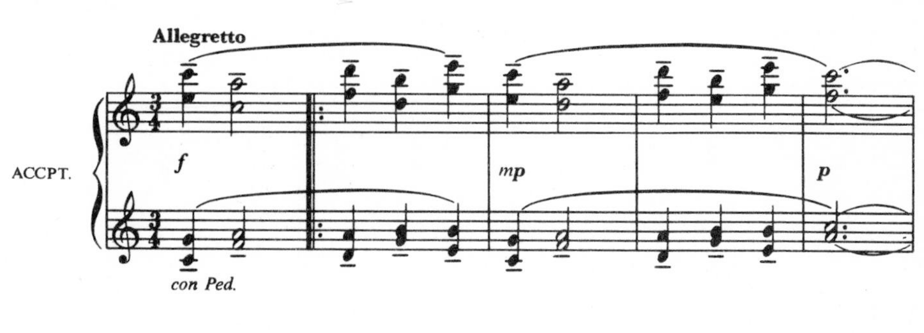
Allegretto
ACCPT.
f
mp
p
con Ped.

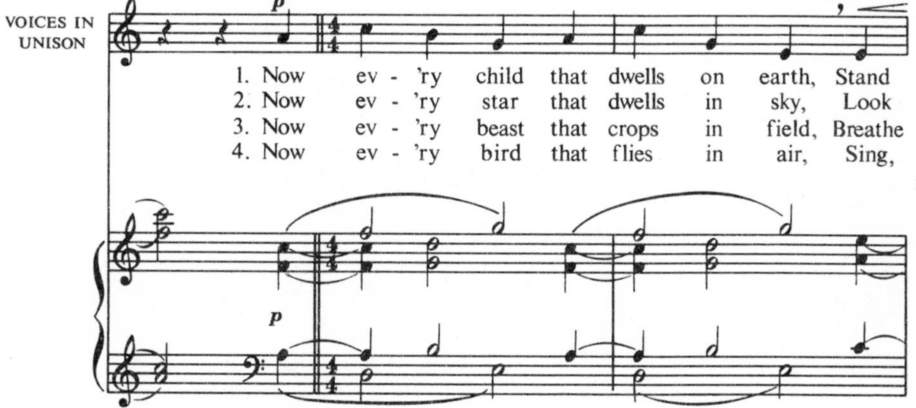
Moderato
p
VOICES IN UNISON
1. Now ev - 'ry child that dwells on earth, Stand
2. Now ev - 'ry star that dwells in sky, Look
3. Now ev - 'ry beast that crops in field, Breathe
4. Now ev - 'ry bird that flies in air, Sing,
p

mf
up, stand up and sing: The pass - ing night has
down with shi - ning eyes: The night has dropped in
sweet - ly and a - dore: The night has brought the
ra - ven, lark, and dove: The night has brood - ed
mf

dim.
pp
giv - en birth Un - to the child - ren's King.
pass - ing by A Star from pa - ra - dise.
rich - est yield That e'er the har - vest bore.
on her lair And fledged the Bird of love.
Sing
pp
sweet as the flute, Sing clear as the horn, Sing
joy of the child - ren,
stars,
creat - ures,
birds,
Come Christ - mas the morn:
cresc.
cresc.
Lit - tle Christ Je - sus Our bro - ther is born.
rit.
f Allegretto
f

p
5.* Now
mp
p
p
Moderato
all the an - gels of the Lord, Rise up on Christ - mas
mf
† Even: The pass - ing night will hear the Word That
mf
f
Poco meno mosso
is the voice of heav'n. Sing sweet as the flute, Sing
f

† Pronounce nearly as one syllable

clear as the horn, Sing joy of the an - gels, Come
Christ- mas the morn:
mp cresc.
allarg.
ff
Lit - tle Christ Je - sus Our bro - ther is
mp
cresc.
allarg.
Allegretto
born.
f cresc.
ff
f

For high voices this carol may be transposed to key E.

189 MERRY CHRISTMAS
(CHRISTMAS, Secular)

Adapted from Sir Walter Scott

Martin Shaw

With animation (𝅗𝅥 = about 84)
(SOLO)
mp
VOICES IN UNISON
On Christ-mas Eve the bells were rung, On
ACCPT.
mp

Christ-mas Eve the mass was sung; The dam-sel donn'd her

kir - tle sheen, The hall was dress'd with hol- ly green;

189—Merry Christmas

mf
Forth to the wood did mer-ry-men go, To gath - er in the
mis - tle - toe:
(CHORUS)
f
Then drink to the hol - ly
f
ber - ry, With hey down, hey down der - ry! The mis - tle - toe we'll
pledge al - so, And at Christ-mas all be mer - ry, At Christ - - mas
cres -

all be mer - ry.
8ve higher
- cen - - - do
ff
loco
2. The fire, with well-dried
dim - in - u - en - do
f
logs sup-plied, Went roar - ing up the chim - ney wide;
Then
came the mer - ry mas - quers in, And car - ols roared with

blithe - some din.
Eng - land is mer - ry

Eng - land, when Old Christ - mas brings his sports a - gain:

Then drink to the hol - ly ber - ry, With

hey down, hey down der-ry! The mis-tle-toe we'll pledge al-so, And at
Christ-mas all be mer-ry, At Christ-mas all be
cres - - - cen - - - do
cres - - - cen - - - do
ff
accel.
mer-ry.
8ve
loco
ff
accel.

The words are taken from *Marmion*, introduction to Canto VI; with a traditional refrain added.

190 WINTER'S SNOW
(CHRISTMAS)

FIRST TUNE

E. Caswall

J. Goss

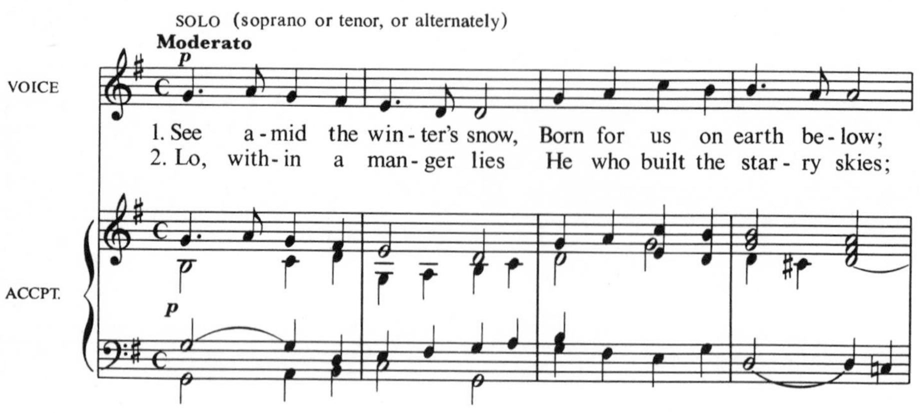
SOLO (soprano or tenor, or alternately)
Moderato
p
VOICE
1. See a-mid the win-ter's snow, Born for us on earth be-low;
2. Lo, with-in a man-ger lies He who built the star-ry skies;
ACCPT.
p

See the ten-der Lamb ap-pears, Pro-mised from e-ter-nal years:
He who, throned in height sub-lime, Sits a-mid the che-ru-bim:

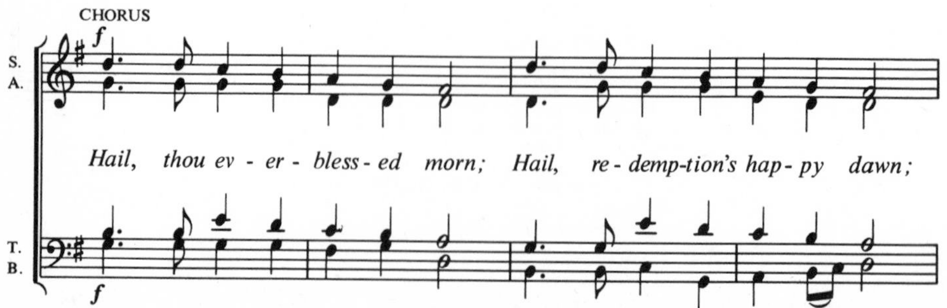
CHORUS
f
S.
A.
Hail, thou ev-er-bless-ed morn; Hail, re-demp-tion's hap-py dawn;
T.
B.
f

Sing through all Je - ru - sa - lem, Christ is born in Beth - le - hem.

3 Say, ye holy shepherds, say
What your joyful news to-day;
Wherefore have ye left your sheep
On the lonely mountain steep?

Hail, thou ever-blessed morn; etc.

4 'As we watched at dead of night,
Lo, we saw a wondrous light;
Angels singing "Peace on earth"
Told us of the Saviour's birth':

Hail, thou ever-blessed morn; etc.

5 Sacred infant, all divine,
What a tender love was thine,
Thus to come from highest bliss
Down to such a world as this:

Hail, thou ever-blessed morn; etc.

6 Teach, O teach us, holy Child,
By thy face so meek and mild,
Teach us to resemble thee,
In thy sweet humility:

Hail, thou ever-blessed morn; etc.

The familiar tune by John Goss appeared in Bramley and Stainer's *Christmas Carols New and Old*.

190 WINTER'S SNOW
(CHRISTMAS)
SECOND TUNE

E. Caswall R.O. Morris

SOLO
Moderato
p
VOICE
1. See a-mid the win-ter's snow, Born for us on_ earth be-low;
2. Lo, with-in a man-ger lies He who built the_ star-ry skies;
ACCPT.
p

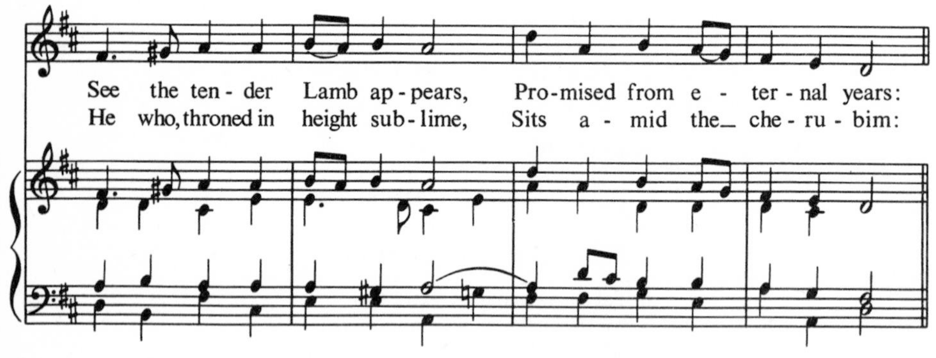
See the ten-der Lamb ap-pears, Pro-mised from e - ter-nal years:
He who, throned in height sub-lime, Sits a-mid the_ che-ru-bim:

CHORUS
S.
A.
f
Hail, thou ev - er - bless-ed_ morn; Hail, re-demp-tion's hap-py dawn;_
T.
B.
f
(Accpt. ad lib.)

Sing through all Je - ru - sa - lem, ___ Christ is born in ___ Beth - le - hem.

3 Say, ye holy shepherds, say
What your joyful news to-day;
Wherefore have ye left your sheep
On the lonely mountain steep?

Hail, thou ever-blessed morn; etc.

4 'As we watched at dead of night,
Lo, we saw a wondrous light;
Angels singing "Peace on earth"
Told us of the Saviour's birth':

Hail, thou ever-blessed morn; etc.

5 Sacred infant, all divine,
What a tender love was thine,
Thus to come from highest bliss
Down to such a world as this:

Hail, thou ever-blessed morn; etc.

6 Teach, O teach us, holy Child,
By thy face so meek and mild,
Teach us to resemble thee,
In thy sweet humility:

Hail, thou ever-blessed morn; etc.

191 THE CHRISTMAS TREE
CHRISTBAUM
(CHRISTMAS)

Peter Cornelius
Tr. H. N. Bate

Peter Cornelius

Allegretto giojoso
cres - - - - cen - - do
ACCPT.
mf
f
VOICES IN UNISON
1. The hol - ly's up, the house is all bright, The
tree is rea - dy, the can- dles a - light: Re - joice and be
con espressione
glad, all child - - ren to - night!
sf

cres - - - cen - - - do
mf
f
2. The
mo - ther sings of our Lord's good grace Where-by the child who
mf
saved our race Was born and a - dored in a
con espressione
sf
low - - - ly place. 3. Once more the shep - herds,
p

as she sings, Bend low, and an - gels touch their strings: With
mf
mf
'Glo - - ry' they hail the King of kings. 4. The
child - ren lis - ten - ing round the tree Can hear the heav'n - ly
p
mf
min - strel - sy, The man - - - ger's mar - - - vel
mf
p cresc.

they can see.
5. Let ev - 'ry house be
rea - dy to - night— The child - ren gather'd, the can - dles a - light— That
mu - - sic to hear, to see that sight.
mf
con espressione
sf
mf
cres - - - cen - - - do
f
sf

For German text and editorial note see overleaf.

191 *CHRISTBAUM*

P. Cornelius Ibid.

WIE schön geschmückt der festliche Raum!
Die Lichter funkeln am Weihnachtsbaum!
O fröhliche Zeit—o seliger Traum!

2 Die Mutter sitzt in der Kinder Kreis;
Nun schweiget Alles auf ihr Geheiss:
Sie singet des Christkind's Lob und Preis.

3 Und rings, vom Weihnachtsbaum erhellt
Ist schön in Bildern aufgestellt
Des heiligen Buches Palmenwelt.

4 Die Kinder schauen der Bilder Pracht
Und haben wohl des Singens acht,
Das tönt so süss in der Weihenacht!

5 O glücklicher Kreis im festlichen Raum!
O gold'ne Lichter am Weihnachtsbaum!
O fröhliche Zeit—o seliger Traum!

Carl August Peter Cornelius, nephew of the painter, Peter Cornelius, was both composer and poet; he was born at Mainz, and worked much with Liszt. Among his most famous works are the *Weihnachtslieder*, from which this carol, 'Christbaum', is taken. Cf. No. 193.

192 THE SNOW LIES THICK
(CHRISTMAS)

Selwyn Image — Geoffrey Shaw

Andante con moto
TENOR SOLO
VOICES
ACCPT.
mf
1. The snow lies thick up - on the earth_ To-night, when God is come_ to birth:
4. But see, but see! the child's a - wake!_ His pret - ty hands stretch out_ to take,
Senza Ped. (organ)
CHORUS
S. A. T. B.
f
O col - lau - dan - tes Do - mi - num, Let's run to give him greet - ing.
O col - lau - de - mus Do - mi - num, The sim - ple gifts we bring_ him:
Ped. (organ)
TENOR SOLO
mf
His lodg - ing but a
Yea, he for-gets for
Senza Ped.

sta - ble, see! Where ox and ass his cour - tiers be, The
ve - ry love The glo - ry of his home a - bove, Nor
might - y Lord in pov - er - ty
cares but on - ly this to prove,
CHORUS
f
Laid low for our sal -
He's come for our sal -
Laid low, laid
He's come, he's
f
f
Ped.
(For verse 5 begin at letter A)
-va - - tion!
-va - - tion.
low for our sal - va - - tion!
come for our sal - va - - tion.
(For verse 5 begin at letter A)

SOPRANO SOLO
2. I hear sweet Ma - ry sing to rest_ The
3. Good Jo - seph, may we en - ter here_ To
Senza Ped.
CHORUS
lit - tle one a - gainst_ her breast: O col - lau - dan - tes
watch her and her child_ a - near, Nos col - lau - dan - tes
Ped.
SOPRANO SOLO
Do - mi - num, We'll make soft mu - sic round_them; For gen - tle as a
Do - mi - num, And kneel a - round his cra - dle? The hum - ble beasts that
Senza Ped.

192—The Snow lies thick

breeze in June_ Must be to-night our car-ol's tune, Lest
hom-age pay, And we as hum-ble sure as they, Would
That's born, that's
O'er him, o'er
CHORUS
p
we_ a-wake the babe_ too soon
keep_ still watch to break_ of day
That's
O'er
That's born_ for our_ sal-
O'er him_ that brings_ sal-
p
p
Ped.
To page 419 for v. 3
D.C. for v. 4
born_ for our_ sal-va--tion.
him_ that brings_ sal-va--tion.
-va--tion.
-va--tion.
To page 419 for v. 3
D.C. for v. 4

A
CHORUS
f
5. Then let us great, and let us small,_ And
young and old, and one_ and all, Nunc col - lau - dan - tes
Do - mi - num, With dance and song_draw hith - er! Bring boughs of hol - ly
Ped.

green and red To deck a-bout his lit-tle bed, This
ve-ry God, who lays his head So low for our sal-
So low, so
ff
ff
ff
rall.
-va- -tion.
low for our sal-va- -tion.
rall.

By permission of Novello & Co. Ltd.

193 THE KINGS
DIE KÖNIGE
(EPIPHANY)

Peter Cornelius
Tr. H.N. Bate

Peter Cornelius

Rather slowly, the accompanying Chorale with breadth
VOICE(S)
ACCPT.
p
1. Three kings from Per - sian lands a - far To Jor-dan fol - low the
point - ing star: And this the quest of the trav - el-lers three, Where the
new born King of the Jews may_ be. Full roy - al gifts they bear for the
King; Gold, in - cense, myrrh_ are their of - fer - ing. 2. The star shines

out with a stead - fast ray; The kings to Beth - le - hem
p
make their way, And there in wor - ship they bend the knee, As Ma - ry's
child in her lap they see; Their roy - al gifts they show to the
p
King, Gold, in - cense, myrrh are their of - fer - ing.

3. Thou child of man— lo, to Beth - le - hem
The kings are trav - 'lling— tra - vel with them!
un poco più mosso
The star of mer - cy, the star of grace, Shall lead thy_ heart to its rest - ing-
p un poco più mosso

rit.
a tempo
-place. Gold, in-cense, myrrh thou_canst not_ bring; Of- fer thy heart_ to the
rit.
a tempo
f

in - fant__ King, Of - fer thy heart!

p

'Die Könige', from the *Weihnachtslieder*. The old Christmas tune 'Wie schön leuchtet' (No. 104) forms the accompaniment, and, as in Sir Ivor Atkins' well-known arrangement, may be sung by the choir.

193 *DIE KÖNIGE*

P. Cornelius Ibid.

DREI Kön'ge wandern aus Morgenland;
Ein Sternlein führt sie zum Jordanstrand.
In Juda fragen und forschen die Drei,
Wo der neugeborene König sei?
Sie wollen Weihrauch, Myrrhen und Gold
Dem Kinde spenden zum Opfersold.

2 Und hell erglänzt des Sternes Schein;
Zum Stalle gehen die Kön'ge ein;
Das Knäblein schauen sie wonniglich,
Anbetend neigen die Kön'ge sich;
Sie bringen Weihrauch, Myrrhen und Gold
Zum Opfer dar dem Knäblein hold.

3 O Menschenkind! halte treulich Schritt!
Die Kön'ge wandern, o wandre mit!
Der Stern der Liebe, der Gnade Stern
Erhelle dein Ziel, so du suchst den Herrn,
Und fehlen Weihrauch, Myrrhen und Gold,
Schenke dein Herz dem Knäblein hold!
Schenk' ihm dein Herz!

194 KINGS IN GLORY
(CHRISTMAS: EPIPHANY)

Selwyn Image

Martin Shaw

SOPRANO SOLO

Allegro

CHORUS

p

SOPRANO
ALTO

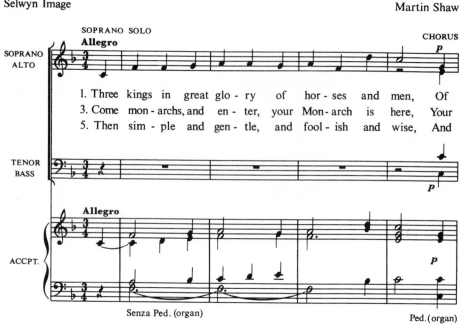

1. Three kings in great glo - ry of hor - ses and men, Of
3. Come mon - archs, and en - ter, your Mon - arch is here, Your
5. Then sim - ple and gen - tle, and fool - ish and wise, And

TENOR
BASS

p

Allegro

ACCPT.

p

Senza Ped. (organ)

Ped. (organ)

SOLO
hor - ses and men, In___ haste come a - rid - ing o'er
Mon - arch is here, Doff___ crowns, on the bare sod fall
fool - ish and wise, Come a - dore the great Lord of the
Senza Ped.

CHORUS
SOLO
p
moun - tain and fen, O'er moun - tain and fen; For their
down and re - vere, Fall down and re - vere; For the
earth and the skies, The earth and the skies, Who
Ped.
Senza Ped.
King is a - wait - ing, and lo they would bring, And
best you can of - fer is lit - tle, I trow, Is
deigns for us all on this night to be born, This
lo they would bring, The best of their trea - sure to
lit - tle, I trow, To the Lord God of heav'n you're a -
night to be born, This night that is fair - er than
Senza Ped.

194—Kings in Glory

CHORUS
p
Fine
SOLO
give to their King, To give to their King. 2. Poor shep- herds lie
-kneel - ing to now, A - kneel - ing to now. 4. Come, shep - herds, and
mid - sum - mer morn, Than mid - sum - mer morn.
Ped.
Senza Ped.
CHORUS
SOLO
hud - dled to - night on the plain, To - night on the plain, Their
fear not, he will not des - pise, He will not des - pise The
Ped.
Senza Ped.
CHORUS
sil - ly sheep guard - ing from dan - ger and pain, From dan - ger and
gifts that you bring him, tho' rude in men's eyes, Tho' rude in men's
Ped.

SOLO
CHORUS
p
pain; For the wolves howl a - round them, and bit - ter the air, And
eyes. See, he's not ar - rayed here in pur - ple and gold, In
p
p
(b)
Senza Ped.
Ped.
SOLO
bit - ter the air, That blows o'er the snow - field all fro - -
pur - ple and gold, God's Lamb lies as help - less as lamb
Senza Ped.
CHORUS
D.C. for vv. 3 & 5
All fro - - - - zen and bare.
As lamb of your fold.
p
- - zen and bare, All fro - - zen and bare.
of your fold, As lamb of your fold.
p
D.C. for vv. 3 & 5
p
Ped.

195 KINGS OF ORIENT
(EPIPHANY)

Words and music by
J. H. Hopkins, Jun.
(arr. M.S.)

CASPAR
1. We three kings of O - ri - ent are; Bear - ing
5. Glo - rious now, be - hold him a - rise, King, and
MELCHIOR
1. We three kings of O - ri - ent are; Bear - ing
5. Glo - rious now, be - hold him a - rise, King, and
BALTHAZAR
1. We three kings of O - ri - ent are; Bear - ing
5. Glo - rious now, be - hold him a - rise, King, and
ACCPT.

gifts we tra - verse a - far Field and foun - tain,
God, and sac - ri - fice! Heav'n sings al - le -

gifts we tra - verse a - far Field and foun - tain,
God, and sac - ri - fice! Heav'n sings al - le -

gifts we tra - verse a - far Field and foun - tain,
God, and sac - ri - fice! Heav'n sings al - le -

moor and moun - tain, Fol - low - ing yon - der star:
-lu - ya, Al - le - lu - ya the earth re - plies:
moor and moun - tain, Fol - low - ing yon - der star:
-lu - ya, Al - le - lu - ya the earth re - plies:
moor and moun - tain, Fol - low - ing yon - der star:
-lu - ya, Al - le - lu - ya the earth re - plies:
REFRAIN (after each verse)
O star of won - der, star of night,
Star with roy - al beau - ty bright, West - ward lead - ing,
still pro - ceed - ing, Guide us to thy per - fect light.

195—Kings of Orient

INTERLUDE

(Fl. or Ob.)

(Clar.)

MELCHIOR
2. Born a king on Beth - le - hem plain, Gold I
CASPAR
3. Frank - in - cense to of - fer have I; In - cense
BALTHAZAR
4. Myrrh is mine; its bit - ter per - fume Breathes a

bring, to crown him a - gain— King for ev - er,
owns a de - i - ty nigh: Prayer and prais - ing,
life of gath - er - ing gloom; Sorrow - ing, sigh - ing,

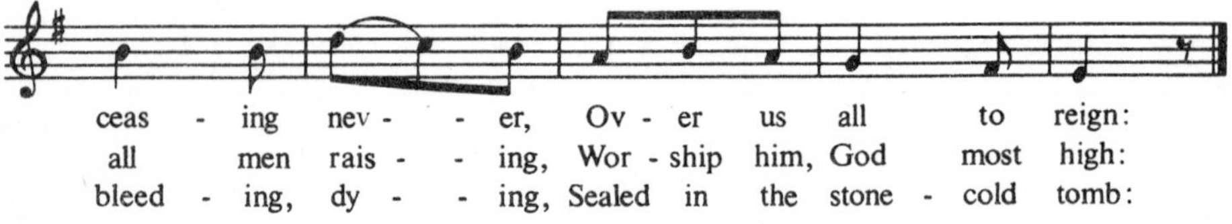
ceas - ing nev - - er, Ov - er us all to reign:
all men rais - - ing, Wor - ship him, God most high:
bleed - ing, dy - - ing, Sealed in the stone - cold tomb:

For verse 5 go back to the beginning. Verses 2, 3 and 4 should be sung as solos for men's voices, the accompaniment and refrain remaining unchanged.

The verses may be sung dramatically, in a hall or in church, the three kings entering in procession as they sing the first verse. Standing together (and each holding a casket), each may turn to the people to sing his verse, all forming round an imaginary crib for the choruses and v. 5. This last verse may then be sung full, the three kings returning to their places during the last two lines of the chorus.

This carol is one of the most successful modern examples. It was both written and composed (c. 1857) by Dr. J. H. Hopkins, Rector of Christ's Church, Williamsport, Pennsylvania, who died at Troy, New York, in 1891. See his *Carols, Hymns, and Songs*, New York, 1882.

196 BLAKE'S CRADLE SONG
(GENERAL)

William Blake
R. Vaughan Williams
Andantino
VOICES IN UNISON
ACCPT.
sempre pp
1. Sweet_ dreams,_ form a shade
5. Wept for me, for thee, for all,
6. Smiles on thee, on me, on all;
O'er my love-ly in-fant's head: Sweet_ dreams of pleas-ant streams By
When he was an in-fant small. Thou his i-mage ev-er see,_
Who be-came an in-fant small. In-fant smiles are his own smiles;_
hap-py, si-lent, moon-y beams._
Heav'n-ly face that smiles_ on thee,_
Heav'n and earth to peace_ be-guiles._
last time
last time
ppp

196—Blake's Cradle Song

2. Sweet sleep, with soft down Weave thy brows an in - fant crown.
3. Sleep, sleep, hap - py child, All cre - a - tion slept_ and smiled;
4. Sweet babe, in thy face Ho - ly im - age I ___ can trace.
Sweet sleep, an - gel mild, Hov - er o'er my hap - - py child. ___
Sleep, sleep, hap - py sleep, While o'er thee thy mo - - ther weep. ___
Sweet babe, once like thee, Thy Ma - ker lay, and wept ___ for me, ___
D.S. for vv. 5 &6

Words from Blake's *Songs of Innocence*, etched in 1789.

197 THE CROWN OF ROSES

(Tchaikovsky's 'Legend')

(GENERAL)

Plechtchéev, tr. G. D.

P. I. Tchaikovsky

Moderato
SOPRANO
ALTO
TENOR
BASS
mf
p
1. When Je-sus Christ was yet a child He had a

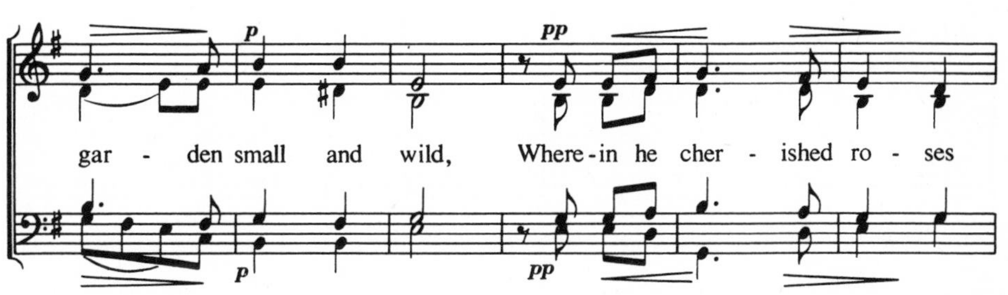
p
pp
gar - den small and wild, Where-in he cher - ished ro - ses

mf
fair, And wove them in - to gar - lands there. 2. Now

p
mf
once, as sum - mer - time drew nigh, There came a

p pp

troop___ of child - ren__ by, And see - ing ro - ses on the

p pp

tree, With shouts they plucked them mer - ri - ly.

f

3. 'Do you bind ro - ses in___ your hair?'___ They cried, in

'Do you bind ro - ses in your hair?' They cried, in

f f

3. 'Do you bind ro - ses in___ your hair?' They cried, in

pp
scorn, to Je - sus there.___ The boy said hum - bly: 'Take, I
pp

p cresc.
pray, All but the nak - ed thorns a - way.' 4. Then of the
p cresc.
ff
thorns they made a crown, And with rough fin - gers pressed it
ff
p cresc.
ff
down, Till on his fore - head fair and young Red drops of
p cresc.
ff
p
blood like ro - ses sprung.
p
p
like ro - ses sprung, like ro - ses sprung.

The Russian composer, Peter Ilich Tchaikovsky, was born in 1840 and died at St. Petersburg in 1893. From his *Chansons pour la Jeunesse*, Moscow, 1883: Plechtchéev wrote the words, which were translated into German by Hans Schmidt. The melody is used by Arensky in his *Variations on a Theme by Tchaikovsky*

THE CAROLS ARRANGED

FOR USE THROUGHOUT THE YEAR

Titles are printed in italic, and when the beginning of the first line is used as a title, this part is printed in italic.

The carols classed under the heading *Nativity* are suitable for Christmas, but can also be sung in church at any time outside Lent throughout the year. On more informal occasions the Christmas carols themselves can sometimes be sung outside the Christmas season. The danger can thus be lessened of many beautiful Christmas carols being never sung, and the spirit of Christmas can be more widely diffused.

ADVENT
(*For the Fourth Sunday, see also* Christmas Eve)

5 *The Praise of Christmas.* All hail to the days
134 *If ye would hear* the angels sing
115 *Joseph and Mary.* O, Joseph being an old man truly
133 *Carol of the Advent.* People, look East
114 *No Room in the Inn.* When Caesar Augustus
41 *Righteous Joseph.* When righteous Joseph wedded was

CHRISTMAS EVE
(*Also for Christmas*)

123 *Chanticleer.* All this night shrill chanticleer
66 *The Cherry Tree Carol.* (*Part* 2) As Joseph was a-walking
168 *Ben Jonson's Carol.* I sing the birth was born tonight
134 *If ye would hear* the angels sing
138 *O Little Town* of Bethlehem
189 *Merry Christmas.* On Christmas Eve the bells were rung
24 *Sussex Carol.* On Christmas night all Christians sing
1 *Christmas Eve.* The Lord at first did Adam make

CHRISTMAS
From the week before Christmas to February 2nd
(*See also under* Nativity)

116 *A Babe is Born* all of a may
73 *Dutch Carol.* A child is born in Bethlehem
2 *A Child this Day* is born
118 *Susanni.* A little child there is yborn
74 *Flemish Carol.* A little child on the earth
4 *A Virgin most Pure*, as the prophets do tell
169 *Tyrley, Tyrlow.* About the field they piped full right
5 *The Praise of Christmas.* All hail to the days
119 *Angels, from the Realms* of glory
3 *Sunny Bank.* As I sat on a sunny bank (I saw three ships)
170 *New Prince, new pomp.* Behold a simple tender babe
6 *Irish Carol.* Christmas Day is come
7 *Hereford Carol.* Come all you faithful Christians
8 *Somerset Carol.* Come all you worthy gentlemen
10 *Come, love we God!*
154 *Courons à la fête*
135 *Earthly Friends* will change and falter
76 *Es ist ein' Ros'* entsprungen
186 *Snow in the Street.* From far away we come to you
11 *God rest you merry*, gentlemen
12 *God rest you merry* gentlemen (*London*)
13 *God's Dear Son* without beginning
14 *Wexford Carol.* Good people all
111 *Grand Dieu! Que de merveilles*
67 *Song of the Nuns of Chester.* He who made the starry skies
18 *I saw Three Ships* come sailing in
168 *Ben Jonson's Carol.* I sing the birth was born tonight
117 *Immortal Babe*, who this dear day
120 *In Bethlehem, that fair City*
75 *Bethlehem.* In that poor stable
187 *Mid-Winter.* In the bleak mid-winter
17 *All in the Morning.* It was on Christmas Day

162 *Je sais, vierge Marie*
77 *Song of the Crib*. Joseph dearest, Joseph mine
140 *Laissez paître vos bêtes*
20 *Yeoman's Carol*. Let Christians all with joyful mirth
23 *Make we joy* now in this feast
137 *Masters in this Hall*
149 *Noël nouvelet*, Noël chantons ici
147 *Nous allons, ma mie*
188 *Our Brother is Born*. Now every child that dwells on earth
173 *The Golden Carol*. Now is Christèmas ycome
115 *Joseph and Mary*. O, Joseph being an old man truly
138 *O Little Town* of Bethlehem
22 *Coventry Carol*. O sisters too
121 *Falan-tiding*. Out of the orient crystal skies
78 *Personent Hodie* voces puerulae
166 *Promptement levez-vous*, mon voisin
164 *Quelle est cette odeur agréable?*
79 *Quem Pastores* laudavere
67 *Song of the Nuns of Chester*. Qui creavit coelum
144 *Quittez, Pasteurs*
25 *A Gallery Carol*. Rejoice and be merry
42 *Remember*, O thou man (*verses* 1, 3, 4, 5, 6)
190 *Winter's Snow*. See amid the winter's snow
79 *Quem Pastores*. Shepherds left their flocks a-straying
133 *Shepherds, shake off your drowsy sleep*
78 *Personent Hodie*. Sing aloud on this day!
27 *The First Nowell* the angel did say
191 *The Christmas Tree*. The holly's up, the house is all bright
192 *The Snow lies thick* upon the earth
76 *Es ist ein' Ros'*. There is a flower springing
29 *This New Christmas Carol*
81 *Torches*, torches
156 *Une vaine crainte* trouble vos esprits
174 *Welcome Yule*, thou merry man
122 *Herrick's Carol*. What sweeter music can we bring
33 *While Shepherds Watched* their flocks by night
82 *Patapan*. Willie, take your little drum
83 *Congaudeat*. With merry heart let all

CHRISTMAS, Secular

171 *Shakespeare's Carol*. Blow, blow thou winter wind
50 *Nos Galan*. Deck the hall with boughs of holly
16 *Good-bye*. God bless the master of this house
15 *Wassail Song*. Here we come a-wassailing
172 *Make we merry*, both more and less
189 *Merry Christmas*. On Christmas Eve the bells were rung
19 *Boar's Head Carol*. The boar's head in hand bear I
32 *Somerset Wassail*. Wassail, and wassail, all over the town!
31 *Gloucestershire Wassail*. Wassail, wassail, all over the town!
21 *Sir Christèmas*. Who is there that singeth so

ST. STEPHEN (December 26th)

136 *Good King Wenceslas* looked out
26 *Saint Stephen* was a holy man
174 *Welcome Yule*, thou merry man

ST. JOHN (December 27th)

174 *Welcome Yule*, thou merry man

INNOCENTS' DAY (December 28th)

120 *In Bethlehem, that fair City*
22 *Coventry Carol*. O sisters too
55 *The Miraculous Harvest*. Rise up, rise up, you merry men all
80 *Three Kings* are here
92 *Puer nobis*. Unto us a boy is born!
174 *Welcome Yule*, thou merry man
140 *The Band of Children*. What songs are these, faint heard and far?

THE CAROLS ARRANGED

NEW YEAR
(*cf.* Christmas)

74 *Flemish Carol.* A little child on the earth has been born
44 *The Lamb of God.* Awake, awake, ye drowsy souls
12 *God rest you merry* (*London*)
15 *Wassail Song.* Here we come a-wassailing
50 *Nos Galan.* Now the joyful bells a-ringing
28 *Greensleeves.* The old year now away is fled
32 *Somerset Wassail.* Wassail, and wassail, all over the town!
31 *Gloucestershire Wassail.* Wassail, wassail, all over the town!
174 *Welcome Yule*, thou merry man
83 *Congaudeat.* With merry heart let all

JANUARY AND FEBRUARY
(*cf.* Epiphany, Candlemas, etc.)

141 *January Carol.* Earth to-day rejoices

EPIPHANY
January 6th to Septuagesima

116 *A Babe is Born* all of a may
118 *Susanni.* A little child there is yborn
119 *Angels, from the Realms* of glory
10 *Come, love we God!*
9 *Dark the Night lay*, wild and dreary
13 *God's Dear Son* without beginning
104 *How Brightly Beams* the morning star!
117 *Immortal Babe*, who this dear day
23 *Make we joy* now in this feast
173 *The Golden Carol.* Now is Christèmas ycome
121 *Falan-tiding.* Out of the orient crystal skies
78 *Personent Hodie* voces puerulae
79 *Quem Pastores* laudavere
25 *A Gallery Carol.* Rejoice and be merry
79 *Quem Pastores.* Shepherds left their flocks a-straying
78 *Personent Hodie.* Sing aloud on this day!
27 *The First Nowell* the angel did say
139 *Infinite Light.* The greatness of God in his love has been shown
140 *The Band of Children.* The stars shall light your journey
121 *Falan-tiding.* The wise may bring their learning
54 *King Herod and the Cock.* There was a star in David's land
29 *This New Christmas Carol*
80 *Three Kings.* Three kings are here
193 *The Kings.* Three kings from Persian lands afar
194 *Kings in Glory.* Three kings in great glory
195 *Kings of Orient.* We three kings of Orient are
83 *Congaudeat.* With merry heart let all

NATIVITY
(*Suitable both for Christmas and for General use*)

85 *Puer Natus.* A boy was born in Bethlehem
34 *Poverty.* All poor men and humble
123 *Chanticleer.* All this night shrill chanticleer
175 *The Virgin's Cradle Hymn.* Dormi, Jesu! (Sleep, sweet babe)
141 *January Carol.* Earth to-day rejoices
124 *Summer in Winter.* Gloomy night embraced the place
84 *The Cradle.* He smiles within his cradle
67 *Song of the Nuns of Chester.* He who made the starry skies
142 *Children's Song of the Nativity.* How far is it to Bethlehem?
86 *In Dulci Jubilo*
176 *Herrick's Ode.* In numbers, and but these few
87 *Rocking.* Little Jesus, sweetly sleep
88 *Waking-Time.* Neighbour, what was the sound, I pray
35 *Sans Day Carol.* Now the holly bears a berry
36 *The Salutation Carol.* Nowell . . . Tidings true
89 *Sion's Daughter.* O Sion's daughter, where art thou?
177 *Out of your sleep* arise and wake

67 *Song of the Nuns of Chester*. Qui creavit coelum
125 *Rorate* coeli desuper!
110 *Jesus of the Manger*. Sing, good company, frank and free!
30 *Lute-book Lullaby*. Sweet was the song the Virgin sang
91 *In the Town*. Take heart, the journey's ended
37 *The Angel Gabriel* from God
69 *The Saviour's Work*. The babe in Bethlem's manger laid
143 *The World's Desire*. The Christ-child lay on Mary's lap
38 *The Holly and the Ivy*
90 *Song of the Ship*. There comes a ship a-sailing
39 *This Endris Night*
92 *Puer nobis*. Unto us a boy is born!
113 *Spanish Carol*. Up now, laggardly lasses
40 *Wonder Tidings*. What tidings bringest thou, messenger
178 *In Excelsis Gloria*. When Christ was born
41 *Righteous Joseph*. When righteous Joseph wedded was

CANDLEMAS (February 2nd)

126 *Candlemas Eve*. Down with the rosemary and bays. (*And till Refreshment Sunday*)
17 *All in the Morning*. (*Part* 1) It was on Christmas Day
174 *Welcome Yule*, thou merry man

ANNUNCIATION (March 25th)

100 *The Message*. A message came to a maiden young
52 *Angelus ad Virginem*
102 *Gabriel's Message* does away
36 *The Salutation Carol*. Nowell . . . Tidings true
37 *The Angel Gabriel* from God
41 *Righteous Joseph*. When righteous Joseph wedded was

LENT

First four weeks

71 *My Dancing Day*. (*Part* 2) Into the desert
144 *White Lent*. Now quit your care
45 *Sussex Mummers' Carol*. O mortal man, remember well
42 *Remember*, O thou man (*verses* 1, 2, 3, 6)
38 *The Holly and the Ivy*
66 *The Cherry Tree Carol*. (*Part* 3) Then Mary took

Also General Carols, especially:—

51 *The Sinners' Redemption*. All you that are to mirth inclined
61 *Down in yon forest*
102 *Gabriel's Message* does away
105 *The Garden of Jesus*. Lord Jesus hath a garden
184 *All Bells in Paradise*. Over yonder's a park
139 *Infinite Light*. The greatness of God
46 *The Bellman's Song*. The moon shines bright
166 *Carol of Service*. Up, my neighbour, come away
72 *Wondrous Works*. When Jesus Christ was twelve years old
197 *The Crown of Roses*. When Jesus Christ was yet a child
167 *Carol of the Kingdom*. When Jesus was a baby

REFRESHMENT SUNDAY

4th Sunday, Mid-Lent

145 *Mothering Sunday*. It is the day of all the year

PASSIONTIDE

Last fortnight in Lent

43 *The Seven Virgins*. All under the leaves
146 *The Merchants' Carol*. As we rode down
44 *The Lamb of God*. Awake, awake, ye drowsy souls
71 *My Dancing Day*. (*Part* 3) Before Pilate the Jews me brought
71 *My Dancing Day*. (*Part* 2) Into the desert I was led
17 *All in the Morning*. (*Part* 2) It was on Holy Wednesday
35 *Sans Day Carol*. Now the holly bears a berry
45 *Sussex Mummers' Carol*. O mortal man, remember well
93 *Mary's Wandering*. Once Mary would go wandering
179 *The Quest*. Saint Mary goes a-seeking
46 *The Bellman's Song*. The moon shines bright

66 *The Cherry Tree Carol.* (*Part* 3) Then Mary took
197 *The Crown of Roses.* When Jesus Christ was yet a child
72 *Wondrous Works.* (*Part* 2) When they bereaved his life

PALM SUNDAY
(*cf.* Passiontide)
146 *The Merchants' Carol.* As we rode down

HOLY WEEK AND GOOD FRIDAY
See Passiontide

EASTERTIDE
Easter Day till Ascension Day
(*cf.* Spring)
71 *My Dancing Day.* (*Part* 3) Before Pilate the Jews me brought
147 *Easter Carol.* Cheer up, friends and neighbours
148 *Christ the Lord is risen!*
94 *Easter Eggs*
102 *Gabriel's Message* does away
104 *How Brightly Beams* the morning star!
152 *Festival Carol.* How great the harvest is
71 *Mv Dancing Day.* (*Part* 2) Into the desert I was led
17 *All in the Morning.* (*Part* 2) It was on Holy Wednesday
95 *Now glad of Heart* be every one!
149 *Love is come again.* Now the green blade riseth
35 *Sans Day Carol.* Now the holly bears a berry
96 *Hilariter.* The whole bright world rejoices now
150 *The World Itself* keeps Easter Day
97 *The Secret Flower.* This child was born
151 *Athens.* 'Twas about the dead of night
72 *Wondrous Works.* (*Part* 2) When they bereaved

ASCENSIONTIDE
71 *My Dancing Day.* (*Part* 3) Before Pilate the Jews me brought
127 *God is Ascended* up on high
152 *Festival Carol.* How great the harvest is
95 *Now glad of Heart* be every one!
72 *Wondrous Works.* (*Part* 2) When they bereaved

WHITSUNTIDE
And the Holy Spirit
59 *Welsh Carol.* Awake were they only
152 *Festival Carol.* How great the harvest is
97 *The Secret Flower.* This child was born
153 *Song of the Spirit.* When Christ blessed his disciples
154 *The Spirit.* Winds of God unfailing

TRINITY SUNDAY
(*cf.* General: Praise)
152 *Festival Carol.* How great the harvest is
95 *Now glad of Heart* be every one!
96 *Hilariter.* The whole bright world rejoices now

OTHER FESTIVAL OCCASIONS
(*cf.* General: Praise)
Saints' Days
100 *The Message.* A message came to a maiden young
156 *Summer Time.* Lift your hidden faces
132 *Psalm of Sion.* O mother dear, Jerusalem
97 *The Secret Flower.* This child was born
99 *Flower Carol* (*verses* 3, 4, 5). Through each wonder

Dedication, etc.
162 *Bell Carol.* In every town and village
44 *The Lamb of God.* (*Part* 2) It was early (*Missionary, etc.*)
88 *Waking-Time.* Neighbour, what was the sound, I pray (*Missionary, etc.*)
111 *The Builders.* Sing, all good people gathered
139 *Infinite Light.* The greatness of God (*Missionary, etc.*)
121 *Falan-tiding.* The wise may bring their learning
166 *Carol of Service.* Up, my neighbour, come away (*Missionary, etc.*)

SPRING

126 *Candlemas Eve*. Down with the rosemary and bays
155 *April*. Now April has come
98 *Spring has come*. Now the spring has come again
129 *Pleasure it is*
99 *Flower Carol*. Spring has now unwrapped the flowers
96 *Hilariter*. The whole bright world rejoices now

MAY

47 *May Carol*. Awake, awake, good people all
48 *May-Day Garland*. I've brought you here a bunch of may!
49 *Furry Day Carol*. Remember us poor Mayers all!

SUMMER

101 *Gems of Day*. All the gay gems of day
156 *Summer Time*. Lift your hidden faces
128 *Welcome, Summer*. Now welcome, Summer, with thy sunnè soft
129 *Pleasure it is*
157 *Summer Carol*. The dawn-wind now is waking
96 *Hilariter*. The whole bright world rejoices now

HARVEST

158 *Thanksgiving Carol*. Fields of corn, give up your ears
129 *Pleasure it is*
159 *Golden Sheaves*. Sing to the Lord of harvest

AUTUMN

158 *Thanksgiving Carol*. Fields of corn, give up your ears
63 *Green grow'th the Holly*
38 *The Holly and the Ivy*

WINTER

63 *Green grow'th the Holly*
50 *Nos Galan*. Now the joyful bells a-ringing
133 *Carol of the Advent*. People, look East

GENERAL

(*Carols classed under* Nativity *are also suitable for general use*)

100 *The Message*. A message came to a maiden young
101 *Gems of Day*. All the gay gems of day
51 *The Sinners' Redemption*. All you that are to mirth inclined
57 *Dives and Lazarus*. As it fell out upon one day
58 *Jacob's Ladder*. As Jacob with travel
59 *Welsh Carol*. Awake were they only
60 *Job*. Come all you worthy Christian men
9 *Dark the Night* lay
161 *The Shepherd*. Down in the valley
61 *Down in yon Forest*
103 *The Birds*. From out of a wood
102 *Gabriel's Message* does away
63 *Green grow'th the Holly*
104 *How Brightly Beams* the morning star!
145 I know a lovely angel-game
162 *Bell Carol*. In every town and village
163 *The Three Traitors*. It was about the deep of night
17 *All in the Morning*. It was on Christmas Day
65 *The Decree*. Let Christians all with one accord rejoice
165 *Paen* (*Part* 2). Lift up your heads
105 *The Garden of Jesus*. Lord Jesus hath a garden
131 *Coverdale's Carol*. Now blessed be thou
106 *So, Brother*. Now, brothers, lift your voices
108 *The Kingdom*. O, I have seen a King's new baby
109 *O Little One* sweet
132 *Psalm of Sion*. O mother dear, Jerusalem
181 *Balulalow*. O my dear heart
184 *All Bells in Paradise*. Over yonder's a park
111 *The Builders*. Sing, all good people gathered
110 *Jesus of the Manger*. Sing, good company, frank and free!
69 *The Saviour's Work*. The babe in Bethlem's manger laid

70 *Joys Seven*. The first good joy that Mary had
139 *Infinite Light*. The greatness of God
46 *The Bellman's Song*. The moon shines bright
165 *Golden Mornings*. They saw the light
68 *The Truth from Above*. This is the truth sent from above
112 *Eia, Eia*. To us in Bethlem city
71 *My Dancing Day*. Tomorrow shall be
166 *Carol of Service*. Up, my neighbour, come away
64 *A New Dial*. (*In those twelve days*.) What are they
72 *Wondrous Works*. When Jesus Christ was twelve years'old
197 *The Crown of Roses*. When Jesus Christ was yet a child
167 *Carol of the Kingdom*. When Jesus was a baby
41 *Righteous Joseph*. When righteous Joseph wedded was
154 *The Spirit*. Winds of God unfailing

GENERAL, Cradle Songs

(*cf.* Nativity *for Cradle Songs of the Nativity*)

130 *Watts's Cradle Song*. Hush! my dear
185 *Wither's Rocking Hymn*. Sweet baby, sleep!
196 *Blake's Cradle Song*. Sweet dreams, form a shade

GENERAL, Legendary

53 *The Carnal and the Crane*. As I passed by a river-side
56 *The Holy Well*. As it fell out one May morning
163 *The Three Traitors*. It was about the deep of night
66 *The Cherry Tree Carol*. Joseph was an old man
55 *The Miraculous Harvest*. Rise up, rise up, you merry men all
54 *King Herod and the Cock*. There was a star in David's land
197 *The Crown of Roses*. When Jesus Christ was yet a child

GENERAL, Medieval

180 *Adam lay ybounden*
52 *Angelus ad Virginem*
62 *All and Some*. Exortum est in love
182 *Lullay my Liking*. I saw a fair maiden
183 *I sing of a Maiden*
177 *Out of your Sleep* arise and wake

GENERAL, Praise

160 *Angels Holy*, high and lowly
152 *Festival Carol*. How great the harvest is
165 *Golden Mornings* (*verses* 3, 4). O every thought be of his grace
107 *Praise to God* in the highest!
164 *Carol of Beauty*. Praise we the Lord
99 *Flower Carol* (*verses* 3, 4, 5). Through each wonder

SUITABLE FOR USE IN PROCESSION

2 *A Child this Day* is born. (*Christmas*)
4 *A Virgin most Pure*. (*Christmas*)
119 *Angels, from the Realms of glory*. (*Christmas*)
160 *Angels Holy*, high and lowly. (*General*)
152 *Festival Carol*. How great the harvest is. (*Easter to Trinity*)
17 *All in the Morning*. It was on Christmas Day (*Christmas to Easter*)
105 *The Garden of Jesus*. Lord Jesus hath a garden. (*General, and Saints*)
137 *Masters in this Hall*. (*Christmas*)
173 *The Golden Carol*. Now is Christèmas ycome. (*Christmas*)
111 *The Builders*. Sing, all good people gathered. (*General, and Dedication*)
27 *The First Nowell* the angel did say (*Christmas*)
192 *The snow lies thick* upon the earth. (*Christmas*)
194 *Kings in Glory*. Three kings in great glory. (*Epiphany*)

For Conclusions of Services or Concerts, see Praise; *also the following verses:* 16 *Good-bye*, 44 (*Pt*. 3), *Good Wishes*; 45 (4-6), *Sussex Mummers*; 49 (6), *Furry Day*; 99 (5), *Flower Carol*; 104 (3), *How brightly*; 129, *Pleasure it is*; 152 (4, 5), *Festival Carol*; 165 (Pt. 2). *Paean*; etc.

NOTES ON THE USE OF CAROLS

THE following notes are the result of consultation and experiment.

Waits customarily sing during the week before Christmas. Properly organized from good choirs, they might supplant the casual choir-boys and sturdy but unmusical beggars who are a nuisance at so many front doors. Waits may be accompanied by wind instruments, but harmoniums are as fatal to carols as to hymns. It is often worth while to announce the day and the district beforehand, together with a charity to which the money will be given after expenses have been deducted.

Carol Parties. Sometimes a dozen or two men and women from a choral society visit people by arrangement in their own houses, the host inviting a party to listen to carols for an hour, and making a small contribution to a charity. A whole round of half-hour parties can be managed by car on Christmas Eve.

Private Houses and Schools. There is often amateur carol singing in private houses and at school breaking-up parties. But sometimes on such occasions nearly all the carols sung are poor imitations: amateur singers and school teachers need the warning that strong commercial interests are engaged in pushing inferior songs of all descriptions; and the true carol is still obscured by the false, because the nature of carols has not been fully understood. The simplest remedy is to choose from the traditional tunes.

Concert Rooms and Parish Halls. No concerts are so popular as those which consist of carols. Since crowded audiences are assured, it is worth while to obtain the best musical help and to pay professional musicians, and local orchestras and bands. Such concerts can be made even more delightful by interspersing two or three carols sung dramatically (*e.g.* Nos. 20, 26, 48, 49, 64, 77, 88, 90, 173, 195). Costume can also be used; and in any case it is perhaps best to avoid evening clothes. Some may come on as a party of waits to sing carols like Nos. 15, 30, 31. Carol concerts need not be only in the period between Advent Sunday and Septuagesima: Lent, Easter and Spring carol concerts should, for instance, be very popular.

In Church. Groups of carols, both during and after a service, are a good way of marking Easter and other festivals as well as Christmas. In some churches carols are sung on Easter Day and other festivals instead of an evening sermon. On ordinary Sundays appropriate carols would form a sound and very popular substitute for anthems in many churches.

Children's Services. It has been found a good plan to sing a carol to the children on any Sundays throughout the year when a good singer can be got.

Carol Services. We suggest a new type of informal popular service, to be announced as a 'Carol Service', and to be held on every Sunday throughout the year, in the afternoon, or in the evening. The name will at once attract; and, if the music chosen is really carol music, the whole service will have a delightful character. We suggest that this Carol Service should last from one hour to an hour and a quarter, but not longer; and that it should take something like the following form:—

1 Short Prayer; 2 Hymn or Carol: 3 First Reading; 4 Carol A; 5 Poetry; 6 Carol B; 7 Notices; 8 Carol C; 9 Second Reading; 10 Carol D; 11 Short Lecture or Address; 12 Hymn or Carol; 13 Lord's Prayer and Grace.

In this scheme, perhaps the carols marked A and B might be in the main for a choir or quartet, and those numbered C and D of a more congregational character. If carols are sung for Nos. 2 and 12, the people's share would be further increased. Should still more carols be wanted, a solo carol might be substituted sometimes for No. 5, or for some other number. The First Reading in this example is from the Bible, the Second is from some other source, as a rule. All the readings and other parts are meant to be short—about the length of the Gospels in the Prayer Book. It has been found that improvised versicles and responses have a remarkable effect upon the general tone of these gatherings; they may be taken from the carol itself, announced when it is given out, and then repeated by the person in charge and the people before the carol is sung. Sometimes the refrain can be thus used, sometimes the opening lines, sometimes another couplet from the carol. The congregation can also be brought in by some verses being allotted to them, as well as by their joining in the choruses.

INDEX OF COMPOSERS, SOURCES, ETC.

(There are sometimes two traditional tunes to one number.)

INDEX OF AUTHORS, SOURCES, ETC.

(The word 'Traditional' may cover any date or era from the fifteenth to the eighteenth century)

INDEX OF AUTHORS, SOURCES, Etc.

INDEX OF TITLES

INDEX OF TITLES

INDEX OF FIRST LINES

INDEX OF FIRST LINES

INDEX OF FIRST LINES